Earl Stanhope

History of England comprising the reign of queen Anne until the peace of Utrech

Earl Stanhope

History of England comprising the reign of queen Anne until the peace of Utrech

ISBN/EAN: 9783742817051

Manufactured in Europe, USA, Canada, Australia, Japa

Cover: Foto ©ninafisch / pixelio.de

Manufactured and distributed by brebook publishing software (www.brebook.com)

Earl Stanhope

History of England comprising the reign of queen Anne until the peace of Utrech

EACH VOLUME SOLD SEPARATELY.

COLLECTION
OF
BRITISH AUTHORS

TAUCHNITZ EDITION.

VOL. 1089.

THE REIGN OF QUEEN ANNE
BY
EARL STANHOPE.

IN TWO VOLUMES. — VOL. I.

LEIPZIG: BERNHARD TAUCHNITZ.
PARIS: C. REINWALD & Cᴵᴱ, 15, RUE DES SAINTS PÈRES.

This Collection is published with copyright for Continental circulation, but all purchasers are earnestly requested not to introduce the volumes

TAUCHNITZ EDITION.
Each volume 1/2 Thlr.

W. ADAMS: Sacred Allegories 1 v.
AGUILAR: Home Influence 2 v. The
 Recompense 2 v.
 ...t Rita 1 v. Carr of Carrlyon 2 v. The
 ...ns 2 v.
...SWORTH: Windsor Castle 1 v. Saint
 ...s 1 v. Jack Sheppard (w. portr.) 1 v.
 ...ue Lancashire Witches 2 v. The Star-Chamber 2 v. The Flitch of Bacon 1 v. The Spendthrift 1 v. Mervyn Clitheroe 2 v. Ovingdean Grange 1 v. The Constable of the Tower 1 v. The Lord Mayor of London 2 v. Cardinal Pole 2 v. John Law 2 v. The Spanish Match 2 v. The Constable de Bourbon 2 v. Old Court 2 v. Myddleton Pomfret 2 v. South-Sea Bubble 2 v. Hilary St. Ives 2 v.
"ALL FOR GREED," AUTHOR OF: All for Greed 1 v. Love the Avenger 2 v.
MISS AUSTEN: Sense and Sensibility 1 v. Mansfield Park 1 v.

"THE LAST OF THE CAVALIERS,"
AUTHOR OF: The Last of the Cavaliers 2 v. The Gain of a Loss 2 v.
S. T. COLERIDGE: The Poems 1 v.
WILKIE COLLINS: After Dark 1 v. Hide and Seek 2 v. A Plot in Private Life 1 v. The Dead Secret 2 v. The Woman in White 2 v. Basil 1 v. No Name 3 v. Antonina 2 v. Armadale 3 v. The Moonstone 2 v.
"COMETH UP AS A FLOWER," AUTHOR OF: Cometh up as a Flower 1 v. Not wisely but too well 2 v. Red as a Rose is She 2 v.
FENIMORE COOPER: The Spy (w. portr.) 1 v. The Two Admirals 1 v. Jack O'Lantern 1 v.
THE TWO COSMOS 1 v.
MISS CRAIK: Lost and Won 1 v. Faith Unwin's Ordeal 1 v. Leslie Tyrrell 1 v. Winifred's Wooing and other Tales 1 v. Mildred 1 v.
MISS CUMMINS: Lamplighter 1 v. Mabel Vaughan 1 v. El Fureidîs 1 v. Haunted Hearts 1 v.
DE-FOE: Robinson Crusoe 1 v.
CHARLES DICKENS: The Pickwick Club (w. portr.) 2 v. American Notes 1 v. Oliver Twist

COLLECTION
OF
BRITISH AUTHORS

TAUCHNITZ EDITION.

VOL. 1089.

HISTORY OF ENGLAND 1701—1713.
BY EARL STANHOPE.

IN TWO VOLUMES. — VOL. I.

TAUCHNITZ EDITION.

THE HISTORY OF ENGLAND FROM THE
Accession of James the Second till 1701. By LORD MACAULAY.
10 vols.

HISTORY OF ENGLAND COMPRISING THE
Reign of Queen Anne until the Peace of Utrecht. 1701—1713.
By EARL STANHOPE. 2 vols.

HISTORY OF ENGLAND FROM THE PEACE
of Utrecht to the Peace of Versailles. 1713—1783. By
LORD MAHON (EARL STANHOPE). 7 vols.

HISTORY
OF
ENGLAND

COMPRISING

THE REIGN OF QUEEN ANNE

UNTIL THE PEACE OF UTRECHT

BY

EARL STANHOPE.

1701—1713.

COPYRIGHT EDITION.

TWO VOLUMES. — VOL. I.

LEIPZIG
BERNHARD TAUCHNITZ
1870.

The Right of Translation is reserved.

PREFACE.

THESE VOLUMES have been written, in accordance with the wish expressed to me by several persons, as a connecting link between the close of Lord Macaulay's History of England and the commencement of that from the Peace of Utrecht, which I published while still bearing the title of Mahon. It is to be observed, that Lord Macaulay did not live to complete, as was hoped, the reign of William the Third. It is sometimes supposed that he did so, since his final volume, as published by his family, contains an excellent account of the last illness and decease of the King. But this is only a detached passage which stands separate from the rest. Of the last part of that reign, a period of between one and two years, there is unhappily with one other exception no record from his pen. That deficiency has here to be supplied.

In the reign of Anne the main figure in war and politics—around which it may be said that all the others centre—is undoubtedly Marlborough. I have to the best of my ability endeavoured to weigh his character in the scales of impartial justice—believing as I do that these scales have not been held even in the hands of preceding writers. In some we may trace blind adulation; in some others most unsparing hostility.

Although in several points of my narrative I differ from the conclusions which Archdeacon Coxe has formed, I have constantly derived the greatest advantage from the ample extracts of the Blenheim Papers which he has inserted in his Life of Marlborough. I allude especially to the confidential correspondence of the Duke with the Duchess and Lord Godolphin. There are some further extracts from these Papers which Archdeacon Coxe had made but did not publish, and which (forming part of his large manuscript collection) are now at the British Museum. Of these also I have been able to make use. But, on the other hand, I cannot acknowledge any obligation to the series of Marlborough's letters, taken from Mr. Cardonnel's copybooks, and published by Sir George Murray in 1845. Of these letters, filling five large volumes, by far the greater part as I conceive was neither written nor dictated by the Duke but prepared by his Secretaries, at his order and for his signature. They are merely formal or relative to matters of minute detail, and scarce ever in my judgment afford any thing of historical interest.

It will be seen by my notes, where and how far I have availed myself of other family papers hitherto unpublished. But I desire at this place to express my great obligation to the Government of His Majesty the Emperor Napoleon, which in the most liberal manner allowed me access to the Archives of the Foreign Office at Paris during the last years of Louis the Fourteenth. Thus I was enabled to obtain transcripts of the secret letters addressed to M. de Torcy by Abbé Gaultier, during his negotiations in England,—letters of the highest value to the history of parties at that time. Considerable extracts from them had been already made by Sir James Mackintosh in 1814; but these have remained in manuscript, with the exception of some passages cited in the Edinburgh Review, as I had occasion to explain in a note (vol. I. p. 32, Tauchnitz Ed.) to my History of England.

It should be borne in mind throughout this work that, as in my previous History, dates when not otherwise specified are given in England according to the Old Style which was then the legal one; but in foreign countries, except Russia and Sweden, according to the New. There is some inconvenience in this method, but, as it seems to me, there would be more in any other.

GROSVENOR PLACE, *February* 1870.

CONTENTS
OF VOLUME I.

CHAPTER I.

A.D.		Page
1700	Prospects of the Spanish Succession	1
	Death of Charles the Second of Spain	2
	His Will	3
	Philip, Duke of Anjou, proclaimed	4
	Close of the Session in England	5
	Lord Somers dismissed	6
	Disturbances at Edinburgh	7
	Death of the Duke of Gloucester	9
	Jacobite intrigues	10
	Bombardment of Copenhagen	11
	William returns to England	12
	Calls the Tories to his Councils	13
1701	The General Election	15
	Intercepted letters from France	16
	"Jack Howe"	17
	Negotiations at the Hague	18
	Act of Settlement passed	20
	The Electress Sophia	21
	Impeachment of Lord Somers	22
	Articles of charge against him	24
	The Kentish Petition	25
	The five Kentish gentlemen sent to prison	27
	The Legion Memorial	27
	Case of Lord Haversham	29
	Lord Somers acquitted	30
	Basis of the Grand Alliance	32
	Death of James the Second	33

CONTENTS OF VOLUME I.

A. D.		Page
1701	General Election in England	34
1702	Change of Ministry	35
	Case of Thomas Colepepper	36
	Act of Abjuration	37
	Death of William the Third	38
	His character	39

CHAPTER II.

	Page
Accession of Anne	42
Her character	43
Her first speech in Parliament	44
Ascendency of Marlborough	46
His embassy to Holland	47
The Coronation	48
Godolphin named Lord Treasurer	50
Rochester dissatisfied	51
Prince George named Lord High Admiral	52
Progress of the Grand Alliance	53
Marlborough takes the field	54
Siege of Kaiserswerth	56
The Hanoverian troops	57
Campaign upon the Meuse	58
Fort St. Michael stormed	59
Liege surrendered	60
Marlborough seized by freebooters	60
His escape	61
Plot of the French in North Holland	62
The Elector of Bavaria	63
Philip of Spain	64
Victor Amadeus of Savoy	66
English expedition against Cadiz	66
The Spanish galleons destroyed at Vigo	68
General Election in England	69
Visit of the Queen to Oxford	70
Meeting of Parliament	71
Election Petitions	72
Marlborough created a Duke	74
Great generosity of the Queen	75

CHAPTER III

A.D.		Page
1702	Character of Marlborough	76
	His great qualities	78
	Charm of his manner and address	79
	His two acts of treachery	81
	His love of money	83
	Parallel between him and Belisarius	85
	Death of his only son	86
	Provision for Prince George	87
	Bill to prevent Occasional Conformity	89
	Eagerly pressed by the Queen	91
1703	But defeated by the Lords	92
	Rochester resigns	93
	Cabals of the High Tories	94
	Project of Union with Scotland	95
	The new Scottish Parliament	97
	Letter from the Queen to the Privy Council	98
	Resentment of the Estates	99
	Fletcher of Saltoun	100
	The Act of Security	100
	Close of the Session at Edinburgh	102
	Order of the Thistle revived	103
	Rising of the Protestants in Languedoc	104
	Accession of Portugal to the Grand Alliance	105
	Campaign in Southern Germany	106
	Victory of the French at Hochstädt	108
	And at Spires	109
	Marlborough at the Hague	110
	Dilatory counsels of the Dutch	111
	General Obdam defeated	112
	Insurrection in Hungary	114
	The Archduke Charles	116

CHAPTER IV

	Page
The Great Storm	117
Havoc throughout the country	119
Loss of life	121
Proclamation for a General Fast	121

A.D.		Page
1703	The Houses of Convocation at strife	122
	The Occasional Conformity Bill revived	123
	But again defeated	125
	The Methuen Treaty with Portugal	125
	The Archduke at Windsor	126
1704	And at Lisbon	127
	The Queensberry Plot	128
	Trial of David Baillie	129
	Arrest of Sir John Maclean	130
	Case of Ashby and White	132
	Queen Anne's Bounty	133
	The Session closed	135
	Nottingham resigns	136
	Robert Harley	137
	Henry St. John	138
	Armies set on foot by France	139
	Marshal Marsin in Bavaria	139
	Plans of Marlborough	141
	Politics of the Court of Berlin	143
	Marlborough marches to Mayence	144
	Prince Eugene	145
	The Margrave of Baden	146
	Marlborough on the Danube	148
	His victory on the Schellenberg heights	149
	Negotiations with the Elector of Bavaria	151
	Advance of Marshal Tallard	153
	He marches with the Elector to Dillingen	154
	Marlborough and Eugene at Dapfheim	155
	Preparations for battle	156

CHAPTER V.

	Page
Strength of the two armies	157
The ground at Blenheim described	158
The Allies march forward	160
Public prayers	161
The battle begins	162
Conflict of Eugene on the right	164
And of Marlborough on the left	165

CONTENTS OF VOLUME I.

A.D.		Page
1704	The victory is decided	166
	Marshal Tallard made prisoner	167
	The French infantry surrenders	169
	Flight of the Elector and Marsin	170
	Interview of Tallard with Marlborough and Eugene	171
	Losses of the French	172
	Magnanimity of Louis the Fourteenth	173
	Marlborough and Eugene at Ulm	175
	Cabals in England	176
	Siege and reduction of Landau	178
	The campaign in Italy	179
	Marlborough goes to Berlin	180
	Jean Cavalier	181
	War in Portugal	182
	British fleet in the Mediterranean	183
	Gibraltar taken	184
	Meeting of the Scottish Parliament	185
	And of the English	186
	Conflict between them	187
	Occasional Conformity Bill	189
	Marlborough returns to England	190
	Grant to him of Blenheim	192
	And of Mindelheim	193
1705	Case of Ashby and White continued	194
	Visit of the Queen to Cambridge	195
	The Whig Junto of Five Peers	197
	They negotiate with Godolphin	198
	The General Election	199

CHAPTER VI.

	Page
Plans for the next campaign	200
Death of the Emperor	201
Marshal Villeroy advances	202
Marlborough joins Overkirk	204
And forces the French lines	205
Affair at Neer Ische	206
General Slangenberg	206
Marlborough marches to Genappe	208

A.D.		Page
1705	Battle designed at Waterloo	209
	The Dutch chiefs	210
	Prince Louis of Baden	212
	Gibraltar besieged by the Spaniards	213
	Lord Peterborough in command	213
	He touches at Altea	215
	And proceeds to Barcelona	216
	His design on Montjuich	217
	His entire success	219
	Lord Charlemont's failure	219
	Retrieved by Peterborough	220
	Barcelona surrenders	221
	Great energy of Peterborough	222
	His railing correspondence	224
	State of affairs at Edinburgh	226
	The "Squadrone Volante"	227
	Lord Sunderland sent to Vienna	229
	Cowper appointed Lord Keeper	229
	Address moved by Lord Haversham	230
	The Regency Bill	232
	Cry of "the Church in danger"	233
	Debate in the Lords	234
	Marlborough at Vienna	235
1706	His return to England	236
	Commissioners for Union with Scotland	237
	Their first meetings	238

CHAPTER VII.

	Page
Design of Marlborough upon Italy	240
His discussions with the Dutch	242
His command in Flanders	242
He comes in sight of the French army	243
Battle of Ramillies	245
Losses on both sides	247
Brussels and Ghent surrendered	249
Antwerp and Ostend reduced	249
Siege of Menin	250
And of Dendermond	251

A.D.		Page
1706	Government of the Low Countries	252
	Eugene marches to Turin	254
	His victory over Marsin	255
	Success of Peterborough at San Mateo	256
	And at Fuente de Higuera	257
	Barcelona besieged by the French	258
	Peterborough summoned back	259
	He goes on board the British fleet	260
	And raises the siege	261
	A Council of War	263
	Peterborough returns to Valencia	264
	Balls and Bullfights given by him	265
	The Portugal army	266
	It marches to Madrid	267
	Aragon rises in revolt	269
	"The Vienna crew"	270
	King Charles at Zaragoza	271
	Madrid relinquished by the Allies	271
	Complaints of Peterborough	273
	He quits the army	274
	His adventure at Huete	275
	He embarks for Italy	277
	Retreat of the Allies from Castille	277
	Disappointment in England	278
	Overtures for peace	280
	Opposed by Marlborough	281

CHAPTER VIII

	Page
Progress of the Scottish Treaty	284
The Equivalent	285
The National Debts	286
Political arrangements	288
The Houses of Parliament	288
Articles of Union agreed to	290
State of parties in Scotland	291
The Cameronians	292
Petitions and addresses	293
Great speech of Lord Belhaven	294

A.D.		Page
1706	Decisive division	297
	Riots at Glasgow	298
	The Act of Security	299
	Points of Excise and Finance	300
	Lord Sunderland, Secretary of State	301
	Promotions in the Peerage	302
1707	Supplementary Estimates moved by St. John	303
	The Scottish Parliament meets	304
	Intended Protest	306
	Death of Lord Stair	307
	The Treaty of Union passed	308
	The Scottish Peers	309
	Debates upon the Union in England	310
	Views of the High Churchmen	311
	Sir John Packington	313
	Talbot, Bishop of Oxford	313
	Speeches of Halifax and Nottingham	314
	The Royal Assent	316
	Subsequent results of the Union	317
	Charge of bribery in its passing	319
	Case of Lord Banff	321
	Lingering national prejudices	322
	Apprehended frauds in trade	324
	The new Great Seal of the United Kingdom	325
	Last patents of Scottish peerage	326

HISTORY OF ENGLAND.

CHAPTER I.

THE first year of the new century found the Peace of Ryswick still unbroken. All the great nations desired its continuance, all shrunk from any possible renewal of the conflict. Yet all felt that one black cloud still remained upon the sky. So long as the Spanish succession was unsettled no peace in Europe could be deemed secure.

To guard against this danger so far as human foresight could avail the second Treaty of Partition was signed in March 1700. The contracting parties were England, Holland and France. In this treaty as in the preceding, dominions were parcelled out as more or less convenient to their rulers, and with no view whatever to the welfare or the feeling of the nations to be ruled. The sole object was to trim the balance between the rival claimants, the Dauphin and the Archduke Charles. It was stipulated that the Archduke should succeed as King of Spain, his monarchy to comprise besides Spain itself, the Indies and the Netherlands. The Dauphin on the other hand was to receive the kingdom of Naples and Sicily and the province of Guipuzcoa. There were further clauses, enabling him to obtain the Duchy of Lorraine in ex-

CHAP.
I.
1700.

change for the Duchy of Milan, and providing against any possible junction on the same head of the Spanish and Imperial Crowns.

To make this scheme effectual it should have been kept secret; and this among other causes the popular forms of the Dutch Government forbade. Even the first rumours that such a treaty was pending aroused all the pride of Castille. It was not against France however that the resentment of the Spanish statesmen was directed. Their only chance to maintain their monarchy entire lay in some possible change of purpose in Louis the Fourteenth. It was against England that their anger blazed high. While the Dutch and French diplomatists were suffered to remain at Madrid, Mr. Alexander Stanhope the English Envoy received an order from the King of Spain to depart from the Spanish dominions.

Charles the Second, the unhappy King of Spain, was already a decrepit old man before the age of thirty-nine. Childless, and without the hope of children, weak alike in body and in mind, he faltered in helpless perplexity when pressed to make a Will. Sometimes his inclination pointed to the Austrian Princes as his nearest kinsmen, and sometimes to the Bourbon Princes because they might keep his monarchy entire. Cardinal Porto Carrero the Archbishop of Toledo and at this time his principal adviser took the latter side. So did also the courtiers that were most around him. One of whom he sought counsel was the Count San Estevan. "Speak freely," said the King. "Tell me what you think would be the evil of the Partition Treaty." "Sir," replied the Count in a mystic tone, "recollect that our Saviour in the Garden of Olives found consolation in the thought 'of them which thou gavest me have I lost none.'"[1] The King, it is added, was moved even to tears.

Under such impulses the poor King decided, or, to speak more truly, allowed others to decide for him. He signed and sealed in due form the Will which they prepared. On the 1st of November, at three o'clock in the morning, that "long disease his life" came to a close. Then all was stir in the palace. The antechamber was thronged with priests and nobles, with diplomatists and statesmen, while the Will was opened by the Ministers within. At length they came forth, and the great result was publicly announced. It appeared that Philip Duke of Anjou, the second son of the Dauphin, was named the heir to the universal Spanish Monarchy. In the event of the King of France refusing the succession for his grandson, Charles Archduke of Austria was named as the next heir.

The paramount object was of course to avert all projects of partition; and, in that point of view, the will was most gladly acquiesced in by the leading statesmen and by the popular opinion in Castille. It was to Versailles however that all eyes at this juncture turned. Would the King of France accept or reject the Spanish Will? Louis seemed for a time to waver. On the one side were the faith of the recent treaties, and the fear of a formidable war; on the other the entreaties of his family, and stronger even than the feeling of family affection, the feeling of family pride. Louis could not withstand the temptation to see his own grandson installed as the successor of his constant rival. His decision once taken was announced with

[1] St. John, Gospel ch. xviii. ver. 9; Mémoires de Louville, vol. i. p. 99.

all that majestic grace in which Louis far exceeded all the princes of his time. One morning the folding doors at Versailles were thrown open and the flood of courtiers poured in. Louis advanced, and pointing to the youthful Duke of Anjou by his side, "Gentlemen" —thus spoke LE GRAND MONARQUE, and never did he seem greater than that day—"behold the King of Spain."[2]

Philip the Fifth—for by that title was the new Sovereign proclaimed—found his rule acknowledged, not only in Spain, but in all the European dependencies of the Spanish Crown; at Naples, at Milan, and at Brussels no less than at Madrid. Setting out from Paris in the first days of December, he made a joyful progress through Biscay and Castille, and entered the Spanish capital with loud acclamations from the people. It seemed as though his accession to the Crown would be easy and secure. It seemed as though under his name the Court of Versailles would rule all things at its pleasure beyond the Pyrenees. We find the English ambassador at Paris express at this period a feeling of almost despair. "I fear," he writes, "that the affairs of Europe are in a very ill condition, and that in a few years France will be master of us all."[3]

The circumstances of the time may excuse these gloomy forebodings. France and Spain united could only be withstood by a combination of other Powers, and such a combination could not at that period be obtained. Portugal looked coldly on. The Princes of Germany showed no concern. The Princes of

---

[2] Mémoires de St. Simon, vol. III. p. 39, ed. 1829.
[3] Earl of Manchester to Mr. Alexander Stanhope, at the Hague, Dec. 3, 1700.

Italy rather inclined to the French side. The Emperor Leopold, indeed, as the heir male of the House of Austria and the person most affected by the transfer of the Spanish Succession to the House of Bourbon, was prompt and eager in his wrath; he recalled his ambassador from Madrid and prepared himself for war. He looked in this emergency to the support of at least the Maritime Powers, as England and Holland were at that period termed. He clung to the hope that England would follow the impulse of its Sovereign and Holland the impulse of its Stadtholder. The personal wishes of King William could not be for a moment doubtful. Resistance to French aggrandizement had been the main pursuit, the main passion, of his life. But his authority both as Sovereign and Stadtholder had been for some time past upon the wane. Domestic discords, foreign influences, were rife around him. He had to face the most formidable difficulties while bereft of the popular favor in both countries, with resolute antagonists and lukewarm friends, and while, at the same time, his health was failing and his energy impaired.

It has been related by Lord Macaulay—and this is the last consecutive passage in his History which he was enabled to complete—how painful and humiliating for William had been the Session of 1700; how abruptly he had closed it on April the eleventh; and how for the first time since the Revolution without any Speech from the throne. The close of that Session had left his affairs in evil plight; with his Dutch Guards dismissed; his grants of Crown property to his former mistress, Elizabeth Villiers, brought to light and denounced; and his most trusted Minister, the Lord

CHAP. I.
1700.

Chancellor Somers, threatened with a vote of censure. Moody and secluded the King remained at Hampton Court, while his young favourite the Earl of Albemarle was plied in every quarter with remonstrances, which, it was hoped, would through that channel reach the Royal ear.

The Tory chiefs above all, eager to strike a blow at their arch-enemy, urged on Albemarle that the Lord Chancellor was in fact the main obstacle in the way of reconciliation. Of no man had the conduct given so much umbrage; of no man would the dismissal cause so much satisfaction. It may be doubted whether William in his hey-day of health and fame would have listened for one moment to such representations. He would have stood by his faithful servant and tried a Dissolution of the Parliament before a rupture of the Ministry. But now he was bowed down both by increasing illness and by conscious unpopularity. He exhorted Somers when next he saw him to resign his office; but Somers declared that he had consulted his friends, and was resolved to take no step that should indicate either guilt or fear. Then, on the 17th of April, the King sent to him the Earl of Jersey with a peremptory order to return the Seals; and sent back they were accordingly by Somers to the King.

It might be easy to dismiss Lord Somers but it was found a hard matter to replace him. In that precarious state of politics the highest prize of the Law seemed to be no longer an object of ambition. Both the Lord Chief Justice Holt and the Attorney General Trevor declined the Seals. At length, after more than a month's delay, they were accepted with the title of Lord Keeper by Sir Nathan Wright—"in whom" writes Bishop

Burnet "there was nothing equal to the post; much less to him who had lately filled it."[4]

Other changes were expected, tending to the Tory side; but they did not at this time take place. Meanwhile there was no one who appeared to take a lead in the conduct of the Ministry. There was a lull in public affairs corresponding with the languid condition of the King.

In Scotland as in England the Session of Parliament proved unprosperous and stormy. The disasters of Darien which Lord Macaulay has so well related roused a vehement flame to the north of Tweed. It was felt to be a transaction concerning the national honor as well as the national interest. It was taken up accordingly with all the uncompromising firmness that a proud people could display. Moreover, as commonly happens in such cases, there arose some personal bickerings to embitter the sense of public wrong. Lord Basil Hamilton had been deputed to go to London and lay the Scottish grievances before the King: but the King refused to admit Lord Basil to his presence. The Duke of Queensberry had been appointed by William as his Lord High Commissioner to the Estates, but the Estates would enter into no concert of measures with His Grace. It is difficult to say to what extremities the Scottish Parliament might have proceeded, had it not been for a timely prorogation.

The animosity in Scotland was of course most welcome to the very numerous adherents of the Stuarts in that kingdom, and they kept up the flame by a studied misrepresentation of the views and motives of the King. It was alleged that his repugnance to take vigorous

[4] History of his own Times, vol. iv. p. 446, ed. 1833.

measures of reprisal against Spain arose in no degree from his just anxiety to avert a war, nor yet from his punctual observance of treaties, but solely from his tenderness to the Dutch, who dreaded lest the Scottish company might injure their own trade from Curaçoa. Such calumnies found ready credence. Thus reports the Earl of Melville of the malcontents on the 27th of June:—"It is certain whatever number of the Parliament be with them, they have almost all the people on their side.... There is no more speaking to people now than to a man in a fever."[5] Only a week before, indeed, Edinburgh had one evening witnessed some insolent successes of the mob, with abundance of bonfires and of broken panes. The rioters forced open the Tolbooth doors and set free some prisoners of their party. And as a token of their feelings towards their Sovereign they made the bands of music play as their first tune the song: "Wilful Willy, wilt thou be wilful still?"

On the 4th of July the King, having first appointed Lords Justices to govern in his absence, and turning his eyes in disgust from the affairs of both his kingdoms, embarked for his native country. It is probable that he felt as much pleasure as he was still capable of feeling when he found himself again amidst the trim gardens of Loo. There he applied himself to carry on the manifold negotiations resulting from the recent Treaty of Partition. But in less than a month after his arrival most painful tidings came to him from England. The Duke of Gloucester was the only surviving child of seventeen whom the Princess Anne had borne, though not all to the full time. He had now attained the age of

[5] See the Carstares State Papers, p. 544.

eleven, and was Heir Presumptive to the Crown. William with most laudable zeal had spared no pains for the young Prince's training. Notwithstanding his own rooted distrust of the Earl of Marlborough he had named him Governor; accompanying the appointment with some gracious words most unusual in his mouth. "Teach him to be like yourself" he had said "and he will not want accomplishments."

As Preceptor William had selected a Prelate far from welcome to the largest party in the Church, yet certainly distinguished by great learning, great diligence, and peculiar aptitude for teaching—Bishop Burnet. The young Duke was growing up with the reputation of an amiable temper and promising abilities when he was seized with a malignant fever. He expired on the 29th of July after an illness of only four days. William was deeply moved. Thus he writes to Marlborough: "It is so great a loss to me as well as to all England that it pierces my heart with affliction." [6]

The death of the Duke of Gloucester set adrift the Succession to the Crown. William, as every one knew, was in most precarious health. There was no probability of any further issue from Anne. If then the English people desired—as no doubt they would desire—that the Succession should be continued in the Protestant line, it would be needful in a new Act of Parliament to depart very widely from the regular order—to exclude entirely the descendants of Charles the First—and to revert to Sophia Electress Dowager of Hanover, a daughter of the Queen of Bohemia and a grand-daughter of James the First.

[6] Letter of August 4, 1700, in Coxe's Life of Marlborough. Coxe, by a slip of the pen, has made the month October.

One immediate effect of this altered prospect was to add greatly to the chances of the titular Prince of Wales at St. Germain's—the Pretender as soon afterwards he began to be called. A large majority of Englishmen had been well content to reject his claims in favor of the Duke now deceased—who, though his nephew, was of almost exactly the same age, and who was bred in an Englishman's faith, in an Englishman's feelings, at home. But there was a strong repugnance to adopt in his place the aged Princess at Hanover, who, except by remote descent and the Protestant religion in another form, had nothing at all in common with this country. It was a repugnance which only the strongest sense of danger or of duty could surmount. Under these circumstances the Jacobites in England who had lain by inactive and languid ever since the peace with France again took heart. They despatched one of themselves, Mr. Graham brother of Lord Preston on a secret mission to St. Germain's, and they planned not indeed the restoration of the aged tyrant but the succession of his son.

It is very remarkable that the Princess Anne herself appears to have participated in this change of views. So far as any feelings of family affection might remain to her, they would probably, on the loss of her only child, turn towards her father and brother. We learn that she made a secret overture to the exiled King, requesting his permission to accept the Crown on the demise of him whom she styled the Prince of Orange, and expressing her wish to restore it to the rightful heir on a favourable opportunity.[7] The date of this singular communication is not given, but it seems

[7] See Clarke's Life of James the Second, vol. II. p. 559.

natural to suppose that it did not take place in the life-time of the Duke of Gloucester. "His Majesty" we are further told from the Stuart Papers "excused himself from that." It was indeed his fixed intention, in case he survived as he said "the Prince of Orange" to land in England even though he found but three men to follow him, and to throw himself on the good feeling of the English people.

In the north meanwhile a new war arose. Denmark, Russia and Poland had formed a combination against Charles the Twelfth, the youthful monarch of Sweden. William, beset as he was with dangers and perplexities of other kinds, was not willing to see that ancient kingdom, the bulwark of the Protestants in Germany, overpowered. He assumed, as well becomes at any time the Sovereign of England, the character of an umpire. He made earnest remonstrances to Denmark but in vain. Then he had recourse to more powerful arguments. He sent into the Baltic a fleet of thirty ships, English and Dutch, under Sir George Rooke, which drove the Danish ships to their harbours and proceeded to bombard the Danish capital.

This bombardment proved very different from that which England was destined to inflict upon the same capital a century afterwards. We are told that there was very little damage to their city and none at all to our fleet. But the very appearance of this fleet gave fresh spirit to the Swedes, and its timely aid was much more than seconded by the martial spirit which Charles himself displayed. In the month of August he appeared off Copenhagen, at the head of a well-appointed expedition, and compelled the Danes to sue for peace. Next turning his arms to the opposite shores of the

Baltic, he inflicted a signal defeat upon the Muscovites at the battle of Narva, and prepared next year to pursue his victorious progress to Poland.

William did not return to England till past the middle of October. Besides the discontents arising from other causes he found a flame stirred up by the second Treaty of Partition. That Treaty which had been divulged in the course of the summer was little relished on the Continent and not at all in England. It was represented by the Tories and even by many of the Whigs, as tending to entangle us without necessity in foreign complications; as designed to benefit Holland at the expense of Great Britain; as having been framed by Dutch favourites instead of English Ministers. It was indeed on Portland and on Albemarle that William had mainly relied during these negotiations. Lord Somers seems to have been the only Minister of English birth whom William consulted or advised with in this affair; and when the fact was known or at least surmised, it tended not a little to swell the outcry against both Somers and the King.

It was in this state of public feeling that there came the news to England—first of the death of the King of Spain—and next of the acceptance of his Will by the King of France. William was filled with resentment— the greater as he felt that it must for the present be restrained. He wrote in confidence as follows to Pensionary Heinsius: "The blindness of the people here is incredible. For though this affair is not public yet, it was no sooner said that the King of Spain's Will was in favor of the Duke of Anjou than it was the general opinion that it was better for England that France should accept the Will than fulfil the Treaty of

Partition. . . . . It is the utmost mortification to me in this important affair that I cannot act with the vigour that is requisite and set a good example, but the Republic (of Holland) must do it; and I will engage people here, by a prudent conduct, by degrees, and without their perceiving it."[B]

In the course which William thus proposed to himself of imposing upon English politicians, and artfully leading them forward to a point beyond what they desired or designed, his first object was of course to postpone any present decision. Mr. Secretary Vernon announced that His Majesty must be allowed to consider a little what might be the consequence of so sudden a change in the Court of France. Meanwhile the King, eager to obtain popular support by whatever channel, resolved to carry out the policy which he had indicated in the previous spring—to dissever himself from the Whig connection and to call the Tories to his councils.

The Earl of Rochester was then regarded as the chief of the last named party, not so much from any weight or talents of his own, but as the uncle of the late Queen Mary and of the Princess Anne. On the 12th of December he was declared Lord Lieutenant of Ireland. At the same time were appointed Lord Godolphin, First Lord of the Treasury, Lord Tankerville Privy Seal, and Sir Charles Hedges one of the Secretaries of State in the room of the Earl of Jersey. Then it was that the faults of the Royal character dawned for the first time upon the party thus excluded. As we find it stated by an early writer of their own side

[B] Letter, dated Hampton Court, Nov. 16, 1700 (N.S.) and printed in the Hardwicke Collection.

CHAP. I.
1700.

"the Whigs also began to complain of the King's conduct, of his minding affairs so little, of his being so much out of the kingdom, and of his ill choice of favourites."[9] Yet William had not forgotten his old friends. The title of Halifax had become extinct in the course of this very year by the death of the only son of the great Marquess; and that title, though with the inferior rank of Baron, was now conferred by William on Charles Montague, so lately his Whig Chancellor of the Exchequer.

It was natural that the Whigs as a party should look mainly to an important public measure which the King at the same time adopted. To gratify his new advisers and to increase their probable power William agreed that the Parliament should be dissolved. Writs were issued accordingly at the middle of the month, the new Parliament being summoned to meet on the 6th of February.

In so momentous a crisis of home politics it is obvious that William could form no decisive resolution on foreign affairs. Nor could he return any satisfactory answer to Count Wratislaw who at this period was despatched to him upon a special mission from the Court of Vienna. Meanwhile the agitation of his mind seriously impaired his health; nor did his Ministers past or present make any secret of the fact. Thus in one despatch for instance writes Secretary Vernon: "His Majesty is not very well; his appetite abates, and his legs are more swelled; but it chiefly arises from great thoughtfulness in relation to the public."[1]

1701.

It was manifest even in the first days of the New

[9] Tindal's History, vol. III. p. 75.
[1] To the Earl of Manchester, Dec. 30, 1700.

Year that the Tories would altogether prevail in the Elections. The cry against the Partition Treaties, against the Dutch favourites, and against the late Ministry as an abettor of such measures and such men, was too strong to be withstood. And when the two Houses met, first on the 6th and then by Prorogation on the 10th of February, there was an immediate trial of strength in the choice of Speaker. The Tories put forward their principal man, as he had rapidly grown to be, Robert Harley. On the other side there was proposed Sir Richard Onslow, a respectable gentleman but of no especial note. A division being taken the former was elected by 249 against 125; and this first triumph of the Tories gave as it were its colour to the entire Session that ensued.

The King, in his opening speech which he delivered in person, urged upon the Houses two objects of paramount importance—first to provide for the Succession to the Crown in the Protestant line—and next to consider maturely the altered state of affairs abroad in consequence of the death and the Will of the King of Spain. As regards the last point, His Majesty found it requisite only three days afterwards to announce to them some further and far from favourable news. The States of Holland under the influence of Pensionary Heinsius had resolved, as William did in England, to postpone for the present the paramount question, whether or not to recognize the Duke of Anjou as heir to the Spanish monarchy. But the King of France found means to quicken their decision. Under a former treaty with the Court of Madrid, they had 15,000 of their troops in the Low Countries, designed to garrison the chief towns on the French frontier.

These troops were now surprised and overpowered by the sudden and well-concerted march of a French division.

Such a step on the part of Louis might seem bold yet in truth it was the boldness of consummate skill. It proved a master-stroke of policy. It changed in a moment the entire policy of the Dutch, who, to obtain the release of their captive troops, instantly, as was asked of them, acknowledged Philip as King of Spain.

It was expected by William that this further aggression on the part of France would kindle a resentful feeling in his English Parliament. With the same view he sent down to both Houses an intercepted letter from a leading Jacobite abroad. It was written by the Earl of Melfort to his brother the Earl of Perth. It boasted of "the favourable audience I had of Madam Maintenon," and discussed the chance of a landing in England with the aid of France. But when this letter was published it seems to have stirred the French diplomatists much more than the English legislators. M. de Tallard the ambassador in London loudly complained that so much weight was given to the words of a man whom he called a madman and enthusiast— a man he said who was banished from the Court of King James, and had nothing at all to do with the Court of King Louis. His waiting upon Madame de Maintenon, Tallard added, was only to obtain the admission of two of his daughters into the nunnery of St. Cyr.[2] To the same effect spoke the Ministers at Paris; and as a token of their displeasure with Melfort, they issued a Lettre de Cachet by which he was exiled to Angers.

[2] Secretary Vernon to the Earl of Manchester, Feb. 20, 1701.

The House of Lords, in answer to the communication of Melfort's letter, readily agreed to thank the King and to pray "that he would be pleased to order the seizing of all horses and arms of Papists and other disaffected persons, and have those ill men removed from London according to law." But the Commons were chiefly intent upon denouncing the measures of the former Ministry. They took occasion in another Address a short time afterwards "to lay before His Majesty the ill consequences of the Treaty of Partition passed under the Great Seal of England, during the sitting of Parliament and without the advice of the same."

In the debates which now occurred on the Partition Treaty no man took a more active, it might be said, a more scurrilous, part against the Court than Mr. Howe, one of the members for Gloucestershire, commonly talked of as "Jack Howe." Thus it was quickly noised abroad how he said on one occasion "that His Majesty had made a felonious treaty to rob his neighbours!"[3]

William was at this time busily employed in a new negotiation. He had instructed Alexander Stanhope his Envoy at the Hague to deliver to Comte d'Avaux the French ambassador a series of proposals, by which he hoped to secure the Netherlands from French control, in spite of the succession of a French Prince. He asked that the Court of Versailles should agree to withdraw its troops from those countries, and not to introduce them again, and that the two cities of Ostend and Nieuport should be made over to himself, to be garrisoned by his own troops or the troops of his allies,

[3] See the Kentish Memorial, charge XI.

CHAP. I.
1701.

as he might think fit. The States of Holland backed this Memorial by another from themselves, claiming in like manner to hold and garrison ten cautionary towns which they named. On the other hand Comte d'Avaux tossed aside these proposals with much disdain. "As to the demand" he said "of withdrawing the French troops from the Spanish Netherlands, I expected it and came prepared to give satisfaction on that point; but as to the other articles, they could not be higher if my master had been defeated in four pitched battles." And the haughtiness of d'Avaux prevailed.

It was at a juncture so unpromising for William that Philip of Anjou, being duly installed at Madrid, addressed a solemn letter in Latin to his "most dear brother and cousin" in England. This epistle was read at a Cabinet Council on April the 13th. The Earl of Rochester and the rest of the new Ministry entreated William to own the King of Spain and to answer the letter accordingly. They alleged the example of Holland, and they urged the point so strongly that William was obliged to yield. But he yielded with the worst possible grace, and with a repugnance which he made apparent to the world. The letter which he wrote in reply as to "Philip the Fifth" was not communicated either to the Privy Council or to the two Houses; nor did the King speak of it to any of the Foreign Ministers. It was through the Paris Gazette that it first became publicly known.[4]

The States of Holland were more and more disquieted at finding in spite of their representations the Netherland fortresses remain in possession of Louis.

[4] Philip V. to William III. March 24, 1701, N. S. William to Philip, April 17, 1701, O. S.

These ancient bulwarks against French ambition, so lately garrisoned in part by their own troops, were now turned, into instruments of menace to themselves. They apprehended a speedy attack on their own territory, and they sent to William a formal demand for those succours which under the Treaty of 1677 England was bound to supply. William referred their Memorial to both Houses of Parliament; and received in reply an assurance of their readiness to fulfil their obligations, and to stand by their ancient Allies. But the Lords in their Address could not forbear one parting taunt against the King: "In the last place, with great grief we take leave humbly to represent, that the dangers, to which your kingdoms and your allies have been exposed, are chiefly owing to the fatal counsels that prevented your Majesty's sooner meeting your people in Parliament."

It must be owned that the advice which the King had given to the Houses in his opening Speech, with regard to foreign affairs, had not been answered in any degree to his satisfaction. Nor was he much better pleased with the mode in which they treated his other counsels for the Succession in the Protestant line. It was determined by the Commons at the suggestion of Harley that the person to be named should be taken last; and that as preliminaries there should be settled the conditions of the future Government. Each of these conditions when voted was found to convey a most severe reflection on the conduct and measures of the King. Thus in reference to his frequent visits to Holland, it was provided that the future Sovereign should never go out of the country without consent of Parliament. Thus again bearing in mind his lavish

CHAP. I.
1701.
rewards to his Dutch favourites, the Bill proposed to enact that from the time its other clauses took effect no person born out of the kingdom, unless of English parents, should be capable of holding any office or place of trust, or receiving from the Crown any grant of land.

Inured to patience, both by his Dutch temperament and by the vicissitudes of his chequered and eventful life, William most wisely dissembled his chagrin. He calmly looked on and watched the progress of the Bill in the Commons. It advanced but very slowly. Yet the limitations were voted with little demur. One party thought them desirable; the other was determined to do nothing that could obstruct the passing of the Bill. Then the preliminaries as Harley called them having been accepted the name of the Electress Sophia as of the intended heir was first proposed by a member of very little weight and authority. It was Sir John Bowles, who was thought even then disordered in his senses; and who soon afterwards entirely lost them. Nor were there wanting persons to suspect that Sir John had been purposely put forward, by the secret ill-wishers of the Bill, with a view to make the matter less serious when moved by such a man.[5]

Certain it is that even after the name of the Electress had been brought forward and as it were agreed to, the Bill continued to linger. Though scarcely at all opposed it was most languidly supported. There were seldom above fifty or sixty members attending the Committee. All parties seemed to feel the calling of a stranger to the throne as a great evil, although in the opinion of many or of most it was by far the least

[5] Burnet's History, vol. IV. p. 499.

of the evils then before us. In the Lords the progress of the measure was as easy and as listless. Finally then it passed both Houses; and on the 12th of June received the Royal Assent from the King on the Throne; an Assent accompanied by an expression of his thanks.

Some further details of the Act of Settlement and of the conditions which it imposed will be found in the first chapter of the History of England from the Peace of Utrecht—just before the time when it came into practical effect. At the period of its passing it may upon the whole be said that there was a warmer feeling for it in the country than in Parliament. It might have been less warm perhaps, had the public in general surmised that the Electress was very far from zealous for the doctrines of the Reformation. A singular proof of her own and of her husband's slackness is given in the Memoirs of Gourville, a most able Frenchman, the manager for the great Prince de Condé. Gourville states that being on a visit at Hanover in the year 1681, he saw by the side of the Duchess her daughter then a blooming girl of thirteen, and he inquired of the Duchess which was her religion. "She has none at all as yet," replied Sophia. "We are waiting to know what Prince she is to marry, and whenever that point is determined she will be duly instructed in the religion of her future husband whether Protestant or Catholic." [6] This was the princess who subsequently became the first Queen of Prussia, and was the friend and correspondent of Leibnitz.

Of Sophia herself we may add, that until the year 1701, when her claim to the Succession was for the

---

[6] Mémoires de Gourville, vol. II. p. 244, ed 1782.

CHAP. I.
1701.

first time taken up in earnest by the King and Parliament, she had an inclination to the Exiled Family. There is an interesting letter from her written in French to Mr. Stepney who had been British Minister at her daughter's Court. Lord Chancellor Hardwicke used to call it the Princess Sophia's "Jacobite letter." In this we find her bewail the fate of the "poor Prince of Wales," who she says if he were to be restored would be warned by the misfortunes of his father, and might be easily guided in a right direction.[7]

Thus in 1701 the Houses of Parliament had set before them two questions of surpassing magnitude— to maintain if possible the balance of power in Europe; and to provide for the Protestant Succession of the Crown in England. But the majority of the Lower House at least deemed these by no means the paramount objects. They showed far more interest and spent far more time in vindictive measures against their political opponents. They desired to renew the proceedings against Lord Somers for his share in the first Partition Treaty; and it was their wish to include in the same accusation the Earl of Portland, who was especially obnoxious to them as the chief of the Dutch favourites, the Earl of Orford and the newly made Lord Halifax.

Lord Somers being apprised of the measures that were designed against him appeared by his own request, at the Bar of the Commons, and offered some explanations of his conduct. To defend the Treaty itself might be a thorny task, but to vindicate his own share in it was not so hard. He declared that when consulted by

[7] Letter first printed in the Hardwicke Collection, vol. II. p. 442. It was written from Pyrmont in the summer of 1700—not 1701 as the Editor alleges.

the King he had offered his best advice as a Privy Councillor, and objected to many particulars if there were room for it. But when His Majesty again wrote to him declaring that he could not bring the French to better terms, then as His Majesty's Chancellor he would not refuse at His Majesty's desire to set the Great Seal to the document.

So full and clear was Lord Somers's personal defence that, as many persons thought, the vote would have turned in his favor, if it had been taken at once. But the debate which arose was protracted till past midnight—a most unusual hour at that period—and the question being then put, "That John Lord Somers by advising His Majesty in the year 1698 to the Treaty for partition of the Spanish monarchy, whereby large territories of the King of Spain's dominions were to be delivered over to France, is guilty of a high crime and misdemeanour," it was affirmed by the narrow majority of 198 against 188. It was then ordered that Mr. Simon Harcourt—destined one day to sit in Somers's chair—should go up to the Lords and impeach him. Similar Resolutions of impeachment were carried against the Earl of Portland (this indeed came first in point of time), against the Earl of Orford and against Lord Halifax.

The framers of these impeachments however looked forward to little fruit from them, being well aware that whenever the trials came on the Lords accused would in all probability have a majority in their own House. But they would not thus be baulked of their prey. They had recourse to another expedient. They carried an Address to the King, praying that His Majesty pending the impeachments would dismiss the four Peers from his presence and councils for ever. Hereupon the Upper House took the field and certainly on strong grounds. The Lords presented a counter-address which was carried by a majority of 20, and which besought the King not to pass any censure upon the four Lords until they were tried upon their impeachments, and judgment given according to the laws of the land. William was much perplexed by these conflicting Addresses. He could only evade the difficulty by returning a vague answer and obtaining a brief adjournment.

When after the adjournment the two Houses met again the impeachments were earnestly pressed, and the charges in due form prepared. Somers was arraigned not only for his share in the Partition Treaties, but also as an abettor of Captain Kidd who at this very time was hanged with three of his crew, under their conviction for piracy on the coast of Malabar. It was moreover alleged against Somers that he had passed the exorbitant grants from the Irish forfeited estates; that he had begged a share of them; that he had made arbitrary orders in the Court of Chancery, and been the cause of numerous delays. Against Portland were urged first the Partition Treaties concluded by his counsel; and next the vast part which had accrued to himself from the exorbitant grants of Crown lands. Halifax was charged on several points with official malpractices, as for waste of the timber to his own profit in the Royal forest of Dean; and while Chancellor of the Exchequer appointing his brother Christopher Montague to the office of Auditor in trust for himself, so that in fact he had impudently audited his own accounts. In the case of Orford it was imputed that he had given his countenance to Kidd the pirate, and been guilty of gross abuses in managing and victualling the fleet off the coast of Spain.

Such then were the Articles exhibited against these four Peers, of whom it may with truth be said that the Commons would have been quite ready to punish them before trial, and the Lords equally ready to protect them after conviction. With views so far divergent a controversy soon arose between the Houses—a long and tangled controversy, which there would be little interest to pursue through all its mazes. The main point grew to be that the Commons required further time to prepare their evidence, which the Lords were not willing to grant; and there really seems little to choose between the factious feelings displayed on either side.

But although the spirit of faction might be nearly equal in each of these contests, it was certainly far most conspicuous when directed against Lord Somers, from his acknowledged genius and his wide renown. From abroad we find the Duke of Shrewsbury, so lately at the head of public affairs, write in a strain of the |utmost bitterness at the tidings which had reached him. "Had I a son" he adds "I would sooner breed him a cobbler than a courtier, and a hangman than a statesman!"[a] At home we find a similar indignation aroused in the county of Kent. At the Quarter Sessions held in Maidstone on the 29th of April there was a strong desire expressed to make some representation of their feelings to the House of Commons. A Petition being drawn up accordingly by William Colepepper of Hollingbourne, the Chairman of

[a] Letter dated Rome June 17, 1701, and first printed in the Hardwicke Collection, vol. II. p. 440.

CHAP. I.
1701.

the Sessions, it was signed by the Deputy Lieutenants present, above twenty Justices of the Peace, and a large number of freeholders. In its prayer it deprecated "the least distrust of His Most Sacred Majesty," and it implored the House "that your loyal Addresses may be turned into Bills of Supply."

The petition thus prepared was sent up to London by the hands of its framer William Colepepper. Four other Kentish gentlemen offered themselves to go with him. Their names (for they well deserve to be recorded) were Thomas Colepepper, David Polhill, Justinian Champneys and William Hamilton. Mr. Polhill, it may be noted, was the head of a family long settled and most honourably remembered at Chipstead Place in the parish of Chevening; descendants in the female line of Ireton and Cromwell.

These five gentlemen accordingly took charge of the petition to London. But the question then arose who should present it to the House. There was understood to be some peril in the performance of this duty. One of the County Members Sir Thomas Hales excused himself. The other Mr. Meredith would only consent, on condition that when he presented the Petition, he might be able to tell the House that several persons of good quality who had signed it were at the door, quite ready to avow their deed. The five gentlemen were perfectly willing, and Mr. Colepepper exclaimed in allusion to some words of Luther at the Diet of Worms: "Though every tile upon St. Stephen's Chapel were a Devil I would have the petition presented!"

Presented the Petition was accordingly. The five gentlemen being then called in appeared at the Bar, and in reply to the Speaker's questions owned the signatures which were shown them to be truly theirs. They were directed to "withdraw and expect the order of the House." Meanwhile a fierce debate began. In its terms the Petition was certainly less strong than many which in recent times have been presented without rebuke. But in the reign of William the Third it seems to have been held that the electors, having once returned a House of Commons, had little right to cavil at its conduct, and were bound to sustain the assembly they had chosen.[9] On this ground the majority called out for vengeance on the audacious men of Kent.

Several attempts were made to shake their constancy during the debate. Members came out to them with pretended pity, and declared that if they would only yield a slight submission they would be excused. "If you will but say that you are sorry"—whispered Sir Theophilus Oglethorpe. "We will have no sorry!" one of the gentlemen exclaimed. Finally the debate, which lasted for five hours, having terminated, the House came to a vote that the Kentish Petition was "scandalous, insolent, and seditious," and that the five gentlemen who had avouched it should be taken into custody. They were accordingly received as prisoners by the Serjeant-at-Arms.[1]

The matter did not end here. The petitioners or their friends employed an able pen believed to be Defoe's. A Memorial to the House of Commons was drawn up conveying divers charges and demands. It bore no signatures but was afterwards called the Legion Memorial because it concluded with—"Our name is Legion and

---

[9] Observe a note upon this subject, with some additions dated 1845 in Hallam's Constitutional History, vol. iii. p. 272, ed. 1855.

[1] On this whole transaction see "The History of the Kentish Petition" printed in the Somers Tracts, second collection, vol. iv. p. 300.

we are many." Its language was extremely violent, which of course requires no great effort of courage where the accusation is anonymous and is intended to remain so. Besides the graver and weightier questions of national politics, it also alleged some theological and some personal points. Thus we find the writer complain that the arm of the law is not raised against the Unitarians as they would now be termed—"having among you impudent deniers of our Saviour's divinity; and suffering them unreproved and unpunished to the infinite regret of all good Christians." Oh for the good old days of Calvin when Servetus could be burned alive!

Thus again as to another point the writer requires: "That John Howe aforesaid be obliged to ask His Majesty's pardon for his vile reflections or be immediately expelled the House."

This party pamphlet—for in truth it was no more —seems however to have assumed large dimensions in the eyes of its contemporaries. For this two reasons may be given. First it was drawn up with telling force. In the second place it accurately represented the feelings and the temper of the time. The Whigs were ready to adopt its sentiments and the Tories quite as ready to resent them. No measures could of course be taken by the last against an author whose name they did not know. But the majority in the Commons seemed as though a real Legion were in arms against them. Mr. Howe declared in the House that he was in danger of his life. Other Members talked as they might have done with a rebellion in prospect. An Address was carried to the King praying him to provide for the public peace and security; and a Committee was appointed to meet in the Speaker's chamber and to sit from day to day.

If it be considered that on this occasion as on others the Tory majority in the Commons overstepped all bounds of temper and discretion, the same may be said with equal truth of the Whig majority in the Lords. A Protest against their precipitation in the case of Somers's trial had been signed by thirty-two Peers—some of these among the foremost as Marlborough and Godolphin. Its terms were extremely moderate, since it did no more than express an apprehension that "our proceeding now to this trial may tend to the disappointment of all future trials on impeachments." Nevertheless this Protest was declared by the majority injurious to the honor of the House, and was ordered to be expunged from the Minutes.

The angry feeling, which had sprung up between the Lords and Commons, was further inflamed by the indiscretion of a very new Peer, John Thompson by name, and by title, Lord Haversham, who, at a Free Conference held between the Houses on the 13th of June, referred to a demand of the Commons that the Peers should not vote in their own case, and said that the Commons had plainly showed their own partiality in impeaching some Lords for facts, in which others were equally concerned with them, who yet were not impeached. At hearing these words the Managers of the Commons immediately withdrew from the Conference, although they were assured as they went by the Duke of Devonshire that Lord Haversham had no authority from their House to use any such expressions. Mr. Harcourt reported the affair to the House of Commons, which immediately resolved that Lord

Haversham had used false expressions, and that the Lords be desired to proceed in justice against him. Several other proceedings passed. The Lords showed no desire to screen Lord Haversham, but considering themselves a Court of Justice could not inflict upon him a summary punishment, as the Commons appear to have expected.

Finally so far as Lord Somers's trial was concerned the Peers fixed it for the 17th of June. The Commons much incensed at having no further time allowed them resolved that they would not appear. Therefore on the day appointed the Lords having solemnly marched from their own House to Westminster Hall, and finding no prosecutors present after the articles of impeachment and the answers had been read, as solemnly marched back whence they came. Then it was carried by a large majority that John Lord Somers be acquitted and that the impeachment be dismissed.

The resentment of the Commons was both promptly and fiercely shown. They passed some votes severely reflecting on what they termed "the pretended trial of Lord Somers" and declaring "that the Lords have refused justice to the Commons." The Lords passed some counter votes in a strain of equal violence. Scarce ever in our History had the flame between the two Houses blazed so high. But fortunately by this time the House of Commons had gone through the principal Bills and granted the desired supplies. It was found practicable to bring this stormy Session to an immediate close. On the 24th of June the King came down in person, and in proroguing the Houses delivered a speech of three sentences, in which, notwithstanding his many causes of displeasure with the Commons, he expressed himself to them in very gracious terms.

Immediately on the close of the Session the Kentish gentlemen imprisoned by order of the House of Commons were as the law required set free. They had been treated with much distinction by their party as though Confessors of the Faith, and before they returned to the country, they were splendidly entertained at Mercers' Hall at the charge of the citizens.[a]

Domestic affairs being now disposed of, the King gave orders to send at once to Holland the succour that the Dutch States had asked—new levies and other regiments amounting in all to 10,000 men. Of this force he with excellent judgment overcoming his former prepossessions entrusted the command to the Earl of Marlborough, naming Marlborough also his ambassador to carry on the intended negotiations at the Hague.

A few days from the close of the Session the King as was his wont embarked for Holland. He appeared before the States at the Hague and delivered an Address to them, causing great pain to all present by his haggard countenance and altered looks. But his ill health could never divert him from his public cares. He watched with great anxiety the war which was waging this summer in Southern Europe. The Emperor still refused to acknowledge Philip as the rightful heir of Spain, and sent across the Alps an army for the conquest of the Milanese. On the other hand a French

---

[a] Oldmixon's History of William III. &c. p. 238, folio ed. If we may rely on this writer (p. 235) confirmed by the Somers Tracts, vol. IV. p. 306, they had not been allowed to converse during their captivity, and "the Serjeant seeing two of them talk together drew his sword upon his Deputy for permitting it."

CHAP. I.
1701.

force advanced in support of—who could lately have supposed it?—the Spanish dominions. But besides this aid Philip had contracted a marriage with the second daughter of the Duke of Savoy,—the elder was already Duchess of Burgundy,—and thereby received the military alliance of that politic and wavering Prince. Little however was achieved on either side, and after a desultory campaign the two armies withdrew to winter quarters.

Meanwhile William was intent on framing a new system of alliances which might give a wider extension to the war. He felt the necessity of proceeding cautiously and step by step, while the disposition of many European Courts was doubtful and a majority of his own House of Commons hostile to his schemes. Some Conventions of smaller import were negotiated with Denmark and with Sweden. But on the 7th of September there was concluded at the Hague under William's own direction a treaty of alliance between England, the States of Holland and the Emperor. This treaty bore only the signature of Marlborough on the part of England. It declared that nothing could be more conducive to the establishment of the general peace, than to procure satisfaction to the Emperor in the Spanish succession, and sufficient security for the dominions and commerce of the Allies. Amicable means were to be employed for this object within a period of two months. But if the satisfaction aimed at were not in this manner attainable the Allies should then seek to recover the Low Countries from the hands of the French so as to be as heretofore a barrier between Holland and France, and to recover also for the Emperor's security the Duchy of Milan and other

Italian territories. It was added that the English and Dutch should keep whatever they might conquer in the West Indies. This last article it is said was first suggested to the King by Lord Somers at the time of the Partition Treaty.

It is clear even from this slight summary that the first step which the new Allies had contemplated was a peaceful overture to France. Taking Louis as at this period supreme ruler of the governments both at Paris and Madrid, it would be easy for him by some moderate concessions on the side of Flanders, and some other concessions more or less considerable on the side of Italy, to establish his grandson without any contest as acknowledged Sovereign of Spain and the Indies. Or if only any fresh causes of offence were to be avoided, it might be practicable, the negotiation once begun, to spin it out from month to month until the fatal progress of disease had done its work on a noble frame—until he died who had been and who was the soul and spirit of the new confederacy—until the main hope of European independence should languish and expire with William of Nassau.

Happily for the balance of power, there occurred at this very crisis, the series of events which Lord Macaulay in a separate fragment has related with his usual felicity of diction and fullness of detail. He has told us how the exiled monarch James the Second died at St. Germains on the 17th of September—how Louis in opposition to all his ablest counsellors acknowledged the titular Prince of Wales as King of England—how in consequence the fiercest flame of indignation burst forth in the British people—how William seized the opportunity to overrule his Tory Ministers and dissolve his Tory Parliament—and how the current of the new Returns ran steadily in favor of the Whigs. The narrative of Lord Macaulay breaks off abruptly in the midst of the Gloucestershire Election. It would have given him pleasure to record its close—how "Jack Howe," the personal assailant of King William in the House of Commons, was put to the rout by an obscure antagonist of the Court party, Mr. Maynard Colchester, while his late colleague Sir Richard Cocks as a Whig retained his seat.

It was the same in other places. Wherever the popular voice was freeest the Whig candidates most commonly appeared at the head of the poll. The Tories maintained their ground chiefly in those bodies where family influence and ties of neighbourhood prevailed. Still, though no longer a majority in the House of Commons, they formed a compact and numerous party. They were always strong; they might sometimes be victorious. This was apparent even at their first meeting for the choice of Speaker. There were two gentlemen put forward; Sir Thomas Littleton who was favoured by the Court, and Mr. Harley recommended by his Parliamentary knowledge and recent experience of the Chair. It was felt that party spirit apart Harley was much the fittest of the candidates, and he was elected accordingly by the narrow majority of four—216 against 212.[3]

William was determined that the flame which Louis had kindled should not be allowed to cool. He had summoned his new Parliament to meet as early as pos-

[3] Commons Journals, vol. XIII. p. 645. The "Complete History of England in 1701" (p. 361) had made this majority fourteen instead of four, and has been followed by Tindal in his Continuation of Rapin, Coxe in his Life of Marlborough, and several other compilers.

sible. Even before the New Year—on the 30th of December—he came down to the Houses and delivered his opening Speech. It was wholly free from that cold and conventional tone which the Royal Speeches have displayed more or less through the entire Hanoverian period. This Speech on the contrary, which came from the pen of Lord Somers, bears throughout, unrestrained by forms, the impress of his clear sense and lofty spirit. "It is fit I should tell you" he said "the eyes of all Europe are upon this Parliament; all matters are at a stand till your resolutions are known; and therefore no time ought to be lost. . . . Let me conjure you to disappoint the only hopes of our enemies by your unanimity. I have shown, and will always show how desirous I am to be the common father of all my people. Do you in like manner lay aside parties and divisions. Let there be no other distinction heard of amongst us for the future, but of those who are for the Protestant religion and the present establishment, and of those who mean a Popish prince and a French government."

These patriotic sentiments received a prompt reply. Both Houses passed unanimously Addresses expressing the highest indignation at the conduct of the French King "in owning and setting up the pretended Prince of Wales." A sum of 600,000*l.* for the service of the fleet was voted by the Commons; and they further agreed to support the proportion of land-forces, namely 40,000 men, which the King had stipulated to act in conjunction with those of his Allies.

Encouraged by the spirit which the Houses manifested, the King proceeded, though by cautious steps, to make some changes in the Ministry. Already at the close of December he had named the Earl of Carlisle

CHAP. I.
1702.

First Commissioner of the Treasury in the room of Lord Godolphin. Now he replaced Sir Charles Hedges as Secretary of State by the Earl of Manchester late ambassador at Paris, and he called the Earls of Radnor and of Burlington to the Privy Council. Some other appointments followed all tending to reinstate the Whigs in office. Rochester the great Tory chief, strong in his kinsmanship to the late Queen, had gone some months before to take possession of his Vice Royalty of Ireland, and there he was left for the present, receiving however an intimation from the King that His Majesty intended to put an end to his commission.

It is worthy of note nevertheless that although this House of Commons had been elected on wholly different principles, which it manifested on national questions, it adhered to the worst precedents of the former wherever its own dignity and grandeur might be thought to be concerned. The case of Thomas Colepepper is a strong example. He had been one of the candidates for Maidstone at the last General Election and was defeated by a majority of only two votes. He now presented a Petition praying for the Seat, in which far from succeeding he was himself judged guilty of corrupt practices. For these he might perhaps be well deserving of censure or punishment. But the members took occasion to revive the proceedings of last Session against the Kentish Petition, which they again voted to be "scandalous, insolent, and seditious," and they ordered that Colepepper as one of its main instruments should be committed to Newgate, and be prosecuted by the Attorney General.

The two Houses however passed with great expedition a Bill for attainting the pretended Prince of Wales, who had now taken the title of King James the Third. There was even a question of including in the same attainder his mother the Queen Dowager, as claiming to be Regent during his minority. Holding any correspondence with him or remitting any money for his use was in like manner declared High Treason. So far great unanimity appeared.

But this unanimity ceased when there arose the question of another Bill for the purpose of abjuring the young Prince, and of taking an oath to William and to each of his successors according to the Act of Settlement, as the "rightful and lawful King." This measure was introduced with the specious title of "An Act for the further security of His Majesty's person and the succession of the Crown in the Protestant line." It was begun in the House of Lords; and the first design was that the oath should be only voluntary—to be tendered to all persons, and their subscription or refusal to be put on record without any other penalty. To this the Earl of Nottingham and other Tories took exception, and not without good cause. Besides that it would place in a most invidious light all those who for whatever causes—and the causes might be very various—omitted to take the oath, it would raise a new theological difficulty, since many persons deemed it unwarrantable to take any oath of free will and without being required and bound to do so by some lawful authority. Nevertheless the Bill passed the Lords with the oath left free; and, in the Commons after long debate, the question that it should be imposed was carried but by one vote. In this form the oath was made a necessary qualification for every employment either in Church or State.

At that period so far as we are now enabled to judge, and for many years afterwards, there was a feeling very prevalent in England though scarce ever publicly avowed—a belief that the restoration of the titular Prince of Wales like that of his uncle Charles the Second would probably in the end take place—that it was rather a question of time and of terms. Men who had no sort of concert or engagement with his partisans, and who looked forward with complacency to the Princess Anne as next heir, were yet unwilling to give any vote, or take any step that should irretrievably dissever them from their eventual Sovereign. Hence the progress of the Bill in both Houses was marked by some strange fluctuations, and divers pretexts and devices; and there was at work a latent opposition rather felt perhaps than seen.

Another underhand proceeding of certain politicians at this time was the attempt to sow dissension between the King and the Princess. It was whispered that the secret object of William was to obtain the succession of the House of Hanover, immediately on his own decease. This appears to be an utter calumny, without even a shadow of foundation or excuse; nevertheless it is thought to have produced some effect on the mind of Anne. The opposition, affecting great concern for her safety, proposed a Clause making it High Treason to compass her death, as in the case of a Prince of Wales, she standing then in the same relation to the Crown; and this Clause being at once conceded by the Government was duly inserted in the Bill.

This Bill which stirred up so much of party passion was still depending when on the 20th of February William fell from his horse and broke his collar-bone.

Lord Macaulay, with a mournful interest in the close of his hero's career, has anticipated the order of time, in a separate fragment tracing the accident to its fatal result on the morning of March the 8th. I content myself with only this brief notice, being not able—and were I even able scarcely willing—to add anything to Lord Macaulay's full and excellent narration.

The character of William has been sketched by Lord Macaulay with a friendly, and as some may think a partial, hand. He has done justice to the lofty qualities of that great Prince, but has overlooked or scarcely touched the not inconsiderable drawbacks that must be made. Confining our attention now to these, as seeking in the present instance only to complete the picture, we may in the first place observe of William how unsympathetic was his nature. There can be no stronger contrast than between the enthusiastic allegiance which Henri Quatre for example knew how to inspire in France and the cold and sullen respect which only—here at least—was shown to William. The longer he was known in this country the less he was beloved. It may be doubted whether, at the time of his decease, there was a single Englishman who entertained for him a feeling of personal attachment.

The demeanour of William was certainly in no common degree, dry, forbidding, and austere. He spoke little, and very seldom in praise. Indeed it has been said of him that he never appeared quite at ease or quite to his advantage except on a day of battle. There and there alone the hero was fully manifested. For this coldness and reserve there might be perhaps in some degree a physical cause assigned. When his body came to be dissected in the presence of ten physicians and four surgeons, the most eminent of their day, we may observe that they state at the conclusion of their joint Report: "It is very rare to find a body with so little blood as was seen in this."[4] Yet on the other hand his general demeanour was, it may be thought, no untrue reflex of his feelings whenever his own countrymen were not concerned. Beyond the sphere of Holland he appears to have viewed mankind too much as mere instruments to carry out his great designs.

In the same spirit it was perhaps that when once satisfied as to the end he did not at all times concern himself enough about the means. Thus he resolved to establish order in the Highlands, and with that view he signed an order to extirpate the Macdonalds of Glencoe. Thus he wished to preserve the peace of the world, and with that view he was willing to let perish the adventurers of Darien. Thus again in the last few months of his life, he was desirous to have a government in England that should cordially cooperate with his foreign policy, and with that view, while still retaining and employing his Tory Ministers, he consulted with their rivals how and by what means he might most easily supplant them. His secret overtures to Lords Somers and Sunderland, dated in the autumn of 1701 and published by Lord Hardwicke in his State Papers, reveal a course which in the present day would be denounced on all sides as wholly unbecoming the honor and duty of a British Sovereign.

Moreover, in estimating the character of King William, great attention is certainly due to the remark of Bishop Burnet that "he had no vice but of one sort in which

---

[4] The Report is given at length in the Complete History of Europe for 1702, p. 76.

he was very cautious and secret."—"If you live to read my History," said the Bishop one day to Lord Dartmouth, "you will be surprised to find I have taken notice of King William's vices; but some things were too notorious for a faithful historian to pass over."[5] Swift on his part, in annotating his own copy of Burnet, has appended to this sentence a very caustic, not to say a cynical, remark.[6] Without pursuing the subject further it may suffice to say that the words of Bishop Burnet should be carefully weighed. It is no light charge that is here implied. It is no light quarter from which the charge proceeds. It comes from a familiar friend and a constant follower—from one who owed to William not only his return from exile but his Episcopal rank—from one who had no imaginable motive to deceive us, and who was most unlikely to be himself deceived.

[5] Note by Lord Dartmouth to this passage in Burnet's History, p. 690 of the folio or vol. III. p. 133 of the octavo edition.
[6] See Swift's Works, vol. x. p. 281, ed. 1814.

CHAPTER II.

CHAP. II.
1702.

Queen Anne at her accession was thirty-seven years of age. Her powers of mind were certainly not considerable. She had no wit of her own nor appreciation of wit in others. No one could have less share, or less sympathy, in the great intellectual movement which took place in her reign. But at the same time she had many most estimable qualities. As a wife and mother her conduct was at all times exemplary. Not even the shadow of a shade rests on the perfect purity of her wedded life. As a mother it is touching to trace how losing child after child, and childless at the last, her poignant grief was blended with pious resignation. In her intimacy with others of her sex she was most warmhearted; and wherever such intimacy ceased the fault was not I think upon her side. If we look at the whole course of the transactions between herself and the Duchess of Marlborough in William's reign and in her own, it may be said that scarce any person ever endured more for a friend—or from a friend.

In her religious tenets Queen Anne was most earnest and sincere. She was warmly attached to the Church of England, receiving the Sacrament once every month, according to its rites; and she had steadily resisted all the attempts at her conversion or perversion that were made in her father's reign. She was liberal sometimes even lavish in her benefactions; kindly and compassionate in all her private feelings. Upon the whole it may be said of her that she fairly merited the popular appellation of "good Queen Anne"—as applied to her not only in her lifetime but down to the present day.

As to the affairs of Government the Queen's principles were sometimes such as might rather deserve the name of prejudices. She was impressed with a strong distaste of the Whigs whom she had been taught to regard as enemies of the Church and Republicans at heart. But on all political questions, the Church Establishment excepted, she distrusted her own judgment too much. Hence she surrendered herself far too implicitly to the counsels of the leading spirit whom for the time she admitted as a guide. And as a Sovereign it was her great infelicity that such a leading spirit could not be supplied from the sphere of her own family. If there were in England any person duller than Her Majesty, that person was Her Majesty's consort, Prince George of Denmark.

Happily for England, the choice of the Queen at this period called to the highest honors of the State a man of transcendent abilities, the Earl of Marlborough. It was only by a fortunate accident, since in the first place the partiality of Anne appears to have been formed in a great degree from personal liking, and secondly since it was not in fact on Marlborough but on his wife that her partiality rested.

On the day of the King's demise—it was Sunday the 8th of March—both Houses promptly met, when loyal Addresses were voted, as also an order for proclaiming Queen Anne that afternoon. This was done accordingly with the usual solemnities, and amidst the acclamations of the assembled multitude. In the evening, the Privy Council came in a body to pay their respects to their new Sovereign. She answered them in some well-considered sentences which had been prepared for her, expressing her great concern for the religion and laws and liberties of her country, as also for maintaining the Succession in the Protestant line.

Three days later the Queen, going down to the House of Peers, delivered her first Speech in Parliament. "My Lords and Gentlemen," she began, "I cannot too much lament my own unhappiness succeeding so immediately after the loss of a King who was the great support not only of these kingdoms but of all Europe."—Her concluding sentence however had this expression, "as I know my own heart to be entirely English." Notwithstanding the high compliments at the outset this expression was resented by some persons as conveying a reflection on the memory of William. Yet surely the Queen cannot be blamed for putting forward her own strong claim to popular favor, even although the Sovereign whom she succeeded might lack that claim altogether.

The Queen in this Speech urged two points on the attention of her Parliament. The first expressed a sentiment which both Houses in their Addresses had already conveyed to her—"that too much cannot be done for the encouragement of our Allies to reduce the exorbitant power of France." The second was "to consider of proper methods towards obtaining of an Union between England and Scotland which has been so lately recommended to you." It was indeed the parting recommendation of King William, delivered in a Message to the Commons, only one week before his death.

QUEEN ANNE. 45

The Parliaments of England before the Revolution CHAP. II.
were held to expire immediately upon the demise of the 1702.
Crown. In this instance our ancient law-givers appear
to have proceeded on a very fanciful and surely a very
foolish analogy. The King they said is the head of the
Parliament, and as the human frame cannot continue
to exist when the head is cut off, so no more can the
body politic.[1] But as the powers of Parliament gradually increased, it was felt and more inconvenient that
these powers should be suspended or annulled at so
critical a period as the commencement of a reign. This
was foreseen especially after the events of 1688, when
the evils of a disputed Succession rose in view. In the
reign of William accordingly there was passed an Act,
enabling the Parliament which existed at a demise of
the Crown to continue during a period of six months
and no longer.[2] Even with this latitude, the rule has
been several times the cause of most needless expen-
diture, and serious interruption to the public business,
without even the shadow of an advantage alleged on
the other side; and it seems strange that the clear and
simple change in the law, of rendering a Dissolution
at the death of the Sovereign permissive instead of
compulsory, should have been deferred until the year
1867 on the motion of the present writer.

This Parliament of Anne was therefore the first in
our Annals that was entitled to sit and vote after the
demise of the Crown. It showed itself worthy of the
privilege by its prudence. There was no peevish attempt
to embarrass the government or to withhold the sup-

---

[1] Blackstone's Commentaries, vol. 1. p. 177, ed. Kerr, 1857. The relation of the Sovereign to the Parliament was described as *caput, principium et finis.*
[2] Act 7 & 8 Will. III. c. 15.

plies. There was on the contrary a cheerful readiness to clear the path of the new Queen. Undoubtedly the framers of her first Speech had touched precisely the right chord of popular feeling. As many persons thought, the late King had been "entirely Dutch;" the Pretender if restored must be "entirely French;" the Electress of Hanover if she succeeded might be "entirely German;" delightful then to bask in the sunshine of an "entirely English" Queen!

Some such sentiment indeed was much required to soothe the Whig majority of the Commons—that Whig majority so recent and so hardly won—as they saw the current of promotions, just now flowing in their favor, all at once turned aside. There was no sudden or abrupt change of Ministry; that was left to be accomplished by degrees; but it was plain from the first that the Queen's entire favor would rest on the Earl of Marlborough; and through Marlborough on his Tory friends. Only three days from her coming to the Crown she named him a Knight of the Garter; then Captain General of her land-forces both at home and abroad; then Master General of the Ordnance; and earlier still ambassador to Holland for a special object. That object was to give fresh spirits to the leading statesmen of the Hague, and assure them of the Queen's continued support, disheartened as they were and almost bewildered by the loss of their great Stadtholder.

Lady Marlborough had even a larger share—if that be possible—of honors and rewards. She was named Groom of the Stole—strange as seems that title for a lady to bear. She was named also more appropriately Mistress of the Robes. She was named Keeper of the Privy Purse. The Rangership of Windsor Park for life was affectionately pressed upon her by the Queen. Both her married daughters, Lady Henrietta Godolphin and Lady Spencer, were appointed Ladies of the Bedchamber.

It appears from the papers which are now preserved at Blenheim, and which were consulted by Archdeacon Coxe, that the intimate correspondence which had been carried on for many years past between Lady Marlborough and the Princess Anne under cant names —Lady Marlborough as Mrs. Freeman and the Princess as Mrs. Morley—was still continued with wholly unabated ardour on the Royal side. We find however that ever since the decease of her last surviving child the Duke of Gloucester, Anne invariably added to her name a new epithet referring to her loss. Instead of "your faithful Morley" it was now "your poor unfortunate faithful Morley."[3]

Mr. Freeman—as in these letters Marlborough is commonly termed—set out on his Dutch embassy without delay, and reached the Hague on the 17th of March Old Style. Thus writes Mr. Alexander Stanhope the English Minister to the Dutch States: "The Queen's letter was the greatest comfort and cordial they could receive." . . . "My Lord Marlborough is continually busy with the Pensionary, and several of our foreign Ministers, by which indefatigable diligence he hopes to have despatched all his affairs so as to return in three or four days. . . . He has done a great deal of business in a short time here, and now his presence will be as necessary with you."[4] Thus did Marlborough, by his timely visit and his great diplomatic skill, succeed in

---

[3] See Coxe's Marlborough, vol. I. p. 218.
[4] To Secretary Vernon, March 28 and 31, April 14, 1702 (MS.).

CHAP. once more thoroughly combining the scattered threads
II. of the confederacy against France—the "Grand Al-
1702. liance" as it was now commonly termed. It was agreed
that a Declaration of War against France and Spain
should be issued simultaneously by each of the three
Powers—on the 4th of May Old Style in London, and
on the same day, that is the 15th New Style, at Vienna
and the Hague.

On one point nevertheless Marlborough did not
prevail. Prince George of Denmark notwithstanding
his entire want of military experience had conceived
the silly ambition to lead the Allied army. With this
view Marlborough was instructed to press for his appointment as commander of the Dutch forces. The
States however steadily refused; partly as distrusting
the Prince's capacity; and partly because they feared
that with his exalted rank he would resist the control
of their own field-deputies. There were several other
princes competitors for this high post, and Marlborough
at his departure from the Hague left the question still
depending.

Marlborough returned to England in sufficient time
to take part in the solemnities that attend a change
of reign. On the 12th of April the late King was interred in Westminster Abbey; and there on the 23rd,
St. George's Day, the Queen was crowned. Dr. Sharp
Archbishop of York preached on this occasion. He
was a Prelate believed to stand high in the Queen's
confidence; and he preached "a good and wise sermon"
says Bishop Burnet. Immediately afterwards Her Majesty gave orders for naming the Princess Sophia in
the Prayer for the Royal Family, as next in succession
to the throne.

Meanwhile the Parliament had not been inactive. The Abjuration Bill having become law, the members of both Houses were sworn as was required, in due form. There was nothing of that schism or party division which had been apprehended. It was found that the same persons who had sturdily resisted the imposition of the oath took it with no apparent reluctance when it was imposed.—The two Houses passed a Bill for taking and examining the public accounts by means of certain Commissioners. There had been for many years a most defective system of audit, and large fortunes it was said were made from the Treasury charges.—Another Bill which passed through the Houses with great unanimity was to grant to Anne for life the same revenue that William had enjoyed. When the Queen came down to the House of Peers to pass this Act and to thank her Parliament for it, she declared that, while her subjects remained under the burden of such great taxes, she would straiten herself in her own expenses, and would give directions that 100,000*l.* from her Civil List should be applied to the public service in the current year. This well-timed generosity added not a little to the popular favor which greeted the new reign.

Another Bill which passed without difficulty was designed to carry out the recommendation of the Queen in her opening Speech. It empowered Her Majesty to name commissioners for treating of an Union with Scotland.

Since the return of Marlborough and through the influence of "Mrs. Freeman," a change of Ministry was now in progress entirely transferring the reins of government from the Whig party to the Tory. Marl-

CHAP. II.
1702.

borough's chief reliance at this time was on Lord Godolphin. For many years there had been a political alliance between them, since cemented by a near family connection, Marlborough's eldest daughter having married Godolphin's eldest son. By Marlborough's advice Godolphin was named Lord Treasurer. Thus he would have the supreme control of the finances, while the main direction of the war and of the foreign alliances would remain in Marlborough's hands. There were two new Secretaries of State, the Earl of Nottingham and Sir Charles Hedges, in the room of the Duke of Manchester and Mr. Vernon. The Marquess of Normanby was appointed Lord Privy Seal, and soon after created Duke of Buckingham. The Earl of Pembroke became Lord President; the Earl of Jersey had a place at Court. Mr. Harcourt, henceforth Sir Simon, was Solicitor General. Two Tories of great weight in the House of Commons, Sir Edward Seymour and Sir John Levison Gower, were named respectively Comptroller of the Household and Chancellor of the Duchy of Lancaster. Nay more—such are the necessities of party—there was one among the subordinate posts, a Joint Paymastership, which was bestowed on Mr. Howe, the insolent and unscrupulous defamer of King William.

Not less significant of the prevailing temper in high places were the nominations to the Privy Council. That body as in former times the Parliament itself was held to expire at the demise of the Crown. It became necessary for the new Sovereign to reappoint such members as were sought to be retained. Now in the Privy Council which Anne was advised to name there were omitted the most eminent Whig chiefs—Somers above all and Halifax and Orford.

One leading Tory continued much dissatisfied. This was Rochester, who had expected to be himself Lord Treasurer and had no wish to live at Dublin as Lord Lieutenant. Flinging the government of Ireland into the hands of Lords Justices, he hastened up to London full of ire. This he had an opportunity of venting at a Council held on the 2nd of May to issue the Declaration of War against France and Spain. Then Rochester stood up supported by some of his colleagues and spoke against the Declaration; urging that it was safer for the English to act only as auxiliaries. Marlborough took the lead on the other side and maintained that France could never be reduced within due bounds, unless the English entered as principals into the quarrel. In this view the majority of the Council concurred; and the Declaration of War specifying reasons was framed accordingly. On the 4th of May, in pursuance of the agreement made at the Hague, it was solemnly proclaimed before the gate of St. James's Palace and other usual places; like Declarations being issued on the same day both by the Emperor and by the States of Holland. Loyal and approving Addresses were presented to the Queen from both the Houses.

It was not merely on questions of foreign policy that Rochester and his followers differed from their other colleagues in the Council. He wished for a more entire change of men down to all subaltern employments—to extend perhaps even to the Judges and Lords Lieutenant of Counties, since all those Commissions were then terminable at the Royal decease. But the prudence of Marlborough and Godolphin forbade any course so extreme. No new Whigs were appointed,

CHAP. II.
1702.

but many were continued at the posts which they held in the preceding reign. This was especially the case when they were of rank and character, and at the same time of no abilities which could cause alarm. The Duke of Devonshire for example was reappointed Lord Steward.

One main anxiety of Anne at this juncture was to satisfy her consort. She could not obtain for him as he wished the command of the army in the Netherlands, but she named him Generalissimo of all her forces and also Lord High Admiral. In this latter capacity the Ministers took care to provide him with an efficient Council, which comprised Sir George Rooke and other seamen of mark, and which might if necessary administer the navy in his name. Prince George had moreover a seat in the House of Lords, having been created Duke of Cumberland in 1689. He was therefore in a position to acquire an honourable fame in the public service had either activity or ability fallen to his share. But without these the highest employments serve only to render the want of them more clear. Little was expected of Prince George by any portion of the public, but even that little was more than he performed.

The Parliament having now despatched the necessary business, was prorogued on the 25th of May. By that time Marlborough was already at the Hague, where he remained through the month of June, intent alike on diplomacy and on the preparations for war, and fully equal to the calls of both.—Several accessions had been recently obtained to the Grand Alliance. The Elector of Brandenburg was induced to join it on his title as King of Prussia being conferred or acknowledged by the Emperor; and this was the origin of that powerful monarchy now become predominant over all the German States. "King Frederick the First" was the title which the Elector now assumed. Vanity was a leading principle in his mind, and it was skilfully wrought upon by Marlborough, who clenched his resolution by the promise that the Queen would grant to his Ministers the same ceremonial as to those of other Crowned Heads.

The Elector Palatine also joined the Grand Alliance, inflamed by the recollection of the wrongs which his country had suffered when laid waste by order of Louis the Fourteenth. A desire to secure the favor of the English people and the succession to his family influenced in the same direction the Elector of Hanover. Many smaller princes were borne along by the example of the greater. Two brothers indeed who held high rank in the Empire, the Electors of Bavaria and of Cologne, were well known as devoted friends of France, but they professed at this period their intention to remain neutral in the contest. On the whole then the German Diet was induced to take the same course which its chief had already taken as sovereign of the Austrian states. It issued a Declaration of War against France and Spain, and engaged to supply the usual contingents of troops.

The command of the Dutch troops was also at this time decided. Among a host of candidates for it there were two especially in view; first the Prince of Naussau Saarbrück who might point to his dignity as a Prince of the Empire and to the great name of Nassau; secondly Van Ginkell, Earl of Athlone, recommended to the States by his Dutch birth and by his military services. Each of these chiefs had already taken the field at the head of a separate corps. On the other hand Pensionary Heinsius and other statesmen, forming what was termed the party of England, warmly pressed the superior claims of Marlborough. Not only were they convinced of his genius for war but they felt the importance of ensuring, as his nomination would ensure, the union of the British and Dutch forces under one command. Finally, the Prince and Athlone seeing that they could not prevail took to themselves the merit of withdrawing their pretensions and allowing Marlborough to be named General in chief.

On the 2nd of July Marlborough set out to take the field. Most truly arduous was the part which he had to fill. For nearly two centuries the rivalry had been between the monarchies of France and Spain. Other European States had by turns allied themselves with either side; and it was this that made the balance of power. But for many years past the effort had been to sustain the power of Spain which constantly dwindled against the power of France which constantly increased. Now on the other hand by the succession of the Duke of Anjou and his dependence on his grandfather, the whole monarchy of Spain and the Indies with its vast appendages of Sicily, Naples, Milan, Flanders, was suddenly thrown into the scale of France. It was only the extreme decrepitude into which Spain had fallen, and the almost entire annihilation of its fleets and armies, that enabled other Powers to band themselves against this portentous junction with any prospect of success. The change was a great one, and to the Dutch most of all. The Low Countries once their barrier and bulwark against France had become well-nigh one of its provinces. They would have to conquer the territory which had hitherto shielded them, to besiege the very towns in which till lately they had held their garrisons.

The Dutch armies at this period were moreover weakened by their divided counsels and dilatory forms. These had been overruled by the ascendant of their Nassau princes, but appeared in full force under the command of a foreign chief. The States were wont to send out field-deputies, men who had no experience of war but who loved to prate of it. Whenever any new operation against the enemy was proposed they claimed to sit in council upon it; and they were found to bring forward so many criticisms and objections, doubts and scruples, misgivings and anxieties, that most commonly they defeated the object in view, or at least delayed it until the favourable opportunity for it had wholly passed away. It will be seen in the sequel how constantly these troublesome meddlers baffled the skilful designs of Marlborough and tried his admirable temper. They may well recall the exclamation which it is recorded that Hannibal made in his later years when the sophist Phormio had favoured him with a lecture on the Art of War, "Many an old fool have I known, but such an old fool never!"

The Governor of the Low Countries for the King of Spain was at this time the Marquis de Bedmar; a man wholly devoted to the French. He commanded for them a corps near the mouth of the Scheldt. But their principal force was upon the Meuse, holding the fortresses in the bishoprick of Liege. It was headed by an experienced officer Marshal Boufflers, and had been joined by the young Duke of Burgundy, eldest son of the Dauphin and heir apparent of the Crown.

The Allies had in the first place a small force to protect the mouth of the Scheldt and to threaten the district of Bruges; this was commanded by Cohorn the celebrated engineer. Their main army consisted of the two divisions of Athlone and Nassau Saarbrück which have been already mentioned. They began the campaign at the end of April by investing Kaiserswerth, a small town upon the Rhine below Düsseldorf, which had been placed in the enemy's hands by the Elector of Cologne. Kaiserswerth made a long and resolute resistance but was compelled to capitulate on the 15th of June; nor could Marshal Boufflers prevail in effecting a diversion by an attempted COUP DE MAIN, though very near success upon Nimeguen.

At this period also of mid-June a German army commanded by the Margrave Louis of Baden, and 40,000 strong, came over the Rhine and laid siege to the important fortress of Landau — the bulwark of Alsace as it was then regarded. The Margrave was subsequently joined by the Emperor's eldest son the young King of the Romans, who desired to share in the glory, though not in the toils, of the expected conquest.

Early in July the Earl of Marlborough reached the head-quarters at Nimeguen, taking the supreme direction not only of the English and Dutch but of the Prussian and Hanoverian contingents. Of these last however the obedience was by no means prompt or ready. The Prussians made difficulties before they would consent to join, and Marlborough could only satisfy the King by writing to him a renewed assurance that the Queen would grant him in the fullest manner the Crowned Heads ceremonial. Thus also the Hanoverian General before he would bring his troops put forward three demands; first that they should not be required to take an oath to the Queen; secondly that they should not be kept beyond the 5th of November; and thirdly that they should not be led across the Meuse. "The two first" writes Marlborough to Godolphin "are not worth disputing; for they assure me it shall be in my power to keep them [through November]; but I think we were almost as good to be without them as agree to the last. Our misfortune is that if we have not these troops we shall not have strength to act. By these difficulties you may see the great disadvantage a confederate army has."

How like to this and beyond all doubt how true the observation of Prince Metternich in a letter during the Congress of Chatillon addressed to Caulaincourt: "I answer to your Excellency that it is no easy matter to be the Minister of an alliance."[5]

Having by patience and skill overcome these obstacles, and obtained the desired junction without the onerous terms, Marlborough called in the troops lately engaged in the siege of Kaiserswerth, drew the English from Breda, and in a few days was at the head of almost 60,000 men. With these he was eager to cross the Meuse and advance into Brabant, giving battle to the French if they would accept it. Here however the Dutch formalities were very quickly—if at that period any thing with them could be quickly—interposed. Lord Athlone and the other Generals in the service of

---

[5] "Ce n'est pas chose facile que d'être le Ministre de la Coalition." Troyes, le 15 Février 1814. Fain, 'Manuscrit de 1814.'

CHAP. II.
1702.

Holland did not agree among themselves, and appealed to their government for instructions. But when the Generals had thus referred the project to the States, the States referred it back to the Generals. They left it to their own decision, adding only, as an additional perplexity, a vague recommendation for "the safety of the Rhine and of Nimeguen."—"However" says Marlborough "we came last night to a resolution of marching to-morrow and passing the Meuse a little below Grave. Accordingly we have this day made three bridges over that river." [6]

At the news of Marlborough's advance Marshal Boufflers quitted his strong position at Gennep, and also crossed the Meuse. Just at this period he had been compelled by orders from the King to send a large detachment of his army towards Alsace for the relief as was hoped of Landau. His force was so much reduced that he would by no means risk a battle, as Marlborough even before that detachment had desired. Relinquishing the line of the Meuse, Boufflers proceeded by rapid marches to the defence of Brabant, and the Duke of Burgundy, seeing that there were no laurels to be gathered, set out ere long on his return to Versailles.

But though Boufflers avoided a battle it might be forced upon him, and for this two good opportunities occurred, first in the defile of Peer, and secondly in his camp at Zonhoven. Marlborough pressed warmly for an attack; and it was the opinion of the Duke of Berwick that had this attack been made upon the camp at Zonhoven where the French were very ill posted, it would certainly have succeeded.[7] Here again the ir-

[6] To Lord Godolphin, July 13, 1702.
[7] Mémoires de Berwick, vol. I. p. 121, ed. 1778.

resolution of the Dutch field-deputies proved of signal service to their enemies. They doubted and wavered until the promising occasion slipped away. "I have but too much reason to complain;" wrote Marlborough on a similar incident a few days afterwards. "However I have thought it for Her Majesty's service to take no notice, as you will see by my letter to the States."[8]

Still however the retreat of the French was of great importance as leaving open to attack the line of fortresses along the Meuse. Marlborough at once applied himself to their reduction. First he invested Venlo. After some days of open trenches he resolved to direct an assault against Fort St. Michael, which was on the other side of the Meuse and connected with the town by a bridge of boats. The storming party on this occasion consisted almost wholly of English troops: it was headed by a very brave officer Lord Cutts, who had under him also Lord Huntingdon, Lord Lorne, Sir Richard Temple and other distinguished volunteers. They carried the fort with irresistible gallantry, taking prisoners or putting to the sword 700 men who formed the garrison. Batteries were then raised in the captured fort against the town, and within a few hours a practicable breach had been effected.

Just at this juncture the besiegers were greatly cheered by the tidings which came to them of the reduction of Landau. The FEUX DE JOIE which they forthwith fired in honor of this auspicious event were mistaken by the besieged for the commencement of the expected assault; and they immediately hung out a flag of truce as preliminary to their own surrender. Thus as it chanced it was the capitulation of one town which

[8] To Lord Godolphin, August 27, 1702.

CHAP. II.
1702.

obtained or at least which hastened the capitulation of another.

Marlborough in the next place turned his arms against Ruremond. In this siege as in the preceding he was assisted by Cohorn who had hastened from the Scheldt; a most skilful engineer but so cautious and captious that he came to be surnamed by one of his countrymen "the General of difficulties." Ruremond made but a faint resistance, and Marlborough then proceeded to invest the important city of Liege. Boufflers had returned from Brabant in hopes of effecting a diversion; but he was overmatched by Marlborough, and Liege surrendered, October 29, on the first fire from the batteries. The season was then so far advanced that the Allied army was withdrawn into winter quarters. Marlborough had closed the campaign very much to his own honor and to the good of the common cause, reducing Guelders, Limburg, and the entire bishoprick of Liege, and cutting off the communication of the French with the Lower Rhine.

The esteem and value which were in consequence felt for Marlborough through the provinces of Holland, were signally shown, in consequence of an adventure which befell him on his return. He had embarked on the Meuse with the Dutch deputies, and a guard of twenty-five men. A larger boat conveyed Cohorn with a guard of sixty, while a body of horse acting as a further escort rode along the bank. In the night however after leaving Venlo the two boats parted company, and the escort of cavalry missed its way. Thus amidst the darkness Marlborough's boat was surprised, and his guard overpowered by a band of French partisans, thirty-five in number, who in quest of booty were lurking among the reeds and sedges. Happily they had no suspicion of the rank and importance of their captives, and there were shown to them some French passes with which the Dutch deputies had prudently provided themselves. Marlborough had disdained to solicit such a safeguard; but one of his servants, Gell by name, saved him at this critical moment by his promptitude. Gliding up close to him, he slipped into his hand an old pass preserved by accident, which had been granted to his brother General Churchill when obliged by ill health to quit the army. Marlborough though aware that the date had expired presented this pass with the calmness that never forsook him. The freebooters were completely deceived. After plundering the boat and extorting some money as presents from those whom they believed to be protected by their passes, they retained the guard as prisoners but they allowed the travellers to proceed. The news flew apace into Holland, and was magnified into a rumour that the General had been recognised and retained. Two days later we find Marlborough writes as follows from the Hague: "Till they saw me here they thought me a prisoner in France, so that I was not ashore one minute before I had great crowds of the common people; some endeavouring to take me by the hands, and all crying out, Welcome! But that which moved me most was to see a great many of both sexes cry for joy."[9]

Many other were the testimonies to Marlborough's great merits at this period. None could be stronger than that which was nobly, nay magnanimously, given

---

[9] To Lord Godolphin, Oct. 28, 1702. This account is fully borne out by the other letters from Holland.

by his rival Lord Athlone. "The success of this campaign" he said "is solely due to this incomparable chief, since I confess that I, serving as second in command, opposed in all circumstances his opinion and proposals."[1]

In relating the war which at this time was waged in the Low Countries we may observe that it was not always concluded with due regard to the feelings of humanity or to the rules of international law. Of this a strong instance may be adduced from the despatches (not hitherto published) of Alexander Stanhope our Envoy at the Hague: "Here is discovered a most villanous design to pierce a DIGUE in North Holland to drown the whole country. It was first proposed by a Papist gentleman of this country of a good estate, bred by the Jesuits at Emmerick; his name Van Eysel. He proposed it to Monsieur d'Avaux when last here, who recommended him to Boufflers then in Flanders, who relished it so well as to send him with it to Monsieur Torcy at Paris, and after it had all their approbations, and the man came back hither to execute it, he and two of his accomplices were seized, and finding their own letters produced against them besides two witnesses vivâ voce they have confessed the fact."[2]

The wrongs however were by no means all on one side as the following extract from the next year's despatches will show. It was when Baron Spaar—or Sparre as the French have spelled it—with some Dutch troops forced the lines into Flanders by the Pays de Waes: "The Baron found great opposition from five

---

[1] See Coxe's Marlborough, vol. 1. p. 196.
[2] To Mr. Yard, Under-Secretary of State, May 23, 1702 (MS.). In the December following the two villains were publicly beheaded.

French regiments, and a much greater number of the French Boors of the country who fought like devils, and maintained their posts after the regular troops had given way, which cost them dear, for Spaar ordered no quarter to be given them and their houses to be burnt."[3]

The Maréchal de Catinat, one of the soldiers of whom France has most reason to be proud—the virtuous Catinat as Rousseau terms him[4] —held command at this period in Alsace. So inferior were his numbers that he could make no attempt to relieve Landau. But after its reduction an opportunity appeared in which by detaching a portion of his army he might retrieve the fortunes of France in another quarter. The Elector of Bavaria after much irresolution had openly espoused the cause of Louis. He seized upon the city of Ulm and issued a proclamation in favor of his new ally. To support his movements an enterprising and ambitious officer, the Marquis de Villars, was sent across the Rhine with part of the army of Alsace.

The declaration of the Elector of Bavaria and the advance of Villars into Germany disquieted in no slight degree the Prince Louis of Baden. Leaving a sufficient garrison in Landau, he also passed the Rhine. The two armies met at Friedlingen on the 14th of October. Louis of Baden, a ponderous tactician bred in the wars against the Turks, might out-manœuvre some Grand Vizier but was no match for the quick-witted Frenchman. He was signally defeated with the loss of 3000 men; soon after which the season being

---

[3] Hon. A. Stanhope to Secretary Hedges, June 29, 1703 (MS.).
[4] Confessions, livre x. He is describing "le simple mais respectable château de St. Gratien," to which Catinat retired after this campaign of 1702.

CHAP. II.
1702.

now far advanced, Villars led back his army to winter quarters in France. His victory of Friedlingen gained for him at Versailles the rank of Maréchal de France; and, as combined with the Bavarian alliance, seemed to offer an auspicious prospect to his countrymen in the next campaigns.

Beyond the Alps there had been some warfare even in mid winter. Marshal Villeroy who commanded for the French had his head-quarters in Cremona; while beyond the Oglio lay his far superior adversary the Imperial chief, Prince Eugene of Savoy. One dark morning in February Villeroy was suddenly roused by the sound of firing in the streets. This came from Eugene who with singular boldness and skill had brought a body of six thousand men unperceived beneath the walls of Cremona, and entered the city through the channel of an aqueduct. The French though surprised made as usual a most gallant resistance. There was sharp fighting continued for ten hours. Finally Prince Eugene was compelled to relinquish his prey and to leave the half-won city as he had found it, bearing with him however Marshal Villeroy and some other prisoners. Villeroy remained in captivity for nine months, when he was exchanged, and to the misfortune of France sent back to her service. Meanwhile the Duke de Vendome had been appointed to his place in Italy.

As the spring advanced Philip of Spain determined to head his own troops in this campaign. On Easter Day he landed at Naples amidst the loudest acclamations. Naples had never seen its Sovereigns for a period of two centuries; and had been grievously misgoverned in their absence. Nevertheless, and in spite of the first Lazzaroni cheers, it was found that the Neapolitans in general were ill affected to the House of Bourbon, and inclined to the Austrian cause. Philip reembarked in June and pursued his voyage along the Italian coast to his own port of Finale. It had been designed that he should touch at Leghorn and have an interview with the Grand Duke of Tuscany. But the training of Philip at the Court of Versailles had imbued him with the deepest veneration for all points of ceremonial; and he thought that as King of Spain it was his duty to maintain that ceremonial in its utmost rigour. He declared that he could not allow to the Grand Duke the honor of taking place at his right hand; that the Grand Duke must be at his left; and the Grand Duke upon this declined to meet him. Some similar, and as silly, punctilio prevented him from seeing the Doge of Genoa.

Still worse was the effect of the interview which did take place at Acqui between the young King and the Duke of Savoy. Not only did Philip refuse the right hand to the Duke his own father-in-law, but he would not allow him even the use of an arm-chair. Yet these questions of right and left, of arm-chairs and single chairs were at this period held as all important by the German and Italian Princes. To deprive them of any such privilege seemed to be like tearing the very vitals from their bosom. How very far wiser was Marlborough! It is observed by Voltaire that the English General having once agreed at some state-banquet to hand a napkin to the new-made King of Prussia, never afterwards experienced any difficulties with regard to the seven or eight thousand men of the Prussian contingent. [5]

[5] Siècle de Louis XIV., vol. I. p. 300, ed. 1752.

Victor Amadeus of Savoy did not on these points rise above the level of the Princes of his age. He was most deeply irritated by the pride of Spain. There were some considerations of policy and personal advantage at this period which might and no doubt did incline him to the Imperial party rather than the French, but it is thought that his change of sides, which shortly afterwards ensued, had its first origin in the disgust which he conceived from this interview at Acqui.[6]

Proceeding to Milan and from thence towards Mantua, King Philip took the nominal command of his forces, which in fact were directed by the Duke de Vendome, and which were now confronted by those of Prince Eugene. There was in both camps a readiness to give battle, and the two armies met at Luzzara on August the 15th. The action was warmly contested but remained indecisive. Both sides claimed the victory, and a Te Deum of thanksgiving was chaunted with equal fervour in the cathedrals of Paris and Vienna. Certain it is that each army had sustained a heavy loss of men, and that only slight skirmishes ensued between them during the rest of the campaign. Early in the autumn the news of an English expedition against Cadiz induced Philip to set out from the army with a view to repel this new attack; but the further tidings which he received at Milan enabled him to prolong his stay in that city for some weeks; and he then returned to Spain which he never left again.

King William was the first to plan this expedition against Cadiz and after his decease the project was resumed. But had King William lived he would cer-

[6] Sismondi, Histoire des Français, vol. xxvi. p. 338, ed. 1841.

tainly not have selected as chief the Duke of Ormond, a princely nobleman, endowed with many amiable qualities, but destitute of the skill and the energy which a great enterprise requires. Under him Sir Henry Bellasys commanded the English and General Spaar a contingent of Dutch troops, amounting together to fourteen thousand men. Admiral Sir George Rooke had the direction of the fleet. Their proceedings have been related at full length in another history [7]—how the troops were set on shore near Cadiz in the first days of September—how even before they landed angry dissensions had sprung up between the Dutch and the English, the landsmen and the seamen—and how these dissensions which Ormond wanted the energy to control proved fatal to the enterprise. No discipline was kept, no spirit was displayed. Week after week was lost, while the small towns of Rota and St. Mary's were shamefully plundered, while the small fort of Matagorda was feebly bombarded, and while the Spaniards were completing their measures of defence. Finally at the close of the month it was discovered that nothing could be done, and a Council of War decided that the troops should reembark.

The only comfort of the chiefs, as usual in such cases, was to cast on each other the blame of their ill success. The Duke of Ormond inveighed against Sir George Rooke; and Sir George Rooke inveighed against the Duke of Ormond. But on their return and off the coast of Portugal an opportunity arose to recover in some part their lost fame. The Spanish galleons from America laden with treasure and making their yearly voyage at this time, were bound by their laws of trade

[7] War of the Succession in Spain, p. 45-64.

CHAP. II.
1702.

to unload at Cadiz, but in apprehension of the English fleet they had put into Vigo bay. There Ormond determined to pursue them. On the 22nd of October he neared that narrow inlet which winds amidst the high Gallician mountains. The Spaniards, assisted by some French frigates which were the escort of the galleons, had expected an attack and made the best preparations in their power. They durst not disembark the treasure without an express order from Madrid—and what order from Madrid ever yet came in due time?—but they had called the neighbouring peasantry to arms; they had manned their forts; they had anchored their ships in line within the harbour; and they had drawn a heavy boom across its mouth. None of these means availed them. The English seamen broke through the boom; Ormond at the head of two thousand soldiers scaled the forts; and the ships were all either taken or destroyed. The greater part of the treasure was thrown overboard by direction of the French and Spanish chiefs; but there remained enough to yield a large amount of booty to the victors; and on the whole the undoubted bravery of Ormond at Vigo might well, in the judgment of his numerous friends in England, atone for his no less undoubted slackness at St. Mary's.

From the West Indies there came some painful tidings. A squadron of seven ships was there commanded by a brave rough veteran Admiral Benbow. In the month of August he engaged a French fleet of superior force and gallantly sustained the fight for five days until deserted by several of his captains. He had received wounds in the arm and face, and his right leg was shattered to pieces by a chain-shot. Even then he bade himself to be carried back in his cradle to the main deck that he might continue to give his orders. One of his lieutenants near him expressed sorrow for the loss of his leg. "I am sorry for it too" said Benbow "but I had rather have lost them both than have seen this dishonor brought upon the English nation."[8] He put back into Kingston of Jamaica where soon afterwards he died of his wounds. He did not die however until after he had caused three of his captains to be tried by Court Martial for their shameful conduct. Two were condemned to death, and after the orders from the Admiralty had been taken, were shot accordingly; the third was cashiered; and another died a few days before his trial could come on.

    The Parliament of England had been dissolved by Proclamation on the 2nd of July. In the elections which ensued the influence of the new reign and of the change of Ministers was strongly felt. The decision of the preceding winter was entirely reversed. As the Tory candidates were then in most contests defeated, so now they were commonly victorious. It was found that they would have a vast numerical preponderance in the new House. As on the last occasion great interest was centered in the Gloucestershire election. Mr. Howe strove gallantly to regain his seat; he was nevertheless at the bottom of the poll. But a scrutiny being called for the High Sheriff declared him duly elected, not without some strong remonstrances, and subsequently an election petition, from Sir John Guise his baffled competitor.

    During this summer the Queen accompanied by Prince George made a Royal Progress. They went

---

[8] Campbell's Lives of the Admirals, vol. III. p. 345, ed. 1744.

first to Oxford, Her Majesty being met on the borders of the county by the Earl of Abingdon as Lord Lieutenant with the High Sheriff and principal gentlemen; and at some distance from the town by the Vice-Chancellor, Doctors and Masters who wore their robes on horseback. She was conducted in due state to the lodgings prepared for her in Christ Church, where the Dean and Canons expressed their compliments to Her Majesty in English, and to Prince George in Latin; a language which, considering his scanty erudition, was probably quite as unintelligible to him as it could be to the Queen. Next day Her Majesty repaired to the Convocation House where she saw some Degrees conferred, as also to a concert (then called "consort") at the Theatre, and accepted an entertainment to dinner from the University. Lastly she received what in the official accounts are termed "the usual presents" to a Sovereign at Oxford namely, "a Bible, a Common Prayer-book, and a pair of gloves."[9]

From Oxford the Royal Pair travelled to Cirencester and thence to Badminton, where they were entertained with great magnificence by the Duke of Beaufort. On the borders of Gloucestershire Her Majesty was met and addressed by the High Sheriff with a great number of gentlemen, clergy, and free-holders, the Sheriff being introduced to her by the person who since his accession to office was described as "the Right Honourable John Howe, Esq." This complex title, wholly unusual at the present time, may require some elucidation. In the reign of Anne and for some time subsequently, the designation of Esquire was taken to imply for the most part either gentle birth or territorial possession,

[9] Complete History of Europe for 1702, p. 309.

and was not therefore held to be superseded by the honor of admission to the Privy Council.

The Queen did not stay the night at Badminton but proceeded the same evening to Bath. The reception is described as follows: "Her Majesty was met at Hyde Park within half a mile of the city by a handsome company of the citizens all clad like grenadiers, and about two hundred virgins, richly attired; many of them like Amazons with bows and arrows, and others with gilt sceptres and other ensigns of the Regalia in their hands; all of them with a set of dancers who danced by the sides of Her Majesty's coach. . . . All the streets were illuminated and a great number of flambeaux were carried."—The furthest point of this Royal progress was Bristol, where we read of as great though different rejoicings; the houses decked with carpets and tapestry, while flags and pendants were waving from the ships in the river.

On the 20th of October the two Houses met; and Mr. Harley was for the third time—this time without opposition—elected Speaker. The Queen, in her opening Speech, mentioned with due regard, the many expressions of joy and satisfaction which she had met with in all the counties through which she had lately passed. She said nothing of the success in the Low Countries but referred in pointed terms to the "disappointment" at Cadiz, as also to the "abuses and disorders" at St. Mary's. But the Commons in their answer put forward the prosperous scene in such a manner as to provoke a hot debate. It was said in the proposed Address that "the vigorous support of your Majesty's allies, and the wonderful progress of your Majesty's arms under the conduct of the Earl of

Marlborough, have signally retrieved the ancient honor and glory of the English nation." Here then was a direct and cruel stab at the memory of King William. Here then it behoved the Whigs to make their stand. They moved an Amendment not at all disparaging the recent services of Marlborough, but only that instead of "retrieved" the word should be "maintained." On this occasion as on most others at this period we may regret that there is not preserved to us a report of the speeches, nor even a list of the speakers. Finally a division being taken the word "retrieved" was affirmed by 180 against 80 votes.

This division gave it may be said a tone to the entire Session. Every thing continued to flow in the Tory current. First as to Gloucestershire, the Commons, notwithstanding some very doubtful circumstances, rejected by a large majority Sir John Guise's prayer and declared Mr. Howe duly elected.[1] Worcestershire came next. The Commons eagerly welcomed a petition from Sir John Packington, a high Tory and member for that county. He complained that Dr. Lloyd Bishop of Worcester had unduly interfered in the election, and endeavoured through his influence with his clergy to prevent Sir John's return. The charge was fully proved by the Bishop's own very silly letters, but the Commons need not have gone so far as to vote that his conduct was "unchristian." They further addressed the Queen to dismiss him from his post as Lord Almoner, and the Queen complied, in spite of some murmurs from the House of Lords, which resented this step as an infringement of its privileges.

[1] Commons Journals, Oct. 24 and Nov. 19, 1702.

Meanwhile there had come to London the tidings of the affair at Vigo, which were received with a transport of joy far greater than the occasion warranted. The Queen issued a Proclamation appointing the 12th of November as a day of Thanksgiving and naming as the three commanders for whose successes thanks to God should be returned, Marlborough, Ormond, and Rooke. On the 12th accordingly the Queen proceeded in state to St. Paul's, attended by her officers of State and by both Houses of Parliament. Her Majesty, attired in purple, and wearing her Collar and George, sat in her "body-coach" drawn by eight horses, and in which were also the Countesses of Marlborough and Sunderland. The Duke of Ormond who by this time had landed, and who chanced to be in his turn the Staff Officer in waiting was in another coach, and as he passed was greeted with loud cheers, cheers due to his amiable qualities far more than to his military skill. "From that day" says an historian "may be dated the great popularity which he afterwards acquired, and which in the end proved fatal to him." [a]

The Commons in the same spirit passed separate Votes of Thanks to the three commanders; and cheerfully granted the supplies required for the year. They voted 40,000 seamen: and that the proportion of land-forces for England to act in concert with those of the Allies should be 33,000 foot and 7,000 horse.

Such was the general aspect of English politics when towards the close of the month Marlborough returned from the Hague. Ever since his successes on the Meuse the Queen had been most desirous to raise him to the

---

[a] Tindal's Hist. vol. III. p. 436.

rank of Duke. Lady Marlborough however was adverse to the scheme as thinking that their fortune was as yet not adequate to the higher rank. Finally Mrs. Morley prevailed with her dear Mrs. Freeman; and the patent for the Dukedom was accordingly made out in the first days of December. To meet in some degree the objection on the score of income, the Queen at the same time granted to Marlborough for the term of her own life a pension of 5,000*l.* a year, derived from the Post Office revenue. She further sent a Message to the House of Commons desiring that this pension might be settled for ever on the title.

Both the title and the pension were it may be thought premature. Had they been granted two years later they would have been received with general approbation, nay enthusiasm, as the just prize of most eminent exploits. Now on the other hand they were but coldly looked upon. The successes on the Meuse though substantial had not been splendid; they had not comprised a battle nor even a skirmish; and they did not seem to require such exuberance of rewards. It was remembered that Marlborough, besides his great appointments in England, was now in receipt of 10,000*l.* a year from the Dutch, as commander-in-chief of their troops. It was remembered that the Duchess centered in her own hands no less than four Court offices, each of them well paid.[3]

Under these circumstances the proposal to settle the pension for ever on the Dukedom found no favor in the House. Sir Christopher Musgrave in particular

---

[3] The official income of the Duke and Duchess at the height of their favor, amounted jointly to the prodigious sum of 64,325*l.* See the exact items in the History of England from the Peace of Utrecht, vol. 1. p. 21, (Tauchnitz Ed.).

spoke warmly against it. Far from complying, the Commons voted an Address to Her Majesty, fully acknowledging the Duke's great services but stating though with "inexpressible grief," the apprehensions they had "of making a precedent for the future alienations of the Revenue of the Crown, which has been so much reduced by the exorbitant grants of the last reign."

The Queen was much chagrined. She wrote at once to the Duchess expressing her wish "to do something towards making up what has been so maliciously hindered in the Parliament. And therefore I desire my dear Mrs. Freeman and Mr. Freeman would be so kind as to accept of two thousand a year out of the Privy Purse besides the grant of the five. This can draw no envy for nobody need know it." The Duchess however in a disinterested spirit firmly declined this further bounty. But the end of this story is not quite so edifying. At a later time and upon her disgrace at Court the Duchess claimed and received the whole pension since the date of the offer, that is for the preceding nine years.[4]

[4] Coxe's Marlborough, vol. I. p. 708 and vol. V. p. 415.

CHAPTER III.

CHAP. III.
1702.

IT has been shown how, notwithstanding a slight check from the House of Commons, Marlborough had at this time attained the highest pinnacle of rank and dignity, unbounded influence at Court, and supreme command in the field. At this point then it may be convenient to pause in the narrative, while it is attempted in some detail to delineate his character. To judge him rightly we should avoid both that eagerness in his depreciation which Lord Macaulay shows; and that servile spirit in which certain other writers have striven to conceal his faults, and to flatter his descendants. We should neither seek to dim the lustre of his glory, nor yet be dazzled by its rays.

A parallel between Marlborough and Wellington, beyond all doubt our two greatest military chiefs, would be a most tempting topic were we further removed from the period of the last. On some points it has already been sketched with perfect fairness by the Duke of Wellington himself.[1] But there would remain many other points to pursue. One of the most curious lies in the difference of age at which their respective triumphs were achieved. Marlborough can scarcely be said to have commanded an army in chief, or on any great occasion, till the campaign of 1702. Born in 1650 he was then fifty-two years of age. Wellington had no

[1] The Duke's Memorandum on Marlborough is dated Sept. 18, 1836, and published in the Stanhope Miscellanies, p. 97.

further service in the field since the battle of Waterloo. Born in 1769 he was then forty-six years of age. It follows, on this comparison of ages, that the victorious career of Wellington ended before the victorious career of Marlborough commenced.

Leaving a fuller parallel to the coming age, there is yet one slight point of difference that may here be noted. The Duke of Wellington—as is well remembered by all his familiar friends—was fond of writing. Scarce a day when it did not engage some hours of his time; and from constant habit it had become almost a necessary to him. Marlborough on the contrary, whose training had been at a most frivolous Court where in early youth his AIR INDOLENT is commemorated,[2] did not work willingly at his desk. When his duty came to require it he did write, and he wrote clearly and well. But he says of himself in a letter to his wife during his first great campaign: "I am on horseback or answering letters all day long. . . . So that if it were not for my zeal in the Queen's service I should certainly desert, for you know of all things I do not love writing."[3]

It was said by Voltaire that Marlborough had never besieged a fortress which he had not taken, never fought a battle which he had not won, never conducted a negotiation which he had not brought to a prosperous close. The full significance of this praise will scarcely be appreciated until it is seen to how few of the greatest chiefs it would apply. It could not be said of the Black Prince, of Condé or Turenne, of Eugene or of Frederick. It could not be said of Wellington when we remember

[2] Mémoires de Grammont, p. 302, ed. 1792.
[3] Camp at Over Asselt, July 17, 1702.

that he raised the siege of Burgos. It could not be said of Napoleon even had he died before the battle of Leipsick when we remember that he raised the siege of Acre. —

To what then are we to ascribe this uniform success in Marlborough? Not so much to good fortune, though of that he had his share, but rather to the rarest combination of high qualities. His courage was not of that impetuous and inferior kind which kindles at the approach of danger, and rushes beyond the control of prudence. On the contrary it was always well-poised, calm, sustained, and exactly adequate to each occasion. It would not be easy to show even a single case in any part of his military life, in which he deserved like Charles of Burgundy the epithet of TÉMÉRAIRE, nor yet any other case in which for want of daring, he let a favourable opportunity slip by. His genius for war was not formed by tactics and by rules, but rather from the dictates of an excellent though untutored understanding. Never misled by passion, nor warped by any other disturbing influence his clear good sense could form a decision calmly on the balance of opposite advantages; and then abide the issue prosperous or unprosperous as calmly. With him there were none of those after-thoughts and waverings—those painful doubts—"have I judged rightly? might I not have decided better?"—which perplex a common mind.

His expectant calmness was indeed, in Marlborough's own opinion, one secret of his great success. "Patience will overcome all things" so he wrote to Godolphin in 1702. Five years later we find him repeat nearly the same sentiment, with something of that fatalist view which has often been a favourite with great commanders,

Cæsar for example and Napoleon: He says—this also to Godolphin:—"As I think most things are governed by destiny, having done all that is possible one should submit with patience."[4]

Most men it is probable would acknowledge the great value of calmness in human affairs, but many are or think they are, impelled beyond their strength to swerve from it. Marlborough on the contrary had no bursts of passion. No man ever observed the smallest flurry in his demeanour nor the least variation in his countenance. Nature had gifted him with an admirable sweetness and serenity of temper. Nothing in public life at least could ruffle his composure; neither the scruples of the Dutch deputies which so often interposed between him and an almost certain victory; nor the pretensions as unseasonably urged of his German colleagues; neither the calumnies of his opponents nor the changes in his friends; an attack in Parliament as little as an onset from the French. It is recorded of him that once as he heard a surly groom mutter some words of anger behind him, he quietly turned to Commissary Marriot who was riding by his side and said: "Now I would not have that fellow's temper for all the world."

With the suavity of mind in this great chief there was also no less suavity of manner. So competent a judge as Lord Chesterfield speaks of him in the following terms: "Of all the men that ever I knew in my life (and I knew him extremely well) the late Duke of Marlborough possessed the Graces in the highest degree, not to say engrossed them."[5] These Graces enhanced

---

[4] Letters, as printed in Coxe's Life, July 13, 1702, and August 2, 1708.
[5] To his son, November 18, 1748. See some remarks on this passage in Lord Macaulay's History, vol. VIII. p. 204, (Tauchnitz Ed.).

CHAP. the effect of his noble cast of countenance, and of his
III. singular beauty both of face and form. They gave him
1702. on every occasion a most fascinating influence; they
enabled him wherever he desired it to please and to persuade. Even so hostile a witness as Mrs. Manley, and
one so unscrupulous in her assertions, acknowledges
his irresistible charm.[6] Nor was it that he condescended
too far or stooped to those below him. Lord Chesterfield
in the same passage already cited goes on to state:
"With all his gentleness and gracefulness no man living
was more conscious of his situation nor maintained his
dignity better."

It is gratifying to record that the gentleness of Marlborough was not on the surface only. Though not as I
imagine warm-hearted beyond the precincts of his home,
he was an humane and compassionate man. Even
in the eagerness to pursue fresh conquests he did not
ever—as might sometimes be alleged of Napoleon—
neglect the care of the wounded. To his prisoners he
showed a kindly courtesy and was careful to exhibit no
exultation in their presence. He was in general glad
to render a service to any one to whom he bore good
will, whenever it did not put him to expense nor clash
with his own views. This may be called very moderate
praise, yet it will not seem so to any one who has had
experience of public affairs.

The great qualities of Marlborough were not confined
to a narrow circle. No man in English History has
had more influence on the fate of other nations or on
the fame of his own. It was he who gave to the
Germanic Empire another century of life, since but for
him it would have ended in 1704 instead of 1806. It

[6] New Atalantis, vol I. p. 22, &c. ed. 1736.

was he who step by step—siege after siege and battle after battle—wrested the Low Countries from the portentous union of France and Spain. It was he who was the soul, the animating genius, of the whole confederacy, not merely in the army where he commanded, but in all where he advised. But above all, our gratitude as Englishmen is due to him, because he so "signally retrieved" (let us adopt those words from the Commons' votes) the ancient glory of England. That glory had been dimmed during the ignoble reigns of James the First and Charles the Second, while William who succeeded them had upon the Continent far more of merit than success. To Marlborough beyond all others belongs the praise of bringing back to our arms the full lustre that beamed upon them in the days of the Edwards and the Henries. The days of Queen Anne need fear no comparison with those. Ramillies and Blenheim are worthy to be enrolled side by side with Agincourt, Cressy, and Poitiers.

If from the merits of this great man we pass—and how far less welcome the task!—to his errors and defects, we may first observe in his politics a laxity or disregard of principle. To correspond with King James at St. Germain's, after taking the oath to King William at St. James's and accepting posts in his service, is a grievous fault not to be excused, and only in some measure to be palliated, by the too general practice of other politicians of that age. But of that fault, not confined to offers of service or entreaties for pardon, but carried to a most treacherous extreme, there are in the career of Marlborough two signal and painful examples.

The first of these was his secret disclosure of the Brest project to the French Government in 1694—a dis-

CHAP. closure by which as is well known the expedition was
III. defeated, and several hundred English lives were lost.
1702. The fact rests on his own letter to King James, first
made public in 1775, and seems to admit of denial as
little as it does of defence.[7]

The second instance is of 1715. It is alleged that
Marlborough being then in name at least Commander
in Chief for King George, sent over in secret a sum of
money to assist the exiled Prince in his invasion of the
kingdom. Of this second charge the public in general
are not so fully aware nor is it quite so clearly established. The first indication as also the sole proof of it
is contained in a letter which I found among the Stuart
Papers at Windsor and published in the first volume
of my History of England.[8] This letter bearing date
September 25, 1715, is in the hand-writing of Bolingbroke who was then at Paris acting as Secretary of
State for the Pretender. Writing to his Royal Master
he complains how much his proceedings are divulged.
"I must still say" he writes "that since I have been in
business I never observed so little secret as there has
been in your Majesty's affairs. For instance a gentleman belonging to Stair named the very number of battalions which we expected from Sweden; and the Marquis d'Effiat told me the very sum which Marlborough
has advanced to you."

Here the evidence is no doubt only indirect. But I
must observe that Bolingbroke writing a private letter
to James, and alluding to Marlborough's loan as to a
certain fact, could have no imaginable motive for mis-

[7] See Macpherson's Original Papers, vol. I. p. 487. Coxe glides over this transaction as rapidly as possible (vol. I. p. 75), while Lord Macaulay dilates on every detail (vol. VII. p. 320. Tauchnitz Ed.).
[8] Appendix to vol. I. p. 413. (Tauchnitz Ed.).

representation on this point, and I must own myself convinced that even by these two sentences the second charge is sufficiently proved.

Another fault of Marlborough was his love of money. This was shown alike in his large accumulations and in his petty savings. Sometimes though rarely it peeps forth in his own familiar letters. Thus when two years after the event, he refers to his remarkable escape from the French freebooters on the Meuse through the ready wit of his servant, Gell, the Duke makes only this one comment upon it: "He has cost me 50*l.* a year ever since."[9]

This love of money in Marlborough, as in a few years it became generally known, was the topic of numerous taunts from his opponents. It drew forth on several occasions the ribaldry of Swift.[1] But even Swift never showed so much wit in pressing this imputation as did once Lord Peterborough. The mob, misled probably by the likeness of the General's uniform, mistook him for the Duke, and the Duke being then out of favor with them, they were preparing to ill-treat him. "Gentlemen" said Peterborough "I can convince you by two reasons that I am not the Duke of Marlborough. In the first place I have but five guineas in my pocket; and in the second place here they are, much at your service!"[2]

In the same spirit we find St. John then Secretary

---

[9] To the Duchess, Oct. 3, 1704. See Coxe's Marlborough, vol. I. p. 192.
[1] As for instance in "An excellent new Song," where he makes Lord Nottingham "Orator Dismal" pay a visit at Blenheim:

> The Duke showed me all his fine house and the Duchess
> From her closet brought out a full purse in her clutches.

&c. &c. This was in 1711. Works, vol. x. p. 375, ed. 1814.
[2] Seward's Anecdotes of Distinguished Persons, vol. II. p. 243, ed. 1804.

of State write as follows to his friend at the Hague: "I am sorry that my Lord Marlborough gives you so much trouble; it is the only thing he will ever give you."³ Such might be the taunt of St. John; such was not the opinion of Bolingbroke. Years afterwards when the heats of that party strife had passed, Bolingbroke was one day descanting on the many admirable qualities of Marlborough, and some one present let fall a word on his avarice, "He was so great a man" rejoined Bolingbroke "that I forgot he had that defect."

The deliberate opinion of Bolingbroke on Marlborough—and it is equally to the honor of both—may be seen in those eloquent Letters which he drew up in 1736 during his retirement in Touraine. "Over the confederacy, he (the Duke of Marlborough) a new, a private man acquired by merit and by management a more deciding influence than high birth, confirmed authority, and even the Crown of Great Britain had given to King William. . . . . I take with pleasure this opportunity of doing justice to a great man whose faults I knew, whose virtues I admired; and whose memory as the greatest General and the greatest Minister that our country or perhaps any other has produced I honor."⁴

— Another point in the character of Marlborough may be as the reader pleases termed either a merit or defect: it was in fact a virtue carried to a faulty extreme. I mean his devoted attachment to his wife. It is pleasing to observe him, at the busiest moments of his high

---

³ To Mr. Drummond, March 13, 1711. Diplomatic Correspondence of Bolingbroke, published 1798 in two quarto volumes.
⁴ Letters on the Study of History, vol. II. p. 60, ed 1752.

commands, fondly revert to his favourite retreat of Sandridge near St. Alban's. Thus he says to Lady Marlborough at the opening of his first important campaign: "We have now very hot weather which I hope will ripen the fruit at St. Alban's. When you are there pray think how happy I should be walking alone with you. No ambition can make me amends for being from you." Two years later, on his march to the Danube, we find him pass a day at the beautiful village of Weinheim well known to modern tourists. Thence he writes: "I am now in a house of the Elector Palatine that has a prospect over the finest country that is possible to be seen. I see out of my chamber window the Rhine and the Neckar, and his two principal towns of Mannheim and Heidelberg, but I should be much better pleased with the prospect of St. Alban's which is not very famous for seeing far."[5] Such expressions may be compared with those equally tender which Nelson from his flag-ship, and on his way to Trafalgar applies to his beloved cottage, and beloved companion at Merton. But there is one important difference wholly in favor of the former—the endearments of Marlborough were addressed to his own wife and those of Nelson to another's.

But while allowing with all due commendation, that Marlborough in a most dissolute age was ever affectionate, ever constant, to his wife, we may think that like another great chief Belisarius he was no hero at home. Not that there were in the Duchess any moral frailties to forgive as there were in Antonina; but with a temper which Nature had made imperious, her animosities were fierce and her bursts of passion

[5] To the Duchess, July 17, 1702, and June 2, 1704.

frequent. It would have been greatly to her own happiness had there been to curb them a husband's resolute will. We find Marlborough on the contrary as judged by his own letters constantly suffer under them but never rebel. We find him almost sunk in despair until the Duchess herself relents. A single instance out of many may suffice. When Marlborough left England for the campaign which was to culminate in Blenheim, there had been between him and the Duchess "some petty bickerings" as Archdeacon Coxe has called them, using the term perhaps not quite correctly where the violence was solely on one side. The Duchess however wrote to him in terms of reconciliation and Marlborough rejoined in a letter which will be subsequently quoted and which declares that he had been careless of life so long as her displeasure endured."[6]

We have seen that Marlborough had been raised to a Dukedom in December 1702. He valued that dignity in the hope of its transmission to his only son lately called Lord Churchill and now Marquess of Blandford. But the Nemesis too often the attendant on high prosperity was now close behind him. In February 1703 the young nobleman who was pursuing his studies at Cambridge fell ill of the small-pox and in two days expired. The grief of both parents was extreme. They were cheered in some measure by the great kindness of the Queen, who mindful of the like affliction to herself, offered if they wished it to go and stay with them at Sandridge, for as she says "the unfortunate ought to come to the unfortunate."[7]

[6] To the Duchess, Hague May 5, 1704. See page 128 of this volume.
[7] The Queen to the Duchess, Tuesday night (Feb. 23, 1703).

In the letters that passed soon after this sad bereavement it is curious to observe, in token of that ceremonious age, how formally the Duke mentions his children. Writing to Godolphin he refers to his lost son as "poor Lord Churchill;" writing to the Duchess he expresses his satisfaction that their youngest daughter —"dear Lady Mary"—is then with her.[8] It will be found in like manner on examining the letters of the period, that sons most commonly address their parents as "Sir" and "Madam."

It is also worthy of note how little value was set by Marlborough on that female succession which alone remained to him. He passionately longed for another son to inherit his titles. When the Duchess during the next summer complained to him of being indisposed he rejoined as follows: "Pray let me have in every one of your letters an account how you do. If it should prove such a sickness as that I might pity you, but not be sorry for it, it might yet make me have ambition."[9]

From this digression we may now return to the proceedings in Parliament. There were two measures at the commencement of the Session on which the Court laid especial stress. The first was introduced by a Message from the Queen desiring that a further provision might be made for the Prince her husband in case he should survive her. The House being in Committee thereupon Mr. Howe rose and moved a grant to the enormous amount of 100,000*l.* a year. The prodigality of this proposal will best appear when we are told that it was double of what any Queen of Eng-

---

[8] See Coxe's Marlborough, vol. l. p. 226 and 229.
[9] To the Duchess, June 3, 1703.

land ever had in jointure,—double also of what was voted for Prince Leopold on his marriage with the Princess Charlotte of Wales. But on the other hand there was the dread of displeasing Her Majesty; and so the Bill which embodied this lavish grant passed the Commons with only a semblance of debate. In the Lords the case was altered. Even then however the Peers did not take battle on the main question but rather on a collateral issue. The Lower House had inserted a Clause declaring that Prince George should not be liable in any future reign to the incapacity of holding employments which was imposed upon foreigners by the Act of Settlement. This was regarded by the Peers as what is termed a tack upon a Money Bill. They had quite recently passed a Standing Order that the annexing any clause to a Bill of Supply the matter of which is foreign to the matter of the said Bill "is unparliamentary and tends to the destruction of the constitution of this Government."[1]

On this ground the Bill for the Prince's annuity was stoutly resisted in the House of Lords; while on behalf of the clause it was contended that it formed no real tack, since both parts of the Bill referred to the same person. There were some warm debates, but in the end the Court prevailed. The Bill passed with the obnoxious Clause, while Protests against it were signed by some Peers of great name and wealth, as Devonshire and Somerset, as also by the Archbishop of Canterbury, Bishop Burnet, and others of the Bishops of King William.

Marlborough was of course among the warmest supporters of this measure. Greatly to his chagrin the

[1] Lords Journals, December 9, 1702.

opposite course was taken by the husband of his second daughter, who had recently succeeded his father as Earl of Sunderland. The young Earl not only voted but signed a Protest, and drew upon himself in consequence a storm of rage from the Duchess. A family quarrel ensued; only composed after some time and with the utmost difficulty, through Lady Sunderland's affectionate entreaties.

The second measure for which the Queen showed sympathy was the Bill for preventing Occasional Conformity. It was not however a Ministerial measure. We learn from the Commons Journals that it was brought in by three private Members of that House; one of them Henry St. John who had sat for Wotton Basset since 1700 and was rapidly rising into fame.[2] "Occasional Conformity" in those days was held forth by the High Churchmen as a thing to be abhorred. By that phrase was meant the compliance of Dissenters with the provisions of the Test Act, only in order that they might qualify themselves to hold office or to become members of a Corporation. It was found that the persons so admitted gave in general their support to the Whigs; and the Tories had therefore a party motive in seeking to exclude them. But when it was attempted to show that some danger to the Church arose from this Occasional Conformity, the alarm whether real or feigned was certainly ill-founded. It is shown by Mr. Hallam in a lucid argument that the Church on the contrary derived advantage from the practice.[3] To carry his argument further—can we

---

[2] Commons Journals, November 4, 1702.
[3] Constitutional History, vol. III. p. 248, ed. 1855.

doubt that it is the interest of the Church as much as her duty to open the door as widely as possible to her ministrations? If she holds, as hold she must, that these ministrations are of all others most agreeable to Divine truth and to human reason, has she not every thing to gain by inviting not her sons only but strangers also to attend them? We are told by an excellent poet that in some cases those who came to scoff remain to pray; and it may no less justly be presumed that those who came only from interested motives, and to fulfil the requirements of an unwise law, might be touched and won over by what they heard and saw.

Considerations such as these had no weight with the Tories of Queen Anne; and dislike of the Dissenters carried every thing before it. In the preamble of the measure all persecution for conscience sake was expressly condemned; nevertheless it proposed that all those who had taken the Sacrament and Test for offices of trust or the magistracy of Corporations, and who afterwards attended any meeting for religious worship of Dissenters, should be disabled from holding their employments, and pay a fine of 100*l.* besides 5*l.* for every day in which they continued to act in their employments after having been at any such meeting. They were also made incapable of holding any other employment till after one whole year's conformity to the Church to be proved at the Quarter Sessions; and upon a relapse both the penalties and the period of incapacity were to be doubled.

With these provisions the Bill passed rapidly through all its stages in the Commons. But in the Lords it was encountered with sturdy resistance by the Whig Peers

QUEEN ANNE.   91

and a large majority of William's Bishops. They forbore any direct opposition, rightly judging that the best means to defeat the measure would be to move a great number of mitigations and exceptions, some of these to touch the pecuniary fines which would rouse the Constitutional jealousy of the House of Commons. On these tactics therefore they proceeded.[4] On the other hand the Queen in her mistaken zeal for the Church strained all her influence to promote the passing of the Bill. Not only the heads of her government as Marlborough and Godolphin but her Royal Consort went down to vote for it. Yet Prince George's was in truth a melancholy case, since this voter against Occasional Conformity was himself an Occasional Conformist. While he had received the Sacrament according to the rites of the Church of England to be qualified for his office as Lord High Admiral, he had continued to attend the private Lutheran Chapel which he maintained. Accordingly he seems to have voted with a very rueful countenance. It is said that just before they went to a division he came up close to Lord Wharton, a strenuous opponent of the Bill, and whispered: "My heart is vid you."[5]

CHAP.
III.
1702.

Notwithstanding this Court influence not perhaps very wisely exerted, the Whig Peers carried their amendments. On the other part the majority in the Commons was not at all disposed to yield. A Free Conference between the Managers of the two Houses took place in the Painted Chamber—crowded beyond all precedent—on the 16th of January 1703; and some

1703.

[4] The Lords Amendments and the Commons Amendments to theirs are given at full length in the Parl. History, vol. vi. p. 62-92.
[5] Tindal's History, vol. iii. p. 452.

CHAP. Reasons carefully drawn were on several occasions
III. interchanged. It was in vain. As the Lords had hoped
1703. from the beginning, no agreement could be come to
on the Bill. And to allay the rising heats between the
Houses it was found desirable for the Queen to put a
close to the Session with some abruptness, at the end
of February.

There were some other proceedings however before
the Session was closed.—The Commons overhauled the
accounts of the Earl of Ranelagh, Paymaster-General
of the Forces.—They passed a Bill which, with an
amendment making it High Treason to endeavour to
defeat the Succession as now limited by Statute, was
agreed to by the Lords and became law; it gave one
more year as a further term of grace to those who were
required to take the Oath of Abjuration.—There was
also a conclusion, very tame and impotent to the affair
of the famous Kentish Petition. Mr. Colepepper being
proceeded against by the Attorney-General according
to the order of the House tendered his absolute submission. He was called to the Bar and asked whether,
he was sorry for his conduct. He replied that he was
sorry; upon which the action against him was stayed
by an Address to the Queen.

The victory of the Tories at the last General Election had not been to them an unalloyed advantage. As
may often be observed in the working of our English
parties, they had lost in cohesion while they gained in
numbers. On the accession of the Queen they were
content to follow in the wake of Marlborough and
Godolphin. But many more of them now began to
think, as Rochester had thought from the first, that we
should beware of plunging too far into continental

affairs—that it behoved us to be auxiliaries rather than principals in the contest, and to carry on the war so far as possible by sea instead of land. The large expense which it involved was terrifying to their minds. Above all it greatly galled them to be told—bearing in mind their bitter aversion to the memory of King William—that the Ministers taken from their ranks professed to be and were in truth, only the continuators of his foreign policy.

Of all the discontented Tories Rochester was chief. He had aspired to be at the head of the Treasury, and regarded the Lord Lieutenancy of Ireland as only a kind of banishment. During many months he had been absent from his post to which he showed no sign of returning—a circumstance of course not unnoticed nor left unimproved by the Whig writers of that day.[6] The Earl preferred remaining in London and caballing with his friends.

Under these circumstances Marlborough and Godolphin had several anxious consultations. They wished to free themselves of their troublesome colleague, but if possible by his own act, and they resolved "to open the trenches" as Marlborough might have termed it, whenever the Session had closed and Marlborough set out for the army. At that time therefore an order was obtained from the Queen bidding Rochester repair forthwith to his government in Ireland. Rochester haughtily refused; and the order being repeated, he angrily resigned. This was the very course which his

---

[6] Thus for instance William Walsh, then the colleague of Sir John Packington in Worcestershire—the "knowing Walsh" of Pope—inserted these lines in his "Golden Age" written at this period:

Vice-roys, like Providence, with distant care,
Shall govern kingdoms where they ne'er appear.

CHAP. rivals had expected and designed. His resignation
III. was accepted, and the Duke of Ormond was appointed
1703. in his place.

His removal however did not avail to compose the dissension in the Tory ranks. The Earl of Nottingham the new Secretary of State had cordially embraced his views, and continued to act in concert with him. Their objects, shortly stated, were to render the war in the Low Countries so far as possible defensive, and to press hard on the Dissenters, and the favourers of Dissenters, at home.' Towards these aims Nottingham was supported more or less openly by several men holding office in both Houses, by the Duke of Buckingham and the Earl of Jersey in the Lords; by his brother Secretary Sir Charles Hedges and by Sir Edward Seymour in the Commons. It seemed probable that a breach between the moderate and the high Tories could not be much longer averted. All through the next campaign we find Marlborough harassed with letters from Godolphin and the Duchess filled with complaints against Nottingham and Nottingham's allies. It was a most vexatious addition to Marlborough's other and weighty cares. Thus on one of these occasions he writes in reply: "What you say of Lord Nottingham concerning the park is very scandalous but very natural to that person. I wish with all my heart the Queen were rid of him, so that she had a good man in his place, which I am afraid is pretty difficult. . . . We are bound not to wish for any body's death, but if Sir Edward Seymour should die I am convinced it would be no great loss to the Queen nor the nation." And again a week later; "I cannot say a word for excusing the Dutch of the backwardness of their sea preparations this year; but if that or any thing else should produce a coldness between England and Holland, France would gain her point, which I hope in God I shall never live to see; for our poor country would then be the miserablest part of all Christendom." [7]

In Ireland the Ministers were thought to have done well in the appointment of the Duke of Ormond, who possessed and who deserved the popular favor. But Ireland at this time gave little disquiet or anxiety to England. The large Roman Catholic party, trodden to the ground by the iron heel of William and bound fast by the Penal Laws, showed scarcely a sign of life. There was nothing, on the surface at least, to trouble the strong current of the Protestant Ascendency.

The case was far otherwise in Scotland. There the most numerous party, the mass of the people, had triumphed at the Revolution. They had beaten down Episcopacy; they had set up their cherished form of Presbyterian rule; they were supreme in their Parliament; and inflamed by their wrongs at Darien, they were now prepared to manifest by many tokens a most inconvenient independence. These tokens must now be detailed.

First then as to the project of Union. The Queen had been empowered by a Scottish as by an English Act of Parliament to name Commissioners for the discussion of this momentous subject, and they held their first meeting at the Cockpit, Whitehall (then the Privy Council Chamber) in October 1702. They comprised the chief officers of State in both countries, and seemed rather too numerous for business, there being

[7] To the Duchess: Camp at Henef, June 14 and 21, 1703.

CHAP. III.
1703.

twenty-three for England and twenty-one for the sister kingdom.[8] In practice however the fault as to the numbers proved to be the other way. Such was the slackness of attendance in the English members that at one time a quorum could not be formed upon their side; and this greatly chafed the temper of the Scots.

The two first and fundamental propositions—to establish the succession to the Throne according to the Act of Settlement—and to provide one legislature for the united kingdom were readily agreed to. But the unanimity ceased as soon as questions of finance came on. The Scots put forward divers claims of privilege or of exemption. To these it was answered, almost sarcastically, that the Scottish proposals, the one for an equality of duties, the other to be exempt from the debts of England, were self-contradictory, since the duties in England were mainly levied to pay the National Debt.[9]

Of some other answers the Scots had good reason to complain. When they claimed "a free trade between the two kingdoms for native commodities" the English replied that there must be an exception with respect to wool. When they claimed a free trade with the plantations they were reminded "that the plantations are the property of Englishmen and that this trade is of so great a consequence and so beneficial . . . . ." On the other hand the Scots not quite so justly asked that their own Darien Company should be preserved—a demand scarcely compatible with the existence of the East India Company in England.

[8] See the lists in the "Complete History of Europe for 1702," p. 458.
[9] Burton's History of Scotland from 1689 to 1748, vol. I. p. 344.

They were further desirous it would seem that there should be some compensation to the sufferers of Darien from the Treasury of England. On the whole it was soon apparent that taking both sides together there was little earnestness and no conciliation. They held meetings however till the 3rd of February when they were adjourned by a Royal Letter till the autumn following; but in fact they never met again.

During this time there had been in Scotland a General Election, the first since the Convention of Estates in 1689; for there not being in that country a Triennial nor even a Septennial Act there was no reason in law why a Parliament should not subsist so long as the Sovereign survived, and perhaps as some contended even longer still. The new Scottish Parliament however did not meet till many weeks after the English had been prorogued. It assembled at Edinburgh on the 6th of May with the post of Royal Commissioner once more filled by the Duke of Queensberry, a man of good parts but wanting application to business.

The first matter to which this new Parliament applied itself was to provide for the security of the Presbyterian Church establishment. There was a rumour that the High Tories in England had much at heart the restoration of the Episcopal form in Scotland. Nor was this rumour without foundation, as appears from some secret letters which have but lately come to light. The Archbishop of York, who was known to enjoy the Royal favor, had said at a meeting of some friends relative to the project of Union, "Now is the time for restoring Episcopacy in Scotland; and if that be not intended by the Union both the nation and the

Church will be losers by it," Lord Rochester was more cautious as it behoves a statesman to be: "I know not" he said, "when if ever it would be seasonable to restore Episcopacy in Scotland, but I am sure this is not the season to speak of it."[1] We may easily perceive however which way his wishes tended.

These words were not publicly known. But there was also a rumour of sympathetic tendencies in a letter addressed by the Queen to the Privy Council of Scotland. The letter when printed was found to contain only a plea for Toleration. It signified "our Royal pleasure" that the Episcopalians, or as the letter cautiously termed them the "Dissenters," might be "protected in the peaceable exercise of their religion and in their persons and estates according to the laws of the kingdom. And we recommend to the Clergy of the established discipline their living in brotherly love and communion with such Dissenters." At present no exception could be taken to these words. But in Scotland, during the reign of Anne, the principle of toleration was abhorred by the prevailing party. And then brotherly love! Brotherly love with Bishops and favourers of Bishops! It was almost too shocking to think of! Such were the impressions under which the rulers of the Kirk appear at that time to have acted. When therefore in pursuance of the Royal Letter the Earl of Strathmore brought in a Bill "for a toleration to all Protestants in the exercise of religious worship," the Presbyterian chiefs contemptuously tossed aside the project, or rather let it die away. Instead of this

[1] James Johnstone (late Secretary) to George Baillie of Jerviswood, February 13, 1703. Jerviswood Correspondence, edited by the Earl of Minto for the Bannatyne Club and printed in 1842.

they applied themselves to frame and pass a Declaratory Act ratifying and confirming the Church Establishment of the Revolution; while at the same time it was made High Treason to impugn any article of the Claim of Right.

It is worthy of record that in this Act—brought in by the Earl of Marchmont lately Chancellor of Scotland—to satisfy the Presbyterian Church Establishment it was described as "the only Church of Christ within this kingdom." Some members—and more especially Sir David Cunningham of Milncraig—took exception to this phrase as wanting in charity to other denominations of Christians. But the Marquess of Lothian in his zeal started up and cried that the clause was right, since he was sure the Presbyterian government was the best part of the Christian religion—a reply which as we are told and as we might have supposed "set all the House in a merry temper."[2] Nevertheless the Act was passed with these obnoxious words.

In temporal affairs these "Estates" were no less forward. Their great object seemed to be to make Scotland in fact as in name a kingdom separate from England. An Act was passed by them declaring that after Her Majesty's decease no King or Queen of Scotland should have the power to make peace or war without consent of Parliament. And as if to show that they held themselves free of the war against France which was already waging, they brought forward another measure to remove even in the midst of war the restrictions on the importation of French wines. The Jacobites, or as they termed themselves the Cavaliers,

[2] Lockhart Papers, or Memoirs by George Lockhart of Carnwath, vol. I. p. 65, ed. 1817.

who mustered strong in this Parliament, cordially supported the Bill, foreseeing that it would afford them constant and easy means of communication with their exiled Court at St. Germain's. It passed accordingly, notwithstanding the opposition of Fletcher of Saltoun at the head of a party of Whigs. The Ministry in London, contrary to the expectation of some persons, subsequently allowed both these measures to become law—giving leave that the Queen's Commissioner should touch them with the Sceptre, which according to the Scottish forms was held to be equivalent to the Royal Assent—the LA REYNE LE VULT—of England.

Much stronger measures were in contemplation. Fletcher, whose principles were in truth not Whiggish but anti-monarchical, framed a scheme which received the name of the Limitations, its object being to take the patronage of office from the Crown and to exercise it in the Estates by the mode of ballot. "A republican project!" said some of the Court party. "Not at all" answered Fletcher, "it merely transfers the power of governing Scotland from a knot of English placemen to the Scottish Parliament."

It was indeed a turbulent scene that Edinburgh all through this summer displayed. The wildest measures debated—the most utter disregard as to their final consequences—and the parties, each far more violent and reckless than the corresponding party in England. Each party, it might appear, was willing even to injure itself, provided only it could in a still greater degree injure its opponents. All were now intent on framing the so-called Act of Security—to provide for the succession to the Crown in the too probable event of the Queen dying without children. It had been supposed that the Scottish Parliament would take the same part as the English, and declare the Princess Sophia as the nearest Protestant the presumptive heir. But the very fact of England having so decided seemed to be held a sufficient reason why Scotland should not.

Fletcher of Saltoun whose energy gave him a great ascendant in this Assembly was especially active in framing this new Bill. It proposed that, on the decease of Her Majesty without issue, the Estates should name a successor from the Protestant descendants of the Royal Line, but should be debarred from choosing the admitted successor to the Crown of England, unless there were to be such forms of government settled as should fully secure the religion, freedom and trade of the Scottish nation. In that shape was the measure completed after a stormy summer of debate. It passed the House and awaited the decision of the Government.

During this interval however the Earl of Marchmont made an attempt, however hopeless it might seem, to assimilate the law of Scotland upon this point to the law of England. He rose and asked leave to present another Act for settling the Succession; and the House listened with curiosity while the Clerk proceeded to read it. But when the Clerk came to the words "Princess Sophia" there was a burst of uncontrollable rage. "Let the overture be burned!" exclaimed some members.—"Call the mover to the Bar!"—"Send him to the Castle!" was the cry of others. Finally it was resolved that no record of so heinous a proposal should be allowed to stand; and that all notice of it should be omitted from the Minutes.

This occurred on the 6th of September. On the 10th

CHAP. III.
1703.

after much pressing, the Duke of Queensberry as Commissioner said that he was empowered to touch with the Sceptre all the Acts that had been passed, except only the Act of Security. The loss of this their favourite object inflamed the Estates into fury. They were preparing to pass some violent measures which Fletcher had devised, as to disqualify all officers of the army and civil office from being elected members of Parliament, when on the 16th the Duke hastily closed the Session and adjourned the House without any subsidy having been obtained.

The Act of Security which thus fell to the ground began to excite much attention and remark in England. It had been urged forward by men who for the most part were vehement against the project of a Legislative Union, and it is curious to observe how completely they counterworked their own intention. They had wished to make the Union difficult, but in fact they made it inevitable. When reflecting men in England came to see to what lengths a Scottish Parliament would go—how in the midst of an European war it would refuse or elude any grant of supply—how sooner than fail in its party objects it would put to eventual hazard the union on the same head of the two Crowns—they judged and rightly judged that an union of the two Legislatures also had become essential to the welfare nay the safety of both countries. They therefore began to feel for that contemplated measure a growing earnestness which they never till then had manifested, and which, at no distant period as will be shown, succeeded over many obstacles in attaining its fulfilment.

For the Scottish people at this period they were

disposed to blame their own office-holders—the Commissioner, Chancellor and so forth—as having thwarted their wishes and entangled their affairs. In fact however these Ministers had only the shadow of power; as regards the substance they were entirely dependent on Marlborough and Godolphin. They were seen next winter to attend in humble guise the Levees of these two Magnates at Whitehall, and found on some occasions their ill success in Scotland visited upon them. Thus writes Lockhart of Carnwath: "I myself out of curiosity went once to their Levees where I saw the Commissioner, Chancellor, Secretary, and other great men of Scotland, hang on near an hour, and when admitted treated with no more civility than one gentleman pays to another's valet de chambre."[3]

It was no doubt with a view to the state of affairs in Scotland, and to reward some of her loyal adherents in that country, that the Queen at this period revived the Order of the Thistle, which had been called from desuetude by James the Second but let fall in the succeeding reign. The number of Knights at this its fresh foundation was limited to twelve. There were also some new promotions and new peerages. Both the Marquess of Douglas, though under age, and the Marquess of Athol, were raised to the rank of Dukes.

As regards the conduct of the war in this campaign, Louis had resolved to make a most vigorous effort and to strike home at the Allies. Above all he hoped by the aid of the Elector of Bavaria to make a strong impression on Southern Germany. Nor as will presently be seen was his effort unattended with success. But in the course of the year there were three events, each,

[3] Lockhart Papers, vol. i. p. 77.

CHAP. III.
1703.

and that in no slight measure, adverse to his arms. In the first place the Duke of Savoy notwithstanding his close family ties with the Courts both of Paris and Madrid forsook their cause. Early in 1703 he entered into secret engagements with the Emperor. For many months longer he continued to dissemble, but his treachery becoming well ascertained at Versailles, the Duke of Vendome, by order from his Court, took measures for suddenly disarming and detaining as prisoners some four thousand Piedmontese soldiers serving in his army, on the frontiers of Tyrol; and Victor Amadeus thereupon declared war against France. Under these circumstances, Vendome, though at the head of considerable forces, could achieve nothing of note beyond the Alps.

The second event boding ill to France was an insurrection in Languedoc. There the poor Protestants had for some years past groaned under most cruel persecution. The exercise of their religion was denied them; and if ever they presumed to meet for worship among the bleak hills of the Cevennes, they were pitilessly tracked, pursued, and cut down. Scarce any worse persecutors are recorded in history than M. de Baville, Intendant of the Province, and Abbé du Chaila, inspector of the missions, and arch-priest, as he was called, of the Cevennes. The latter, among other atrocities, was wont to renew upon his prisoners the torments sustained by the early Christians in the reign of Nero when they were smeared with combustibles, and set on fire as living torches. In the same spirit, though not to the full perfection of his model, Du Chaila would direct that wool steeped in oil should be tied around the hands of the Protestants whom he succeeded in seizing, and should burn until their fingers were consumed. At last a party of insurgents surprised at Pont de Montvert the house of this ferocious priest, who barricaded himself in the upper chambers while the vaults below were thrown open, and some of his maimed victims were seen to issue forth. At this sight the excited multitude heaped wood and kindled it around the house; and it seems as a just retribution of Providence that Du Chaila himself perished in the flames.[4]

Roused to resistance by their wrongs, small bands of insurgents began to appear in the hill country of the Cevennes. The bands were at first of no more than forty or fifty men, but they gradually increased both in numbers and in daring. They bore the name of Camisards, and they had for chief Jean Cavalier, once for some months a baker at Geneva, and scarce twenty-two years of age, but of inborn ability and commanding the full respect of his co-mates. Louis found it necessary at the beginning of 1703 to send against them a Mareschal of France, De Montrevel, with some troops that were thus withdrawn from other service. The insurrection continued to linger for many months with varying success; never quite triumphant and never quite subdued.

A third event of this year unfavourable to the cause of Louis was the accession of the King of Portugal to the Grand Alliance. For some time past the Court of Lisbon had been wavering, but it was fixed at last by the promise of the Emperor that if the Archduke Charles

---

[4] Sismondi, Hist. des Français, vol. xxvi. p. 395. A portrait of Abbé du Chaila appears among the curious Protestant caricatures which were drawn up by the refugees in England, and published in the Mémoires de Maurepas, vol. iii. pp. 328-358, ed. 1792.

CHAP. III.
1703.

should succeed in establishing his claim to the Spanish monarchy he would cede to Portugal some towns on the several frontiers, as Vigo, Bayona and Badajos, besides the province of Rio de la Plata in America. This promise was reduced to writing in two separate articles of the treaty, but these were to be kept most carefully secret, as certain to offend in no slight degree not merely the pride but the patriotism of the Spaniards. With this reserve the treaty between Portugal and the Allied Powers was concluded at Lisbon on the 16th of May. Mr. Methuen our Minister Plenipotentiary signed it on the part of England.[5] "His Most Faithful Majesty" as the King of Portugal was always styled, acknowledged Charles as King of Spain and espoused his cause, agreeing to maintain at his own charge 15,000 men, and to receive subsidies for raising 13,000 more. Besides these, it was stipulated that 12,000 auxiliary troops should be sent to join his army.

From the terms of this treaty it will be seen how much the design of the Grand Alliance had been widened. It was no longer a mere question of satisfaction to the Emperor in Italy or of security to the Dutch in Flanders. As more Allies came in the pretensions grew. It was now avowed as the final object to substitute the son of Leopold for the son of Louis—to dethrone Philip for the sake of Charles.

The campaign of this year began in Southern Germany. Marshal Villars was again at the head of an army in Alsace eager to gain fresh laurels and to justify his recent promotion. Even in February he crossed

[5] Strictly speaking Mr. Methuen did not sign the general treaty with the other Ministers, but a duplicate alone: *vitandæ controversiæ causâ quæ est de loci prærogativâ inter Coronas Britannicam et Lusitanam.* (Collection de Lamberty, vol. II. p. 508.)

the Rhine at Hüningen, misled his old adversary Louis of Baden by a forward movement, and then suddenly wheeling to his left invested Kehl. Still keeping Prince Louis in check, he compelled the fortress to surrender after thirteen days of siege. In April as soon as the snows of the Black Forest began to melt, and allow a passage through its rugged defiles, he once more deceived the dull prince opposed to him, gained some marches in advance, and plunged boldly into that mountainous region. With some risk he reached the banks of the Danube at Donau-eschingen; and a few marches further, was enabled to join the Bavarian army. The Elector who had been close-pressed by the Imperial forces hailed the approach of his ally with rapturous delight. Villars has himself described the scene: "Although the Elector did not expect me till noon, and although the weather was most inclement, he mounted his horse at seven and climbed some heights from which he could discern my line of march. As soon as he saw me draw near, he came up to me full gallop, shedding tears of joy and declaring that I had saved his person, his honor, his family and his dominions. In his eagerness to embrace me he nearly threw me over and nearly himself fell down."[6]

A wide scope was open to the powerful army thus combined. It might have pressed forward, entered into concert with the insurgents of Hungary, and made the Emperor tremble in his capital. The Elector took a narrower view. He preferred to march with his own troops into the Tyrol, where he reduced Kuffstein and Inspruck and hoped to win the province. But finding

[6] Maréchal de Villars au Roi, 16 Mai 1703. Mémoires militaires de la Succession d'Espagne, vol. III. p. 583, ed. 1838.

the peasantry rise in revolt around him, and learning that the Imperial forces had already entered Bavaria, he relinquished his conquests and rejoined Villars on the Danube. It was owing to the skill and boldness of Villars, that the army, thus again combined, entirely defeated the Imperial general Count Stirum detached by Louis of Baden. This was at Hochstädt on the 20th of September. It was found impossible however for the Elector and the Marshal to agree as to their further movements. A violent dissension had broken out between them; they had grown personal enemies, and Villars apprehensive of disaster solicited recall. His request was granted at Versailles and there was sent in his place the Comte de Marsin, named a Maréchal de France. Even before he arrived the prospects had brightened. A large number of Austrian troops had been called back to repel the more pressing danger in Hungary, so that the French on the Danube and the Lech were enabled to continue their successes, and to co-operate with the Bavarians in the reduction of Augsburg before the close of this campaign.

While Villars was advancing into Germany another French army led by Marshal Tallard had gathered in Alsace; but the month of August came before it could take the field. Then it invested Old Brisach under the experienced eye of Vauban, who in bygone years had himself fortified the place. Brisach surrendered in the first days of September, and Tallard then turned his arms against Landau. The Allies were eager to relieve this important fortress, their conquest of the previous year, and for that object the Prince of Hesse Cassel was detached from the army in Flanders. He took with him twelve battalions of foot and twenty-four squadrons of horse; and on his march was joined by the General of the Elector Palatine with about an equal number. The combined troops encamped in the vicinity of Spires on the 13th of November. The morning but one after as it chanced was the day of St. Leopold,[7] Leopold it will be remembered being the Emperor's name; and the German officers felt it their duty to go into the city and drink His Majesty's health. No doubt they did full justice to the generous vintage of the Rhine, and some of them at least may have been still engaged in this genial occupation when their camp was suddenly assailed by Marshal Tallard. The Prince of Hesse made a gallant defence, but the result was his entire overthrow with four thousand killed and three thousand prisoners. The French according to their own account suffered very little. "Your Majesty's army"—thus wrote Tallard to King Louis—"has gained in this action more flags and standards than it has lost soldiers."[8] Nor was this all. Landau hopeless of relief capitulated two days later; and thus on the Rhine as on the Danube the warfare closed triumphantly in favor of the French.

Such having been from the outset the aim at the Court of Versailles for this campaign, and Southern Germany being designed to bear the brunt of its attacks, it resolved to maintain in great measure the defensive in the Low Countries. Boufflers and Villeroy, the Marshals who commanded the two Corps d'Armée in that region, received orders to avoid engaging in any general action against Marlborough.—Marlborough

[7] Not the Emperor's birthday as stated by Tindal (vol. III. p. 560), for that was the 9th of June. See the "Complete History of Europe for 1703," p. 448.
[8] Voltaire, Siècle de Louis XIV. vol. I. p. 308, ed. 1752.

CHAP.
III.
1703.

himself had reached the Hague from England on March the 17th. He found an eager rivalry prevailing for the chief command under him of the Dutch troops. Since last year the Earl of Athlone and the Prince of Saarbrück had been removed by death from the scene, but three Generals were still competing, Overkirk, Slangenberg, and Obdam. It was mainly to the influence of Marlborough that we may ascribe the judicious selection of Overkirk. But he could not prevent Obdam from being appointed to a separate Corps between Breda and Bergen-op-Zoom. Nor yet could he shake himself free from Cohorn, who was to be with him at the main army, to second him as they said, but much more frequently to cavil and to thwart.

An extensive design had been formed by Marlborough for the invasion of French Flanders and the reduction of Antwerp and Ostend. He was confident of success, and warmly pressed his scheme upon the States. But he had to make the ever recurring complaints of slowness and irresolution both in themselves and in the Deputies whom they sent out. It is hard to understand such a state of things in the government of such a people—the same people which had achieved a wonderful deliverance from the tenfold might of Spain —the same people whose triumph over the higher level of the surrounding ocean was if possible more wonderful still—the same people whose commercial enterprise and skill had raised to equal terms with the proudest European kingdoms a small slip of country hardly rescued from the waves—the same people which had made itself the asylum and the safeguard of the exiles finding there, what they sought in vain at home, freedom of conscience and of laws—the same people whose

courage, energy and hardihood had been signalised on
fields of battle no less than on marts of trade. How
are we to explain the fact that all through the Succession War the counsels of this very people were marked
by an utter indecision, by a procrastinating slowness
which well nigh exhausted the lofty patience of Marlborough, and which again and again defeated his most
skilful combinations? How are we to conceive the
ridiculous reasons or the sorry jests which we find
successfully pleaded as excuses for delay? Thus for
instance on one occasion when there was a conference
at the Hague relative to the Munster troops, Alexander
Stanhope who was present as British Minister heard
one Deputy declare: CANIS FESTINANS CÆCOS PARIT
CATULOS! [9]

Day after day did Marlborough urge his project of
Antwerp and Ostend. The States answered that there
would be risk. But as Marlborough observes at a later
period: "If you have a mind to have Antwerp and
a speedy end of the war you must venture something
for it."[1] At length he partially prevailed. The States
reluctantly consented, provided he would first secure
them from any possible risk on their Rhenish frontier,
by reducing Bonn, the fortress and the residence of the
Elector of Cologne. Marlborough against his own
judgment gave the priority to this siege. He drew his
troops from their quarters, left to Overkirk a Corps of
observation on the Meuse, and opened the trenches
against Bonn on the 3rd of May. He took the fort
on the 9th, and, with a little more time, might have not
only secured the town but made the garrison prisoners

[9] Despatch to Sir Charles Hedges, March 2, 1703 (MS.).
[1] To Pensionary Heinsius, July 15, 1703.

of war. The French however were already making a movement on the Meuse, and Marlborough was so disquieted by it that he deemed it best, on the 15th, to grant the besieged a capitulation, according to which they marched out with all the honors of war.

The siege of Bonn at this juncture had certainly left leisure for preparation to the French in Flanders. Nevertheless Marlborough was full of hope. Thus he wrote to Godolphin on returning to the Meuse. "I shall to-morrow send an express to the Hague to see how far they have prepared for what I call the great design, so that we may not lose time. . . . If this design of Antwerp can be brought to perfection, I hope we shall make it very uneasy for them to protect Brussels and the rest of their great towns. I am speaking as if we were masters of Antwerp but as yet the two Marshals threaten." [2]

The skilful project of Marlborough was however doomed to be disappointed by the silly precipitation of Obdam, who, instead of awaiting his arrival, marched forwards at once from Bergen-op-Zoom, and took up his position at the village of Eckeren a few miles to the north of Antwerp. Marlborough with his usual sagacity discerned the impending danger. "If" he says to Godolphin "M. Obdam be not upon his guard he may be beat before we can help him." And then in a hasty postscript: "Since I sealed my letter we have a report come from Breda that Obdam is beaten. I pray God it be not so, for he is very capable of having it happen to him." [3]

The report proved only too true; and the circum-

[2] Camp near Maestricht, May 19, 1703.
[3] Camp of Moll, July 9, 1703.

stances are so extraordinary that they may deserve to be told in the words of the despatch which Alexander Stanhope wrote home on this occasion: "We were all here in great consternation before yesterday at night, when about six a courier arrived with letters from Monsieur d'Obdam then at Breda, with a lamentable relation, how the Marshal de Boufflers with a great detachment from the French main army had on a sudden surrounded him and cut in pieces or defeated his whole army, desiring the States's orders whether to stay at Breda, or return to the Hague since he had now no army left to command. The States, upon this letter, met extraordinarily at nine and sat till one next morning, to give the best orders to their affairs they could in such an exigency. Mr. Geldermaesen with two other Deputies were immediately sent away with money to try to get together all the scattered debris of the army, if any were left; and luckily the same morning, met on their way a courier despatched by Mr. Hop with letters to the States, which having commission to open, they found things were not so bad as had been represented; on the contrary that our army had beaten Marshal Boufflers though above double the number, taking cannon, standards, and remaining masters of the field. . . . . All here wonder how M. d'Obdam could be so mistaken, but we ought not to censure him till we know what he can say for himself." [4]

The explanations which followed were by no means clear. It appears that General Obdam mistook a column of Frenchmen for a cloud of dust, or a cloud of dust for a column of Frenchmen; that riding onwards to this object he was cut off from his troops; that he left

[4] To Sir Charles Hedges, Hague, July 3, 1703 (MS.).

CHAP. III.
1703.

them to their fate; and that he announced their entire destruction when he came in headlong flight to Breda. On the other hand we find, that General Slangenberg, who succeeded to their command, availed himself of the dykes and natural defences of the country so as not indeed to gain a victory as Monsieur Hop had claimed for him but to arrest the current of the defeat. The strangest point in this strange story still remains to tell. Obdam instead of being punished for his negligence was after some time by his private influence restored to his command.

The reverse of Eckeren proved fatal to the "great design" of Marlborough. He found, in consequence of it, the scruples of the Dutch Generals and Deputies come back with redoubled force. They declared that the enterprise against Antwerp was too hazardous and the enemy too strong. To add to these embarrassments, a violent quarrel having broken out between Cohorn and Slangenberg, the former quitted the army in a burst of anger. Marlborough with deep chagrin found it necessary to relinquish his well-concerted and promising scheme. He returned with his army to the Meuse, where he besieged and took the small fortress of Huy, midway between Liege and Namur. Subsequently he reduced Limburg, while Guelders which had been invested since the spring yielded to that long blockade. Yet taken as a whole, the events of this year in the Low Countries were rather to the enemy's advantage. There had been only one action, and in that one action the French had been victorious.

Moreover, as regarded the prospects of the next campaign, the revolt in Hungary was much more than a set off to the revolt in the Cévennes. For a long time past the Hungarians had chafed under the arrogant dominion of the House of Austria. The persecution of the Protestants, the forced levies of men, and the illegal imposition of taxes were especially obnoxious to them. The renewal of the war with France seemed to afford them a favourable opening; and they found a leader in Francis Ragotzky great grandson of the former Prince of Transylvania. Once already—this was in 1701—the young Magnate had attempted to raise his countrymen in arms; he had failed and was thrown into prison, but made his escape to Warsaw. There he carried on a secret correspondence with the disaffected nobles of Hungary; and thence, while the Imperial troops were drawn off into Bavaria, he suddenly returned. He received some supplies of money and also some officers from France, and, passing the Polish frontier, appeared on the Carpathian hills at the head of a half-armed and half-savage multitude. But descending into the plains of Hungary he gathered strength as he went on. He was joined by some members of the chief Magyar families, as by Count Caroly, a powerful Magnate, and two nephews of the Palatine, Prince Esterhazy, and he found himself ere long at the head of 20,000 men. Through his adherents the flame of rebellion was extended to Transylvania; and the open country up to the Theiss was overrun. The insurgents, who still gained strength, took many of the smaller forts and blockaded the Austrian troops in the larger. Even when more Austrian troops had been brought against them from Bavaria they still maintained the upper hand. All through the winter and spring they negotiated, as though on equal terms, with the Imperial Court, first

CHAP. III.
1703.

through Prince Eugene, and at last by the mediation of the Maritime Powers. But their demands gradually augmented until they seemed almost intolerable to the Jesuit-governed Court of Vienna. They required among other things that Ragotzky should be acknowledged as independent Prince of Transylvania; that the Jesuits should be expelled the kingdom; and that the Protestants should be reinstated in four hundred churches.

There was another event of the year which on the contrary gave the Emperor high hopes; this was the undertaking of the King of Portugal to set his army in motion and assert the Archduke Charles as King of Spain. It was felt that the young Prince ought at once to repair to the scene of action, and draw his own sword in support of his own pretensions; and this step was warmly pressed by the Maritime Powers; but it was not accomplished without that long procrastination which was then characteristic of the Court of Vienna. At last, a public Court being held at Vienna on the 12th of September, the Emperor solemnly renounced his claim to the Spanish Crown, as did also his eldest son the King of the Romans; and the second son was, thereupon, as the next heir, in due form proclaimed Charles the Third, King of Spain and the Indies. The young Prince was not yet fully eighteen years of age. Setting out from Vienna a few days afterwards, he met Marlborough at Düsseldorf disposing his troops into winter quarters. In company with Marlborough he journeyed on to Holland, where he was acknowledged and received with Regal honors. Strange sound to those who bore in mind the history of the two last centuries, to be told that a King of Spain was now upon a visit at the Hague!

CHAPTER IV.

PARLIAMENT met on the 9th of November; and the Queen in her opening Speech, while she announced the accession of the King of Portugal and the Duke of Savoy to the Grand Alliance, made known also the less welcome fact that both the King and the Duke would require the aid of subsidies and lead to "a further necessary charge." The House of Commons however showed itself in a complying humour so far as money was concerned; and the public business was proceeding in its customary course when it was broken through by a sudden convulsion of nature. There occurred the most terrible tempest that was ever known in England. For several years afterwards it was mentioned not as A storm but as THE storm.[1]

This hurricane, comparable to the worst in tropical climes, began about eleven o'clock at night on the 26th of November, and continued in its full fury till about seven the next morning. Its violence was chiefly felt in the southern parts of the kingdom and the adjoining seas; being far less apparent to the north of Trent. All through that month the weather had been very boisterous, insomuch that the Archduke could not

CHAP. IV. 1703.

---

[1] There are several tracts relative to "the Storm" in the Library of the British Museum. Besides the well-known compilation of Defoe and the letters in the 24th volume of the Philosophical Transactions, I have mainly consulted "An exact relation of the late dreadful tempest faithfully collected by an ingenious hand," London, 1704, and "An historical narrative of the great and tremendous storm," London, 1769.

CHAP. pursue his voyage to London, but was detained against
IV. his wish on the coasts of Holland. When the stormy
1703. wind arose upon the 26th it blew from the South West, and was so high that between the gusts it sounded like thunder in the distance. Of real thunder and lightning there was none, but in some places the air was full of meteoric flashes which resembled the latter. In general however the darkness added to the terror, for it was just New Moon.

The palaces of England, both Royal or Episcopal, had their share in the general calamity. A narrative of the time informs us that "part of the palace of St. James's was blown down; and a woman killed by the fall of a chimney. Her Majesty was alarmed and got up with His Highness the Prince and all the Maids of Honor."—At Wells, the Bishop of the Diocese and his wife Mrs. Kidder were killed as they lay in bed, by the fall of a stack of chimneys. He was a prelate held in high esteem, eminent for his knowledge of Hebrew and Arabic.

In humbler life the casualties were numerous and terrible. Many persons were crushed in their beds; while others who had taken alarm and run out into the streets or gardens were struck dead by the fall of bricks and tiles. Many more were maimed or severely bruised. At the same time there were instances of marvellous escape or deliverance. Thus in the case of Mr. Hanson, Registrar of Eton College, who was in London and sleeping in a garret near Ludgate Hill, the roof being blown down he was carried to the ground without any hurt, and as he declared, knew nothing of the storm till he found himself lying on his bed in the open street. Thus also in Aldersgate Street, a man and a woman were forced into a cellar by the fall of a chimney; and as it seemed buried alive. Being however extricated about eight o'clock the next morning, it was worthy of note that the first question the man asked was respecting his clothes which he had left in the next room with fifty shillings in a pocket. The woman on her part demanded what was become of her trunk in which were some pieces of gold; neither expressing any gratitude to either God or man for their timely deliverance.

The Thames also became an agent in the metropolitan havoc. The tide rushed up with great violence, flowing even into Westminster Hall, and flooding the lower parts of the city, while London Bridge was almost choked up by the wrecks. Many barges and boats were submerged or dashed together and several persons drowned. At Bristol in like manner the Avon rose; and the tide was so high in the streets that the people had to pass over in boats. Hogsheads of tobacco and other goods were floating about the city; and the damage in Bristol alone was computed at £150,000. In other towns there was equal havoc. "Portsmouth," says a writer of the time, "looks like a city bombarded by the enemy."

Many great buildings were shattered, and some subverted, by the fury of the blast. In several churches the spire was beaten off the steeple; and the lead upon the roofs rolled up like a scroll of parchment. The Chapel of King's College at Cambridge, one of the noblest fabrics not in England merely but in the world, lost many of its pinnacles; and had some of its painted glass dashed in. The Eddystone Lighthouse, only three years since completed on a new plan by Mr.

Winstanley, was severed into fragments and swept into the sea; and among the three men drowned on that occasion was the ingenious projector himself, then as it chanced upon a visit to his work. It had been built not of stone but of timber; and judging from the designs of it that remain, it resembled in some degree a Chinese Pagoda.[2]

The trees also were in large numbers uprooted or torn asunder. Through the ancestral parks of Southern England, and its richly wooded glades—as the Chace of Cranbourn or the Forest of Dean—the ground was strewn with prostrate trunks and severed branches. In London we find especially commemorated the loss of above an hundred elm trees in St. James's Park, several of large growth and planted it was said by Cardinal Wolsey; and some also in Moorfields of still greater size, being about three yards in girth. Defoe states that he was induced from curiosity to make a circuit on horseback over most part of Kent, and to count as he rode the fallen trees. He counted up to 17,000 and then being weary desisted.

On the coasts the shipping also suffered severely. The main fleet under Sir Cloudesley Shovel rode safe upon its anchors; but several of the smaller men-of-war and many merchantmen foundered at sea, or went to pieces on the Goodwins and other shoals. Particular commiseration was excited by the fate of the Mary, a sixty-four gun ship, having on board Admiral Basil Beaumont of the family of the present Lords Hotham. This vessel perished in full view—though perhaps only by glasses—of the town of Deal; the Admiral using all possible means to save his men's lives and his own. He

---

[2] Smiles's Lives of the Engineers, vol. II. p. 19.

stood on the deck, and, to encourage the people to venture out to him, he showed plate and money by holding it on high. But in vain. Intrepid as the Deal boatmen were and are, none of them would offer to put out in such a sea. The Admiral was drowned and with him his whole crew of 269 except only one single sailor who was cast by a wave to shore.

There seems some reason to suspect that in compiling the Bills of Mortality or other official accounts for London, an endeavour was made to lessen the public consternation, by keeping out of sight as many fatal accidents as possible. Nevertheless we find it stated that taking all throughout the country, one hundred and twenty-three persons were struck down and killed. The number of men lost, including those on the coast of Holland, those in ships blown away and never again heard of, and those drowned in the floods of the Severn and the Thames, could not of course be accurately ascertained, but has been computed to exceed 8,000. Above 800 houses were blown down, in most of which the inmates received some bruise or wound. Above 400 windmills were overset and broken to pieces. Great numbers of cattle were swept away from the river-banks; 7,000 sheep on a single level of the Severn.

In view of this dire calamity, the House of Commons presented an Address to the Queen lamenting the diminution of the Royal Navy, and beseeching Her Majesty to give orders for building some new ships. The Queen's answer was in suitable terms; and two or three days later she issued a Proclamation for a General Fast, which was observed throughout England with great signs of devotion and sincerity on the 19th of January following. Lord Macaulay has noticed that no other tempest was ever in this country the occasion of a Parliamentary Address or of a Public Fast.[3]

Besides the promise of funds which was implied in the Address to build some "capital ships" as the Address had termed them, the Commons cheerfully voted not only as before 40,000 men to act in conjunction with the Allies, but 10,000 augmentation for the next campaign, and a further force of 8,000 designed to serve in Portugal and Spain. For these, for guards and garrisons, and for payments to the Allies the total sum of £1,800,000 was granted, and the vote for seamen was of 40,000 including 5,000 marines.

The House of Commons was in truth at this time much less intent on finance than on theology; so far at least as theology is concerned in the treatment of Dissenters. The flame upon the question of Occasional Conformity had been kept alive by the heats which prevailed between the two Houses of Convocation. To this period may be ascribed the origin of those bywords of High Church and Low Church which have ever since, though under very various phases, divided the Church of England.[4] Both these parties, as they existed among the clergy of Queen Anne's reign, were espoused by men of eminent ability. If the Upper House of Convocation could boast of its Bishop Burnet, the Lower House had its Dean Atterbury. But neither party if tried by our present notions could claim the praise of superior toleration. For while the

---

[3] Essay on Addison first published in the Edinburgh Review for July 1843, p. 218.
[4] Tindal's History, vol. III. p. 481.

High Church clergy desired a stern repression of the Protestant Dissenters, the Low Church clergy were eager to smite the Roman Catholics, hip and thigh. The only point on which, with some few eminent exceptions, they cordially agreed was in denouncing all moderate counsels, which they called latitudinarian and carnal.

The Tory politicians, incited at this time by the High Church Divines, came to Parliament in November 1703 fully resolved to aim another blow at the Occasional Conformists. But they no longer found the same support from the Queen or the Queen's Government. Marlborough and Godolphin had discerned the deep offence caused by the measure of the preceding year. They felt, moreover, in proportion as their differences with Nottingham and Jersey grew wider, that they might have to rely in some degree at least on Whig votes; and they felt reluctant to take a course more than any other distasteful to Whig leaders. Therefore, without as yet breaking away from their High Tory adherents, they did their utmost to dissuade them. By their advice the Queen in her opening Speech expressed her earnest desire to see all her subjects in perfect peace and union among themselves; and these words were clearly understood as conveying the Royal wish that the Dissenters might not at this juncture be again assailed.

Nevertheless the High Tories persevered. Within a few days of the opening of the Session, they brought in once more, with only some slight modifications, their favourite Occasional Conformity Bill. The debate upon this subject as nearly all others of that period has passed by unreported. Only one speech here remains to us; no doubt through the obliging care of the oratoi himself. This was Sir John Packington of Westwood Park in Worcestershire, a cross-grained and conceited politician. One passage of his speech will serve to show with how little respect the heads of the Church were sometimes treated, by those who claimed to be exclusively its friends: "I did wonder last year to hear so many Bishops against this Bill, but that wonder ceased when I considered to whom they owed their preferment. The Archbishop of Canterbury I think was promoted to that See by my Lord Sunderland's interest; and being asked what reasons he had against this Bill replied he had not well considered the Bill, but that my Lord Sunderland told him it ought not to pass. This was a very weighty reason for the head of our Church to give; and yet I dare say none of the rest of them could give a better."[5]

The Bill being thus urged forward in the Commons received the sullen support of the Ministers; and it passed the House by 223 against 140. In the Lords Godolphin and Marlborough also gave their votes in its favor, although the first acknowledged in his speech that he thought the time unseasonable. The Queen's secret inclination was still in favor of the Bill. But, to gratify her "dearest Mrs. Freeman," she determined to mark some change of sentiment, by sanctioning the absence from the House of her Royal Consort. That illustrious Occasional Conformist was no longer required to vote against Occasional Conformity. Some other Peers who had voted for the Bill last year likewise staid away from the House. The Bishops were almost equally divided, but the speech of Burnet—soon after-

[5] Parl. Hist. vol. vi. p. 154.

wards printed by himself at the desire of his friends —excited particular attention. "I myself" he said "was an Occasional Conformist in Geneva and Holland. I thought their Churches were irregularly formed and with great defects in their constitution; yet I thought communion with them was lawful, for their worship was not corrupted. But at the same time I continued my communion with our own Church, according to the Liturgy of this Church, with all that came about me." Finally the Bill was rejected on the Second Reading by, including proxies, 71 against 59. Godolphin and Marlborough, very little to their credit under all the circumstances, endeavoured to gratify their friends, by signing a Protest against its rejection.

It was the ill humour of the Commons resulting from the loss of their cherished Bill, that was at the root of the serious differences, which soon afterwards sprung up between the two Houses, first on the Scottish Plot and secondly on the Aylesbury Case. Both of these shall be presently detailed.

In the last days of this year was concluded at Lisbon the Methuen Treaty, as it has been termed from Mr. John Methuen who signed it on the part of England. There were only two articles. By the first the King Don Pedro agreed to admit into Portugal the woollen manufactures of England. By the second Queen Anne engaged to grant a differential duty in favor of the wines of Portugal, so that the duties on these wines should always be less by one third than those on the wines of France. Many Portuguese proprietors it is said consequently increased their culture of the vine;[6] and the treaty produced no less effect on the taste for

[6] Macpherson's Annals of Commerce, vol. II. p. 729, ed. 1805.

CHAP. wine in England. Till 1703 and even for some years
IV. beyond it, Burgundy, whenever it could be obtained, ap-
1703. pears to have been the favourite wine.[7] But the Methuen
Treaty, in its gradual influence, gave to Port it may be
said the supremacy for above an hundred years.

On the 28th of December the titular King of Spain
having at last arrived from Holland disembarked at
Portsmouth. He was received with Regal honors by
the Dukes of Somerset and Marlborough, and conducted
in state to Petworth where he slept that night. Next
day pursuing his journey he stopped to dine at Guild-
ford, and reached Windsor Castle in the evening.
The ceremonies at Queen Anne's Court differed much
in some respects from those at Queen Victoria's. We
are told how "the Marquess of Hartington, Captain of
the Yeomen of the Guard, received the King at his
alighting out of the coach; and the Earl of Jersey,
Lord Chamberlain, lighted him to the great staircase.
Her Majesty received the King at the top of the great
staircase, without the guard-room, where His Majesty
made a very low bow; and the Queen raising him up
he saluted her, and made his compliment to Her
Majesty, acknowledging his great obligations for her
generous protection and assistance. After which Her
Majesty gave him her hand and he led her into her
bed-chamber. After a little stay there His Royal
Highness (the Prince) conducted his Catholic Majesty
to the apartment prepared for him, where having
remained some time he returned to the presence-
chamber and saluted several ladies presented to him

[7] Burgundy is mentioned as highly relished in Farquhar's comedy, The
Inconstant (act v. scene 2), and in Swift's Journal to Stella, so far at least as
Lord Peterborough and Secretary St. John, no mean judges, were concerned
(Feb. 18, 1711).

by the Queen; and soon after handed Her Majesty to supper which was very magnificent, with extremely fine music played all the while." Next evening at supper, we further read, that the King "would not be satisfied till, after great compliments, he had prevailed with the Duchess of Marlborough to give him the napkin, which he held to Her Majesty when she washed."[8]

On the morning which ensued the Archduke—for so judging by the fortunes of the war we may now prefer to call him—took leave of the Queen and set off on his return to Portsmouth, desiring to reembark and reach Lisbon as soon as possible. With him were to proceed about 8,000 English and 4,000 Dutch troops, the former headed by the Duke of Schomberg, while Sir George Rooke was in command of the fleet. But the expedition was detained week after week by contrary winds, and when at last it did put to sea and had made some progress in the Channel, it was driven back by a violent tempest. Finally it was not till the 8th of March New Style that Charles cast anchor in the Tagus. When we remember that the Treaty with Portugal, acknowledging his claims and requiring his presence, had been signed ten months before, we cannot ascribe these most ill-timed delays in arriving at his destination solely to the weather, but must allow a large share to the procrastinating temper at that time of the Austrian Princes. Certain it is that the storms which prevailed in the month of January did not prevent the Duke of Marlborough from crossing the sea and repairing for a few days to the Hague, there to concert the measures for the next campaign.

[8] Complete History of Europe for 1703, p. 484.

CHAP. IV.
1704.

We may now revert to the proceedings in Parliament, and first as they bore upon that tangled mass of baseness, called in England the Scottish Plot, and in Scotland the Queensberry Plot. In March 1703 the Queen had granted, through the Scottish Privy Council, a general indemnity to all Scotsmen, for political offences, to those at least who would promptly accept it, and qualify themselves by taking the Oaths. It was an humane and a politic measure, yet it came to excite some disquietude in the minds of its framers. It was found that many persons returned to Scotland under colour of this protection, who were believed to have in no degree renounced their Jacobite politics. Such were for example Robertson of Strowan and David Lindsay who had acted as Secretary to Lord Melfort the Pretender's Minister. It was feared therefore that they had come over for the purpose of some rebellious movement, and this apprehension was increased by rumours which reached the Government from other quarters. Alexander Stanhope wrote from the Hague that, as was there believed, a considerable sum in gold had been transmitted to Scotland through a commercial house of Amsterdam. There was, no doubt, the standing conspiracy of the Jacobites always corresponding and caballing, and with their agents going to and fro; but it is difficult to believe that they had seriously in view a rising at this particular time.

Among the turbulent spirits who now reappeared north of Tweed was Simon Fraser of Beaufort, better known in subsequent years as Lord Lovat, one of the most unprincipled men in that far from scrupulous age. He had been convicted and outlawed on a heinous charge in private life brought against him by

Lord Athol; and he now came back to Scotland with a full determination to push his fortunes, and with an entire indifference as to the means. He obtained an interview with the Duke of Queensberry, to whom in the character of a deeply penitent Jacobite, and no doubt with abundance of sobs and tears, he revealed a real or pretended plot for raising the Highlands. He had brought with him he said, while still in the meshes of evil, a secret communication from the Court of St. Germain's to Lord Athol who was then Keeper of the Privy Seal in Scotland. Accordingly he produced a letter expressed only in general terms and signed only with one initial by the Queen Dowager. It had no address and was believed to have been intended for the Duke of Gordon, but Fraser had taken the liberty of writing on the blank cover the address of his old enemy the Marquess of Athol.

Queensberry with much eagerness swallowed the bait which Fraser here set before him. He had conceived a jealousy of Athol as one of his colleagues in the government of Scotland, and he hoped by this device to rid himself of his rival. Accordingly he transmitted to the Queen an account of the supposed conspiracy, as though the proof against Athol were certain and complete. But Athol, having obtained a clue to these secret machinations, was enabled to explain himself and to prove his entire innocence. Both sides turned angrily round on Fraser as the author of the whole; and Fraser secured his own safety by a precipitate retreat to France. David Baillie, who had taken part against Queensberry in another phase of the same transaction, was not so fortunate. Early in 1704 he was brought to trial before the Privy Council at Edinburgh on a charge of defamation or "leasing-making" as it is termed in Scottish law. Being found Guilty the sentence against him was that he should stand in the Pillory at the Tron, and be transported to the West Indies; but of this sentence the first part only came to be enforced.[9]

Meanwhile there had been some arrests. Sir John Maclean, one of the Highland chiefs and up to that time an undoubted Stuart partisan, was taken on disembarking from an open boat at Folkestone. He protested that his object was only to pass through England on his way to claim the Indemnity in Scotland, while the friends of the Government contended that he would never have exposed himself to risk, by touching English ground at all, had there not been some conspiracy to serve. Other men of little note were seized about the same time on the coast of Sussex. Upon the whole the evidence of a Scottish plot was but slight and inconclusive; it was however announced in the most solemn form to the English Parliament. On the 17th of December 1703 the Queen went in person to the House of Peers, and after giving her Assent to the Land Tax Bill for 1704, made a speech declaring that she had "unquestionable information of very ill practices and designs carried on in Scotland," and promising to lay the particulars before both Houses.

The House of Lords in its Whig zeal, and as though seeking to outrun the Tory Government, at once appointed a Select Committee to examine the prisoners, and especially Sir John Maclean. It was however in-

[9] The proceedings against David Baillie, now of very little interest, are elucidated in Lockhart's Memoirs (vol. 1. p. 83), and given at full length in Howell's State Trials (vol. xiv. p. 1035, &c.).

timated to the House by the Lord Steward, that Her Majesty thought the examination of Sir John Maclean a matter of too much nicety and importance to be taken out of its ordinary course, or removed from the officers of the Crown. The House of Lords acquiesced, and there the whole matter might have ended, but that the Tory Commons deemed the occasion favourable for striking a blow at the Whig Peers. They carried an Address to the Queen complaining that "the Lords in violation of the known laws of the land have wrested the persons in custody out of your Majesty's hands, and without your Majesty's leave or knowledge." The Peers retorted by another Address in which they spoke as follows: "The expressions in the Address of the House of Commons are so very harsh and indecent that we may truly affirm the like were never used of the House of Peers in any age, not even by that assembly which under the name of the House of Commons took upon itself not only to abolish the House of Lords but to destroy the monarchy." Such were the compliments interchanged between the Houses through the remainder of the Session. Such was the altercation that prevailed even long after the subject-matter of altercation had been by common consent relinquished and set aside.

Not far unlike in its result though wholly different in its origin was the celebrated Aylesbury case. There had been for many years past complaints of gross corruption at the Aylesbury elections. It was alleged that the four Constables who were the returning officers for the borough were wont to make a bargain with some of the candidates, and then to manage matters so that the majority should be for the persons to whom they had engaged themselves. At the last election they had refused the vote of Matthew Ashby, a burgess who had been admitted to poll on former occasions. For this Ashby brought an Action against William White and the other Constables. The Action was tried in due course at the County Assizes, when the Jury gave a verdict for the Plaintiff with costs.

It was moved however in the Court of Queen's Bench to quash these proceedings. Three Judges, here directly opposed by Chief Justice Holt, were of opinion that no hurt was done to Ashby, and that decisions on the right to vote belonged to the House of Commons. The order of the Queen's Bench was therefore in favor of the Constables. But the question was next brought by Writ of Error before the House of Lords, where it was decided by a large majority to set aside the order of the Queen's Bench, and to give judgment according to the verdict at the Assizes.

The Commons upon this took fire. They passed a string of Resolutions declaring that the qualification of any elector was cognisable only by themselves, and that Ashby in commencing his action had been guilty of a breach of Privilege. The Lords retorted by some well-drawn counter-Resolutions. They maintained: That by the known laws of this kingdom every person having a right to give his vote, and being wilfully denied by the officer who ought to receive it, may maintain an action against such officer to recover damage for the injury: and That the contrary assertion is destructive of the property of the subject, and tends to encourage partiality and corruption in returning officers.—Since that time, the ablest writers who have discussed this question give their judgment in favor of the House of

Lords. Mr. Hallam above all contends that while the House of Commons had an undoubted right of determining all disputed returns to the Writ of Election, and consequently of judging upon the right of every vote, there was no pretext of reason or analogy for denying that this right to vote, like any other franchise, might also come, in an indirect manner at least, before a Court of Justice, and be judged by the common principles of law.[1]

It is pleasing to turn from the petty brawls between the Houses to a noble act of beneficence on the part of the Queen. Her Majesty's birthday, which was the 6th of February, falling this year on a Sunday its celebration had been postponed till the next day. On that day then as well beseeming her pious and princely gift, Sir Charles Hedges as Secretary of State brought down to the House of Commons a message from the Queen, importing that Her Majesty desired to make a grant, of her whole revenue arising out of the First Fruits and Tenths, for the benefit of the poorer clergy. These First Fruits and Tenths had been imposed by the Popes some centuries ago, for the support of the Holy Wars, but had been maintained long after those wars had ceased. The broad besom of Henry the Eighth had swept them from the Papal to the Royal treasury; and there they continued to flow. In the days of Charles the Second they had been regarded as an excellent fund out of which to provide for the female favourites of His Majesty and their numerous children. Under William and Mary Bishop Burnet, as he says, often pressed this question on the Queen, and wrought so successfully with her that she had determined, if she

[1] Constit. History of England, vol. III. p. 274, ed. 1855.

CHAP. IV.
1704.

had lived to see a peace, to clear this revenue of all the charges which had been cast upon it, and apply it to the augmentation of small benefices. The Bishop had also half persuaded King William and laid the matter very fully before the Princess Anne. It was natural therefore that the Bishop should ascribe to himself no small share in the merit of the subsequent grant.[2] He intimates not very graciously that perhaps the time for it was chosen to pacify the angry clergy who resented the loss of their Occasional Conformity Bill. They had now begun, he says, to talk of the danger the Church was in, as much as they had done during the former reign.

Upon the Queen's Message the Commons returned a suitable Address, and proceeded to pass a Bill enabling Her Majesty to alienate this branch of the revenue, and to create a corporation by charter to apply it for the object she desired. But the Commons went further still. They added a clause to the Bill repealing in its favor a part of the Statute of Mortmain—that it might henceforth be free to any man to give what he thought fit, either by deed or will, towards the augmenting of benefices. But this clause so readily passed by the Commons gave rise to great debate in the Peers. "It seems not reasonable" said some of their Lordships "to open a door to practices upon dying men." The Bishops however who had been so much divided on the Occasional Conformity question, united as one man upon this measure, which by their strenuous aid was now carried and passed

[2] See his rather boastful account in the History of his own Times, vol. v. p. 118-123. A summary of Queen Anne's regulations as modified by some later Statutes is given in Burn's Ecclesiastical Law, Phillimore's edition, vol. II. p. 283-295.

into law. This fund has ever since and with good reason borne the name of "Queen Anne's Bounty." Its application has been extended to the building of parsonage-houses as well as to the increase of poor livings; but in one form or the other it has fulfilled the kindly purpose of its founder and rendered most signal service to the Church.

The Session was closed by the Queen on the 3rd of April; and Marlborough set out for Holland on the 8th. But the strife of parties continued among his colleagues at home. Nottingham especially had for many months past shown himself most disputatious and wrangling. Thus, for instance, when during the last year the Protestants in the Cevennes had risen in revolt against the intolerable tyranny of their bigoted rulers, and when Marlborough in his letters was pressing on military grounds that some prompt aid might be afforded them, Nottingham demurred. He had expatiated in Council on the injustice and impolicy of assisting rebel subjects against their legitimate Sovereign.[3] Such doctrines of passive obedience appear inconceivable at the Court of St. James's in 1703, resting as it then did on the Revolution settlement; they could only be expected at the Court of St. Germain's.

The stubborn resistance of Nottingham had not hindered the Government from sending a combined fleet, English and Dutch, on a summer cruise to the Mediterranean. The English ships were commanded by Sir Cloudesley Shovel; supplies of arms and ammunition had been put on board; and they had been instructed by all means in their power to support the

---

[3] Coxe's Marlborough, vol. 1. p. 235.

insurrection, if it should leave the hills and extend along the coast.

Nottingham however was not discouraged from renewing his opposition to his colleagues on many subsequent occasions. He had the support of several men in high places, as the Earl of Jersey and Sir Edward Seymour, and he could reckon on the good wishes at least of a majority in the House of Commons. Before the close of the Session in April 1704 he addressed himself to Godolphin, declaring that he must retire from office unless the administration were cleared of the remaining Whigs. Finding his representations unheeded, he paused until Marlborough had set out for Holland, and then thinking the occasion opportune appealed directly to the Queen. He pressed Her Majesty to choose one of the two parties and abide by that choice. If she chose the Whigs, he and his friends would at once retire. If she continued to abide by the Tories, he must then insist that the Dukes of Somerset and Devonshire be removed from the Privy Council.

The Queen's own views of politics nearly coincided with Nottingham's, but her pride was aroused by his peremptory tone. After some wavering she reverted to Godolphin and, by his advice, determined to deal sharply with the malcontents. She sent a message to Lord Jersey and Sir Edward Seymour dismissing them from office; and Nottingham, who had still hoped to maintain his position, then sullenly resigned.

The secession of Nottingham had for some time past been foreseen by Marlborough as probably impending, and it had been often discussed between himself and the Lord Treasurer. They both desired that, although there might be some change as to persons, the Tory party should still form the basis of their administration. With this view Marlborough had fixed his thoughts on Robert Harley, then Speaker and a personal friend of his own, to succeed Nottingham as Secretary of State. Harley received the offer accordingly. He showed some reluctance, real or pretended, to exchange his more fixed position for the uncertainties of Ministerial life, but he finally yielded. On the 18th of May the Gazette announced his acceptance of the Seals.

Harley like Nottingham was a Tory in politics though by no means so extreme. In every other respect the contrast of their characters was unfavourable to him. Nottingham was an austere and upright man, always avowing his principles and always acting up to them. His enemies nicknamed him "Dismal"; from his tendency to make sad and desponding predictions of public affairs—a tendency which in England is often accepted as a proof of superior wisdom. Harley on the other hand endeavoured to keep well both with Churchmen and Dissenters, and while professing close friendship with the Tory malcontents was in the habit of disclosing their secrets to Marlborough and Godolphin. Thus at this juncture writes Godolphin to the Duchess: "The Speaker is very industrious and has found out things two or three several ways, which may chance to make some of them (the hot angry people) uneasy."

Some other appointments followed. Sir Thomas Mansell who ranked as an ardent Tory took the place of Seymour. The Earl of Kent who ranked as a moderate Whig took the place of Jersey. Blathwayte the Secretary at War, a man of very slight note in politics, was removed from his office in favor of Henry St. John, better known in subsequent years as Viscount Bolingbroke. Since 1700 St. John had been returned to Parliament by his Wiltshire neighbours at Wotton Basset; he had espoused with warmth the Tory side; and he had already signalised his splendid talents by speeches of which unhappily no record now remains.

The successes of the French in the last campaign excited serious apprehension for that which was about to commence. No man had been so mortified as Marlborough. No man had seen more clearly how far the common cause, to say nothing of his own renown, was imperilled by the constant clashing of petty interests, by the innumerable scruples and delays with which his Allies entangled him. Such were his feelings of despondency at the close of the preceding summer that he had formed the secret resolution of resigning his command.[4] He had been dissuaded only by the entreaties of Godolphin in London and of Heinsius at the Hague. During his next visit to Holland in February 1704 the prospect had not brightened, and we find him write as follows to Godolphin: "For this campaign I see so very ill a prospect that I am extremely out of heart. But God's will be done; and I must be for this year very uneasy, for in all the other campaigns I had an opinion of being able to do something for the common cause, but in this I have no other hopes than that some lucky accident may enable me to do good."—But Marlborough even in his sorest trials was serene as ever in his aspect and demeanour. With

[4] See especially his letters to Godolphin from the Hague of October 19 and 22, 1703, Old Style.

an undaunted spirit he was now applying all the resources of his genius to face and overcome the obstacles that lay before him.

The general result of the last campaign was in equal degree inspiriting to Louis the Fourteenth. That sagacious and experienced monarch directing everything in person from his cabinet at Versailles showed himself in his warlike preparations no unworthy rival of Marlborough and Eugene. Through the winter he used every exertion to recruit and supply his troops; and he resolved to have on foot in the coming summer no less than eight separate armies. With one under the Duke of Berwick he hoped to chastise the King of Portugal; with a second under the Duke of Vendome to chastise the Duke of Savoy. Both these princes— so he expected—would have deeply to rue the hour when they had presumed to declare against LE GRAND MONARQUE. The Duke of Savoy was to be further threatened by an army on the frontiers of Dauphiny under the Duke de la Feuillade, and another in Lombardy under M. Le Grand Prieur the brother of Vendome. The Maréchal de Villars with a large body of troops was stationed to repress the revolt in the Cevennes. The Maréchal de Villeroy was named to command the army in Flanders, but with orders to remain on the defensive, since the principal effort to decide the war was designed in another quarter.[5]

That quarter was Bavaria. The Elector had been able in the preceding year not only to maintain but to extend the sphere of his dominion. The Maréchal de Marsin and his army had wintered with him; and it

[5] On these French preparations and equipments see the Mémoires Militaires de la Succession d'Espagne, vol. IV. p. 371.

was now intended that another French army, which we may number as the eighth, should under the Maréchal de Tallard cross the Rhine and march to his assistance. The Elector and the two Marshals would thus combine a force very far superior to any the Emperor could hope to bring against them. While they confronted His Imperial Majesty he would be taken in the rear by Ragotsky and the Hungarian insurgents; and thus supported the French might fairly expect to dictate to him a separate peace involving the dissolution of the Empire beneath—perhaps even within—the ramparts of Vienna. The two Maritime Powers would then be left alone to sustain the brunt of the conflict. Holland, considering the timid counsels which then prevailed at the Hague, would in all probability accept almost any terms, and England would then be reduced to that defensive or naval warfare so much admired by Nottingham and his High Tory friends.

The preliminary steps to this great result were all taken. In the course of May Marshal Tallard entered the defiles of the Black Forest, leading about 15,000 troops as reinforcements to the Elector, whom he met at Villingen. He then returned to the Rhine where he had still about 30,000 men, and was able to make head against Prince Louis of Baden. On the other hand the insurgents in Hungary resumed hostilities, and reduced some more of the Imperial garrisons, sending forward also a considerable body commanded by Karoly, in the direction of Vienna. So great in June was the terror of that capital that many of the citizens prepared to retire, and that the King of the Romans threw up works to defend the suburbs.[6]

[6] Coxe's House of Austria, vol. I. p. 1142, 4to ed.

It was then that Marlborough gradually disclosed the plan which he had formed for the rescue of the common cause. Bearing in mind the circumstances of the time and people, his plan was singularly daring —so daring indeed that he could not venture to unfold it completely and at once, to any of the chiefs combined with him, except in secret letters to Prince Eugene alone.

The plan of Marlborough shortly stated was to march forward at the head of all the troops that could be spared from the defence of Holland; to leave the enemy's fortresses in his rear, while moving into Germany; and to give battle to the French upon the Danube. Even to Godolphin as to the Queen and Prince, it appears that in the first instance he communicated merely a part of his design; but he caused his instructions to be drawn in general terms so as to leave him the required latitude. When he came to the Hague he laid before the States only the much humbler project of a campaign on the Moselle as was desired by Louis of Baden. Even this greatly reduced scheme seemed to the States very far too bold. They opposed it with the utmost vehemence, not desiring that even a single soldier should be withdrawn from their immediate defence.

Marlborough however was firm; and at last declared that if even the Dutch troops were not allowed to follow him he would proceed with the English alone. At the same time he imparted his real project to Godolphin. Thus he writes on April 29: "By the next post I shall be able to let you know what resolutions I shall bring these people to; for I have told them that I will leave this place on Saturday. My in-

CHAP. IV. 1704. tentions are to march all the English to Coblentz; and to declare here that I intend to command on the Moselle; but when I come there to write to the States that I think it absolutely necessary for serving the Empire to march with the troops under my command, and to join those in Germany that are in Her Majesty's and the Dutch pay. . . . The army I propose to have there will consist of upwards of 40,000 men. . . . What I now write I beg may be known to nobody but Her Majesty and the Prince."

The firmness of Marlborough, aided as usual by the friendship of Heinsius, at length prevailed. In a formal conference with the States on the 4th of May he obtained from them sufficient powers for the campaign on the Moselle—powers which he saw might be extended beyond what they then designed. But although the opposition of the Dutch was overcome their repugnance still remained. Of this we may judge by a despatch as follows from Mr. Alexander Stanhope: "The Duke has sent away already all his equipage, and will post himself in three days directly to Coblentz; and whither afterwards you will know from himself better than I can inform you. Only this I can tell you, that the design he goes on is much against the grain of the people here, who never think themselves safe at home without a superiority of 40,000 men, and never dare think of hazarding any thing to make an acquisition upon their enemies." [7]

It is not to be supposed that the timidity of the Dutch States was the only obstacle against which Marlborough had to strive. In a confederacy that ranked together so many members great and small, there was

[7] Hon. A. Stanhope to Sir Charles Hedges, May 2, 1704 (MS.).

scarce upon the Continent one General Officer, there was scarce one petty prince, who did not put forward some selfish and undue pretensions. Thus for instance at this very juncture, there arose a personal dispute between Marlborough's brother General Churchill and the Dutch General Overkirk—a question of course far more important than the successful prosecution of the war! Thus again—to give only one example out of many—the Sovereign of Prussia deemed it most consistent with his dignity as a new-made King to keep back his regiments of Guards—all excellent troops—from active service, and employ them to escort himself in solemn state, whenever he went from Berlin to Potsdam or from Potsdam back again to Berlin. Thus writes Lord Raby, the English Envoy: "Revolutions happen daily in the councils of our little Court, for what is advised one day and agreed on by one party of councillors, is obstructed and altered the next day by another party; each being willing to insinuate themselves with their master and to make him believe they seek nothing but his grandeur. For now they have persuaded him not to let his Guards march, for it is neither safe nor great for a Prince to be without a great number of Guards. I am very sorry of this resolution because they were indeed very fine troops."[8]

All such obstacles were met, and for the most part overcome, by Marlborough, with his usual patience, with his usual skill. This is the more remarkable since we find him at this very juncture a prey to domestic chagrin. The shrewish temper of his Duchess had inflicted upon him a quarrel on his leaving England.

[8] Lord Raby to the Hon. A. Stanhope, Berlin, March 4, 1704 (MS.).

Now at last after some weeks she wrote to him in relenting terms, and Marlborough in his answer can scarce restrain the transports of his joy. "If you will give me leave it will be a great pleasure to me to have it in my power to read this dear dear letter often and that it may be found in my strong-box when I am dead.... You have by this kindness preserved my quiet, and I believe my life, for till I had this letter I have been very indifferent what should become of myself."

Marlborough wrote this letter from the Hague on the 5th of May, and on the evening of the same day he set out to join the army. From Bonn he led his troops to Coblentz, and from Coblentz still along the Rhine to Mayence. On his route he received intelligence of the 15,000 French led by Tallard to the further aid of the Elector of Bavaria; and this afforded him a new argument to justify his own march to the Danube. Hitherto his project had been kept a profound secret both from friends and foes. The French especially had been at a loss to guess what he might design. When at Coblentz he was thought to have in view a campaign on the Moselle; when at Mayence, an attack on Alsace. It was only on leaving Mayence that his real object was disclosed by his passage of the Neckar and his advance through the Duchy of Wurtemberg. It is due to the Dutch politicians as well as to the Dutch Generals to record, that when Marlborough had apprised them of his plan by letter they seeing that its execution was inevitable waived their objections, and did their best to forward its success. The States of Holland sent him as he asked reinforcements instead of reproaches.

Pursuing his march to Mundelsheim the Duke there found Prince Eugene, who came across from his own army to see him. It was the first time that these two renowned commanders ever met; and they remained together three days while the troops were either resting or reviewed.—Prince Eugene of Savoy born at Paris in 1663 was thirteen years younger than Marlborough, yet had already seen as much of active service. In a happy hour for the Court of Vienna he was refused the commission which he had at his outset solicited in the French service; and taking the other part he became probably the greatest General who has ever in any age led the Austrian armies. The position of Eugene in this station was certainly singular. He was an Italian by descent, a Frenchman by training, and a German by adoption; and in his usual signature of three words he was wont as we are told to combine not less strangely the three languages, EUGENIO VON SAVOYE.[9]

Marlborough from the first was greatly prepossessed in his favor. "Prince Eugene"—so he writes to the Duchess—"was with me from Monday till Friday (the 10th to the 14th of June) and has in his conversation a great deal of my Lord Shrewsbury, with the advantage of seeming franker." It was this intercourse of three days that laid the foundations of lasting friendship between these two eminent men. Ever afterwards there prevailed between them an entire concert of measures, an entire cordiality of feeling. Equally to the honor of Marlborough and of Eugene they almost always viewed public affairs in precisely the same light, and they were never disjoined by the least spark of personal jealousy. "I dare say"—thus we find Marlborough

[9] Vehse, *Geschichte des österreichischen Hofs*, vol. VI. p. 220.

write four years after this time—"Prince Eugene and I shall never differ about our share of laurels."[1] Nor indeed without such concord could these laurels have been gained.

On the last of the three days that Marlborough and Eugene now passed together they were joined by Louis of Baden, the interview with whom was by no means as satisfactory. The Margrave was extremely jealous of command and—a frequent combination—extremely unfit to hold it. He would by no means agree to the plan which his colleagues pressed upon him, that he should go back to his native country of Baden where his influence would be greatest, and defend the lines of Stollhofen against Tallard, while Eugene should co-operate with Marlborough against the Elector of Bavaria. The latter post as the most brilliant was preferred by Prince Louis, who as elder in rank insisted on priority of choice. With ludicrous presumption he deemed himself superior even to Marlborough, and was with great difficulty brought to consent that they should share the command when the two armies joined, each chief to hold sway on alternate days.

In pursuance of these resolutions Prince Eugene set out for the Rhine and Prince Louis for the Danube. Marlborough on his part led his troops by the narrow pass of Gieslingen through that difficult chain of hills known in Wurtemberg by the name of RAUHE ALP— the rugged Alps. At no time was it easy to lead troops through that defile, but then some heavy rains had swelled the runlets into torrents and broken up the road. It was only by great exertions that Marlborough and his men could struggle through. Even

[1] To Mr. Travers, July 30, 1708. Coxe's Marlborough, vol. iv. p. 164.

after they had passed he might still complain of some days of almost wintry weather in the midst of that summer season. Thus he writes to the Duchess from Langenau on the 25th of June: "As I was never more sensible of heat in my life than I was a fortnight ago we have now the other extremity of cold, for as I am writing I am forced to have fire in the stove in my chamber. But the poor men that have not such conveniencies I am afraid will suffer from these continual rains."

At the entry of this pass of Gieslingen, the Duke was further harassed by the receipt of some timid letters from the Hague. When Marshal Villeroy found that Marlborough was marching up the Rhine, he had hastened from Flanders with some of his best troops and joined Marshal Tallard in Alsace. But there now arose a rumour that Villeroy was returning to his former post. The States General at all events returned to their former fears. They declared themselves in imminent danger of invasion, and wrote to Marlborough in earnest terms pressing him to send back their troops.

The great mind of Marlborough was not to be thus diverted from pushing forward with all his forces to the real post of danger and of duty. At the same time he contrived, with much adroitness, to soothe the alarm of the States, by sending orders to collect a sufficient number of boats upon the Upper Rhine so as to facilitate the rapid return of their troops, if their territory should be indeed assailed.

It is less pleasing to find Marlborough at this period, or earlier still, receive and not reject—only refer to the Queen in England—a proposal from the Emperor to bestow on him a grant of lands and create him a Prince of the Empire. Far better for his fame that the proposal did not at once take effect and that on this occasion the service preceded the reward.

Having emerged from the pass of Gieslingen and entered on the open plains, the Duke speedily joined the army of Prince Louis. Their combined force was very formidable, amounting probably to 60,000 men, but it was composed of most various materials. Marlborough besides his English had under him Dutch, Danes, and Hanoverians; the Margrave besides the Imperialists had Suabians, Prussians, and Franconians.

Marching onwards the Duke and Margrave came to Elchingen, a village rendered memorable by a gallant feat of arms a century later, and which gave in consequence the title of Duke to Marshal Ney. As they advanced the Elector withdrew in haste from his headquarters at Ulm. He did not nevertheless relinquish the left bank of the Danube, but stationed his army in a fortified camp which he had prepared lower down the stream at Dillingen. Ulm meanwhile was left with strong works, and a sufficient garrison.

Ulm however was not Marlborough's object. The plan, which he had formed but not yet disclosed, was to secure Donauwerth with its bridge across the Danube, and there establish his magazines. It was with some difficulty that he could induce his colleague to join in this design, and to march in that direction. Then their aim becoming manifest the Elector took the alarm. Besides the garrison which he had already placed in Donauwerth he sent forward in hot haste a body of 12,000 men, horse and foot, to occupy and defend the

Schellenberg, a mountain of gradual ascent, which overhangs the town.

On the 1st of July, which on the system of alternate command was the Margrave's day, the Allies in their progress defiled before the Elector's camp. They were watched but not attacked by the Elector's cavalry. When they encamped for the night they were still fourteen miles from the foot of the Schellenberg. But on the morrow, which was Marlborough's day, the first detachment was set in motion by three in the morning, under the command of the Duke himself; and the army followed at five. After some hours of toilsome marching the antique towers of Donauwerth rose on the horizon—beyond them the rapid Danube—above them the Schellenberg heights. Count Arco who commanded the Bavarians had well employed his time. He had posted his men along the mountain slope and begun to intrench the ground. A little more leisure would have enabled him to complete his preparations. Marlborough felt also that were the attack to be postponed the next day would be wasted by the Margrave in waverings or, as the Margrave might prefer to say, in deliberations. Therefore though the men might be weary and many of the troops not yet arrived, Marlborough gave orders for the onset that very afternoon.

The brunt of the action which ensued was borne by the English foot. Most gallantly did they mount the well-defended hill; twice were they arrested or repulsed, but in the third attack supported by the Imperialists who were led by Prince Louis in person they prevailed. The Bavarians disbanded and fled in disorder. Many made their way to the Donauwerth bridge, and some two or three thousand of their number passed, but the hindmost broke it down by their weight and were drowned in the Danube. Arco himself escaped with difficulty, and his son was one of those who perished in the river. Sixteen pieces of artillery and all the tents were taken.

The Allies and especially the English sustained a heavy loss in this conflict—1,500 killed and 4,000 wounded. But the victory was to them of the highest importance. By this hard fought action Marlborough had in no common degree cheered and inspirited his men; he had gained for them a strong position; he had destroyed great part of the Bavarian division; and he had flung the rest across the Danube. Next day we find him write to his Sarah an account of his success, and add the following words: "Now that I have told you the good, I must tell you the ill, news; which is that the Marshal de Villeroy has promised the Elector that he will send him by way of the Black Forest 50 battalions of foot and 60 squadrons of horse—and as he tells him in his letter the best troops of France—which would make him stronger than we. But I rely very much on the assurances Prince Eugene gave me yesterday by his Adjutant General, that he would venture the whole rather than suffer them to pass quietly as the last did."

The alarming news which Marlborough here mentions had reached him by an intercepted letter just before the commencement of the action. But it had not distracted his attention nor ruffled his composure. Ever serene and self-possessed he applied himself with undivided zeal to the duty which was then before him.

There is no doubt, as regards the battle of the

Schellenberg, that it was the genius of Marlborough which first planned and then brought it to a successful issue. But as the Margrave had been the first to enter the intrenchment his partisans desired to ascribe to him the chief honor of the day. They struck a medal representing on one side the head of the Margrave, and on the other the lines of Schellenberg with a pompous Latin inscription. Pity that there was not also another medal to delineate Esop's fable where a frog attempts to swell itself to the full dimensions of an ox!

The Elector of Bavaria disheartened by the Schellenberg action, now withdrew his garrison from Donauwerth and retired to another intrenched camp near Augsburg, there to await the promised succours from France. "It is very plain" so writes Marlborough "that if Her Majesty's troops had not been here the Elector had been now in Vienna." Marlborough himself with the Margrave hereupon took possession of Donauwerth, which they made their place of arms. Next day the army ranged in five columns crossed the Danube. But to gain the heart of the Elector's country it was necessary to pass another deep and rapid river the Lech. A suitable point for this passage near the village of Gunderkingen was selected by Colonel Cadogan, one of the officers on whom Marlborough most relied. There he proceeded to lay down the pontoons; and there the army went over the Lech on the 7th of July.

Having thus the Elector's country at his mercy Marlborough deemed the moment opportune to bring him to terms. A negotiation previously commenced and broken off was now resumed. The Duke offered

—an offer not very willingly concurred in by the Emperor who rather desired the Elector's ruin—that His Highness should be reinstated in his dominions, and receive a subsidy of 200,000 crowns provided he would break with King Louis and furnish 12,000 men to the High Allies. The Elector at first seemed willing to accept such favourable terms. But the near approach of the French succour kept him firm to the French cause. He sent his secretary to the appointed place of meeting with a message that he could not desert his ally; and upon this his unfortunate dominions were given up to military execution. Here is Marlborough's own account to the Duchess: "The succours which the Elector expects on Sunday have given him so much resolution that he has no thoughts of peace. However we are in his country, and he will find it difficult to persuade us to quit it. We sent this morning 3,000 horse to his chief city of Munich, with orders to burn and destroy all the country about it. This is so contrary to my nature that nothing but absolute necessity could have obliged me to consent to it, since these poor people suffer for their master's ambition."

In another letter of the same month and to the same person Marlborough says: "I have great reason to hope that everything will go on well, for I have the pleasure to find all the officers willing to obey without knowing any other reason than that it is my desire, which is very different from what it was in Flanders, where I was obliged to have the consent of a council of war for everything I undertook."—It must not be supposed however that these acquiescing officers included Prince Louis of Baden. On the contrary the letters of Marlborough at this very period teem with complaints of his Highness's jealous and impracticable temper.

From the Danube we pass to the Rhine.—Villeroy and Tallard, in the conferences which they held together consequent on the march of Marlborough into Germany, framed and transmitted to Versailles four separate schemes for a diversion. They might besiege Mayence; they might besiege Friburg; they might assail the lines of Stollhofen; or they might detach one of their two armies to join the Elector. Louis the Fourteenth, being warmly pressed for immediate succour by Legall the Elector's Envoy, decided for the last of these plans.[a] Accordingly, while Villeroy remained for the defence of Alsace, Tallard crossed the Rhine and once more traversed the Black Forest at the head of 25,000 men. He lost five days in a fruitless attempt on the town of Villingen, but on the 3rd of August made his junction with the Electoral army in its Augsburg camp.

This second march of Tallard through the defiles of the Black Forest differed greatly in one respect from that which he had made in the preceding spring. He had no longer on his flank the formal Margrave of Baden who had let him pass and repass without a blow. There was now the far more active Prince Eugene, who was no sooner apprised of his movements than he began a parallel march at the head of 18,000 men. He reached the banks of the Danube at Hochstädt between Dillingen and Donauwerth at nearly the same time that the Augsburg junction was effected.

At this news Marlborough and the Margrave, who had advanced as far as Friedberg, made a retrograde

[a] Mémoires militaires de la Succession d'Espagne, vol. IV. p. 495.

movement by way of Aicha to draw nearer to Eugene. It was not long ere Eugene himself appeared in their camp, having left his troops in order to confer with his colleagues. They resolved that in spite of the enemy's superior force they would not let go their hold upon Bavaria. On the contrary they trusted to secure it by the reduction of Ingolstadt, a virgin fortress as it boasted itself which had never yet yielded to any conqueror. Prince Louis was persuaded to undertake its siege with a separate division of 16,000 men. Marlborough and Eugene viewed this enterprise with especial pleasure. Perhaps it might gain them an important fortress, certainly it would rid them of an insufferable colleague.

Early on the 9th of August Prince Louis set out for the siege of Ingolstadt; and later on the same day Prince Eugene set out also to rejoin his army. But within two hours he hurried back to Marlborough with intelligence that the enemy had broken up from Augsburg and were in full march to Dillingen. Manifestly it was their design to pass over to the left bank of the Danube and overwhelm if they could the scanty forces of Eugene. The two chiefs immediately concerted their measures, and Eugene then set out for the second time. His army was directed to retire from Hochstädt to the line of the Kessel, and Marlborough made all speed to support it with his own. The first division of his cavalry under the Duke of Würtemberg at once received its orders, and began its march at midnight. General Churchill followed with the first division of foot, and at daybreak Marlborough himself moved with the main body. To avoid incumbrances, the last divisions went over the Danube by the aid of pontoons at Merx-

heim, a point below the junction of the Lech; while
the first divisions passed the Lech by the newly formed
bridge at Gunderkingen, and the Danube by the old
bridge of Donauwerth.

During his few hours of anxious halt upon the 10th
we find Marlborough write as usual in confidence to
Godolphin: "The French" he says "make their boasts
of having a great superiority; but I am very confident
they will not venture a battle. Yet if we find a fair
occasion we shall be glad to embrace it, being persuaded
that the ill condition of our affairs in most parts requires it."

Pressing onwards all through the 11th Marlborough
late that evening effected his junction with Eugene.
His artillery and baggage however did not come up
till sunrise the next day. The combined armies were
then encamped with the small stream of the Kessel in
their front, and the river Danube on their left. The
enemy it was known was before them, having moved
upon Hochstädt from Dillingen.

To obtain exact intelligence, and to concert a forward movement, Marlborough and Eugene rode out on
the forenoon of the 12th at the head of the Grand
Guards. It was not long ere they descried some
squadrons of the enemy's horse. Ascending the church
tower of Dapfheim, the two chiefs saw the whole army
in the distance, and the Quarter-Masters busy in preparing an encampment on the rising ground beyond
the Nebel. The opportunity seemed favourable to Marlborough and his colleague; and they determined to
give battle the next day. Riding back to their own
camp they issued in the evening the needful orders,
received by the troops with joyful alacrity.

CHAP.
IV.
1704.

On the morrow then, the 13th of August, was to be fought that great battle on which the liberties of Europe depended. Marlborough was deeply impressed with the awful crisis before him. He passed a part of the night in prayer, and received the Sacrament according to the rites of the Church of England from his chaplain Mr. Hare. Then after a short rest he started up to hold council with Eugene. The two chiefs, while anxiously watching for the first grey streaks upon the eastern sky, concerted together in detail the various arrangements of the coming conflict.

CHAPTER V.

BEFORE I proceed to the events of the battle of Blenheim, it may be proper that I should examine the amount of the forces engaged, and also explain the configuration of the ground.

It is by no means easy to state with entire exactness the strength of any army in that age. We find it in most cases expressed only by the number of battalions of foot and squadrons of horse. We may allow upon a general average 500 men to each battalion and 120 to each squadron, but these numbers varied a little in particular services and also at particular times. The German squadrons for example were rather larger than the English; and thus even in the most careful computations some margin for conjecture must remain.

Marlborough himself, in his letter to the States of Holland, writes that the Allied army on the day of battle consisted of 64 battalions and 166 squadrons, which, with due allowance for the strength of the German squadrons, would make 52,000 men. That is also the number stated by writers of authority on either side, as by Archdeacon Coxe on the part of England, and by Voltaire on the part of France.

The army of France and Bavaria on this day is stated by Marlborough as of 82 battalions and 152 squadrons. Nor does the account of Tallard greatly differ, since he allows the same number of battalions and only a few more squadrons. Archdeacon Coxe computes the entire number at 56,000 men, but expresses in a note his doubt whether he has not rather underrated it. For my own part I see no reason to dispute the accuracy on this point of Voltaire, who had subsequent opportunities as he tells us to converse with several of the General Officers engaged, and who gives the entire force as of 60,000 men. Such is also the force assigned by some of the latest French writers on that period, as for instance M. Latena, author of a short biography of Prince Eugene.[1]—At all events there is nothing in these numbers to disparage that military prowess for which the French nation has ever been renowned. The difference between fifty-two and sixty thousand men by no means fully measures the disproportion of genius between the opposite chiefs— between Tallard and Marlborough—between the Elector and Eugene.

As respects the ground, the small town of Hochstädt with its marshy plain was a little behind the position of the French; and might seem to them of favourable augury as the scene of the victory of Villars in the preceding year. To their right was the Danube, there about three hundred feet broad and on no point fordable, but rolling rapidly between banks either steep or swampy. To their left the valley was bounded by a range of wooded hills. It widened to nearly three miles along the little stream of the Nebel, but contracted again to little more than half a mile at the village of Dapfheim. Near the confluence of the Nebel with the Danube stands the village of Blindheim which was also called Plintheim, but which in England

[1] In the volume published 1856 of the *Nouvelle Biographie Universelle* of Didot.

has gained immortal fame under the less accurate form of Blenheim. It was however divided from the Nebel by a narrow strip of swelling ground. Between one and two miles higher up were two other villages, first Unterglau and then Oberglau, standing on opposite sides of the Nebel, and higher still near the sources of the little stream was Lützingen. The ground bordering the Nebel, especially between Blenheim and Unterglau, was little better than a morass, and in some places impassable. Straight through it however ran the great road from Dillingen to Donauwerth which crossed the Nebel by a stone bridge, and a little above Blenheim were two water-mills well adapted to serve as redoubts and to defend the passage of the stream.

Moreover, on the right bank of the Nebel and beyond its morass though still following its course was a range of gentle uplands. They began behind the village of Blenheim and continued to the village of Lützingen, where they blended with the hills. It was along their summit and their side that the French had chosen their position, and from the morass and the stream in their front, they could not be approached without considerable difficulty. Tallard and his army held Blenheim and the ridge beyond it; the Elector and Marsin with theirs held Lützingen and Oberglau. But the dispositions of Tallard have been severely blamed. He had stationed his best infantry in Blenheim and they had fortified the village with palisades. Here "this great body of troops were so pent up and crowded that they had not room to make use of their arms." So writes, perhaps with some exaggeration, Brigadier-General Kane, one of the officers who that day led the attack upon them. And besides that the massing of these troops in that one place, impeded their movements and led to their disaster, it had further tended in no small degree to weaken the main body where Tallard himself commanded, and where a favourable opening to an enemy might perhaps appear.

Long before the sun had risen on the memorable 13th of August the Allied troops left their camp. They crossed the Kessel at three in the morning and marched onward. Marlborough with much the larger army held their left and would thus confront Tallard; Eugene with the less force held their right and would thus confront the Elector and Marsin. Towards six o'clock they descried the advanced posts of the enemy falling back on their approach; and the morning haze dispersing, the two armies were in sight of each other. Still the French chiefs were far from understanding the full magnitude of the issue before them. Tallard who had written a letter to the King of France added at this hour a few hasty lines of postscript: "Our enemies are now in view and ranged as if for action; but according to appearances they will march further this day. The report is that they are going to Nordlingen. If so they will have to leave us between them and the Danube; and will find it very hard to maintain the settlements they have made in Bavaria."

It was not long however ere the Allies deployed, and gave other indications of their intention to attack. Tallard started at once from his false security and hastened to make the needful preparations. He drew up his troops in line and placed his artillery where it could best command the passable points of the morass. And in cannon as in men the French were that day superior to the English. It is computed that they had 90 pieces of artillery against 66; and of these they were impatient to make use. Within a short period a heavy cannonade was opened from every part of the enemy's right wing.

Meanwhile Prince Eugene had taken leave of Marlborough and was leading his troops to their appointed ground. He promised to send notice to his colleague as soon as his lines were formed, so that the joint attack might be then commenced. He found however great impediments to his progress. The country was rough and the watercourses were so broad that they required to be filled up with fascines before they could be passed by the guns. Thus to the chagrin of Marlborough though by no means to the blame of Eugene considerable delay ensued. During the interval Marlborough gave orders for public prayers; and Lord Macaulay has described the scene with his usual animation. "The English Chaplains read the service at the head of the English regiments. The Calvinistic Chaplains of the Dutch army with heads on which the hand of Bishop had never been laid poured forth their supplications in front of their countrymen. In the meantime the Danes might listen to their Lutheran Ministers; and Capuchins might encourage the Austrian squadrons, and pray to the Virgin for a blessing on the arms of the Holy Roman Empire. The battle commences and these men of various religions all act like members of one body."—We may observe that this passage does not occur in any of Lord Macaulay's historical narratives. It is to be found in one of his critical essays. The accomplished writer is here contending with a no less accomplished adversary. He seeks to controvert the arguments of Mr. Gladstone's "Church and State"; and in order to controvert not a little magnifies them.*

The public prayers having ended, Marlborough with his usual humanity pointed out to the surgeons the most suitable posts for the care of the wounded. He then rode forward to inspect his lines. As he passed along the front a ball from one of the opposite batteries struck the ground beneath his horse and covered him with earth. The troops within sight showed a lively concern, but the composure of Marlborough himself was not disturbed. Having completed his inspection he sat down on the ground to breakfast in company with his principal officers. There soon after midday he received the long expected message from Eugene. An aide-de-camp came spurring up with tidings that the Prince was ready. "Now gentlemen to your posts!" cried Marlborough as he rose and mounted his horse.

His call was promptly answered. Lord Cutts, one of the bravest men in the British army—surnamed by his brother officers "the Salamander" from his utter disregarded of fire—put himself at the head of his division—a large body of foot soldiers—and dashed full upon the French at Blenheim. The cavalry led by Marlborough in person was designed to force the passage of the stream and the morass, in the centre of the line, between Blenheim and Unterglau. On the

---

* See the passage as first published in the Edinburgh Review for April 1839, p. 243.

further wing Eugene with equal gallantry engaged the foes before him.

Lord Cutts's division descending to the bank of the Nebel took possession of the water-mills under a heavy fire of grape. Having crossed the stream they drew up on the further bank where they were covered by the small strip of rising ground. Moving on to Blenheim village which the French held within the palisades they encountered at only thirty paces the first full volley of small arms. Many of their best men fell. But still the advance continued. The gallant General Rowe who commanded the leading brigade stuck his sword into the palisades before he would give the word to fire. Then, thus closely pressed, the slaughter was terrible and chiefly on the side of the Allies. One-third of the troops composing their first line were either killed or wounded. Down went the intrepid Rowe; and both his Lieutenant-Colonel and his Major while seeking to extricate his body shared his fate.

Protected by the palisades and superior in numbers the French were enabled to repulse this first attack. The Allied forces fell back in disarray and were further charged in flank by three squadrons of gens-d'armes. The colours of Rowe's regiment were captured but only for a moment being almost immediately recovered by a body of Hessians. Lord Cutts, seeing that some fresh squadrons were preparing to charge, sent in all haste to General Lumley who commanded the nearest Allied horse for reinforcements. Five squadrons were immediately detached across the Nebel to his succour; and by their aid he was enabled not only to repel the enemy's advance but to charge them in their turn.

11*

There were some furious encounters. Once again the Allies were forced back to their lines.

On their right where Eugene commanded, the Danes and Prussians under the Prince of Anhalt marched first to the assault. They threw into confusion the first line of the Bavarian horse, and took one of the French batteries. But the battery was quickly recovered and the assault was turned back on the assailants. The French fought with admirable spirit as they almost always have done, even when indifferently led. The prowess of the Irish brigade in their service —alas to find it so often in strife with England!—is also on this day especially recorded. Nor have historical writers failed to commemorate with all due praise upon the other side, the conduct of Prussians and Hanoverians, of Dutch and Danes. But loud complaints are made on this occasion of the Imperial cavalry, which although a large body proved of little avail. Their onset was irresolute and feeble, and three times over were they broken and routed. So eager was Prince Eugene to rally the fugitives and retrieve the failure that in his endeavours—which finally succeeded—he exposed his own person with most inconsiderate daring. He was nearly shot dead by a Bavarian dragoon, who came up within a few paces, and who was already levelling a pistol to his breast, when one of his own men, by a sabre-stroke at that critical minute, cut the trooper down.

Marlborough, meanwhile perceiving that Lord Cutts could not prevail in his repeated assaults upon the French at Blenheim, sent him orders to keep up only a feigned attack by firing in platoons over the crest of the rising ground. This would afford to Marlborough the time of coming to his aid after the main body should have passed the Nebel and morass. Already the horsemen under Marlborough's own eye were casting fascines into the stream, or forming bridges with the planks of the pontoons, while others plunged into the water and waded through the swamp. It was only with great difficulty that the horses could be brought across. As thus they struggled onwards, the French brought a part of their artillery to bear upon them and to enfilade the crowded columns which painfully advanced. But Tallard forbore any general onset against them while here entangled and impeded, and only attempted a charge after they had got over; an omission which, whether it resulted from neglect or from over confidence, has been urged as a severe reproach upon his military skill.

Having overcome all obstacles, the troops under the immediate direction of General Lumley were formed in two lines, on the further side of the morass. At this time however the news came that the Danish and Prussian cavalry were charged by the right wing of Marsin bearing down from Oberglau. The two foremost of their battalions were nearly cut to pieces and their chief the Prince of Holstein was mortally wounded. Marlborough seeing the peril set spurs to his horse and galloped at once to the scene of action. He passed the village of Unterglau which the French had set on fire and which was now in flames, and he led the brigade of Bernsdorf against the enemy across the stream. He further brought into play some of the wavering Imperial cavalry, and by great exertions, entirely retrieved the alarming impression which the enemy had made on this side. Through this prompt

CHAP. V.
1704.

and skilful movement he had also reestablished his direct communication with the army of Eugene.

This duty achieved, Marlborough came back to his cavalry now ranged in two lines beyond the morass and opposite the cavalry of Tallard. At five in the afternoon he was ready for a general charge which should decide the fortune of the day. He bade the trumpets sound the advance, and drawing his sword put himself at the head of the troops. In full array and with quickening pace they rode up the gentle ascent before them, amidst a terrible fire from both sides of artillery and small arms. Thus drew near the two great masses of horsemen. The Allies might muster 8,000 sabres and the French 10,000. But the latter had not been skilfully posted, and were disheartened by having been kept so much on the defensive. Still the Allies were repulsed in their first onset and fell back some sixty paces. But in their renewed charge which Marlborough after a short interval directed they had better success. The French horse at this crisis failed in steadiness as even their countrymen have proclaimed. "Our cavalry did ill; I repeat it they did very ill"—so writes Tallard in his official report. They discharged their carbines at a considerable distance and with slight effect. Then immediately they wheeled about and galloped away. The day was decided; the Allies had gained the battle.

The victorious troops pressing close on the defeated, the latter broke into two parts; the one making in wild haste for the Danube, and the other for Hochstädt. Marlborough himself undertook to urge the former, and entrusted the Dutch General Hompesch with the pursuit of the last. The General did his part with vigour.

So long as the daylight lasted he pressed closely on the fugitives who entirely broke their ranks and fled in utter disarray.

Marshal Tallard had remained with the other mass that was driven to the Danube. He was very nearsighted, and it is said that as he galloped onwards he mistook a hostile squadron for some of his own countrymen. According to his own account he and his suite became entangled with a regiment of Hessians, when his rank was discovered by the star and riband which he wore, of the Order of the Holy Ghost. His son was struck down at his side; and the Marshal himself was made prisoner as were also some other chief officers with him. Marlborough, with his usual courtesy and kindness, sent at once his own equipage for their accommodation.

Thus deprived of their chief the panic-stricken cavalry came dashing down upon the Danube, hoping against hope to find a ford. Pressed by Marlborough from behind some were made prisoners on the brink; many more plunged into the stream and attempted to wade or to swim across. But the waters were too deep, and the current was too strong; man and horse were quickly whirled along and overwhelmed. Not hundreds only but thousands are thought to have perished in this manner.

Marlborough was no sooner well assured of the result than he resolved to despatch that very evening one of his officers with the news to England. He tore a blank leaf from a pocketbook and wrote in pencil a few lines as follows to the Duchess: "I have not time to say more but to beg you will give my duty to the Queen and let her know her army has had a glorious victory. Monsieur Tallard and two other Generals are in my coach; and I am following the rest. The bearer, my aide-de-camp Colonel Parke, will give her an account of what has passed. I shall do it in a day or two by another more at large. MARLBOROUGH." This pencil note is still preserved among the archives at Blenheim, and a facsimile of it has been published by Archdeacon Coxe. It bears on the back a note of some tavern expenses.

Still however there remained in arms the French infantry which had so gallantly defended Blenheim. There stood eleven thousand men; "the best troops of France" as Tallard had lately boasted them to be. They had continued to hold their position in that village though cut off by the rout of Tallard from all communication with their countrymen. Hemmed in by their victorious and now far superior foes, and expecting no succour they made nevertheless some efforts to escape. Their commander the Marquis de Clerambault, son of the Marshal of that name, sought a way across the Danube, but plunging into the waves and attempting to breast them he was drowned as had been his comrades of the cavalry. Another party attempted to break through in the direction of Hochstädt, but was checked by an advance of the Scots Greys under their Colonel Lord John Hay. It is full of interest to find that gallant regiment bear a conspicuous part in the battle of Blenheim as a hundred and eleven years later it did in the battle of Waterloo, when it drew from Napoleon the half angry half admiring exclamation: CES TERRIBLES CHEVAUX GRIS!

The loss of M. de Clerambault had now deprived these French foot of their chief. The loss of one of

Tallard's officers some time since on his way to them had deprived them of orders. Nor was any further respite allowed them. Lord Cutts renewed his attack in their front while Lord Orkney and General Ingoldsby, each at the head of his regiment, stormed the village in two other places. Marlborough himself brought up his field artillery and poured some volleys upon them. Several houses of Blenheim caught fire; and the flames which ere long dispelled the evening darkness enabled the English gunners to take the surer aim. Intrepid as was the spirit of the French there was now no resource for them; they had found escape impossible and valour unavailing. A parley took place and the French proposed a capitulation, but General Churchill, who had his brother's orders, rode forwards and told them that there must be an unconditional surrender. Another English officer present, Lord Orkney, when many years later he conversed with Voltaire in London, said that in his judgment there was nothing else that the troops surrounded in Blenheim could have done. It was a bitter pang to these high-spirited soldiers—these proud battalions which for the last forty years had given the law to Europe. The regiment of Navarre in its despair tore to pieces and burnt its colours, that they might not become a trophy to the foe. Then as the bravest must, they submitted to their doom. That same evening eleven thousand French foot-soldiers laid down their arms as prisoners of war.

On the right wing of the Allies and all through that afternoon Prince Eugene had been constantly renewing his attacks: "I have not a squadron or battalion"—so said the Prince next day—"which did not charge four times at least." The Elector and Marsin found them-

CHAP. selves wholly unable to send to Tallard any succour, as
V. Tallard in his need had urgently demanded. The in-
1704. telligence of his rout was a signal for their own retreat.
They set fire to the villages of Lützingen and Oberglau
to obstruct the pursuit of their foes, and then filed off
in good order along the slope of the hills. Eugene
endeavoured to overtake and charge them, but his
troops were much exhausted, and theirs were soon con-
cealed from him by the growing shades of night. Next
day they passed the Danube by the bridges of Dillingen
and Lauingen which they burned behind them; and in
utter consternation pursued their flight to Ulm.

Late that same evening Marlborough took up his
quarters in a little water-mill near Hochstädt, where
he snatched three or four hours of rest. He had been
on horseback for seventeen hours; Wellington at
Waterloo was so for fifteen.—Next day we find him in
a letter to his Duchess sum up as follows the results of
the great battle: "In short the army of Monsieur de
Tallard, which was that I fought with, is quite ruined;
that of the Elector and Marshal de Marsin, which
Prince Eugene fought against, I am afraid has not
had much loss, for I cannot find that he has many prisoners. As soon as the Elector knew that Monsieur
de Tallard was like to be beaten he marched off, so
that I came only time enough to see him retire. . . .
Had the success of Prince Eugene been equal to his
merit, we should in that day's action have made an end
of the war." [3]

Here on the other hand is the testimony borne to
Marlborough himself many years afterwards by one of
his own officers who was present in the action: "No

[3] Coxe's Marlborough, vol. II. p. 6.

General ever did behave with more composure of temper and presence of mind than did the Duke on that occasion; he was in all places wherever his presence was requisite, without fear of danger, or in the least hurry, giving his orders with all the calmness imaginable."[4]

Early next morning, the French garrison having fled from Hochstädt, Marlborough and Eugene entered the little town together. There they issued the needful orders for the day. Next they went to pay their compliments to Marshal Tallard at the quarters of the Prince of Hesse. They found him much dejected and wounded in one of his hands. But in conversing with them he referred of his own accord to the events of the preceding day which they would rather have avoided. He spoke in the spirit of a brave man grieving for his failure, yet conscious of his courage. He told the Duke in courtly phrases well worthy of Versailles, that if His Grace had deferred his visit, meaning his attack, a day longer, the Elector and he would have waited on him first.

On taking leave of Marshal Tallard the Duke and Prince marched onwards from Hochstädt a few miles and encamped that evening at Steinheim. There they gave directions for repairing the bridges across the Danube; and there they halted four days to rest the troops and to tend the wounded.

The French and Bavarians made prisoners in this battle amounted to about 14,000 including a large number of officers. Of these prisoners however the two regiments of Greder and Zurlauben together 2,000 strong, which had been in the pay of the Elector, and

[4] Memoirs by Brigadier General Kane, p. 55. ed. 1746.

CHAP. which now saw the ruin of his cause, consented to change
V. sides and to engage in the Imperial ranks. Several
1704. hundred other soldiers, acting singly, took a similar course, so that the number of captives to be treated as such was brought down to 11,000. All these had surrendered to the troops of Marlborough, and were therefore at the sole disposal of that chief. But he in a generous spirit and knowing that the exertions of his colleague had been fully commensurate to his own, determined as a compliment to share the prisoners equally with him. The exact numbers allotted were 5,678 to the army of Marlborough and 5,514 to the army of Eugene. Marlborough reserved only Marshal Tallard and a few superior officers to be sent at leisure to an honourable captivity in England.

The number of the French and Bavarians who were slain in the action or who perished in the Danube was more difficult to compute with precision; it has however been stated at 12,000 men. To these would have to be added several thousand wounded. But the French themselves have acknowledged that their entire loss of all kinds scarcely fell short of 40,000; since they found that of the 60,000 who were in arms on the morning of the 14th not more than 20,000 either remained beneath, or returned to, their standards. All their tents and baggage, and a very large proportion of both their artillery and their colours had been taken.—On the other hand it is not to be supposed that so vast a victory over so martial a race could be achieved without heavy loss of men to the victors also. The Allies had 4,500 killed and 7,500 wounded; of these the largest proportion in the army of Eugene.

Such then was the battle of Blenheim as we say, or

of Hochstädt as the French have with less accuracy called it—a battle in which it pleased God to grant to the English commander a triumph so signal over his opponents. "He gave them as the dust to his sword, and as driven stubble to his bow." Nor was it the mere battle alone. The tidings of that battle broke the spell which had been cast over Europe by the prosperous and haughty reign of Louis the Fourteenth. William in former years had done little more than arrest his advance and balance his successes. Marlborough was in truth the first to turn these successes to defeat. That Sun which in his youth Louis had taken for his emblem and device seemed now for the first time overclouded; men saw that its light had paled; men thought that its setting was near.

But the magnanimity of Louis in this as in later reverses was truly admirable. There were none of those bursts of passion on his ill fortune, those fiery invectives against his unsuccessful chiefs, which Napoleon so often indulged in. The heir of forty Kings on the contrary, as viewed in his most secret correspondence, evinces a serene and lofty fortitude—abstaining from useless complaints—allowing in the fullest manner for involuntary errors—and seeking only how the past disaster might be most effectually retrieved. Of Marlborough's captive the monarch writes only, "I am sorry for the Maréchal de Tallard, and I take true interest in the grief which he must feel at the loss of his son."

Still more magnanimous if possible and still more kindly is the tone of Louis towards his unfortunate ally. "The present position of the Elector of Bavaria gives me more concern than even my own loss. If he should now conclude a treaty with the Emperor, to preserve his family from being made prisoners or his country from being laid waste, that treaty, whatever it be, will cause me no displeasure. You may assure him that there shall be no change in my sentiments towards him; and that I shall never sign any peace that does not provide for his reinstatement in his dominions. If on the other hand the enemy is resolved to grant him no terms, he shall go to command in Flanders, where he could maintain the war with more hopeful opportunities, and with better success."[5]

Marlborough was far from desiring to press hard on the Elector. "I had much rather"—so he writes on the 18th to the Duchess—"the Elector should quit the French interest if it might be upon reasonable terms; but the Imperialists are for his entire ruin." In these conciliatory views Marlborough induced his colleague in command to join. "Prince Eugene and I"—so he writes again on the 21st—"have offered the Elector by a gentleman who is not yet returned, that if he will join in the common cause against France, he shall be put in possession of his whole country, and receive from the Queen and Holland 400,000 crowns yearly, for which he should only furnish the Allies with 8,000 men. But I take it for granted he is determined to go for France, and abandon his own country to the rage of the Germans."

Such was indeed the case. The part of Maximilian was already taken. He had made up his mind to follow the fortunes of Louis; and he left his consort with her

[5] Letters from Louis to Marshal Marsin, August 21 and 23, and to Marshal Villeroy, August 23, 1704. All these are printed in the fourth volume of the *Mémoires militaires*, edited by General Pelet in the reign of Louis Philippe.

children at Munich to make her submission to Marlborough, and endure the hard conditions, which the Emperor imposed. Throwing then a garrison of three or four thousand men into Ulm, and leaving there the worst of the wounded brought from Blenheim, though only with the hope of obtaining for them an honourable capitulation, he joined Marshal Marsin in a rapid march through the defiles of the Black Forest. Marshal Villeroy had made a movement to meet them, so as if need were to protect their retreat; and all three in mournful mood arrived together at Strasburg, having crossed the Rhine by the bridge of boats at Kehl.

Marlborough and Eugene after their four days' halt at Steinheim marched on to Sefelingen within one English mile of Ulm. Here they were rejoined by Prince Louis of Baden full of wrath and regret, as we may conceive, at having had no share in the laurels of Blenheim. That victory had enabled him to turn the siege of Ingolstadt into a blockade, leaving before it only a small body of troops. It was now agreed between the three chiefs, that, after the surrender of Ingolstadt which was soon expected, the same body of troops should remain for the reduction of Ulm, while they with the main army should carry the war into the country beyond the Rhine.

It is worthy of note how little Marlborough spared himself and how greatly his health was affected by the toils of this campaign. He writes to Godolphin as follows from his camp at Steinheim: "I am suffered to have so little time to myself that I have a continual fever on my spirits which makes me very weak. Nothing but my zeal for Her Majesty's service could have enabled me to go through the fatigues I have had for the last three months; and I am but too sure that when I shall have the happiness of seeing you, you will find me ten years older than when I left England." And to the Duchess he adds: "For thousands of reasons I wish myself with you. Besides I think if I were with you quietly at the Lodge I should have more health, for I am at this time so very lean that it is extreme uneasy to me, so that your care must nurse me this winter or I shall certainly be in a consumption."

The tidings of Blenheim as first conveyed by Colonel Parke, the bearer of the pencil note of Marlborough, were most joyfully received both by high and low. The Queen at once addressed a few lines of warm congratulation to her dearest Mrs. Freeman. The common people threw up their caps and huzzaed. Yet amidst the general exultation there were traces—at all times too frequent amongst us—of malignant party rancour. As some extreme Whigs repined at the battle of Waterloo, so did some extreme Tories repine at the battle of Blenheim. From the first the followers of Rochester and Nottingham in the Lords, and of Sir Edward Seymour in the Commons, had denounced the expedition into Germany. They exclaimed that Marlborough was exceeding his powers—that he was deserting the Dutch—that he was imperilling the English on a distant and uncertain enterprise. He should be attacked in Parliament they said, nay more be impeached if he should fail. Nor did the news of his successes greatly change the tone of his accusers. The battle of Schellenberg—that was no victory at all! The battle of Blenheim—that was a victory no doubt but a bloody and a useless one, tending to exhaust England of its soldiers, and without any commensurate injury to

France. "It is true," so said a leading politician on this last conflict, "a great many men were killed and taken, but that to the French King is no more than to take a bucket of water out of a river." Mrs. Burnet, wife of the Bishop, wrote this saying to the Duchess of Marlborough and the Duchess wrote it to the Duke. He appears to have been greatly nettled and he replied as follows: "As to what the gentleman says of a bucket of water, if they will allow us to draw one or two such buckets more I should think we might then let the river run quietly and not much apprehend its overflowing and destroying its neighbours. . . . . But I will endeavour to leave a good name behind me in countries that have hardly any blessing but that of not knowing the detested names of Whig and Tory."[6]

With this section of the Tories, which had at least the merit of allegiance to Queen Anne, there was also at this time especially opposed to Marlborough that larger and separate branch, which bore the name of Jacobites, and which adhered to the fallen family. It was natural that these men should look with little favor on any victory that humbled France, since it was from French territory and through French aid that they expected their rightful Prince—their own "James the Third"—to return. Bearing all these party cries in remembrance, and being mindful also how much since the downfall of the Fronde the voice of opposition had been hushed in France, it would scarcely perhaps be an exaggerated statement to affirm that, after the battle of Blenheim, there were more complaints in England against Marlborough, than there were in France against Tallard.

[6] To the Duchess, Sept. 2, and Oct. 20, 1704.

CHAP. V.
1704.

Meanwhile the Allied chiefs having led their troops by divers routes beyond the Rhine, combined them once more in the neighbourhood of Philipsburg. There they found themselves confronted by the French army under Marshal Villeroy, and another general action was expected. But the French had been greatly weakened and even more dispirited by the day of Blenheim. They withdrew from their position without a blow, and left the Allies at full liberty to attack as they desired Landau. That unfortunate city had therefore to sustain another siege—the third within two years. It was invested by Prince Louis on the 12th of September, while the covering army was commanded by Marlborough and Eugene. Within ten days however, Joseph King of the Romans arriving from Vienna assumed the nominal direction of the siege.

The French garrison of Landau made a most resolute resistance, but since Villeroy could not hazard a battle for its relief its surrender was only a question of time. It seemed to Marlborough that during a part of this time his army might be employed with great advantage on another enterprise. He led his troops at some hazard across the rugged and difficult uplands which separate the valley of the Queich from the valley of the Moselle —"the terriblest country that can be imagined for the march of an army with cannon," as he says in one of his letters. By his rapid movements he anticipated the arrival of a division of French and occupied without resistance the city of Treves. Thence he took measures for the siege of Trarbach, the conduct of which he entrusted to the Prince of Hesse. It is very remarkable that King Louis, writing from his palace at Fontainebleau, had with great sagacity surmised these to be the very operations which Marlborough had in view.[7]

Before the close of November both Landau and Trarbach had surrendered; and the fall of the latter enabled the army to take up its winter-quarters on the Moselle from Coblentz to Treves. The campaign was virtually over even at an earlier date, and Marlborough might have at once repaired to the Hague and from thence to London, but for another affair which was unexpectedly claiming his attention. This affair arose from the course of events this year in Northern Italy.

Victor Amadeus had been assailed by very superior forces from France. He was wholly unable to meet them in the open field, and could only hover round them at any siege they undertook, endeavouring to protract that siege as much as possible. Vercelli and Ivrea were successively reduced by the Duke de Vendome, and Verrua the key of Turin was next invested. It was clear that, unless some succour could be sent to the Duke of Savoy, before the next campaign his capital must fall, and he must submit to whatever terms the French King might impose. The Duke of Savoy wrote therefore to the Emperor in most pressing terms beseeching aid; and applications to the same effect came to the allied chiefs beyond the Rhine. Mr. Hill the English Minister at Turin urged the case more especially on Marlborough, as the leading spirit of the whole confederacy; and he added, "We expect salvation from no side but from your Grace, but from thence we do expect it."

---

[7] "Il y a grande apparence que M. de Marlbnrough fera . . . occuper Trèves s'il peut, et même attaquer Trarbach." Lettre au Maréchal de Villeroy, 20 Septembre 1704. The movement of Marlborough was not made till mor than a month afterwards.

CHAP. V.
1704.

Marlborough saw most clearly the great importance of affording aid to Victor Amadeus and saving Piedmont from France. But the difficulty was to say from what quarter the required succours were to come. They could not be spared from his own army or from Prince Eugene's, without serious detriment to the common cause. The Emperor's few disposable troops were fully engaged in Hungary. Even money at that period could gain us no more men from the other German Princes. Only one among them, the King of Prussia, from the state of his warlike equipments, was in a condition to send out additional troops, and that prince would be hard, very hard, to persuade. It was strongly pressed upon Marlborough that he should himself go to Berlin, and there propose a treaty for 8,000 further troops in aid of the Duke of Savoy.

In his zeal for the common cause, though with much reluctance, Marlborough undertook this toilsome task. He set out on the 15th of November even before the two fortresses had yielded; and was a full week in reaching Berlin, although as he tells us he was fourteen or fifteen hours daily on the road. At Berlin he wrought so successfully on his Prussian Majesty that in a very few days he was enabled—not however without the promise of an English subsidy—to sign a convention for the required 8,000 men. "It is not to be expressed," so he writes to the Duchess, "the civilities and honors they have done me here, the Ministers assuring me that no other body could have prevailed with the King." Marlborough on his return passed two days at Hanover to pay his respects to the Elector; and then pursued his journey to the Hague and England.

Marlborough at this period was also in communication with the Emperor's Ministers, and attempting at their request to mediate a reconciliation with the Hungarian malcontents. He urged but in vain that the Emperor should freely concede a full measure of religious liberty. Unhappily the Jesuits were still in the ascendant at the Court of Vienna, and Leopold preferred to look to the probable triumph of his arms. The victory at Blenheim gave him means to send some reinforcements into Hungary; and the insurgents who had so lately threatened Vienna began to tremble for themselves. Ere long accordingly General Heuster the Imperial chief gained a signal victory over them, killing or making prisoners the best part of their infantry. Ragotsky indeed still continued in arms, and through the Emperor's stubbornness the troubles in Hungary were by no means appeased; but they dwindled in importance and ceased from this period to have any considerable weight in the general politics of Europe.

Louis the Fourteenth grown wiser by late experience pursued a far different course in Languedoc. The prince who had revoked the Edict of Nantes could not indeed by any amount of schooling be brought to concede religious toleration. But he left the new governor the Maréchal de Villars free to renounce the former cruelties and attempt a healing policy. Villars announced that he should in no degree molest those insurgents who quietly returned to their homes, while on the other hand he gave facilities to such as would rather leave the kingdom. Under this system by far the greater number of the Camisards laid down their arms. Their chief Jean Cavalier himself entered into terms. It was proposed to him to engage in the King's army with the command of a regiment composed of his former followers. But since full religious liberty was not to be allowed them he declined the offer. He made his way to Holland and there also obtained a Colonel's commission. He distinguished himself on several occasions, more especially at the battle of Almanza, and subsequently entering the English service attained the rank of General, being also named Lieutenant Governor of Jersey. He died at Chelsea in 1740. "He was of very mean appearance," says Speaker Onslow.[8]

It was not until this year, that the war which arose from the Succession of Spain was waged within that kingdom. There also the Court of Versailles had desired to commence a vigorous campaign. A subsidiary force of twelve thousand French troops crossed the Pyrenees, and joining the old Spanish regiments, made up a disposable army of almost thirty-five thousand. At the desire of King Louis the chief command was entrusted to a good officer in his service—the Duke of Berwick, a son of James the Second by Arabella Churchill; and a nephew therefore on the mother's side of Marlborough. Berwick determined to anticipate the movement which was expected on the side of Portugal; and himself at the beginning of May invaded that kingdom. He surprised and routed the body of Dutch troops commanded by General Fagel, and reduced the fortified towns of Castel Branco and Portalegre. But in part from the violent summer heats—in part from the misconduct of one of his Spanish divisions—and in part from the brave spirit of the Portuguese peasantry who rose in arms against the invaders—he could not

---

[8] Note to Burnet's History, vol. v. p. 165.

pursue his conquests and found it necessary to march back into Spain.

This desultory warfare in Portugal gave rise to loud and well-founded complaints against the Duke of Schomberg—the incapable son of an illustrious sire. With his small body of English troops, he had remained on the southern bank of the Tagus and done little more than march them to and fro. The Court of Lisbon made a formal representation to St. James's before the campaign was over; and Marlborough was consulted on this affair as on most others, even in the midst of Germany. By his advice the Duke of Schomberg was at once recalled, and in his place was sent out the Earl of Galway. This was a Frenchman by birth, the Marquis de Ruvigny by name; who like the elder Schomberg had left his native country when the persecution of the Protestants commenced, and who like Schomberg also had received from the Sovereign of England both a commission in the army and a title in the peerage.

There was warfare also on the opposite side of Spain. A fleet under Sir George Rooke sailed from Lisbon, and appeared off Barcelona at the end of May. It had on board the Prince of Hesse Darmstadt with some five thousand land forces. The Prince, who had been Governor of Catalonia during the last reign, had kept up a secret correspondence with the malcontents of the province, and with them a rising was concerted. But his letters had held out the hope that he would bring to them the Archduke himself with 20,000 men, and seeing that he fell so far short of his promises, they with good reason thought themselves released from theirs. Darmstadt proceeded to land his scanty

CHAP. V.
1704.

troops and to throw a few bombs into the city, but he had no prospect of reducing it without the aid of insurrection, and no insurrection came. After a brief interval he saw no better course before him than to reimbark his men and sail away.

On their return to the Streights from this inglorious expedition our seamen and soldiers came to be better employed. The chiefs resolved to attack Gibraltar, a fortress not as yet surrounded by skilful works, and in which the Spaniards, with their usual remissness at this period, had left a garrison of less than one hundred men. Eighteen hundred under the Prince of Darmstadt were disembarked on the narrow strip of sand which connects the Rock of Gibraltar with the Spanish shore, and on the 2nd of August they began to bombard the place, while the Admiral at the same time opened a fire from his ships. Such was the natural strength of the position that it might have been for some days at least maintained. But the 3rd was as it chanced a Saint's Day, and the Spanish sentinels upon the rock forsook their station to go and hear Mass in the Churches. While they were praying for destruction to the heretics, a party of English seamen scaled the eastern side of the precipice, and obtained possession of the heights which overhang the fortress. Another party of sailors and marines stormed the South Mole Head; and the garrison capitulated, still however obtaining honourable terms. Darmstadt desired to hoist the Spanish colours and to proclaim the Archduke as the King of Spain, but Rooke resolutely interposed and took possession of the place as an English conquest, raising the English flag on those ramparts where to this day it proudly waves, never lowered nor struck down, in the most formidable sieges by the united armaments of France and Spain.

The Prince of Darmstadt notwithstanding his recent claim for King Charles was left Governor of Gibraltar for Queen Anne with a garrison of 2,000 men. The Admiral proceeded to make a slight attempt on Ceuta, in which he did not prevail, and then sailed forward into the Mediterranean desiring to encounter the Count de Toulouse. The Count was one of the sons whom Madame de Montespan had borne to Louis the Fourteenth; the partiality of his father had named him High Admiral of France; and he was now in command of the fleet which had issued from Toulon. Rooke since he left Gibraltar had been joined by some Dutch ships bringing up his whole number as the French compute it to 47, while the French themselves had 49. The two fleets met off the coast of Malaga on the 24th of August and engaged in a heavy cannonade, which was closed by the approach of night, and which can scarcely be dignified with the name of a battle. If a battle at all it was a drawn one. Some thousand men were either killed or wounded, but no one ship was either sunk or taken.

On the 6th of July the Scottish Parliament reassembled. It had seemed wise to the Government to name a new Commissioner in the person of the Marquess of Tweeddale, but it was found that he throve no better than had the Marquess of Queensberry. The so-called Act of Security was again passed, almost without a show of resistance. Involving as it might on the demise of the Queen a separation of the Crowns of England and Scotland, a resolute Prime Minister would have for the second time refused it the Royal

Assent. But Godolphin whose timidity increased with advancing years had come on all occasions to regard the nearer evil as the worse; and in pursuance of these views he gave authority to Tweeddale to touch with the Royal Sceptre the obnoxious Bill. It must be owned as some vindication of this yielding policy, that the chief men in the Estates had declared themselves ready, should the Queen's Assent be withheld, to take an extreme course on their own side, and refuse to vote the funds for the support of the Scottish troops.[9]

On the 29th of October there met a more important assembly—the Parliament of England. The Queen in her opening Speech joyfully commemorated "the great and remarkable success with which God hath blessed our arms;" and congratulations were duly voted by both Houses though not quite in the same strain. The Peers with their Whig tendencies expressed their admiration of the Blenheim victory, and also of Her Majesty's "wisdom and courage in sending that seasonable and necessary assistance to the Empire." The Commons, with their Tory tendencies that were warmly shown to their favourite Admiral, seemed to depreciate the glorious achievement of the Duke of Marlborough, by bestowing nearly similar praise on the indecisive cannonade of Sir George Rooke. Nevertheless the Lower House evinced much alacrity and readiness in voting the supplies for the vigorous prosecution of the war. These amounted to £4,670,000; a sum which was deemed enormous in that age, and

---

[9] On a counter-plan to maintain if necessary an army in Scotland upon English pay see a letter from George Baillie of Jerviswood in the Marchmont Papers, vol. III. p. 263.

which had to be raised mainly by a Land Tax of four shillings in the pound, by continuing the Duties on Malt, and by the sale of nearly one million of Annuities.

The affairs of Scotland were among the first to engage the attention of Parliament. Lord Haversham introduced them in a set speech duly reported by himself, and the Peers resolved to consider them further on the 29th of November. Then the Queen came for the first time in her reign to hear the debates; she is described by an eyewitness as "at first on the Throne, and after, it being cold, on a bench at the fire."[1] She expected that her presence would moderate the attacks on the Lord Treasurer; nevertheless he was sharply aimed at both by Tories and Whigs—by Rochester and Nottingham no less than by Halifax and Somers. The Lord Treasurer made but a feeble defence; if we may trust Lord Dartmouth "he talked nonsense very fast, which was not his usual way either of matter or manner."[2] His fire indeed was nearly burned out; and it might almost be said of him, that henceforth during the remainder of his life he played but a subordinate part in his own administration.

The question was resumed on the 6th of December and the Queen was present again. Lord Somers, speaking as ever with the greatest weight and authority, explained the specific measures which he thought required. He proposed a law to declare the Scots aliens, and to forbid the importation of their cattle—this law to commence after some interval and to determine whenever the Succession to the Crown of Scot-

---

[1] Letter of Secretary Johnstone in the Jerviswood Correspondence, p. 15.
[2] Note to Burnet's History, vol. v. p. 182.

CHAP. V.
1704.

land should be settled. This appeared to be the sense of the majority and a Bill to that effect was introduced. But the Lords went farther still. They carried an Address to her Majesty praying that Newcastle should be put into a condition of defence—that the port of Tynemouth should be secured—that the works at Carlisle and Hull should be repaired—that the Militia of the four northern counties should be disciplined and provided with arms and ammunition.

The Lower House fully concurred with the Upper. But the Bill of the Lords was found to contain some money penalties which—then perhaps for the first time in our annals—roused the jealousy of the Commons as seeming however remotely to invade their own taxing privileges. Therefore they preferred a Bill of their own which obtained the sanction of the other branch of the Legislature, and became law in the course of the Session. It enacted that the Queen should be empowered to name Commissioners to treat of an Union with Scotland—that after Christmas Day 1705, unless the Succession to the Crown of Scotland should be decided by that time, every native of Scotland, not a settled inhabitant of England, nor serving in Her Majesty's forces, should be taken and held for an alien—that from the same date no Scotch cattle nor sheep should be brought into England, nor yet any Scotch coals, nor yet any Scotch linen.[3]

This Act was intended to put, and did put, considerable pressure on the Scots to conclude an Union. Thus dolefully do we find the Earl of Roxburgh for

---

[3] Act 3 and 4 Anne, c. 7. It is entitled "An Act for the effectual securing the kingdom of England from the apparent dangers that may arise from several Acts lately passed in the Parliament of Scotland."

example write from London: "For my part I don't well know what to say; for unless our cattle and linen can be otherwise disposed of we are utterly ruined should these laws take effect."

The Tory party at this time were mainly intent on reviving their favourite measure, the Occasional Conformity Bill. It was brought in again with fiery haste only a few days from the beginning of the Session, and as before it passed through all its stages in the Commons. But it was foreseen that as before it would certainly be rejected by the Lords. To secure its passing its more violent promoters resolved to tack it to the new Land Tax Bill, so that the Peers could not fling out the proposal of intolerance without losing the proposal of Supply. The "tackers," as they were termed, in their ardour to deal a blow on the Dissenters, grew blind to the danger of striking also at the landmarks of the Constitution. Happily these were not the views of all. Harley and St. John now in office, wrought with success upon their friends in the Tory ranks. About a hundred members adhered to them on this occasion rather than to Nottingham; and thus when the division came the tackers were routed by the decisive majority of 251 against 134. It is worthy of note as a thing most unusual in that age, and betokening the general interest which was felt upon this subject, that there was made public a detailed Division List—a statement showing county by county how each of its members had voted.

The Bill went therefore without any tack to the House of Lords, and the Queen was present at the debate upon the Second Reading which was long and well sustained. The Ministers had passed from lukewarm support into no very bold hostility; and Marlborough who had that very day returned from the Continent, gave like Godolphin a silent vote against the Bill. It was rejected by a much increased majority— 71 Peers against 50.

Marlborough who had left the Hague on the 11th of December, landed in London on the forenoon of the 14th. He brought in his train Marshal Tallard and the other General officers made captive at Blenheim. They were treated with all courtesy and sent to reside on parole at inland towns as Nottingham and Lichfield. The reception of Marlborough himself was such as beseemed his services. He was most warmly greeted by the Queen to whom he paid his respects that same morning at the palace of St. James's. Next day he received at his own house a Committee of the Commons who bore him an Address of Thanks which their House had voted; and when he appeared in the House of Lords he was welcomed by the Lord Keeper who read to him another like Address in the name of his brother Peers.

1705. With Marlborough came over not only the principal captives, but the standards and other trophies that were taken at Blenheim. They were first placed for safety in the Tower but on the 3rd of January were removed in solemn procession to Westminster Hall. First came a troop of the Horse Grenadiers, next three companies of the Horse Guards; then in the centre thirty-four gentlemen each carrying a standard taken from the enemy; and lastly a battalion of the Foot Guards; the pikemen to the number of 128 each bearing aloft in the place of his pike one of the enemy's colours. In this manner they marched through the

City, the Strand, and by St. James's Palace, where the Queen from one of the windows viewed them pass, and thus through St. James's Park to Westminster Hall, while the guns in the Park, forty in number, fired their loud salute and the assembled multitudes poured forth their scarcely less loud acclamations. It was, and it was felt to be, the greatest triumph over foreign foes, that England ever had to celebrate since the rout of the Spanish Armada.[4]

Three days later Marlborough was entertained in Goldsmiths' Hall by the Lord Mayor and Court of Aldermen. According to the far different habits and hours of that period he set out for this dinner about noon. He was conveyed in one of Her Majesty's coaches, in which there sat with him the Lord Treasurer, the Duke of Somerset Master of the Horse, and the Prince of Hesse so lately his companion in arms. The Royal carriage was followed by a long train of other coaches conveying the Foreign Ministers and many Englishmen of rank, as also the Generals and other chief officers of the army. At Temple Bar they were received in ancient form by the City Marshal, and both in going and returning the hero of Blenheim was enthusiastically cheered by the crowds that lined the way.

Other and more substantial rewards ensued. The

---

[4] Complete History of Europe, 1705, p. 7. Here are some of the devices and mottoes of the French standards borne aloft on this occasion. An eagle flying in the air. *In regnum et pugnas* (To reign and to fight). A Granado Shell. *Concussus surgo* (Though burst I rise). A plain white standard. *Victoria pinget* (Victory shall paint my device). A bomb. *Alter post fulmina terror* (The terror next to thunder). An eagle shot at on all sides by thunderbolts. *Audentior* (The bolder still). A rocket let off. *Poco duri purchè s' inalsi* (Let it last ever so little so it but rises).

Commons had voted an Address to the Queen praying her to consider of proper means to perpetuate the memory of the great services performed by the Duke of Marlborough. In reply the Queen declared herself inclined to bestow upon the Duke the Royal manor and honor of Woodstock, at the same time desiring the assistance of the House to clear off the encumbrances on that estate, its rents and profits having been already granted for two lives. The Commons cheerfully agreed. A Bill was passed through both Houses without one dissentient voice to settle this noble domain free of charge on Marlborough and his heirs for ever, as a feudal tenure from the Crown, on the sole condition as the Act itself describes it, of "rendering to Her Majesty and her successors on the second day of August in every year for ever, at the Castle of Windsor one Standard or Colours with three Flowers de Luces painted thereupon." It should be noticed that the 2nd of August was the anniversary of the great battle on the Danube when reckoned by the Old instead of the New Style. This feudal tenure is continued at the present day; and the yearly standard of Woodstock may be seen at Windsor Castle ranged side by side with the yearly standard of Strathfieldsaye.

Nor was this all. The Queen gave orders to construct at her expense a stately palace in the park of Woodstock which should bear the name of Blenheim, and be a lasting record of her own and the nation's gratitude. Her Majesty having approved the model the work was at once commenced under the direction of Mr. Vanbrugh, afterwards Sir John. His merits as an architect were highly extolled in his lifetime, but at present are more commonly viewed in the light of the sarcastic epitaph composed at his decease.[5]

The Court of Vienna was no less desirous to show some token of respect to the deliverer of Germany. Marlborough received the title of Prince and a few months later the grant of the principality of Mindelheim in Suabia. The principality was lost at the peace; but to this day the heir of Blenheim is entitled to quarter his armorial bearings on the two-headed eagle of the Germanic Empire, while below stands his Motto in Spanish: FIEL PERO DESDICHADO—"faithful but unfortunate." This Motto was first assumed by the great Duke's father Sir Winston, when oppressed as a staunch Cavalier in the Civil Wars; but in both the epithets it was certainly most inapplicable to the great Duke's own career.

The ascendancy of Marlborough in England was further shown by the conduct of the Government in reference to Rooke. We have seen how the Tory House of Commons at the beginning of the Session had drawn some kind of parallel between the encounter at Malaga and the victory at Blenheim. A similar course was pursued by the Tory University of Oxford. Early in January there came up a Deputation, headed by the Vice-Chancellor Dr. Delaune, to lay before the Queen a printed copy of the speeches and verses recited in the Theatre on New Year's Day. In the Address which they bore they observed that the exercise performed in their Theatre, "was in honor of the great success of Her Majesty's arms the last year in Germany, under the admirable conduct and invincible courage of the Duke

---

[5] Lie heavy on him, Earth, for he
Laid many a heavy load on thee.

CHAP. V.
1705.

of Marlborough, and at sea, under the most brave and faithful Admiral Sir George Rooke," and it classed both the actions together, both being they said "as beneficial as they were glorious." The Queen gave a cold reply and the Duke's friends were much offended. It was felt moreover that observing how very nearly equal in force Rooke had been to Toulouse, and bearing in mind how constantly the English had prevailed at sea, his distant and doubtful cannonade rendered him liable to censure rather than entitled to praise. At this juncture then it was announced that Prince George, as Lord High Admiral, had superseded Rooke as Commander-in-Chief of the fleet, naming in his place Sir Cloudesley Shovel and for Vice-Admiral Sir John Leake. Both these officers it should be noted belonged to the Whig party.

This Session of Parliament after the Christmas holidays was continued for several weeks, but these were almost wholly consumed in disputes and altercations arising from the Aylesbury case of the preceding year. Since Matthew Ashby the Constables of the Borough had been sued by four other inhabitants for denying them the right to vote. These four persons were committed to Newgate by order of the House of Commons. They moved for an Habeas Corpus in the Court of Queen's Bench, but three of the Judges, against the opinion of Holt their chief, decided that the Court could take no cognizance of the matter. Upon this Paty and Oviat two of the prisoners petitioned the Queen for a Writ of Error to bring this question before the Lords.

Both Houses showed equal zeal in this cause though in exactly opposite directions. The Commons not only voted an Address to the Queen against granting a Writ

of Error, but, for greater security removed the prisoners
to the custody of their own Serjeant at Arms. The
Lords passed six different Resolutions against the conduct of the Commons, which they said was an obstruction to justice and contrary to Magna Charta. Conferences took place between the Houses but without
any reconcilement, and the heats on both sides were
rapidly rising, when the other business of the Session
being now concluded, the Session itself was closed on
the 14th of March. The Queen in her final Speech
alleged "our own unreasonable humour and animosity,
the fatal effects of which we have so narrowly escaped."
This allusion was well-understood as referring to the
intended tack on the Land Tax Bill.

Parliament being now close on its triennial period
was dissolved on the 5th of April, and a Proclamation
calling another was issued on the 23rd. The Queen
and Prince availed themselves of the interval to pay a
visit to Newmarket and from thence by invitation to
Cambridge. There she was received with as many
tokens of attachment as greeted Her Majesty at Oxford
in the preceding year. At a mile from the town she
was met by the Mayor and Aldermen with the Earl of
Orford their High Steward and Sir John Cotton their
Recorder, who in the name of the whole body made
Her Majesty a speech and presented her with a purse
of gold. In the town itself the Queen found the
scholars ranged along the streets in their caps and
gowns and welcoming her approach with joyful acclamations, not however in English but in Latin—VIVAT
REGINA—so as to display both their loyalty and learning. The ways were all along strewn with flowers;
the bells rang, and the conduits flowed with wine. In

CHAP.
V.
1705.

the "Regent Walk" which led to the Schools Her Majesty was received by the Duke of Somerset as Chancellor at the head of the Doctors in their Robes. After sustaining one speech from His Grace, and another from Mr. Ayloffe the Public Orator, the Queen entered the "Regent House" and saw the Degrees of Doctor in Divinity and Law conferred on some eminent men. Thence repairing to Trinity College the Queen heard another speech from the Master Dr. Bentley, and conferred the honor of knighthood on several persons, among whom we find commemorated "Isaac Newton, formerly Mathematic Professor and Fellow of that College." Then about three hundred ladies were admitted to kiss Her Majesty's hand. Next she was entertained at dinner in Trinity College Hall and at the expense of the University. She sat upon a throne erected five foot high; and for the other guests there were four large tables with fifty covers each. In the afternoon Her Majesty visited also St. John's College and Queen's, and attended prayers in King's College Chapel; then setting forth again she returned to Newmarket the same night.[6]

Marlborough was at this time in Holland having embarked at Harwich on the 31st of March. By his letters however he could still counsel and guide Godolphin with respect to the coming elections. He advised that any members who had voted for the tack should be if possible unseated. Thus he writes: "As to what you say of the tackers I think the method that should be taken is what is practised in all armies, that is if the

[6] Complete History of Europe, 1705, p. 159. The University had found itself obliged to borrow 500*l.* for the purpose of this entertainment. *Grace Book*, April 2, 1705, as cited in Monk's Life of Bentley.

enemy give no quarter they should have none given to them."[7]

But the case of the Government was full as strong against those non-tacking Tories in the Government ranks, who while they retained office entirely concurred, and secretly caballed, with Nottingham and Rochester. Foremost among these was Sheffield, Duke of Buckingham. Marlborough and Godolphin had some months before come to the resolution that he should be removed. That resolution was now carried out with the reluctant assent of the Queen; and the Privy Seal taken from him was bestowed on the Duke of Newcastle, who was one of the Whig party.

It was indeed to the Whigs that Marlborough and Godolphin were now by slow degrees inclining. They had been in some negotiation more or less direct through the winter with the knot of five Whig Peers—the Junto as it was commonly called—which governed the Whig party at that time. The members of this Junto were Somers and Halifax, Orford, Wharton and Sunderland. Of these five, the first four have been portrayed by Lord Macaulay with his usual felicity, and I may add with entire fairness.[8] He does, not for example, seek in any manner to disguise the fact that Wharton was a man of profligate life and an open scoffer at Revealed Religion. It may be added that as such he was in especial disfavor with the Queen.

Charles Earl of Sunderland did not fall within the

---

[7] Letter of April 14, 1705.

[8] See in his History, for Russell (Lord Orford), vol. vi. p. 167, for Somers, vol. vii. p. 239, for Montague (Lord Halifax), ib. p. 263, and for Wharton, ib. p. 267. (Tauchnitz Ed.).

scope of Lord Macaulay's narrative. I have at some length sketched that character elsewhere.[9]

In their negotiations during the past winter with these powerful "Five," Marlborough and Godolphin had been drawn into a promise, not perhaps quite consistent with fairness to one of their present colleagues. It was, to take some convenient opportunity of dismissing Sir Nathan Wright from the office of Lord Keeper and transferring the Great Seal to William Cowper, who was endeared to the Whig chiefs by eminent qualities no less than by party ties.

There were also at this time, not only in promise but performance, several crumbs of State patronage bestowed on younger Whigs. Thus Walpole, afterwards the great Sir Robert, but then only at the outset of his busy career, was appointed one of the Council to the Lord High Admiral, at the especial recommendation of Marlborough. In the army and navy also the same predilection might be traced. Of Sir Cloudesley Shovel and Sir John Leake I have already spoken. Sir George Byng another officer like them, that is, not only of tried merit but of Whig politics, was placed at the head of the Channel Fleet. Colonel James Stanhope was made a Brigadier General; and Lord Cutts was sent to command the forces in Ireland under the Duke of Ormond.

The favourite object of the Whigs at this time was, however, to find some Cabinet office for the Earl of Sunderland. As son-in-law of Marlborough, they thought that if once in place, he might ere long attain considerable influence and draw in others of the party

---

[9] History since the Peace of Utrecht, vol. 1. p. 247. (Tauchnitz Ed.). At page 218 there is also a character of Lord Somers.

after him. They had already made a convert of the
Duchess. Her letters during the past year or longer
still were filled with railing against the Tories, not un-
mixed with some reflections on her husband for the
more than indifference which he showed to their son-
in-law's promotion. Indifference to promotion was by
no means in general the fault of Marlborough, nor yet
resistance to the wishes of his wife. But in this case
he paused. Sunderland he knew was at this juncture
held to be impetuous and extreme by the Whigs themselves; and he feared lest his nomination to some high
office of home Government might lead Harley and the
other Ministerial Tories to break away from him. His
object and Godolphin's, so far as we can trace it, was
rather at this juncture to proceed most cautiously and step
by step until they saw the result of the General Election.

That result was soon made clear. The Tories
went to the hustings divided and perplexed, as tackers
or non-tackers, as members or as opponents of the
Ministry. The Whigs, even when they might be inferior in numbers, were compact, united and hopeful.
In party watch-words also, the Whigs had this time
the advantage. From the loss of the Occasional Conformity Bill, the Tories raised the cry of the Church
in danger, but except among the clergy produced no
great effect. The Whigs on the other hand might
point to the glorious triumphs of the last campaign as
following the policy and fulfilling the aspirations of
their hero William the Third. It is not strange therefore that the latter party prevailed in these elections.
Wherever there was any contest of a political character
and detached from family influence the Whig candidates for the most part were returned.

CHAPTER VI.

CHAP. VI.
1705.

MARLBOROUGH was three weeks at the Hague before he could obtain the consent of the Dutch States to his plan for the next campaign. That plan had been concerted with Prince Eugene during the siege of Landau. It was to invade France on the side of the Moselle where in the judgment of Marlborough her northern frontier was the least defensible. Early in the spring the two armies, assembling between the Moselle and the Saar, were to commence the siege of Saar-Louis and to open a communication with the Duke of Lorraine, who was overawed by his mighty neighbour but who at heart inclined to the Allies. It was with a view to this design that Marlborough had directed his final operations in the preceding year by taking Treves and Trarbach and quartering his army in the vale of the Moselle.

Louis on his part was not unprepared for such a scheme on the part of the Allies. He had made strenuous and successful efforts to fill up the void both in men and in equipments which the day of Blenheim had caused; and the superiority of numbers was still upon his side. He was able to allege in one of his secret letters dated the 15th of May: "My enemies have not so much infantry as there is in my armies of Flanders, of the Moselle and of the Rhine; though in cavalry they are as near as may be equal."[1] The

[1] Mémoires militaires de la Succession d'Espagne, vol. v. p. 415, ed. 1842.

troubles in Languedoc being now appeased, he summoned Villars from that province and entrusted him with the command on the Moselle. Villeroy he left in Flanders, and Marsin in Alsace.

When Marlborough therefore, having at last extorted the tardy consent of the Dutch States, appeared at the head of his troops on the Moselle, he found in his front an able General and a large well-appointed army. Worse still, he had no longer Prince Eugene at his side. That great chief had been sent by the Emperor to command in Italy, and Marlborough was yoked once again to the untoward Margrave of Baden. It was in vain that Marlborough solicited the co-operation which had been stipulated. Prince Louis remained immoveable in his palace of Rastadt near Baden, sometimes pleading his own illness and sometimes the deficiencies of his troops.

It was at this juncture that news came of the decease of the Emperor Leopold at Vienna on the 5th of May. Marlborough hoped that a more vigorous system might be pursued by the King of the Romans now the Emperor Joseph. But after a short show of activity it soon relapsed into the old torpid system of routine. In compliance however with Marlborough's earnest application an order was sent to Prince Louis to expedite his movements, and Marlborough himself repaired to Rastadt in hopes of conciliating his colleague. He took care to admire the formal palace which the Margrave had built and the trim alleys he had planted. Nor were such courtesies without effect. The Margrave promised that he would begin his march on a day that he named. But he pointed out that the force he would bring must be very scanty; since the

CHAP. VI.
1705.

Court of Vienna, unmindful of its positive stipulations for the quota of troops, and looking mainly to its more immediate objects in Hungary and Italy, had called back the best part of its army from the Rhine, and left the remnant extremely ill supplied.

Slight as were the hopes of any effective co-operation which Prince Louis gave they were much more than he accomplished. When the time came he declared himself sick, threw up his command, and set off to drink the waters of Schlangenbad. Count de Frise whom he named in his place brought to Marlborough only a few ragged battalions, and moreover like his principal showed himself most jealous of the English chief. To add to Marlborough's difficulties at this juncture, the person, Sentery by name, who had been employed all through the winter to superintend the magazines of bread and forage suddenly fled to the enemy, when it was discovered that he had embezzled the money and that the magazines were not half filled.

Marlborough nevertheless took the field and even singly desired to give battle. But positive instructions from Versailles precluded Villars from engaging. He intrenched himself in an extremely strong position at Sirk, where it was impossible for an inferior army to assail him. And while the war was thus unprosperous on the Moselle there came adverse tidings from the Meuse. Marshal Villeroy had suddenly resumed the offensive, had reduced the fortress of Huy, had entered the city and invested the citadel of Liege. In great alarm the Dutch General Overkirk despatched his colleague Hompesch to Marlborough with most pressing applications for immediate aid; and Marlborough with so many Dutch troops in his army saw the necessity for his compliance. Accordingly he set out the very next day on his march to Liege, leaving only a sufficient force as he hoped for the security of Treves.

The chagrin of Marlborough at this period rose to the height of anguish, as may best be shown by some extracts as follows from his private correspondence. Thus to Godolphin, on June the 16th: "I have for these last ten days been so troubled by the many disappointments I have had, that I think if it were possible to vex me so for a fortnight longer it would make an end of me. In short I am weary of my life." And again on the 24th: "I beg you will give my humble duty to the Queen, and assure her that nothing but my gratitude to her could oblige me to serve her after the disappointments I have met with in Germany, for nothing has been performed that was promised; and to add to this they write to me from England that the tackers and all their friends are glad of the disappointments I meet with, saying that if I had success this year like the last the Constitution of England would be ruined. As I have no other ambition but that of serving well Her Majesty, and being thought what I am a good Englishman, this vile enormous faction of theirs vexes me so much that I hope the Queen will, after this campaign, give me leave to retire, and end my days in praying for her prosperity and making my own peace with God. . . . I beg you will not oppose this, thinking it may proceed at this time from the spleen; I do assure you it does not, but it is from the base ingratitude of my countrymen." . . . .

The Great Duke when he wrote these bitter lines was more especially chafed by the news that came to him from his rear. M. d'Aubach, whom he had left in command at Treves, was scared at the advance of a small French detachment, and retired without a blow from both Treves and Saarbrück, leaving our best magazines in possession of the enemy. On the other hand he had the satisfaction of learning that his own advance had produced nearly the same effect on Marshal Villeroy. That chief at once relinquished his design upon the citadel of Liege and fell back in the direction of Tongres, so that Marlborough and Overkirk effected their junction with ease. Marlborough took prompt measures to re-invest the fortress of Huy and compelled it to surrender on the 11th of July.

Applying his mind to the new sphere before him, Marlborough saw ground to hope that with the aid of the Dutch troops he might still make a triumphant campaign. The first object was to force the defensive lines that stretched across the country from near Namur to Antwerp, protected by numerous fortified posts and covered in other places by rivers and morasses. They had been constructed by the French in the earlier years of the war, and were now defended by an army of at least 60,000 men under Marshal Villeroy and the Elector of Bavaria. Marlborough laid his plans before Generals Overkirk and Slangenberg as also those civilian envoys whom the States were wont to commission at their armies. But he found to his sorrow that for jealousy and slowness a Dutch deputy was fully a match for a German Margrave.

Having with great difficulty obtained that obedience to his orders which in a better regulated service would have ensued as a matter of course, Marlborough was enabled to make his intended attack, at daybreak on the

18th of July. The point he had selected was on the banks of the Little Gheet, where the enemy deemed the position so strong as to have left it very bare of troops. A sudden onset from Marlborough here broke through the defences and scattered the defenders, while in the skirmish and surprise which followed he took more than 1,200 prisoners. Thus were the French lines forced to the utter surprise of the Dutch chiefs. To these last the Duke refers as follows in writing to Godolphin: "The bearer will tell you that I was forced to cheat them into this action, for they did not believe I would attack the lines; they being positive that the enemy were stronger than they were." To the Duchess he adds: "I had no troops with me in this last action but such as were with me last year; for M. Overkirk's army did not come till an hour after all was over. This was not their fault for they could not come sooner; but this gave occasion to the troops with me to make me very kind expressions, even in the heat of the action, which I own to you gives me great pleasure and makes me resolve to endure any thing for their sakes."

Having thus successfully broke through the lines so laboriously constructed Marlborough was most eager to pursue his advantage. But the heavy rains which fell during the next following days completely flooded the meadows along the Dyle, and debarred him from attempting the passage of that river. Meanwhile the French chiefs had leisure to recover from their first surprise, and the Dutch—General Slangenberg especially who had a personal spleen against him—to frame anew their cavils and objections.

The floods having subsided and the fair weather returned, Marlborough wrought so far upon the Generals

CHAP. VI.
1705.

and Deputies that they agreed to an attack of the French army, now encamped on the opposite side of the Dyle. The attack was made accordingly on the 30th of July, the troops being well provided with pontoons. The Dutch were on the left, and General Heukelom who commanded their first division not only led the whole of his infantry across the Dyle, but drove three brigades of the enemy from their post at the village of Neer Ische. The object in view, that is the passage of the river, was thus accomplished, and it was only needful to support with steadiness the advantage which Heukelom had bravely gained. Just at this crisis however, an unaccountable doubt or demur was conceived by the Dutch chiefs as to the propriety of moving onward to the support of their first line. Marlborough, who was advancing at the head of his own army, was apprised of their hesitation and instantly despatched an aide-de-camp to urge upon them the necessity of succouring, or, if they would not, of recalling Heukelom. He soon followed with all speed to add his own entreaties.

The scene that ensued has been well described by Mr. Hare, the Army Chaplain, who that day was on horseback and in attendance on the Duke. Marlborough, as he tells us, riding up to the spot where the Dutch chiefs were holding council, was about to exhort them for the immediate support of their detachment, when Slangenberg exclaiming, "For God's sake, my Lord Duke, do not"—took him aside and continued for some time to address him with much gesticulation, as if dissuading him from so hazardous an enterprise.[2] During

[2] Hare's Narrative, MS. from the extract in Coxe's Marlborough, vol. ii. p.156.

this colloquy the other Dutchmen took it on themselves to send their own orders to Heukelom; and the purport of those orders may be guessed. Heukelom accordingly retreated, as did also another detachment which had already passed the river. They were little pressed by the enemy; and the entire loss of the Allies this day fell short of fifty men. But their object had been frustrated, and they were not beyond the Dyle.

Marlborough was deeply moved. Thus he wrote to England: "It is very mortifying to find much more obstructions from friends than from enemies; but that is now the case with me; and yet I dare not show my resentment for fear of too much alarming the Dutch." The latter motive indeed so far prevailed with him, that, in the official letter which he sent to the States of Holland, he ascribed the retreat only to the head of the enemy's army having come up in force. Yet he did not leave the ruling men in ignorance of the fault of their officers. He sent General Hompesch to the Hague with a private letter to Heinsius stating the real fact, and complaining especially of Slangenberg. As he explains it to Godolphin, "besides the danger of resolving every thing that is to be done in a Council of War which cannot be kept so secret, so Monsieur Slangenberg, though he is a brave man his temper is such that there is no taking measures with him."

In relation to the affair at Neer Ische no letter at all from Marlborough appeared in the London Gazette. The Tories and other malcontents in England made the best use they could of this slight check—since how few others could they find! However, they did not very well agree in their complaints. Some declared that the Duke was too rash in making the advance; others that he was too cautious in allowing the retreat.

After this recent failure, it was felt by Marlborough, that it was hopeless to propose any renewed attempt to force the passage of the Dyle. His fertile genius devised another scheme—to move round the sources of the river and to threaten Brussels from the southern side. As this movement would separate him from his magazines, he found it necessary to halt in his camp at Meldert till he could procure a sufficient supply of bread, and during the interval, he celebrated with thanksgiving and rejoicing the anniversary of the battle of Blenheim. On the 15th of August he began his march as did also Overkirk in a parallel direction, and in two days they reached Genappe near the sources of the Dyle. There uniting in one line of battle they moved next morning towards Brussels by the main CHAUSSÉE or great paved road; their head-quarters that day being fixed at Frischermont, near the borders of the forest of Soignies.

On the French side, the Elector and Villeroy observing the march of the Allies had made a corresponding movement of their own for the protection of the capital. They encamped behind the small stream of the Ische, their right and rear being partly covered by the forest. Only the day before they had been joined by Marsin from the Rhine, and they agreed to give battle sooner than yield Brussels. One of their main posts was at Waterloo, which was held by Colonel Pasteur with two regiments of dragoons and one battalion from Béarn; and here ensued a slight skirmish, not to the advantage of Pasteur, with the advanced guard of the Allies; but

"Waterloo is a bad post as I have already explained to your Majesty." So wrote Villeroy to Louis.[3]

It is probable had a battle now ensued, that it would have been fought on the same or nearly the same ground as was the memorable conflict a hundred and ten years afterwards. But the position of the armies would have been reversed, since at the earlier date, as I have shown, the French defended Brussels upon which the English and Dutch were marching. More than once have I heard the Duke of Wellington advert with much interest to this singular coincidence or contrast, of which he had carefully studied the details.

But the expected battle did not take place. On the morning of the 18th of August Marlborough rode forward to reconnoitre the enemy's army, which according to his computation was fully by one-third less in numbers than his own. He discovered also, as he thought, in their position four practicable points for an attack. As he was viewing one of these points, which in his judgment was the weakest of all, he found his party aimed at by the fire of some French artillery; but his usual composure was not ruffled, and he only said with a smile to the officers around him: "These gentlemen do not choose to have this spot too narrowly inspected."

Marlborough came back in high spirits and confident of victory. He met Overkirk, who in his company examined the ground again, and fully approved his intended dispositions. By this time (it was past midday) the Allied troops were ranged in battle order

[3] See the Mémoires militaires de la Succession d'Espagne, vol. v. p. 600, ed. 1842.

within cannon shot of the enemy. The Duke was eager to give the signal for an onset. But the Deputies were quite as eager to interpose. They declared that they could not give their assent to an engagement until they had consulted their Generals, and except Overkirk all the Dutch chiefs thus being consulted declared that the French positions were too strong to be assailed. "Murder and massacre!" cried Slangenberg especially at the head of the malcontents. A small circle was formed, and hour after hour wasted in starting doubts and difficulties, while Marlborough was observed standing by in an agony of impatience. At last after one more survey of the ground the opinion of Slangenberg prevailed, and Marlborough with a heavy heart gave orders for the troops to return to their respective quarters.

Next morning the enemy had strengthened his position; the Dutch chiefs continued obdurate; and the troops could remain no longer at gaze. The supply of bread which they had brought with them was running short; and if they did not advance to Brussels they must fall back on their magazines. Orders were issued accordingly that they should commence their retreat on that same day; and in this manner they marched back to their former camp at Meldert. To the States Marlborough wrote an official report in measured terms, but he added a postscript as follows which was published with the rest: "My heart is so full that I cannot forbear representing to Your High Mightinesses that I find my authority here to be much less than when I had the honor to command your troops in Germany." And in his private letter to Godolphin we find: "I beg you will give my duty to the Queen, and assure her that if

I had the same power I had the last year I should have had a greater victory than that of Blenheim in my opinion; for the French were so posted that if we had beat them they could not have got to Brussels."

It is not surprising after these events that the French, unacquainted with all the circumstances, should be tempted to disparage their principal antagonist. "You will easily persuade me"—Chamillart remarks to Villeroy—"to have but an indifferent opinion of the capacity of the Duke of Marlborough. What he has done this campaign clearly shows that we rated him far too highly after the battle of Hochstädt, which he appears to have gained by his good fortune rather than his genius."[4] So wrote the Ministers in France.

The Ministers in England were much—and surely with good reason—offended. They resolved to send one of their own number, Lord Pembroke, President of the Council, to the Hague, to complain of Slangenberg and the Deputies, and to remonstrate against the system of divided command. But Heinsius, Slingelandt, and other staunch friends of England who were consulted, saw that such a step would give general offence, and Marlborough himself dissuaded it. Lord Pembroke therefore remained at home, and the Dutch were induced of themselves to send a rebuke to their Deputies, and to recall Slangenberg from his command.

But by this time the opportunity had passed. The campaign from which so much had been expected was over. The army after its return to the camp of Meldert did no more than reduce the petty fort of Leuwe, and with some amount of labour level the French lines. This period was however signalised by a feat of arms

[4] Letter dated Versailles, September 5, 1705.

upon the Rhine. Prince Louis so long inactive roused himself as by a sudden effort and succeeded in surprising Drusenheim, forcing the lines of Haguenau, and blockading Fort Louis. This exploit came too late in the season to assist in any material manner the cause of the Allies. But it stood in good stead to Prince Louis himself. The English Government under the guidance of Marlborough was at this very period endeavouring to obtain from the Court of Vienna the recall of the Margrave from his command. It was from the first no very hopeful negotiation since the Margrave had the honor to be first cousin to the first Minister; and at the news of Haguenau, Marlborough at once desired that no further effort against him should be made.

In northern Italy the gallant defence of Verona had been continued through the winter; and it was not till the 10th of April that the place surrendered. The siege of Chivasso was in like manner protracted by the brave spirit of the garrison. Thus during this year's campaign the Duke of Savoy was enabled to make head against La Feuillade, as could also in Lombardy Prince Eugene against Vendome. The two last chiefs came to a pitched battle on the 16th of August at the bridge of Cassano; it was fierce and well contested, and both parties claimed the victory. Through all this warfare the Allies derived very great advantage from the auxiliary force of 8,000 Prussians which Marlborough had negotiated, but their stipulated term of service was only for one year, and their King had threatened that it should not be renewed.

Passing to more southern climes we find the Spanish Court which had so negligently guarded Gibraltar most keenly resent its loss. A body of 8,000 men was at once employed to invest it; and the siege was continued all through the winter, directed first by the Spanish Marquis de Villadarias, and then by the French Maréchal de Tessé. There was also a French squadron under Baron de Pontis sent forward to complete the blockade. But the Prince of Darmstadt made a most brave defence, and no progress was made by the besiegers either on land or sea. At length, early in the spring, came in sight Admiral Leake with a well-appointed squadron from England. Attacking the French ships he took some and dispersed the rest; and on this event the land-forces of the enemy were also withdrawn.—On the other hand the campaign of the Allies was but feebly conducted on the side of Portugal; and they throve no better in their siege of Badajos than had the French in their siege of Gibraltar.

A new turn, however, was given to Peninsular affairs by the appearance of another actor on the scene. This was Charles Mordaunt, third Earl of Peterborough, or Peterborow as it was always spelled by himself. He was now forty-six years of age and hitherto distinguished mainly by his wild adventures and his fickle amours. Marlborough with his usual sagacity had discerned the latent genius for war which lurked in this eccentric man, and had singled him out to command the fresh auxiliary force which was to be despatched from England. That force consisted of about 5,000 men, one-third Dutch and two-thirds English; it was collected at Portsmouth; and with Peterborough on board reached Lisbon on the 20th of June. The first object assigned to the Earl in his instructions was to relieve the Duke of Savoy, who had been loudly calling for aid against the French, but he was allowed a discretionary power if he should rather choose some enterprise on the coast of Spain; and while with sole authority over the land-forces, he owed it to his rank perhaps that he was associated with Sir Cloudesley Shovel as joint Admiral of the fleet.

Such ample authority, so wide discretionary powers, were well suited to the genius of Peterborough. With a bit in his mouth or a spur in his flank he never failed to kick and plunge. But give him the bridle and his inborn mettle appeared. As a subaltern he was heedless of orders. As a colleague he was ever discontented, ever railing. As a chief, on the contrary, he achieved some splendid successes. The same impetuosity of temper which made him overlook an obstacle enabled him also in many cases to overleap it. He was in truth, as Lord Macaulay has well called him, "the last of the Knights Errant." Ever ready to engage in any romantic adventure, either of love or war, and constant to no one person as to no one place, he too often found the reputation which he had earned by his exploits dimmed by his public and his private follies.[5]

Peterborough, when he arrived at Lisbon, found the Archduke Charles pining at the languor of the Portuguese campaign. His Majesty, as he was termed by his allies, though not as yet acknowledged on one

[5] Lord Peterborough is well sketched by Swift in some lively lines beginning: "Mordanto fills the trump of fame" (Works, vol. xiv. p. 67.) Pope's opinion may be gathered from Spence's Anecdotes (p. 294), and the whole is ably summed up by Lord Macaulay (Essays, vol. ii. p. 146. Tauchnitz Ed.). A small volume of Peterborough's confidential letters in Spain was printed in 1834, but only for private circulation, and to the number of fifty copies. I have made great use of it. My own character of Peterborough is given in vol. i. p. 363 of my History of England (Tauchnitz Ed.).

foot of Spanish ground, resolved to quit that inactive scene and to join the English Earl. Embarking accordingly with a large train of attendants the young Prince gave occasion to Peterborough to show his characteristic generosity. During the whole voyage he entertained his guest magnificently and at his own expense, yielding him all honors as to the King of Spain. At Gibraltar they also took on board the Prince of Darmstadt and some veterans from the garrison, and nearly at the same time they were joined by Sir Cloudesley Shovel with the remaining ships and a few more soldiers. Even after these accessions the whole of the land-forces fit for service amounted to no more than seven thousand men.

From Gibraltar the expedition touched next at the bay of Altea in the kingdom of Valencia. There the appearance of a young Prince of the Austrian line raised, as had been expected, considerable enthusiasm in his favor. The country people gathered on the shore with shouts of welcome; and the garrison of the neighbouring fort of Denia surrendered at the first summons. It was there that Charles was proclaimed, for the first time by any Spaniards, as King of Spain.

So favourable seemed the opportunity that Peterborough was eager to pursue it. He observed that the troops of Philip were either at Barcelona where they expected an attack, or on the Portugal frontier where they carried on a campaign. At the capital there were only some squadrons of horse, acting as guards to the King and Queen. No force and only one fortified place lay between the English General and the city of Madrid. It might therefore be practicable for him to push forward with his seven thousand men, and by one bold stroke seat the Archduke in the centre of Castille. Judging from the events of the next few months we may affirm that this design at such a juncture and in such a country held out no inconsiderable chances of success.

But so daring a march could certainly not be undertaken in opposition to the wishes of the Prince whose interests it was designed to serve. Charles, from the time of his being joined by the Prince of Darmstadt, had constantly inclined to the counsels of his countryman, and Darmstadt in this year as in the former, overrating his own influence among the Catalans, was wholly intent on the siege of Barcelona. Peterborough urged with great warmth how far from promising was that design; but a Council of War being called he found it requisite to yield; the troops were re-embarked and to Barcelona they sailed.

The difficulties however proved to be of the most formidable kind. Barcelona was strongly defended by regular works, besides which it had the sea on one side and on another the castled crag of Montjuich—the MONS JOVIS of the Romans, and the MONS JUDAICUS of the middle ages when it was the dwelling-place of the Jews.[6] At this period moreover the garrison that held it was fully equal to the force that would besiege it. The Allied troops when set on shore and encamped at some distance from the city suffered severely from the midsummer heats; and far from any general rising in their favor were joined only by some few hundred

---

[6] See the excellent description in Ford's Handbook, vol. 1. p. 492, ed. 1845. "The present name," he observes, "may be derived from either of the former appellations."

ragged Miquelets. And while the soldiers were sickening the chiefs disputed. Charles and the Germans around him pressed for an attack upon the city at all risks and against any odds. The Dutch General exclaimed against the notion, and declared that not one of his men should stir on such a service. Peterborough railed fiercely against Darmstadt and Darmstadt retorted with no less warmth on Peterborough. Such was the animosity that the Earl and Prince were no longer on speaking terms.

Three weeks passed and nothing at all had been achieved—nay nothing attempted. Even the most sanguine began to own that the enterprise was hopeless. It was reluctantly determined to proceed to Italy and resume the first design of aiding Victor Amadeus. Already was the heavy cannon sent on board. Already had the troops been ordered to prepare for their own embarkation. So certain seemed the prospect that on this same day the 12th of September there were entertainments and public rejoicings in Barcelona to celebrate the raising of the siege and the departure of the heretics.

At this very crisis however the genius of Peterborough was intent on a most daring scheme for a COUP DE MAIN. He had closely examined the defences of Montjuich attended by no person but a single aide-de-camp; and had convinced himself that the garrison confiding in the strength of their rock had grown neglectful of their duty. On this conviction his hopes depended. To no one around him, not even to his closest friends, did he impart any previous hint of his design. Only that night he bade a chosen few— twelve hundred English foot and two hundred English horse—stand to their arms or mount and follow him. Another thousand was entrusted by him to General Stanhope as second in command. These were to form the reserve and to take post at a convent midway between the camp and the city.

At midnight then the Earl at the head of his small force suddenly appeared at the quarters of the Prince of Darmstadt with whom for the past fortnight he had not exchanged a word. The Prince rose in some surprise to greet his unexpected visitor. "I have determined, Sir" said Peterborough "to make this night an attempt upon the enemy. You may now if you please come with us, and see whether I and my men really deserve the ill character which you of late have thought fit to give us." Darmstadt, much surprised, at once called for his horse, and thus they rode on together.

Peterborough led his troops by a winding march along the foot of the hills, till within a quarter of a mile of the works of Montjuich. There he ranged them in order for the coming conflict—selecting for himself and Darmstadt the enterprise of the greatest danger, the storming of a bastion on the Barcelona side. At the first break of day they marched up to the assault. The Spaniards then first descrying them poured on them a heavy fire which the English sustained nothing daunted and still advanced; and upon this the enemy came down to meet them in the outer ditch. This was the very event for which Peterborough had prepared his men. He had bid them in that case not be content with repulsing the enemy but follow close and pell-mell, so that Spaniards and English might enter the fort together. And so it proved.

Fighting hand to hand, and carrying all before them, the English quickly reached the summit of the bastion and were able to throw up a breast-work of some loose stones which they found there, before the garrison could recover from their surprise.

The Spaniards being here engaged and drawing their whole force to this quarter, the second division was enabled with little or no hindrance to scale the rock on the opposite side, and to seize the guns upon the walls. Thus did Peterborough become possessed at all points of the outer fortifications of Montjuich, and he sent at once for Stanhope and the reserve so as to secure what he had gained. The enemy however had still possession of the inner works or the keep of the place. Thence after a short interval they poured forth some volleys of musketry. One of these took fatal effect. It struck dead the gallant Darmstadt who fell by the side of Peterborough so recently his rival and now his comrade in arms.

Almost at the same moment there came a rumour that the Spanish Viceroy in Barcelona learning the loss of Montjuich was sending a division of three thousand men from the city to recover it. The distance was about a mile, and all uneven ground; so that the Spaniards besides being tardily collected could advance but slowly. The Earl at once mounted and rode off to reconnoitre, leaving a Peer of Ireland, Lord Charlemont, to command in his place. But no sooner did his presence cease to animate his men than their hearts began to fail. They reflected how few they were in number and how exposed in position, and they muttered that the only thing left for them to do was to return the way they came. One of the officers

CHAP. VI. 1705.

acting as spokesman made an earnest representation in this sense to Lord Charlemont, a man of personal courage but, as Captain George Carleton then serving under him has mildly put it, "somewhat too flexible in his temper."[7] Carleton who overheard the pressing advice and also the meek answer, and who saw how matters were going, slipped away as he says as fast as he could, and put spurs to his horse until he overtook Lord Peterborough and told him what had passed. Peterborough at once turned round and galloped back. As he drew near he perceived that his troops in one compact body and with Lord Charlemont at their head had relinquished the fort and were already half way down the hill. Coming up to them at full speed he snatched from Lord Charlemont's hand the half-pike borne by that officer in symbol of command; then turning to the men he cried: "Face about and follow me, or you shall have the scandal and eternal infamy upon you of having deserted your posts and abandoned your General!"

The sight, the speech, of this most high-spirited chief had a wonderful effect on both officers and soldiers. The dark cloud passed away from their minds, and left no trace behind it; they faced about, and with the greatest alacrity followed Peterborough up the hill. Happily the Spaniards had not perceived their recent panic, so that all the posts could be regained and anew possessed without any loss and in less than half an

[7] Carleton's Memoirs p. 137, ed. 1808. I have no more doubt than had Dr. Johnson or Lord Macaulay, of the perfect authenticity of this narrative; and I venture to refer to a passage in my History of the War of Succession in Spain (Appendix, p. 130) as affording proof that Carleton was not, as has sometimes been asserted, an imaginary character wrought into a fiction by De Foe.

hour. Nor was this their only good fortune. The Spanish General who was bringing up 3,000 men from Barcelona caught at the report that both the Earl and Prince were in Montjuich, and took for granted that their main army must be with them; upon which he immediately gave his orders for retreat. Soon afterwards Stanhope came up with the reserve; and the English posts were most fully secured.

Next day by Peterborough's orders the heavy cannon were once more landed from the ships, and two mortars were brought to bear upon the keep of Montjuich. Its fall was hastened by the explosion of its powder-magazines, and Peterborough interposed to save its garrison from the fury of the Miquelets. The citadel being thus at all points reduced Peterborough proceeded to invest the city. His late exploit it was found had inspirited all ranks. "Everybody" says Carleton "now began to make his utmost efforts; and looked upon himself as a drone if he was not employed in doing something or other towards pushing forward the siege of Barcelona." The Miquelets poured down in great numbers from the hills. The Admirals and Captains of the fleet offered the aid of their sailors, and came day by day to serve on shore. Such indeed was their zeal that when it was found impossible for horses to drag the heavy artillery up the precipices, harnesses were made for two hundred seamen; and by that means the cannon and mortars were after prodigious labour brought to the points required.

With so much ardour on the part of the besiegers it was not long before a practicable breach was made. Velasco hereupon beat a parley, and articles of capitulation were signed on the 9th of October. In four days, should no succour meanwhile arrive, the Viceroy and the garrison were to march out with all the honors of war. But on the day following there broke out an insurrection at Barcelona. The severities of the Viceroy before and during the siege had incensed many of the townspeople, and they, supported by some Miquelets who had stolen in, were eager to wreak their vengeance upon him. The tumult of the city was plainly to be heard in the English camp. Lord Peterborough rode up boldly to the city-wicket, and was let in; he had with him only a single officer, but was subsequently joined in the same manner by Stanhope and one or two more.[8] Thus entering the city at imminent risk to himself, he succeeded by his personal ascendancy in saving the life of Velasco, whom he sent in due time on board ship to be conveyed by sea to Alicant. He had also the honor of rescuing from danger a beautiful lady whom he met flying with dishevelled hair from the apprehended fury of the Miquelets; she proved to be the Duchess of Popoli whose husband was in command of the Spanish troops. It was not only beauty in distress which as on this occasion claimed the regard of Peterborough. Writing to the Duchess of Marlborough a few months later we find him declare in a moment of spleen that "the most disagreeable country in the world is Spain," with however one exception as follows, "the only tolerable thing your sex, and that attended with the greatest dangers."

The brilliancy of Peterborough's late achievements appears to have produced a strong impression on a people ever lovers of the marvellous. Of the five or

---

[8] Compare Captain Carleton's Memoirs (p. 152) with the narrative derived from Stanhope, in Burnet's History, vol. v. p. 218.

six thousand troops who marched out of Barcelona, and were free to go further according to the terms of the capitulation, not above a thousand went, the rest consenting to take service with Charles as rightful King of Spain. Great part of the open country also declared in his favor. The young Prince himself made his public entry on the 23rd of October, amidst loud acclamations, and with all established forms; he returning every cheer with the movement of his hand to his mouth; "for the Kings of Spain are not allowed to salute or return a salute by any motion to or of the hat."

By Peterborough's orders General Stanhope at once embarked for England to carry the news of the late successes, and to claim in the most earnest manner reinforcements and supplies. Peterborough writes as follows to the Duchess of Marlborough: "I know the good nature of England, especially towards the month of November; but I hope at least they will find no fault..... I think we have met with miracles in our favor. But we are poorer than church-rats, and miracles cannot save us long without money."

Peterborough meanwhile took a step of great political significance in which he was fully justified by the terms of his instructions. He gave a public assurance that his Queen would engage to secure to the province the enjoyment of its ancient FUEROS—the rights and liberties which the Crown of Castille had set aside. This promise joined to the lustre of his arms wrought wonders. Lerida and Gerona, Tarragona and Tortosa, the last of especial importance as commanding the passage of the Ebro, proclaimed the Archduke as their King. The whole of Catalonia was for the time won over. Nay more, the flame spread rapidly to the province, or as the Spaniards love to call it the kingdom, of Valencia. San Mateo and other places to the south of the Ebro declared for the Austrian Prince. And thus also to the south of the Xucar. A partisan chief, a native of that part of the country, General Basset y Ramos in name or names, had been left by the Allies as Governor of the fort of Denia, with a garrison of four hundred men. Sallying out with the greater part of his force he was joined by Colonel Raphael Nebot, a Catalan in King Philip's service, who came over with his whole regiment of five hundred horse. These two chiefs overran the open country and reduced the smaller towns, appearing at length before the gates of Valencia, which were thrown open to them. Entering that great city in triumph they proclaimed Charles as King, and Basset y Ramos as his Viceroy until his pleasure should be known.

Peterborough meanwhile continued at Barcelona making great efforts to sustain his troops. He instructed his wife in London to make earnest applications for him to the Ministers, and meanwhile he continued with most impartial acrimony to rail at almost every thing and almost every person around him. Thus he writes to Stanhope in England, "In the beggarly circumstances of our Princes and Generals, it is certain that nothing can be greater than the affection of all sorts of people to the King; and nothing greater than the contempt and aversion they have to Lichtenstein and Wolfeld, and to the whole Vienna crew. . . . Never Prince was accompanied by such wretches for Ministers; they have spent their whole time in selling places; they have neither money, sense, nor honor.... I have intelligence and correspondence wherever the enemy have troops, who are much more disposed to join us than to fight with us. From Valencia, from Aragon, from Mont Louis, from Languedoc, from the Cevennes, I have every day offers and solicitations, and I cannot want success wherever I go if I could but go."

His own General Officers do not fare much better in Peterborough's correspondence than does "the Vienna crew."—"I believe the Queen will order Charlemont to sell; if so I have agreed with him at £1,500; but he would have been described as a hero. If he be prevented bargaining for the new clothing the regiment will come cheap. . . . . . Cunningham is such an eternal screech-owl, and growing more and more disagreeable; if possible get him removed to some other service more suitable to his humour."

To Alexander Stanhope at the Hague Peterborough writes in more general terms while pressing for Dutch aid. "Give us support and you shall have no Portuguese excuses! We will bring affairs to a speedy issue. We have not hitherto gone the pace of Spaniards though amongst them![9]

From Spain pass we to Scotland. The bitter fruits of the Darien enterprise were not all past. In the summer of 1704 the Worcester, a ship which belonged to the New East India Company, being driven by stress of weather into the Frith of Forth, and anchoring in the harbour of Burnt Island, was there seized by the agents of the Darien Company in requital as they imagined of a former wrong. The Captain Thomas Green and his crew, thirteen in all, were surprised and over-

[9] Tortosa, November 19, 1705 (MS.).

CHAP. VI.
1705.

powered and cast into prison. Then they were brought to trial on charges of piracy upon the coast of Malabar, and of the murder of Drummond one of the Darien Captains who had been missing for three years. They were found Guilty on very insufficient evidence and condemned to death, and though most of them were reprieved and soon afterwards quietly released, three of the number, namely Green the Captain Madder the mate and Simpson the gunner, were left to suffer the extreme sentence of the law. It was felt in England that these poor men would fall a sacrifice to national resentment; and the Queen sent orders to the Privy Council of Scotland to stay the execution and to consider the sentence. But the Privy Council were scared by the apprehension of mob violence; they made no sign; and the prisoners underwent their doom upon the sands of Leith, on the 11th of April 1705. Strange to say there was some evidence at the time, which subsequent inquiry confirmed, that Captain Drummond, for whose murder three men were hanged, was then and for some years afterwards alive—a wanderer among the savage tribes of Madagascar.[1]

The angry temper of the Scottish people was by no means confined to the humbler classes, nor yet to any single subject, and the Ministers in England looked forward with much anxiety to the next meeting of the Scottish Parliament. They adopted at last a timid resolution in which the mind of Godolphin at this period may probably be traced. They determined to change once again the holders of office at Edinburgh, and, in

[1] State Trials, vol. xiv. p. 1199, and Burton's Criminal Trials in Scotland, vol. i. p. 157. "Somers says he knows not the laws of Scotland, but that the proceedings are illegal according to all other laws that he knows." So writes Secretary Johnstone in the Jerviswood Correspondence, April 9, 1705.

spite of his recent failures, reinstate the Duke of Queensberry. His Grace however took on this occasion only the secondary post of Privy Seal, while the function of representing the Crown was conferred on the Duke of Argyle, a young man of signal spirit and ability. Under these new auspices the Estates assembled on the 28th of June; and the Queen's Message at their opening most earnestly pressed upon their notice both the settlement of the Succession, and the appointment of Commissioners to treat for a legislative Union.

A tangled web of party-politics ensued. Lord Tweeddale and his friends who were ousted from office immediately formed themselves into what they termed the "New party;" but keeping close together and throwing their weight from time to time into the divers sides of the divisions, they came to be commonly called the "Squadrone Volante." Italian was then for some reason in vogue with the politicians of that country for their private notes; thus we may observe the Earl of Roxburgh begin to Johnstone—"if you have read my letter in Italian."[2] The Jacobites formed a no less compact mass, and were against the project of a legislative Union at any time or on any terms. The Duke of Queensberry it was found intended to keep aloof in England on the plea of sickness, so that without committing himself he might watch the first direction of events, and meanwhile, says Lockhart, "he sent down the Duke of Argyle as Commissioner, and used him as the monkey did the cat in pulling out the hot roasted chesnuts."[3]

[2] Jerviswood Correspondence, p. 105.
[3] Lockhart Papers, vol. I. p. 114.

In spite of the pressing recommendations conveyed in the Queen's Message, the Estates resolved to consider first the matters of trade. When they came to the Succession, they showed themselves wholly disinclined to settle it so far as the person was concerned. Nevertheless they lent a ready ear to the schemes of Fletcher of Saltoun for all kinds of limitations and securities. They did not indeed go the full length that he proposed, but they passed an Act which, on the Queen's demise, was to make the Officers of State and the Judges of the Supreme Courts elective by Parliament. Another Act provided that a Scottish ambassador should be present at every treaty made by the Sovereign of the two kingdoms with a foreign power. By a third measure, the Parliament was to become triennial at the end of the next three years. None of these Acts however received the touch of the Sceptre, nor was the Royal Assent to them seriously pressed after the all-absorbing debate upon the Union had begun.[4]

As regards the last the Court party, assisted on this occasion by the Squadrone, carried an Act empowering the Queen to name Commissioners to treat for Scotland. This Act was however accompanied by a Resolution that the Scottish Commissioners should not begin to confer with the English, until the clauses in the English Act of Parliament making the Scotch aliens had been repealed. In this manner the Session was closed in tolerable harmony on the 21st of September.

The English Ministers meanwhile had been watching with anxious eyes the result of the English elections.

[4] Burton's History of Scotland, 1689-1748, vol. I. p. 387.

Finding it much in favor of the Whigs, they desired
to make a further movement in conciliation of that
party. Now the first object at that moment of the
Whig Junto was to obtain an office for Lord Sunderland —a home office if possible but if not a foreign
one, which might be a preparatory step to the Secretaryship of State. For this there appeared a favourable
opening. Besides that Mr. Stepney, our Minister at
Vienna, had offended the Austrian statesmen by his
blunt remonstrances, and could not at that moment
continue the negotiation with advantage, there seemed
good reason to appoint a new Envoy Extraordinary to
compliment Joseph on his accession to the throne. The
Duchess of Marlborough threw her whole weight into
Sunderland's scale; Godolphin and Marlborough yielded;
and Sunderland being named Envoy accordingly set out
for Vienna in the course of June.

Another and far more important change in the
same direction had been for some time in suspense,
but was postponed till close upon the Session of Parliament. Then, the Queen's consent having been reluctantly granted, Sir Nathan Wright was dismissed
from the custody of the Great Seal, which was transferred with the same office of Lord Keeper to William
Cowper. The proved incompetency of Sir Nathan and
the rising genius of Cowper made this a welcome
change, independently of its party motive. And here
begins the Private Diary of Cowper which, though in
general meagre, is not without its value for the History
of these times.[5]

[5] The Diary of Lord Cowper has not been published but was printed in 1833 by the Rev. Dr. Hawtrey for the members of the Roxburgh Club. The first entry is on the day of Cowper's taking office, October 11, 1705. And

CHAP. VI.
1705.

The appointments of Sunderland and Cowper being however looked upon as party measures, were in a high degree distasteful to the Tories, both to those who like Nottingham were already in opposition, and to those who like Harley continued to hold office. No sooner had the new Parliament met on the 25th of October than the two parties tried their strength on the first question that arose—the choice of Speaker. The Tory candidate was William Bromley, who on High Church principles represented the University of Oxford; the Whig was John Smith, member for Andover, who under King William had for a short time held an office in the Treasury.[6] The Court gave its full support to the latter candidate; and he was elected by a majority of 248 against 205.

In the Royal Speech which ensued, Her Majesty descanted in general terms on the importance of sustaining the war upon the Continent and of forming an Union with Scotland. She went on to say that it would be ever her chief care to support the Church and leave it secure after her. And she added "I mention this with a little more warmth, because there have not been wanting some, so very malicious as even in print to suggest the Church of England as by law established to be in danger at this time."

It was indeed this cry "the Church in danger!" which Rochester and Nottingham resolved to raise. But they gave precedence to another which they thought would touch the Queen in a still more tender place. On the 15th of November, Lord Haversham,

on the 27th he adds: "Note. The Lords who were against my advancement all wished me joy."

[6] See Lord Macaulay's History, vol. VII. p. 317. (Tauchnitz Ed.).

acting under their auspices, moved an Address in the House of Lords entreating Her Majesty to invite the presumptive Heir "into this kingdom to reside here." It seemed to the High Tory Chiefs that their support of this proposal would effectually clear them from the common charge of acting in secret concert with the Jacobites, and that it would place the Ministers in great embarrassment, it being known that the idea was utterly distasteful to the Queen, who was determined not to yield it.

The Queen herself was present at this debate, and heard the three Tory chieftains, Rochester, Nottingham, and Buckingham, so lately her own confidential servants, urge with all their strength a measure which they knew her to abhor. Nor did Buckingham recommend it by any peculiar amenities of style, since among other things he suggested that perhaps the Queen might live till she did not know what she did and be like a child in the hands of others. It is no wonder if the attachment of Anne to the Tory party was at this time rudely shaken.[7]

The proposal of Lord Haversham was met on the part of the Ministry by the previous question, which was carried without dividing. But the spirit roused by the discussion so far prevailed that two measures for the better security of the Succession (first suggested in the debate by Bishop Burnet) were ordered to be brought in. The first was entitled, "an Act for the Naturalization of the most excellent Princess Sophia" and her issue, with a saving clause that any person naturalized by this Act and becoming a Papist should lose the benefit of the Act and be taken as an alien

[7] Conduct of the Duchess of Marlborough, p. 171, ed. 1742.

born out of the allegiance of the Queen. This measure was passed without any difficulty or discussion.

The second measure of security as sketched by Bishop Burnet was further developed on the 19th in a very able speech by Lord Wharton, and was ordered to be brought in accordingly. Then it came to be commonly known by the name of the Regency Bill. It provided that, in the event of the Queen's decease without issue, the Privy Council then in being should, on pain of High Treason, cause the next appointed successor to be proclaimed as Sovereign with all convenient speed: That, to carry on the Government in her or his absence, seven great Officers of State as specified should act as Lords Justices: That the next heir should be empowered, by an instrument under her or his hand, to nominate any other persons to act in conjunction with these seven as Lords Justices; this instrument to be sent over in triplicate and to be kept sealed; one copy by the Lord Chancellor or Lord Keeper; another by the Archbishop of Canterbury; and a third by her or his own Minister at this Court.

The occasion was also taken to review that clause in the Act of Settlement which, after the accession of the House of Hanover, would exclude all holders of office from the House of Commons. Under the Regency Bill the prohibition ceased to be absolute. A certain number of offices was specified as actually disqualifying; besides all those that might at any time be created since the day the Parliament met—the 25th of October 1705. As to any others, the acceptance of office was to vacate the Seat, but the electors were left free if they pleased to re-elect the office-holder. Such is the law under which, even at the present day, our Ministerial system continues to be ruled. It was at first intended that those clauses like that in the Act of Settlement which they were framed to amend should apply only to the following reign. But the Ministers, on being pressed, agreed that they should take effect at the next Dissolution.[9]

Godolphin and the other Ministers had from the first supported the Regency Bill. It would have been far wiser in the Tory chiefs, had they also given to it their frank adherence rather than raise against it as they did in both Houses a host of petty cavils. This laid them open to the taunt that they were in truth no friends to the Hanover Succession, first urging a security which they knew was unattainable, and next rejecting another security which was placed within their reach. They did not venture however to try their strength by any party vote against the entire Bill, which was finally carried through both Houses; but they brought forward divers amendments, some of a very trifling character. Thus for instance in the Commons, they moved that the Lord Treasurer should not be named among the seven great Officers of State; an omission that could be defended by no possible argument, and proceeding solely from their spleen against Godolphin who filled the post.

The second arrow in the Tory quiver, "the Church in danger," was let fly, not quite willingly, on the 6th of December. Lord Halifax on behalf of the Whigs had accused the opposite party of making a complaint which they were unable to establish, and he had fixed a day for its consideration by the House of Lords.

---

[9] Act 4 and 5 Ann. c. 8, re-enacted after the Union as 6 Ann. c. 7.

Her Majesty came to hear the debate which her uncle Lord Rochester commenced and which on the other side Lord Somers closed. Several Prelates spoke; one or two not greatly to their credit. Thus the Archbishop of York (Dr. Sharp) said that he apprehended danger to the Church from the increase of Dissenters, and particularly from the many academies set up by them; and he moved that the Judges might be consulted what laws were in force against such seminaries, and by what means they might be suppressed. In like manner the Bishop of London (Dr. Compton) warmly inveighed against the sermon which one clergyman, Mr. Benjamin Hoadley, had lately preached before the Lord Mayor, and in which the Bishop said "rebellion was countenanced and resistance to the higher powers encouraged." This provoked a spirited reply from Bishop Burnet. "My Right Reverend brother" he cried "ought to have been the last man to complain of that sermon, for if the doctrine of that sermon be not good, I know not what defence his Lordship could make for appearing in arms at Nottingham."[9]

This debate was taken with the House in Committee on the Royal Speech. A division being called for, the alarm-cry of the Tories was negatived by 61 votes against 30. It was resolved that "under the happy reign of Her Majesty the Church is in a most safe and flourishing condition;" and that "whoever goes about to suggest and insinuate that the Church is in danger is an enemy to the Queen, the Church, and the kingdom." A Protest against this Resolution was signed by two Bishops and twenty-three lay Peers, but the majority, forming the House, sent it to the Commons,

[9] See Lord Macaulay's History, vol. III. p. 379. (Tauchnitz Ed.).

who by a division of 212 against 160 expressed their concurrence therewith. The Resolution was next presented as a joint Address of both Houses to the Queen, who on her part published a Proclamation declaring that with the advice of her Privy Council she would "proceed with the utmost severity the law will allow of against the authors and spreaders of the said seditious and scandalous reports."

These proceedings in Parliament passed before the Christmas holidays. They were all, as has been seen, greatly in favor of the Government. It may be added that the Commons showed much alacrity in voting the required Supplies; and that both Houses cheerfully concurred in expediting the negotiations for a Scottish Union. The only obstacle in the way of beginning to treat lay in the Act of last Session imposing in a certain case divers disabilities on Scotsmen. But Lord Somers who had been the author of that Act saw, that its object was answered from the moment the Estates at Edinburgh had empowered the Queen to name Commissioners for Scotland. He therefore at once expressed his willingness to repeal the obnoxious clauses; and a Bill repealing them was accordingly passed with all despatch.

Marlborough meanwhile was still absent from England. He had been earnestly pressed to pay a visit to Vienna at the close of the campaign, and he desired to try his personal influence at the Emperor's Court. Setting out with the full assent of his colleagues, he found Lord Sunderland installed as the English Minister, and though offered a separate palace he took up his abode at his son-in-law's house. The Emperor showed him every mark of high regard, invested him with the promised principality, and hearkened to his counsels for the next campaign. Marlborough was however disappointed in his hopes of meeting Prince Eugene who was detained with the Italian army.

From Vienna the Duke accompanied by Sunderland proceeded to Berlin. There he soothed the dissatisfaction on various petty grounds of the King, and induced him to renew the treaty for the further subsidiary force of 8,000 men. At Hanover his presence was of still more essential service. The old Electress had been induced to write a letter to the Archbishop of Canterbury expressing her readiness to come over if the Queen and Parliament should desire it.[1] This letter had been made public during the discussions on this subject and had given great displeasure to the Queen, while the Electress was no less incensed when she found her inclination disregarded. In several interviews both with herself and her son, Marlborough was able to convince them that the Ministers in England had meant them no unkindness, and had done their best to secure the succession of their House. On concluding his visit at Hanover Marlborough went on to the Hague, where, as he writes, "I have not been idle one minute," and from whence in company with Sunderland he returned to London, on the last day of the last month.

1706. Already at the Hague Marlborough had received a letter from Godolphin pressing him to draw closer to his recent allies the Whigs, and Marlborough had answered: "I shall with all my heart live friendly with those that have shown so much friendship to you and service to the Queen." On the first Sunday after his

[1] See this letter at length in the Parliamentary History, vol. vi. p. 520.

return, the 6th of January, a dinner was given by Secretary Harley to cement the new alliance. There were present besides Marlborough and Godolphin, Boyle and St. John, Halifax, Sunderland and Cowper. Somers also had been invited but had gone to his country house. The scene is described with much spirit in Cowper's Private Diary. "After Lord Treasurer was gone, who first went, Secretary Harley took a glass and drank to love and friendship and everlasting union; and wished he had more Tokay to drink it in; we had drank two bottles good but thick. I replied his White Lisbon was best to drink it in, being very clear. I suppose he apprehended it, as I observed most of the company did, to relate to that humour of his, which was never to deal clearly or openly but always with reserve, if not dissimulation or rather simulation; and to love tricks even where not necessary but from an inward satisfaction he took in applauding his own cunning." It is plain from this entry how rife jealousies were still.

The two Houses met again as usual after the Christmas holidays, but transacted no further business of importance. Dispirited by its late reverses the Tory party remained at gaze; and the Session was closed in quiet with a Speech from the Queen, on the 19th of March.

Public interest however was now centered, so far as home-affairs were concerned, on the pending treaty for a Scottish Union. The Commission for Scotland was issued on the 27th of February; that for England on the 10th of April. According to precedent in both cases the former was in Latin, and the latter in English. The members were thirty-one on each side. In the

Scottish list, besides many persons of rank and office, there were also several independent country-gentlemen; as Clerk of Pennycook and Lockhart of Carnwath. On the English side there was more attention to routine, the Commissioners being the most part the heads of Church and State, but comprising also some chief men out of office, and above all Lord Somers, whose clear and pervading genius proved to be the master-spirit of the whole.

The two Commissions held their first meeting on the 16th of April in the Council-chamber of the Cockpit near Whitehall, the place which had been appointed for them. Their first day was taken up with introductory speeches from Mr. Cowper the Lord Keeper of the Great Seal in England, and the Earl of Seafield the Chancellor of Scotland; but they proceeded to real business when they met next, on the 22nd of the month. Then the Lord Keeper on the part of England formally proposed: That the two kingdoms of England and Scotland be for ever united into one kingdom by the name of Great Britain: That the United Kingdom of Great Britain be represented by one and the same Parliament; and That the Succession to the Crown of the United Kingdom be fixed according to the stipulations of the English Act of Settlement.

To these terms the Scottish Commissioners made some demur. It is plain from their counter-proposals though most cautiously worded that they desired the Union to be not legislative but only federative like that of the Dutch States or the Swiss Cantons. But the English Commissioners stood firm. They declared that in their judgment nothing but an entire union of the two kingdoms would settle perfect and lasting friendship between them; and they declined to continue the treaty on any other ground. Met at once by this explicit intimation the Scots yielded. Next day they gave in their acceptance of the first proposals on the condition that there should be full freedom of trade, and a communication of all other advantages, between the two kingdoms. The English Commissioners answered frankly that they regarded this condition as the necessary consequence of an entire Union.

Thus the foundation at least was happily and securely laid. The further progress of this treaty and its final issue shall be related after I have traced in some detail the campaigns of this memorable year in Flanders, Italy and Spain.

CHAPTER VII.

CHAP. VII.
1706.

MARLBOROUGH reached the Hague from England on the 25th of April. But although as in former years he made the Hague his starting point he designed a far different sphere. Recent experience disinclined him equally from two proposals which at this time were pressed upon him—the one from the Emperor to co-operate on the Moselle with Prince Louis on the Upper Rhine—the other from the States of Holland to join his army to theirs and act, not unattended by their Deputies, in Flanders. Marlborough on the contrary desired that they should, as in his Blenheim campaign, place a smaller body of their troops under his sole command; with these and his English to march to Italy, and join once more his tried friend Prince Eugene.

Combined with this great project there was a smaller also. Marlborough had been for some time in communication with the Marquis de Guiscard who was a refugee from the Cevennes, and profuse of promises as is the wont of exiles. He was certain, he said, the Protestants of Languedoc would rise in arms once more as soon as a friendly force appeared in sight of their hills. Both Marlborough and St. John lent an ear to his representations, and had directed twelve regiments of foot with some dragoons to assemble at Portsmouth, there to embark, as soon as the arrangements should be ready. The troops were to be headed by Lord

Rivers and accompanied by De Guiscard with other French Protestant officers. Landing at Blaye near the mouth of the Gironde they would endeavour to raise the Cevennes in insurrection, and failing in that object they might burn the ships at Rochefort on their return. In any event it was thought that this expedition would prevent the French from sending reinforcements either to Italy or Spain.

Wisely framed as might be these two projects they were found incapable of actual execution. The jealousies attending every wide confederacy here came into full play. Thus does Marlborough report on the 9th of May: "I am so tired that you will excuse my not giving you any other account of Cadogan's voyage to Hanover but what you will see by the Elector's inclosed letter. He obstinately persists in letting none of his troops march notwithstanding he very much approves the project (of Italy). The Danes and Hessians have also excused themselves upon their treaties; so that though the Pensioner and the town of Amsterdam had approved of sending the forty squadrons and forty battalions, now that they must of necessity be of the English and Dutch only they dare not consent, since it must leave them in the hands of the strangers, for so they call the Danes, the Hanoverians, and the Hessians."

An untoward event upon the Upper Rhine increased the perplexities of the States. Marshal Villars having received a reinforcement from the Netherlands under Marshal Marsin suddenly took the field and attacked the Margrave of Baden with great success, forcing the German lines on the Motter, and reducing Drusenheim and Haguenau which contained the principal magazines.

CHAP. VII.
1706.

With this recent instance of French daring before them, the Dutch were more than ever unwilling to see Marlborough depart for Italy. If he would but remain they offered to give him in secret the choice of their Field Deputies, or to instruct these gentlemen to conform on all points to his wishes. Finally though with great reluctance the Duke yielded. It was agreed that an auxiliary force of 10,000 men should be at once despatched to Prince Eugene; and that besides those on the Upper Rhine, the remaining troops in English or Dutch pay should under the command of Marlborough act on the side of Flanders. The plan being thus determined at the Hague the Duke set out for the army on Sunday the 9th of May. His chagrin is apparent in his letters. "God knows I go with a heavy heart; for I have no prospect of doing any thing considerable."

At this very moment however—so much should gloomy prognostics be distrusted—fortune had in store for him one of the brightest of his triumphs. When he left the Hague the English and Dutch troops were still apart, but they effected their junction at Bilsen on the 20th; and the Danes who were rapidly pressing forward came in shortly afterwards. Thus combining, the army advanced upon Flanders in nearly the same direction as last year. Officers and men were in high spirits, and Marlborough, could he but find the opportunity, was eager to engage.

Marshal Villeroy on his part had already taken the field. Ever too sanguine and vainglorious in temper, he was persuaded that Marlborough could not so soon have gathered his whole force together, and he fully relied on his own superior numbers and superior skill.

He did not even deem it necessary to await the coming of Marsin who was already on his march with eighteen battalions to join him from Alsace. Thus he writes to the King: "I am convinced that it must be for our advantage to risk a battle; above all if the enemy have to come and attack us. Your Majesty's troops are fine; their courage is elated by the news of our late successes; and everything leads us to expect a happy issue if we come to a general action."[1]

The same confident spirit pervaded his ranks. As Marlborough states when writing to Godolphin on the day after the event: "the General officers who are taken tell us that they thought themselves sure of victory, by having all the King of France's Household and with them the best troops of France." The numbers however were most nearly matched. According to Marlborough's statement in the same letter the French had 128 squadrons and 74 battalions, while Marlborough himself had 123 of the former and 73 of the latter. The French may be reckoned at 60,000 and the Allies at 62,000 men.

The English commander was now steadily advancing towards the sources of the Little Gheet. It was just beyond the site of the French lines demolished by the Allies in the preceding year. There on the forenoon of Sunday, May the 23rd, he appeared in sight of the French. General Cadogan led the van at the head of six hundred horse. Two of the columns that followed marched along one of those strange old Chaussées which in France and Belgium are known by the name of Queen Brunehaut; the others proceeded in parallel

[1] Mémoires militaires de la Succession d'Espagne, vol. VI. p. 70.

lines; and Marlborough no longer fettered by Dutch trammels had determined to attack that very day.

Villeroy was well prepared to receive him. Close to the Little Gheet sources stands the village of Ramillies, which has given its name to the battle which ensued. Behind the village the ground rises, and forms a gently undulating plain, the highest ground in all Brabant. It was from this slope of Ramillies that the French Marshal, when the fog of the forenoon had cleared, descried for the first time the approaching columns of his foe. He at once ranged his own army in order of battle on the ground which he had already reconnoitred. His left was at the back of the village of Autre-Eglise; his right at a barrow which is called the Tomb of Ottomond, and which crowns the summit of the plain. From the Tomb of Ottomond the ground falls away to the village of Tavier and the marshes that border the Mehaigne. Tavier was protected by a French detachment, and better still by its swampy ground. Opposite to Tavier also there was swampy ground at the Little Gheet sources; and it was through the interval between these two morasses that the Allied onset on Ramillies must be made. Thus on the whole the French were posted in concave round the segment of a circle extending from Autre-Eglise to Tavier.

While Villeroy was thus drawing out his army he was joined from Brussels by his colleague the Elector of Bavaria. His Highness approved the selection, and acknowledged the strength, of the ground. Marlborough meanwhile accompanied by Overkirk was intently eyeing it and them. He saw that the concave order of the French would expose them to some disadvantage in rapidity of movement. He saw moreover that the

Tomb of Ottomond was in truth the key of their position, since from thence the entire field of battle might be enfiladed. The object was therefore by a sudden effort to overpower the French right, and this as Marlborough thought might best be achieved through a preliminary feint upon their left.

The battle was begun about three o'clock by a mutual cannonade. An hour afterwards Marlborough pursuing his skilful stratagem made a vigorous demonstration against Autre-Eglise. The feint was entirely successful. Both Villeroy and Maximilian hurried off to the threatened quarter drawing with them a considerable corps of infantry from the centre and right. Then Marlborough, seizing his opportunity and masking his onset by the aid of some hollow ground, sent forward his columns and fell with fury upon Tavier and Ramillies. Tavier, where the French were weak, was quickly carried, but Ramillies made a most resolute resistance. The Elector and French Marshal, seeing but too late where would be the brunt of battle, came back with all speed from Autre-Eglise; they could not however regain the ground which Marlborough had already won.

In spite of this early advantage there were still some fluctuations of fortune. The Dutch Marshal, Overkirk, made a gallant charge, and with good effect, upon the French cavalry by Ramillies; but after his first success was himself assailed and his ranks thrown into confusion by a counter charge from the MAISON DU ROI. Marlborough seeing the disarray spurred up to the rescue. Riding in front of his men he was recognised by a small party of French dragoons who closed round and sought to make him prisoner. He

CHAP. VII.
1706.

endeavoured to extricate himself by making his horse leap a ditch, but he failed in the attempt and was thrown to the ground. Upon this his aide-de-camp Captain Molesworth dismounting supplied him with another horse. His equerry Colonel Bingfield was holding the stirrup and helping him up when a cannon-ball carried off the Colonel's head. Thus narrowly was Marlborough's precious life preserved.

Again on horseback however and preserving at all times his presence of mind, Marlborough though severely bruised was enabled to shake off his assailants and to rejoin his lines. The Dutch cavalry was rallied; other foot advanced; and Marlborough, putting himself at the head of his own horsemen in triple rank, led them to a combined charge on Ramillies, where the French taken in flank from Tavier and already wavering now gave way. The village of Ramillies was thus carried at half-past six o'clock. Next was gained the Tomb of Ottomond commanding the entire plain. Then Villeroy and the Elector saw that the day was decided, and thought only of making their retreat in as good order as they could. Like brave men had they behaved in the battle; like brave men also they bore up against defeat.

The object of these chiefs was now to gain the pass of Jodoigne, and from thence the fortress of Louvain. But at the very outset, some baggage-waggons being upset and obstructing the way, while the hindmost of the defeated army still came pressing on, the retreat quickly grew into a rout. Many of the French soldiers disbanded to the right and left, and flung their muskets to the ground. All their baggage and nearly all their artillery was lost. Their rear was pressed by Marlborough and Overkirk far beyond Jodoigne; nor did these commanders halt till two o'clock in the morning and two leagues from Louvain. Even then the pursuit was continued by Lord Orkney with some squadrons of light horse, to the very gates of the city.

Entering Louvain in dismal plight with the remains of the French army Villeroy and Maximilian held a consultation by torch-light in the market-place. They decided that they could not hold the city; and they continued their flight by the Brussels road. Thus on the following day were Louvain and the passage of the Dyle left free to the Allies.

Of this battle of Ramillies it may be noted that the fighting though severe was far less protracted than at Blenheim. It scarcely in its full brunt endured above an hour and a half. The French were from the first out-generalled and appear to have felt that they were so. In killed and wounded, in prisoners and deserters, their entire loss has been computed at 15,000 men. The Allies owned to having above 1,000 slain and above 2,500 wounded. Among the former were five Colonels and the gallant Prince of Hesse.

On the day after the battle Marlborough sent Colonel Richards with the good tidings to England. There it was most cordially welcomed. The Queen appointed the 27th of June as a day of Public Thanksgiving, while Addresses of Congratulation came pouring in from every quarter. Villeroy on the other hand is said to have lingered several days before he could prevail upon himself to send a courier to Versailles with the news of his disaster. A subsequent letter to the King reveals how bitter was his anguish. "Sir, although in my heart I am not conscious of any self-reproach, I

CHAP.
VII.
1706.

know that I can never appear before your Majesty without recalling to you the cause of great affliction; and I assure you, Sir, that death is nothing in comparison of so cruel a thought."² But, as after Blenheim, Louis showed himself magnanimous. When Villeroy came next to Versailles the great King in receiving him said only: "Monsieur le Maréchal, at our age good fortune deserts us."³

Marlborough during this time was pursuing his success. Appearing at the gates of Brussels he found the French retire from the city. Of the brother Electors in exile he of Cologne fled to Lille, he of Bavaria to Alost; while the magistrates admitting the victors hastened to proclaim the Archduke their rightful Sovereign as King Charles the Third. Well might Marlborough write at this time with no unbecoming exultation: "You will see that we have done in four days what we should have thought ourselves happy if we could have been sure of in four years."⁴

Nor could the French on leaving Brussels maintain the line of the Scheldt. Chamillart the Minister of War came for a few days from Versailles to examine with his own eyes the state of the army, but he came only as a witness of fresh reverses. Villeroy felt himself unable with his far diminished numbers to make a stand against Marlborough or to run the risk of another battle. He retired almost to the frontiers of France, leaving Flanders protected by its fortresses alone. Moreover the people of the country showed a strong disposition to side with the victorious. At

² Lettre au Roi, le 3 Juin 1706. Mémoires militaires, vol. vi. p. 41.
³ Voltaire, Siècle de Louis XIV, vol. i. p. 328, ed. 1752. "Cela fut court et sec," says St. Simon of this first interview (Mém. vol. v. p. 132, ed. 1829).
⁴ To the Duchess, Brussels, May 27, 1706.

Ghent and at Bruges the Allies were warmly welcomed. Oudenarde, a stronghold which King William had besieged in vain, opened its gates without a blow. "So many towns" writes Marlborough "have submitted since the battle that it really looks more like a dream than truth."[5]

Marlborough was now intent on besieging Antwerp; but that necessity was spared him. As the army of Villeroy was withdrawn to its own frontier the tie of cohesion between the French and the Flemings loosened. Thus a schism broke forth at once between the French and Walloon regiments which composed the garrison of Antwerp. The latter having at their head the Governor of the citadel, the Marquis of Terracina, acknowledged King Charles the Third and opened their gates to Marlborough, while the French, according to a convention which they had concluded, were permitted to march out with all the honors of war.

Availing himself of this interval of leisure Marlborough repaired to the Hague. He remained there only one day—the 10th of June—but even in that short space was able to reconcile the Dutch Government to his further schemes. Then, returning with all speed to his army, he proceeded in conjunction with Overkirk to invest Ostend. That important fortress, which in the last century had cost the Spaniards a siege of three years and a loss of fourscore thousand men, yielded to the attack of the Allies in nine days. The garrison, about 5,000 strong, beat the chamade on the morning of the 6th of July and were allowed to proceed to France, but without military honors, and under an engagement not to bear arms against

[5] To the Duchess, from near Ghent, May 31, 1706.

the Allies for a period of six months. Ere they left the place however the greater number, being Walloons by birth, consented to enter the service of King Charles. A squadron of ships from England had cooperated in the siege; and in the harbour of Ostend were found two men-of-war, the one of eighty and the other of fifty guns, besides forty-five smaller vessels—these also among the spoils of success. Thus rapidly did the chief cities and fortresses of this much disputed province fall into the hands of the Allies. As Marlborough by the battle of Blenheim had rescued Germany, so it may be said of him that by the battle of Ramillies he conquered Flanders.

Far from resting on his laurels however after the reduction of Ostend the English chief at once proceeded to invest Menin; a stronghold which commanded the line of the Lys, and which in its fortifications was regarded as one of the master-pieces of Vauban. Meanwhile the King of France having learnt from Chamillart how downcast and faint-hearted were now the troops of Villeroy felt it essential to send them a new chief. His choice fell on the Duke of Vendome, who was then commanding in Italy; and in place of Vendome he appointed his nephew the Duke of Orleans with Marshal Marsin as adviser and guide. We find Vendome on assuming his new post write to Chamillart in most anxious terms. He describes the broken spirit of the officers since their late defeat, and the awe which they felt at Marlborough's very name.[6] Under such

---

[6] "Tout le monde ici est prêt d'ôter son chapeau quand on nomme le nom de Marlborough. Si les soldats et les cavaliers étaient de même, il n'y aurait qu'à prendre congé de la compagnie, mais j'espère y trouver plus de ressource." Vendôme à Chamillart, de Valenciennes, le 5 Août 1706. Mém. milit. vol. vi. p. 94.

circumstances Vendome durst not attempt to raise the siege of Menin which Marlborough had commenced on the day before the date of this letter. Menin made a resolute resistance and held out till the 22nd, when, on a capitulation, the garrison retired with warlike honors to Douay. The reduction of this fortress cost the Allies no less than 3,000 men.

Next, Marlborough turned his arms to Dendermond. There the French had let out the water in the sluices, so as to place great difficulties in the way of an attack. Nevertheless Marlborough prevailed, making the garrison prisoners of war. Thus he writes to Godolphin: "That place never could have been taken but by the hand of God which gave us seven weeks without any rain. The rain began the next day after we had possession and continued till this evening. .... I believe the King of France will be a good deal surprised when he shall hear that the garrison has been obliged to surrender, for upon his being told that preparations were making for the siege of Dendermond he said 'they must have an army of ducks to take it.'"

Ath was the subsequent object. Here again Marlborough after a twelve days' siege, made himself master of the place by capitulation on the fourth of October the garrison remaining prisoners of war. He had hoped to proceed to the reduction of Mons; but the backwardness of the Dutch in supplying stores withheld him; so that Ath was the concluding trophy of this glorious campaign.

While thus engaged in conquering the Low Countries, Marlborough had been greatly embarrassed with the question of their future government. The Archduke being acknowledged as King it seemed to follow that the nomination of Governor must rest with him, or with his brother the Emperor as administering his affairs in his absence. Charles had indeed left at Vienna a blank paper signed by himself, and to be filled up by Joseph. When therefore the tidings of the victory of Ramillies came to the Imperial Court, Joseph in a transport of gratitude inscribed the Duke's own name in the vacant space. It was a post of immense emolument as well as power; and Marlborough was much inclined to accept it with the Queen's consent.

The Queen and her Ministers were well pleased. They consulted Somers and Sunderland as chiefs of the Whigs and found them well pleased also. These Lords—so Godolphin writes to Marlborough—"seem to think there is no reason for the Dutch not to like it as much as we do." Here however Lord Somers failed in his usual sagacity. So far from relishing the scheme the Dutch viewed it with extreme aversion. They utterly denied the right of the Emperor to fix the government of the Low Countries before their own Barrier was decided. Nor could they disguise their jealousy at the idea, that so many commands, so many powers, should be concentrated in Marlborough. These sentiments extended even to Pensionary Heinsius and others like him, the warmest friends of Marlborough personally, and the main stay of the English alliance.

It was the more necessary to consult the sensitiveness of the Dutch upon this point since any disregard of it would have inclined them to a separate peace. A secret proposal for that object had already been made to them in the course of the preceding winter on the part of France. They had been lured by the prospect of commercial advantages. They had been promised that the

Low Countries should be erected into an independent State to serve them as the best of Barriers. It was certain that France would renew such offers or higher still at the first favourable opening; and it was probable, considering the strong Gallican party at the Hague, that any disgust given to the friends of England, might turn the scale in behalf of the former, and wholly detach the Republic from the cause of the Allies.

Marlborough therefore saw at once that it was requisite to yield; and he did so with excellent grace. "Assure the States"—thus he writes to Heinsius— "that they need be under no difficulty; since if they think it for their service I shall with pleasure excuse myself from accepting this commission." Finally it was agreed, notwithstanding some angry remonstrances from Vienna, that the two Maritime Powers should for the time share the Government of the Low Countries between them; each to appoint commissioners who should form a council and administer all affairs in the name of Charles the Third.

In Italy the French had formed great expectations. It was intended that the Duke de La Feuillade should undertake the siege of Turin. He was son-in-law of Chamillart, who accordingly strained every nerve to augment his forces and ensure his success. It was also intended that the Duke of Vendome with another body should keep in check and if possible repulse the army of Prince Eugene. Vendome began well. Marching through the night of the 18th of April he fell upon the Germans at Calcinato near the Lake of Garda. Taking them by surprise he put them to the rout with the loss of several thousand men in slain and prisoners. Eugene himself was not present. He had been delayed beyond the Alps in mustering his tardy reinforcements, and he did not arrive till the day after the action. Then he found it necessary to continue the retreat and withdraw the army to the left bank of the Adige.

On the 22nd of May La Feuillade began to invest Turin, while the Duke of Savoy, who had left the city, hovered round with a body of light troops, watching an opportunity and burning to prevent or at least protract the siege. Meanwhile however the position of Eugene was much improving. The reinforcements which he had brought from Germany, and those which Marlborough had despatched to him from Holland, made his army more than equal to Vendome's. Early in July he was enabled to pass the Adige and a fortnight afterwards the Po.

It was then that in pursuance of the orders from Versailles Vendome departed for Flanders while the Duke of Orleans and Marsin arrived. Eugene skilfully availed himself of the slight confusion inseparable from a change of command. Through the month of August he gained post after post and drew nearer and nearer to Turin. Then combining his forces with those of the Duke of Savoy they marched together on the beleaguered city; while the Duke of Orleans and Marsin in like manner fell back on La Feuillade.

From the heights of the Superga and on the morning of the 6th of September, Eugene side by side with Victor Amadeus was surveying the French lines. The enemy might have fifty thousand men; and they no more than forty; still they were decided to give battle. During this time an anxious Council of War was being held by the French chiefs. The Duke of Orleans was for marching forward and charging, but Marsin and De Feuillade counselled—and their counsel prevailed—rather to await the attack within their lines.

Next morning then the 7th of September and at break of day Eugene led his army to the onset, well supported by a sally from the garrison under General Count Daun. The battle was well contested and during two hours doubtful, but the genius of Eugene prevailed. The gallant Marsin fell mortally wounded, according to his own prognostic felt by him in secret ever since he crossed the Alps.[7] The Duke of Orleans also was struck both on the thigh and wrist and compelled to quit the field; and the French were put to flight with the loss of many thousand men. Had they been promptly pursued their entire army might have been destroyed, or dispersed in a few days. But the Ministers at Vienna were intent on the reduction of the Milanese; and had made this a primary object with Eugene. There was little difficulty; as Eugene approached the French found it necessary to retire from all the districts which they held in King Philip's name; leaving only small garrisons in the citadels of Milan and Lodi and other such strongholds.

Spain was now the scene of remarkable vicissitudes. Even before the close of the preceding year, the Court of Madrid, incensed at the sudden revolt of Catalonia and Valencia, had sent a body of seven thousand troops under the Count de Las Torres to recover the lost ground. The first step of Las Torres was to lay siege to San Mateo, where Peterborough had placed a small

[7] This appears from a very curious letter which he wrote to Chamillart the day before the battle; it went inclosed to his Confessor to be delivered only in case of his death as he had predicted it, and it was first printed in the Mémoires militaires de la Succession d'Espagne, vol. VI. p. 277.

CHAP. VII.
1706.

garrison of some hundred Miquelets commanded by Colonel Jones. Peterborough himself had hastened from Barcelona to Tortosa. He had with him no more than a thousand foot and two hundred dragoons, yet even with these was resolved on relieving the place. We find him in the first days of January write to the Governor of San Mateo, by no means in any dry official style: "Be sure upon the first appearance of our troops and the first discharge of our artillery, you answer with an English halloo and take to the mountains on the right with all your men. It is no matter what becomes of the town; leave it to your mistresses! Dear Jones, prove a true dragoon; preach this welcome doctrine to your Miquelets; Plunder without danger." [8] There was another letter with false intelligence, which as was meant Las Torres intercepted. So skilfully was the whole scheme combined that the Spanish General became convinced that he was encompassed by far superior forces, and he raised the siege with precipitation, leaving his artillery behind him.

The officers of Peterborough counselled him to be content with this success. The season was wintry; his men were few; and the troops of Las Torres might at any moment rally and turn round upon him. Still Peterborough pressed onward. He came next to Nules, a walled town which, unlike the others of this province, was zealous for the house of Bourbon. The inhabitants, several hundreds in number, had enrolled themselves in arms, and had closed their gates. But Peterborough riding forward haughtily demanded a parley with their chiefs. When these appeared, he declared that he would

[8] Printed under Lord Peterborough's direction in Dr. Freind's Account, p. 211, ed. 1707.

allow them only six minutes for consideration, and would wreak his full vengeance upon them if they presumed to wait until his artillery came up. The townspeople scared at his confident tone, and ignorant of the fact which Peterborough had omitted to tell them that he had not with him even a single piece of cannon, agreed to a surrender. Advancing in this manner and prevailing by the mere terror of his name, Peterborough on the 4th of February entered in triumph the capital city of Valencia which his partisans already held. "I call it a fine city," says Captain Carleton, "but sure it richly deserves a brighter epithet since it is a common saying among the Spaniards that the pleasures of Valencia would make a Jew forget Jerusalem."

Peterborough might now have expected some repose. But intelligence reached him—for he had always excellent intelligence, the reason being, according to Captain Carleton, that he always maintained a good correspondence with the priests and with the ladies— that a Spanish force of 4,000 men was lazily advancing to support Las Torres, and had encamped in listless security at Fuente de Higuera. The Earl at once devised a scheme to surprise them. He sent forward his troops by a night-march—crossed the river Xucar unperceived—and fell upon the Spaniards before they were aware of his approach. Several hundreds became his prisoners and the rest dispersed. This feat performed Peterborough fixed his head-quarters at Valencia, where he took to himself, much to the advantage of his cause, the duties of the Government, and divided his time between the avocations of love and war.

CHAP.
VII.
1706.

Not many weeks however were allowed him. The Courts both of Madrid and of Versailles felt most strongly the importance of recovering Barcelona. For this object Philip took the field in person, and called back the greater portion of his troops from the frontiers of Portugal. Louis sent a fleet from Toulon, commanded by his son the Comte de Toulouse; and besides some stout soldiers from Roussillon, appointed as a guide for Philip and as the real chief of the besieging army one of the Marshals of France, Tessé. Thus at the beginning of April Barcelona was closely invested both by sea and land. Charles had bravely determined to share the fortunes of the garrison. He was shut up in the place; and might become a prisoner of war in the event of its capitulation. As may be supposed in such a streight there went pressing letters to Peterborough to entreat his aid.

Nor did the Earl linger. He returned to Catalonia by rapid marches; but when there he found that of his English he could muster round him scarce 3,000, to be supported by an irregular body of Miquelets under the Count of Cifuentes. With such means it was manifestly hopeless to give battle to the 20,000 men of Marshal Tessé. All that Peterborough could do for the present was to take post in the neighbouring mountains and do his best to harass the besiegers. His main hope was fixed on the succours that were expected from England.

Meanwhile Tessé on commencing the investment made Montjuich his first object. So careless were Charles's Germans that even the recent breaches in the walls had never been repaired. Nevertheless the citadel which the genius of Peterborough had surprised in a few hours was maintained against Tessé for a period of twenty-three days. Then the commander Lord Donegal having fallen, and the place become untenable, the garrison was withdrawn into the city against which the Spanish batteries began to play. Happily at this most critical juncture the English succours came in view.

These succours were of various kinds. The fleet which, commanded by Sir Cloudesley Shovel, had brought out Charles in the preceding year, and had returned to England to winter, now came forth again commanded by Sir John Leake. In force and in equipments it was fully equal to that of the Comte de Toulouse. There was also a new commission to Peterborough for its command. By the former he was conjoined with equal powers to Shovel; by this he had full authority over Leake, only however on those occasions when he was himself on board. There was embarked the greater part of the sum of 250,000*l.*, which on the news of the first success at Barcelona had been voted by the House of Commons for the service of King Charles. Such a supply was the more required since Peterborough had already with signal generosity strained his personal credit to raise in Italy for the public service the sum of 40,000*l.* On board there was also a body of English troops; at their head General Stanhope, who was moreover invested with diplomatic functions as English Envoy at the Court of Charles.

"Never"—so writes Stanhope—"did succours come in a more critical instant; for the enemies who had besieged the King for five and thirty days had made two breaches, one of which is practicable, and the other in a fair way of being so. Their approaches were brought to the covered way, from which to the breaches they had not 150 yards to march to the assault." [9] Not an hour therefore was to be lost for the relief of Barcelona. Admiral Leake however, a brave and skilful but overcautious man, though already equal or more than equal in force to the Comte de Toulouse, had resolved not to hazard an engagement until he should be joined by Admiral Byng with some further ships. Stanhope most earnestly urged the Admiral to press forward without delay, but the Admiral was not to be persuaded. Nothing remained for Stanhope but to send an express to shore and apprise Lord Peterborough of the Admiral's determination.

At these tidings the Earl took a step of singular boldness. He knew that French cruisers were plying along the coast, but he hoped to pass through them protected by the darkness and to reach the English fleet unperceived. With this view he marched down at once to Sitges a fishing village on the seashore. There his officers greatly astonished and concerned saw him embark with a single aide-de-camp in a small felucca. All that night the Earl and his attendant rowed about but could see nothing of their ships. Next night their attempt was resumed and with better success. They came up with the Leopard, one of the English men of war. Captain Price, a gentleman of Wales, who commanded her was amazed to find in an open boat and at open sea the person who had the Queen's Commission to command the fleet. Peterborough going on board ordered the Royal Ensign to be displayed at the maintop masthead, that the other ships might see it

[9] To Sir Charles Hedges, off Barcelona, May 9, 1706 (MS.).

waving as his symbol of authority so soon as the day should break. Meanwhile the pinnace was sent out with a notification to General Stanhope of his safe arrival, and with his orders to Admiral Leake—those orders being to sail straight on Barcelona and make ready to attack the French.

It seems probable that if Peterborough could have reached the fleet on the first night of his search instead of on the second there would have ensued a naval battle fraught with glory to the British arms. But the time that intervened was not lost upon the Comte de Toulouse. He learnt the strength of Leake's armament; he was informed that it had already been, or would immediately be, joined by the squadron of Byng. To contend with such a force seemed to him too uncertain a venture. He determined rather to raise the siege and return to France. When therefore on the 9th of May Peterborough and the English fleet drew near to Barcelona they found their naval enemies disappeared. They entered the harbour without opposition, and proceeded amidst loud huzzas from the people to land the soldiers and marines. As Peterborough wrote to the Queen: "I must not complain where there is so much occasion for joy; but when I spent two nights in a boat at sea to get on board the fleet, I was in hopes I might have given your Majesty some account of the other trust you have been pleased to honor me with; but a discreet retreat prevented those flattering hopes."

The object however of relieving Barcelona was most fully attained. The enemy's land-forces followed the example of the sea. Marshal Tessé when he found the French fleet sailed away, and the English succours landed, lost heart and desisted from the siege. In the night but one after he struck his tents and spiked his cannon, commending by letter his sick and wounded and not in vain to the generous care of Peterborough. On the early morn of the 11th accompanied by Philip he was in full march for the French frontier; and they scarcely paused until they found themselves within it, namely at Perpignan. Thus it appeared as though the reverses at Barcelona were to drive the Bourbon King of Spain out of his dominions.

There were two things which in popular impression seemed at this time to enhance the triumph of the Allies. As on the morning of the 11th of May the French were marching homeward in utter disarray the sun, that chosen device of Louis the Fourteenth, was obscured by a total eclipse. Secondly, as it chanced, the news of the raising the siege of Barcelona, and of the defeat at Ramillies, reached Versailles within a few days' interval of each other. Louis was perhaps the only man in France whose magnanimity was equal to these misfortunes. We find him late one night write to Chamillart as follows: "Evil tidings pour in upon us from all quarters, but we must not let ourselves be downcast, nor fail to do whatever can be done."[1]

Peterborough had by no means the same well-balanced mind. When things go ill we find him set no bounds to his railing; when prosperously he is full of vaunts. Thus from Barcelona at this period he writes to his wife in England: "You see my toils and

---

[1] "Toutes les nouvelles sont accablantes; mais il ne faut point se laisser abattre ni manquer à faire ce qui est possible pour sortir de l'état où nous sommes." Louis XIV à Chamillart, 1 Juin 1706, à onze heures du soir.

good intentions are rewarded with perhaps the most remarkable successes that ever were." His tone to the Secretary of State is almost as high: "As to what relates to Spain I am a stranger and a heretic, yet I have the power of a Dictator, of a tyrant, when the King is absent. In truth I do all, but the King himself is made use of to obstruct me almost upon all occasions; and it may be easily conceived how I am with his Ministers whose avarice I cannot satisfy and whose plunder I am obliged to obstruct. . . . I took the liberty to think and inquire—a mortal sin in this country!"[a]

The siege of Barcelona being thus successfully raised, and the public rejoicings over, there was held on the 18th of May a Council of War to determine the further proceedings. A forward movement was expected on the part of the Portugal army; and Peterborough urged upon Charles that theirs should advance also—first proceed to Valencia and thence march upon Madrid. Charles, although his personal courage has never been called in question, was by no means equally inclined to adventurous courses. The advice of Peterborough therefore only in part prevailed. It was agreed that the Earl should take the leading part, and be conveyed with his infantry by sea, while the horse should march by land to Valencia. Charles meanwhile with his Court and Ministers was to fix his head-quarters at Tortosa, and hold himself ready to proceed to Madrid as soon as Peterborough should have cleared the way. It was computed that the Earl

[a] To Sir Charles Hedges, June 27, 1706 (MS.). This letter in the transcript fills twenty folio pages closely written. "Lord Peterborough"—so Godolphin says to Marlborough—"has written a volume to Mr. Secretary Hedges." (Coxe's Life, vol. III. p. 38.)

CHAP. VII.
1706.

would have with him in Valencia nearly 7,000 men, about half of them English; and that an equal number would be left in Catalonia to escort the King and to garrison the fortresses.

Before the close of May accordingly, we find Peterborough once again landed from the fleet and fixed at his favourite abode of Valencia—in the brightest of cities and by the bluest of seas. There he applied himself with great zeal to his military objects. He sent forward at once a detachment of 2,000 men under General Wyndham to besiege Requena the only stronghold between him and Madrid. He formed schemes for reducing on his flank the strong castle of Alicant. His singular energy was shown meanwhile in raising a regiment of dragoons with almost unparalleled despatch. He bought them horses, drilled and disciplined them, provided them clothes, arms, and accoutrements, and in six weeks' time had them ready to take the field. At the same time he had another opportunity to manifest his generous temper. There had been many disputes at Barcelona with respect to the money sent from England; Charles claiming it as at his own disposal, and Peterborough pointing out that it was already appropriated to the prescribed services by order of the English Ministers. The Earl loudly complained of the insulting language used to him by the King on this occasion. Nevertheless when in the beginning of July Peterborough received a further sum of 10,000*l*. raised on his own personal credit and all in gold he disregarded the personal affront and sent the whole to Charles. Unhappily he could not bridle his tongue or pen; nor, even in the midst of his largesses, forbear insulting language also on his side. Thus he writes to Stanhope: "I hope you are not so angry as not to take the money I sent you. I desire you take the King's own note to repay me when he comes to Madrid; and I desire—since he wants twenty pistoles!—that you will let him have it in his own power."

We find Peterborough remember also in the kindest manner some of the Valencian nobles. "Make my compliments to the Marquis of La Casta, to the Count of Villa Franquesa, and to the Count of Cassall, telling them that, because I knew they went out of Valencia so suddenly and unprovided, I take the liberty to send you two hundred pistoles a piece for them if they have occasion."

The Earl meanwhile was gaining much popular favor in Valencia by his gaiety and his magnificence. He gave both balls and bull-fights, lamenting only that the tamer race of the Valencian bulls deprived the latter festivities of the zest of danger. Nor, indefatigable as he was in his public cares, did he ever want some leisure for love-making. He was by no means duly mindful of his distant consort, the venerable Countess of Peterborough. On the contrary we find him in his letters a few months afterwards commemorate with much satisfaction "my services to the little Marquesa"[3] — the Marchioness that is of La Casta.

On the frontiers of Portugal there was an able chief for Philip; the Duke of Berwick lately advanced to the rank of Maréchal de France. His force had been reduced to 5,000 men by the drafts made from it for the siege of Barcelona, and was ill able to cope with

[3] To Gen. Stanhope, Jan. 6, 1707. Peterborough, who was born in 1658, had married—even as a minor it would seem—Carey, daughter of Sir Alexander Fraser of Dores. Their eldest son, Lord Mordaunt, sat in Parliament so early as 1700.

the 18 or 20,000 men of the Allies. As leaders of these last were the Marquis Das Minas and the Earl of Galway; the former for the Portuguese; the latter for the English; and both conjoined as colleagues although Das Minas stood first in seniority of rank. A strange result of civil strife and religious persecution, that Berwick an Englishman by both his parents should appear at the head of a French army, and be confronted by Galway a Frenchman by both his parents, yet now in command of English soldiers! So thorough a transposition is scarcely to be traced any where else in History. Berwick seems to have suffered no disparagement from his foreign birth; but it was not so with Galway; and we find his ill-wishers among the other English chiefs, as Peterborough for example, constantly sneering at him as "our French General." Apart from any such unworthy prejudice it can scarcely I think be denied, that he owed his first promotion to his Protestant zeal much more than to his military talents.

It happened besides that Galway, a brave soldier though an indifferent chief, had lost an arm last year at the siege of Badajos. His health since that time had languished, and he was scarcely equal to the toils of high command. Moreover he was unfortunate in being joined to a colleague or rather a superior so stubborn and untoward as the Portuguese Marquis appeared. Thus when Galway seeing the far diminished numbers of Berwick pressed for a speedy advance upon Madrid, Das Minas utterly refused unless the right as the post of honor were yielded to the Portuguese in Spain. Galway sooner than remain inactive gave up the point, and thereby at a later period incurred a censure in Parliament. The House of Lords resolved in 1711 that he had "acted contrary to the honor of the imperial Crown of Great Britain,"[4] — which Crown by the way was so constituted through the Act of Union with Scotland, and therefore at the time of Galway's concession did not yet exist.

Even with this concession however the Portuguese were to be drawn no further than about half-way to Madrid. They halted at the bridge of Almaraz expressing a desire to return to their own country; and it was with some difficulty that Galway could bring them to the intermediate step of investing the frontier fortress of Ciudad Rodrigo. It held out but seven days; and by that time the Allied chiefs animated by the great news from Barcelona agreed to suspend their dissensions and to resume their advance. First they occupied Salamanca and next they marched upon Madrid. Philip on learning the danger of his capital had at once hastened thither from Perpignan by way of Pamplona, but he arrived only to depart again. He found that it would be impossible to make any effectual stand, and therefore sending his young Queen and his Council of State to establish the seat of government at Burgos, he for his own part with a soldierly spirit joined the camp of Berwick on the Guadarrama range.

No further obstacle arising the vanguard of the Allies headed by the Marquis of Villaverde entered the city of Madrid on the 25th of June. Two days later came their main body headed by Galway and Das Minas. They caused King Charles to be solemnly proclaimed but appear to have done little else for his

[4] Parl. Hist. vol. vi. p. 993.

service. They were joined however by some persons of high note hitherto conspicuous on the other side. Thus the Primate of Spain, Cardinal Porto Carrero, not long since chief Minister of Philip, was now living in a kind of honourable exile at his See of Toledo. He combined with the Queen Dowager who was a resident of the same city, and who had always been a German by inclination as by birth. They both eagerly welcomed a squadron of horse sent to Toledo by Das Minas, and hastened to acknowledge the Archduke as their rightful Sovereign. The Queen cast off her sables and appeared with her ladies in festival attire, while the Cardinal donning his Archiepiscopal robes chaunted a Te Deum in the Cathedral, and gave his solemn benediction to the Austrian standards.

Looking to these and other such defections—considering also the ready acceptance of the Allies in Catalonia and Valencia and their prosperous progress along the Tagus and the Manzanares, it might have been supposed that the cause of Charles was now secure and that of Philip irrecoverably lost. But it speedily appeared that the contest in Spain was not of persons nor yet in truth of politics; it was only a renewal of the ancient strife between the provinces of the Crown of Aragon and the provinces of the Crown of Castille. Had the wishes of the Spaniards themselves at this period been able to prevail, they would have been again, as before Ferdinand and Isabella, a divided race. The more enthusiasm was shown to Charles by the people of the one Crown, the more did the people of the other grow from indifference to aversion. Galway and Das Minas at Madrid found themselves most coldly received. Few if any of the common rank would join their banner or give aid to their cause; while at the same period both Philip and his Queen, the one in his camp the other in her Court, received, for the first time in their reign, strong tokens of popular attachment. But on the other hand there now burst forth at Zaragoza a revolution in behalf of Charles—a revolution which seemed to be effected with entire unanimity, and which quickly extended to the whole of Aragon. There were also betrayed to Charles's hands two most renowned strongholds,— Carthagena on the coast of Murcia and Oran on the coast of Barbary.

It seems probable had only some man of active mind filled Charles's place at this period that he might have turned to good account the popular favor of the east of Spain, and triumphed over or anticipated the not yet developed aversion of Castille. His personal appearance was the one thing needful. So great and so unaccountable seemed his torpor at this critical time that in many places they believed him to be dead. "Several towns," writes Peterborough, "are very obstinate upon that persuasion." And in another letter the Earl observes to Stanhope, "You told me once you wondered at my temper upon the retreat of the Portuguese (from the bridge of Almaraz); but though it may seem strange to retire when there is no enemy, I think it more extraordinary not to advance towards a Crown."[5]

Long before the date of these letters Peterborough had reduced Requena—had sent forward the same detachment to invest Cuenca—and had thus most effectually cleared the way to the capital. Stanhope, as the

[5] Letters dated Valencia, July 13 and 20, 1706.

CHAP. VII.
1706.

English Minister at Charles's Court, had been pressing him to carry out the Resolutions of the Council of War held on the 18th of May. But the insurrection along the Ebro had suggested to Charles's mind another scheme. He determined to keep clear of Peterborough and to advance upon Madrid by way of Zaragoza and not by way of Valencia. The true object, as Peterborough vehemently declares in his letters, was that the "Vienna crew" might enrich themselves with the plunder of Aragon. Considering their general character it is far from unlikely that such a motive may have weighed with them. Even the calmer Marlborough writing to Godolphin from Flanders in this same month of July observes that "nothing ever was so weak, so shameful, so unaccountable in every point, as the conduct of the Prince of Lichtenstein and the rest of the King of Spain's German followers." But Charles had another motive of his own. He was extremely offended with Peterborough. The Earl's contemptuous demeanour and insulting sarcasms had stung him to the quick. "I would not"—he once cried to Mr. Crowe, who had been Stanhope's predecessor at his little Court—"I would not accept of Salvation if it came through Lord Peterborough's hands!"[6] As Stanhope reports to the Secretary of State at this juncture: "I find that he will venture the not going to Madrid at all rather than be carried thither by my Lord." Yet at this very time the Ministers in England, little foreseeing such hostility, had drawn a still closer tie between the King and Peterborough, and conferred upon

---

[6] Told by Mr. Crowe himself to Marlborough (Coxe's Life, vol. III. p. 38). But Mr. Crowe appears to have mistranslated the French word *salut* as "health."

the latter the post of Ambassador Extraordinary at the Court of Charles.

After long delays against which Stanhope remonstrated in vain Charles began his advance to Aragon. He did not enter Zaragoza till the 18th of July, more than three weeks since the Anglo-Portuguese were at Madrid. Proceeding onwards he sent instructions to Peterborough to march at the same time from Valencia, and to meet him at Pastrana in Castille. There accordingly they made their junction on the 4th of August, the appointed day. But before that time Galway and Das Minas had found it necessary to leave Madrid. Their troops had wasted most rapidly in numbers, in part from the midsummer heats and in part from their own excesses. Full six thousand had gone to the hospitals and of these the greater part had died. Berwick on the other hand had been receiving large reinforcements, and above all the Count of Las Torres who had fled from Valencia with about four thousand men. Thus Berwick became more than a match for the Allied chiefs in the capital. These determined as a measure of prudence to sally forth and join their army to that of Charles, leaving only a few hundred Portuguese to take post at the Royal Palace. But no sooner had they marched from the gates, than the population rose in arms, and a squadron of Spanish horse rode in. Within two days the Portuguese at the palace were compelled to surrender for want of food; and thus the whole city of Madrid was won back to Philip's power. Salamanca and Toledo in like manner resumed their old allegiance.

Proceeding from Madrid Galway and Das Minas encamped near the small city of Guadalaxara. There on the 5th of August they were joined by the united force of Charles and Peterborough. Each of these divisions appear to have gazed with surprise at the scanty numbers of the other. The Anglo-Portuguese as already shown had much melted away. Stanhope in his despatches home computes them at little more than 3,000 horse and under 10,000 foot. Charles and Peterborough had between them brought 1,400 horse and no more than 2,500 foot; since besides the difficulty of exposing the latter to long and destructive summer marches, it had been necessary to garrison the strongholds left behind them. During this period the army of Berwick had grown by degrees, it was said, to full 20,000 men.

With the Allies the multiplicity of Generals was even a worse evil than the paucity of soldiers. Galway held the older commission, and it was decided this summer by the Ministers in London that in the case of junction Galway should accordingly command. "I think" writes Godolphin "this is right for the Service, but how it may make my Lord Peterborough fly out I cannot answer."[7] It is therefore very highly to Galway's honor that at Guadalaxara he called upon Peterborough and expressed his readiness to serve under his orders until he could obtain his own recall from England. But Das Minas when consulted positively refused to join in the proposal, and insisted on his own seniority of rank, so that if Galway's offer were accepted Peterborough would still be controlled by this arrogant and froward Portuguese.

Peterborough devised a plan of his own. He proposed that there should be four distinct Corps d'Armée

[7] To the Duke of Marlborough, July 19, 1706.

—himself to command the same English as before, with the addition of the Catalan or Valencian levies—Galway the English serving in combination with Das Minas—Das Minas the Portuguese—and the Count de Noyelles the Dutch; each of these Generals to receive no orders except from Charles as King of Spain.[8] Such a scheme might have succeeded when the reference was to some far-famed chief as Marlborough or Eugene; but with a young and inexperienced Prince like Charles it could lead only to confusion and failure. No wonder if Charles himself shrank from the perilous responsibility.

Another offer of Peterborough was to attempt the recovery of Madrid by a COUP DE MAIN, at the head of 5,000 men. Here again he was resisted on the plea of wanting bread. His proud spirit, conscious of great services, chafed at being in such a manner and by such men overruled. It was a situation not unlike to that of Sir Arthur Wellesley when, immediately after gaining the battle of Vimeiro, he found the orders from England place him beneath two other Generals of superior rank and far from equal genius. But Sir Arthur with resolute wisdom remained at his post and Peterborough quitted his. For the Earl in his mortification now proposed to take his departure from the army.

A plea was by no means wanting. Even his first instructions had left him considerable latitude as to assisting the Duke of Savoy. But he had recently received another despatch from the Secretary of State

---

[8] Letter to the King dated Guadalaxara, August 8, 1706, and printed in Dr. Freind's Account, p. 113; a volume that contains many valuable documents, most unskilfully compiled.

CHAP. VII.
1706.

Sir Charles Hedges, dated Whitehall, June the 19th Old Style. When that despatch was written the affairs of the Duke of Savoy were supposed to be in great extremity from the investment of Turin. Sir Charles deemed it "an absolute necessity" to reinforce His Highness, and he therefore enjoined that three at least of the Queen's regiments should be sent to his aid from the coast of Spain. It was left free to Peterborough to join or not to join the expedition as he pleased. This despatch was produced by the Earl at a Council of War held in the palace of Guadalaxara on the 9th of August, and he expressed his wish to act upon it.

Many men of no less genius than Peterborough have on decisive occasions overreached themselves by an exaggerated estimate of their own importance; and it is a hard lesson of life to learn how little we are missed. Considering his talents and his services the English commander may have thought that he should be pressed to stay. But the very contrary happened. Unlike Marlborough he had never understood that conciliation is among the main duties of a chief. His bitter sarcasms both by word and writing had keenly offended those with whom he acted. Soldiers and civilians all rejoiced to be rid of him. King Charles above all was well pleased. Even at Zaragoza, so long as Charles believed the Portugal army to be entire and well-established he had urged the Earl by letter to proceed to the Duke of Savoy's aid, and assured him that his presence would not be needed at Madrid. Now he warmly commended Peterborough's zeal and entirely approved his design. In another respect also he observed, that besides the relief of the Duke of

Savoy the Earl might do good service by his voyage; he might raise among the bankers of Genoa a loan for the subsistence of his army; and with this view the King gave him full authority to mortgage, if it should be requisite, any part of His Majesty's dominions. He might also, it was said, on coming back with the fleet make an attempt on Port Mahon; a conquest held to be most important as affording a good haven and enabling the Queen's ships instead of returning home every autumn to winter in the Mediterranean.

CHAP. VII.
1706.

With these views and well laden both with full powers and with compliments Peterborough set out once more for the coast. He brought away with him only some fourscore troopers for an escort and was to take on board a part of the foot left behind in Valencia or Alicant. On his journey like a true Knight Errant he did not fail of adventures. Before he could come up with his baggage which was on its way to Madrid it was assailed near the small town of Huete and plundered of plate and other valuables to the amount of at least eight thousand pistoles. Peterborough full of ire threatened condign punishment, and the townspeople full of terror promised ample restitution. They offered to pay down the amount DE CONTADO, that is, in ready money. But Peterborough, ever most generous, would take nothing for himself. He desired that an equal value of their newly reaped corn should be forwarded free of charge for the supply of the army whose command he had just relinquished.

Huete supplied a second incident of quite another kind. It was reported to the Earl that on a threat which he had made of burning the town one of the most beautiful ladies in all Spain had taken refuge in

18*

CHAP. VII. 1706.

the Convent. This building stood upon a small rising ground within the walls. Peterborough immediately discovered that no spot could be more proper for a fortification. It might be his duty to construct new works; it might be his duty to leave a sufficient garrison. Making no secret of the scheme, he went with Captain Carleton as an engineer to inspect the place. It was not long ere the Lady Abbess attended by the fair fugitive sallied forth in great alarm to beseech his kind forbearance. Peterborough listened with indulgence to her entreaties; and gazed with admiration at her friend. Nothing further was heard of the fortifications; but the Earl appears to have prolonged his stay at Huete for two or three days.

On resuming his journey Peterborough proceeded first to Valencia and next by sea to Alicant. There he hastened by his presence the capitulation of the castle, which by his orders had been for some time past besieged. There he also conferred with the Captains of the fleet and learnt to his infinite mortification that orders from England had come despatching one-half the ships on a special service to the West Indies. This would put an end for the present year at least to all idea of an attack on Port Mahon. There was also news from Italy not as yet officially communicated but told by Rumour with all her thousand tongues—how the Allies had gained a battle—and how the siege of Turin was raised. As sometimes and strangely happens with great events, the first reports were even a little in anticipation of the real fact—the decisive victory achieved by Prince Eugene on the 8th of September.

Tidings such as these might well have induced Peterborough to relinquish or at least suspend his voyage. But he appears at this time to have set his heart upon Italy, and was determined under any circumstances to go onward. A Council of War consisting both of land and sea officers was held in Alicant on the 17th, when the members acknowledged the pressing want of funds both in fleet and army, "and no money to be hoped for but by the Earl of Peterborough's endeavouring to obtain it at Genoa." Therefore, as the Officers proceed to say, "we have been forced to approve the resolution taken by the said Earl to go in person." It is plain that theirs was by no means a very willing acquiescence. The Earl however embarked, but, considering the news from Italy, decided to leave behind the troops that had been asked.

Setting sail from Alicant on the 22nd of September, a voyage of seven days brought the English chief to Genoa. There he found most fully confirmed the decisive results of the recent victory. His own part was now to fulfil only the duties of a money-broker for which he was least of all men qualified. But besides these he rashly engaged in some secret negotiations with the Duke of Savoy and other Italian princes —negotiations for which no authority had been given him, and from which no advantage either to himself or to the public ensued.

During this time the Allies had marched from Guadalaxara. Desiring to maintain themselves at least a little longer in Castille they had encamped at Chinchon to the north-east of Aranjuez. Das Minas was pressing that their retreat should be made towards the Portugal frontier; and his wish would have prevailed but that Berwick with his augmented army lay between. The Allies therefore fell back in the opposite direction beyond the borders of Valencia and there took up their winter quarters. They could not prevent Berwick from besieging and retaking their last conquest of Cuenca; and they also relinquished Carthagena which was judged to be not tenable. Thus ingloriously to them, ended a campaign which had begun so well.

Nor were their future prospects very cheering. Thus does Stanhope state the case to Godolphin: "I have already hinted to your Lordship the drift of Count Noyelles to form two bodies against next spring, that he may command one of them either alone or under the King. In pursuance of that scheme the Count presses to separate the English troops. My Lord Galway does what he can to keep them together until my Lord Peterborough returns from Italy. If the Queen continues to have two Generals here it may seem proper to have two armies; but if our business be to beat the enemy, I believe we ought to have but one. It is I think evident beyond contradiction, that had our forces been joined this summer the work had been finished. We are now extremely weakened and the enemies grow stronger."

In England these events excited no small surprise. We find St. John as Secretary at War address Stanhope as follows in a secret letter: "Whilst we were rejoicing with the Duke of Marlborough in the City over very bad wine, for the great success of Her Majesty's arms in the last campaign, arrived your brother with letters of the 29th of October from Valencia. What a wretched condition are our affairs in Spain reduced to! And how practicable an enterprise is become desperate! I do not undertake to give you an account of the reflections which people here make on this subject, nor of the measures which the Queen takes to retrieve the great disadvantages which have been sustained in Spain. No doubt but our new Secretary of State my Lord Sunderland does this at large. My own opinion is, that the Court you have to do with must be new-modelled, and that the King stands as much in need of able Ministers as of good troops. .... My Lord Rivers will be with you long before this letter, and with this reinforcement I hope you will be in a condition to support and extend yourselves. I do not yet know what troops, if any, will be sent to Portugal, but sure a diversion must be made on that side; and none of any consequence can be expected unless to a body of Portuguese there be joined a head from our troops."[9]

During the whole of this year Marlborough was intent on diplomacy no less than on war. By the desire of his colleagues in England, he had sought to obtain from the Dutch and subsequently from other Powers a guarantee of the Protestant Succession. The Dutch however declined any positive answer. Their object was to require in return a settlement of their Barrier according to their pretensions; and their pretensions were now most unreasonably high. They desired not merely some cautionary fortresses, such as they held before the war, but whole districts and even provinces to be added to their dominions. Such a scheme was by no means agreeable to England, and it was of course most bitterly resented by the Emperor at whose own or brother's expense it would have to be effected. The displeasure was not confined to the

---

[9] Letter dated Whitehall, December 24, 1706 (MS.).

CHAP. Cabinets of Vienna and St. James's, nor yet limited to
VII. this subject alone. "It is certain"—so writes Marl-
1706. borough at this time—"that the Dutch carry everything with so high a hand as not to be beloved any-
where."¹

Other discussions with Holland arose from the
offers of France. King Louis had for some time past
earnestly desired to put an end to the war; and the
recent disasters to his arms in Flanders, in Italy, in
Spain, added of course not a little to his pacific resolutions. For this object he made overtures through
divers channels. One by the Elector of Bavaria seemed
at first to be without his sanction or knowledge and
on the Elector's own account. Another more direct
came from Count Bergueick, Intendant of the Netherlands, to Pensionary Heinsius. It was as yet only
tentative and not officially avowed. But the proposals
comprised the relinquishment to the Archduke of Spain
and the Indies—a Barrier for the Dutch Republic—a
recognition of Queen Anne's title—and considerable
commercial advantages to both the Maritime Powers
on condition that the kingdom of Naples with Sicily
and Milan should remain as a separate sovereignty to
Philip. Even the mere rumour of such terms made a
great impression on the Dutch. As Marlborough writes
to Godolphin, "It is publicly said at the Hague, that
France is reduced to what she ought to be, and that if
the war should be carried further it would serve only
to make England greater than it ought to be."

It was not long before the Pensionary in confidence
consulted the Duke upon these terms; and here is the

¹ To the Lord Treasurer, from Grametz, Sept. 20, 1706.

Duke's answer. "As a good Englishman I must be of the opinion of my country, that both by treaty and interest we are obliged to preserve the monarchy of Spain entire. At the same time as a friend I must acknowledge that I believe France can hardly be brought to a peace unless something be given to the Duke of Anjou, so that he may preserve the title of King. I think that of Milan is unreasonable since it would make France master of the Duke of Savoy and all Italy." But within a few weeks the objections of Marlborough grew far more intense. We find him say to Godolphin: "As yet nothing has been proposed but a Partition Treaty, which is not only dishonourable to the Allies but in length of time destruction."[2] Acting on these latter views, and straining to the utmost his influence with the ruling statesmen in Holland, Marlborough prevailed so far that the public proposal of France—to open conferences for the negotiation of peace—was solemnly declined, the Dutch Deputies declaring that the Republic would abide by its Allies, and accept no overtures for a pacification without their concurrence and approval. Thus was the continuance of the war decided; and both parties prepared for the next campaign.

On reviewing these transactions, we may probably incline to think that the zeal of Marlborough against France carried him much too far. Even admitting to be valid the objection against the relinquishment of Milan to Philip, no such objection would apply against his retention of Naples and Sicily. It would have been a Treaty of Partition such as King William had planned

---

* Letters of Marlborough, August 21 and November 16, 1706.

CHAP. VII.
1706.

and many leading statesmen, Marlborough himself included, had agreed to. Why then should that Partition which was so readily adopted in 1700 be so bitterly denounced in 1706? It might be deemed inadequate after the glorious successes of Marlborough and Eugene, but how could it have become such utter "dishonor and destruction?"

For my part it does appear to me, as I have elsewhere argued, that the Treaty of Partition during the lifetime of Charles the Second was insulting and unjust. But after the decease of that monarch and his Will in favor of France—after the acceptance of that Will by both the Maritime Powers and by other European States—I conceive that the question had changed. To surrender Spain and the Indies besides the Netherlands to the next Prince of the House of Austria, as France now proposed to do, was to yield the very gist of the dispute. Instead of distant cousins and not friends, as with Leopold and Charles the Second of Spain, it would place two brothers bound in close amity and concert on the thrones of Vienna and Madrid. It would thus provide in the most efficient manner an equipoise to the might of France, and enable the Allies, without any future risk, to assign Naples and Sicily, and perhaps Milan also, as the portion of the retiring King of Spain. I therefore presume to think as did the Dutch statesmen of the time, that the offer of Louis, though no doubt not spontaneous, though no doubt extorted from him by his late reverses, did in fact concede the main object and design of the Grand Alliance, and might well have been accepted as at least the basis of negotiations. Had a peace on that basis ensued it would have averted a large effusion both of blood and treasure in the years to come, and would have secured to the Allies far better terms as regarded the probable balance of power than they finally were able to attain.

CHAPTER VIII.

THE basis for the Union with Scotland having been determined, the Commissioners on both sides applied themselves with vigour to their task. Several of them showed themselves able in their conduct, and many persevering and pertinacious in their claims. But by degrees the genius of Somers won to itself a quiet preeminence, and it was to him rather than to any other person that the prosperous result should in justice be ascribed.

By far the hardest to adjust were the questions of taxation and trade. Debates on them were continued from the 29th of April to the 7th of June. It was proposed by the English Commissioners in one comprehensive phrase "that there be the same customs, excises, and all other taxes, and the same prohibitions, restrictions and regulations of trade throughout the united kingdom of Great Britain." The Scottish Commissioners desired rather to discuss the matter in detail; and their wish was granted; but they quickly came to the same conclusion so far as trade was concerned. Points of taxation on the contrary were fought one by one. It was pleaded on behalf of Scotland that before that country would be able to bear its part in the heavier imposts of England it must enjoy for some years to come the prosperous fruits of the Union. On these grounds it was asked, and finally it was conceded that there should be granted to Scotland an exemption from certain taxes, those especially which by Acts of the English Parliament were at a fixed period to determine. Such were the Window Duties and a portion of the Stamp Duties expiring on the 1st of August 1710, and the tax on coals to cease on the 30th of September the same year. The Salt Duty was more difficult to deal with as being permanent in England; and the Scotch felt its great importance since it bore so much on their curing of fish. At last it was agreed that they should enjoy an exemption for a limited period, namely seven years.

Moreover the English Commissioners had even from the outset owned that since Scotland would sustain an immediate loss from an uniform system of taxation, England might in justice be expected to offer compensation by an immediate payment of money. This sum thus acknowledged in principle, though at first undefined in amount, was discussed under the name of "the Equivalent." Scottish writers have acknowledged that the idea once promulgated tended not a little to reconcile the Scottish statesmen to this measure. It smoothed away a whole host of difficulties real or pretended; it served, as Dr. Johnson once observed of public dinners, "to lubricate business."

To fix the exact sum for this Equivalent proved far from an easy task. Statements and calculations in great detail were now produced.[1] It was computed that the

[1] These documents are inserted in the Second Appendix to De Foe's very ponderous History of the Union (1. vol. folio, 1709). But Mr. Burton who took the pains to verify them found that De Foe has put them together with great carelessness, and that the numbers are not always correctly balanced (Hist. of Scotland, note at vol. 1. p. 412).

total revenue of England came to 5,691,803*l*., that of Scotland to only 160,000*l*. Even this amount was not, as in the case of England, actual but in some measure prospective; since it included the addition—laid on it is true with a most gentle and forbearing hand—which it was designed to make to the Scottish Land-tax, raising it from 3,600*l*. a year to no more than 48,000*l*. as against the 2,000,000*l*. which the same impost produced in England. These last numbers, even allowing for the great indulgence shown on this occasion to the lesser kingdom, manifest how very small when compared to the English were at this time the incomes of the Scottish landowners. Feudal power indeed might make them some amends. They had heritable jurisdiction where their brethren of the south had comfortable rent-rolls; the service of men instead of the payment of money.

The debts of England partly permanent and in part for terms of years gave a total of 17,763,842*l*., while those of Scotland were so complex and varying between nominal and real that they were found to be incapable of any quite accurate statement. They were taken in round numbers at 160,000*l*., being one year of the annual revenue. These Scottish obligations it was intended to discharge at once, so that there might be only one National Debt for the one united kingdom. In the same spirit regulations were framed to establish an uniform coinage and also an uniform system of weights and measures.[2] Some discontent was felt that

---

[2] For the currency in Scotland at this period see especially Leake's Historical Account of English Money, p. 400, ed. 1745. Among these Scottish coins is mentioned "a Darien pistole of King William." Was there also a Glencoe pistole?

in these cases there was no reciprocity; the standard of England being always adopted as the rule. Yet it might not unfairly be pleaded that the customs of the majority if adopted were the more likely to gain a footing and prevail in the entire island; and that if some temporary inconvenience must result even from the changes that tend most to lasting good, it was best that this inconvenience should be borne by what was at that time incomparably the smaller and the less commercial people.

With these documents before them, and computing as best they might the probable results of an uniform or nearly uniform system of taxation, the Commissioners finally fixed the Equivalent at 398,085 *l.* 10*s.* This sum when duly voted by the House of Commons was to be applied—partly in payment of the public debts of Scotland—partly in payment of the stockholders of the Darien Company with interest, that Company itself to be dissolved—and partly in compensation for losses by the coinage. The surplus, it was stipulated, should be spent in the promotion of the Scottish fisheries and such other "manufactories and improvements" in Scotland as might tend to the prosperity of the United kingdom.

So great had been the difficulties which attended these financial questions that the Commissioners more than once almost despaired of solving them. The Queen was advised that her presence might perhaps promote a satisfactory conclusion. It appears from the Minutes that Her Majesty did accordingly attend the Meetings upon two occasions, when she sat down in her Chair of State, exhorted the Commissioners to despatch, and heard the Proposals and Resolutions read.

CHAP.
VIII.
1706.

As the financial questions drew near to a settlement the political were found far more easy to adjust. It was agreed that Great Britain should be the designation of the united island; the name of Scotland to be merged in the name of North Britain. It was agreed that the Crosses of St. George and St. Andrew should be conjoined in the flag of the united kingdom. It was agreed that the Arms of the two countries—the three lions passant and guardant Or, and the lion rampant Or, within a double tressure flory and counterflory, Gules—should be quartered with all heraldic honors. It was agreed that the united kingdom should have a new Great Seal.

As regards the House of Commons the English party proposed that Scotland should be represented by thirty-eight members. Even Scottish writers have observed that if taxation be taken as the measure of representation, and if it be remembered that the Scots of that time had asked and been allowed to limit their share of the Land-tax to one-fortieth of the share of England, it would follow that as an addition to the 513 members of Parliament returned by England, Scotland was entitled to demand no more than thirteen. But even thirty-eight seemed by no means adequate to the claims on other grounds of that ancient and renowned kingdom. The Scottish Commissioners stood out for an increase, and the English Commissioners finally conceded forty-five.

The Peers of England were at this juncture 185 and the Peers of Scotland 154. It was intended that the latter should send representatives to the former, and the proportion was settled according to the precedent that was just decided. The 45 members from Scotland when added to the 513 from England would make one-twelfth of the whole; and 16 Peers from Scotland when added to the 185 from England would also make about one-twelfth of the whole. Sixteen was therefore the number adopted; and the mode of election both of Commoners and Peers was left to be determined by the Parliament of Scotland, before the day appointed for the Union, that is the first of May 1707.

By this treaty Scotland was to retain her heritable jurisdiction, her Court of Session and her entire system of law. The Presbyterian Church as by law established was to continue unaltered, having been indeed excluded from debate by the express terms of the Commission.[3] Such then was the tenor of the Articles of Union as subscribed at the Cockpit on the 22nd of July, 1706, and next day in due form presented to Her Majesty. Some few of the Commissioners were however on divers grounds absent or dissentient. Of the thirty-one on either side the Articles were signed by twenty-seven of the English and twenty-six of the Scots.

It has been observed of the Treaty which was projected in 1706 and accomplished in 1707, that it was indeed a great blessing both to England and Scotland, but a blessing because in constituting one State it left two Churches.[4] There seems to be implied some praise on that account to the framers of the Scottish Union and some blame to the framers of the Irish. In truth however both the praise and the blame are undeserved.

---

[3] "Quod licitum non erit dictis Commissionariis de alteratione cultûs disciplinae aut regiminis ecclesiæ Scoticanae ut nunc per leges stabilita sunt ullo modo tractare." Scottish Commission, dated Feb. 27, 1706.

[4] See the remarks to that effect of Lord Macaulay in his History of England, vol. iv. p. 256. (Tauchnitz Ed.).

CHAP. VIII.
1706.

The framers of each measure did no more than leave untouched and confirm the Church which they found established. To propose a new establishment in either country would have been at these periods the wildest of all wild schemes. In 1707 any attempt for the restoration of Prelacy would have stirred up such a storm of passion north of Tweed as would have made an Union utterly impossible. In 1800 it might have been feasible to endow the Roman Catholic priests as Mr. Pitt proposed, but the idea of rendering their's the Established Church of Ireland in the place of the Protestant never, it may be said, even entered the minds of any statesman of that time.

The Articles of Union having been by Lord Somers laid before the Queen, and Her Majesty having in gracious terms received them, there remained the not less necessary duty of submitting them to both the Legislatures. It was resolved by the Government with excellent policy that they should be first decided by the Parliament of Scotland, so as to avoid any, even the smallest, appearance of constraint or compulsion on the part of the more powerful country.

With this view the meeting of the English Parliament was deferred, while the next and as it proved the last Session of the Scottish began on the 3rd of October. It had been resolved after much deliberation to send once more the Duke of Queensberry as Lord High Commissioner, and it must be owned that this choice was justified by the result. His Grace appears to have profited by past experience, and in the arduous task which was now assigned him to have shown no lack of sagacity and skill. With him went as Secretary of State the Earl of Mar, a young nobleman of ready

talents but versatile politics, recently connected with
the Tory if not the Jacobite party. "Many of them,"
says Lockhart of Carnwath, "esteemed him an honest
man and well inclined to the Royal family"—that is,
to the exiled House.⁵ How fatally for himself that
attachment was manifested nine years afterwards my
readers need scarcely be reminded. He had been one
of the Commissioners for Scotland at the Cockpit conferences, and distinguished himself by his active and
useful support of the Government scheme.

The Session was opened as usual by the reading
of a Royal Letter, in which the Queen earnestly pressed
the proposal for an Union, which she said "will secure
your religion, liberty and property, and remove the
animosities among yourselves." For the moment however these animosities were only the more inflamed.
Eagerly and promptly did the divers parties array themselves for battle. The Government had secured the
powerful aid of that well-organised section which was
called the Flying Squadron. They had also on their
side by no means all but a large part of those who
were interested in the progress of trade and manufacture, and who had the sagacity to foresee how greatly
these would be promoted by a thorough incorporation
with England. Opposed to them there was in the first
place the compact phalanx of the Jacobites, or as they
termed themselves the Cavaliers. There were also many
men with no kind of leaning to the Exiled Family but
jealous in their national pride, and deeply impressed
with the persuasion that the honor and independence
of their country were now at stake. As the foremost

⁵ Lockhart Papers, vol. I. p. 114.

of this class may be named Fletcher of Saltoun and Lord Belhaven.

But the strangest alliance that the friends of the Stuarts formed at this time was with those whom so long as they held the power they had mercilessly persecuted—with whom in the evil days of Charles the Second their favourite arguments had been the boot and thumbscrew—I mean the so-called "hill-folk," the followers of Richard Cameron. These men viewed with horror any closer union with a country which was like England embued with the abominable sin of Prelacy. Sooner than admit such an idea they were ready to make common cause with their ancient persecutors.

But it was not the Cameronians only. The Earl of Marchmont writing at this juncture to Lord Somers complains of the Ministers of the Kirk, "whereof" he declares "by far the greater part being young men of little experience and warm zeal are too easily imposed upon." Thus in some cases at least they gave ready access to the jealousies that were industriously instilled into them; and of these jealousies the Earl of Marchmont further writes: "Truly, my Lord, they have no foundation save one, that is the reckoning and judging the Protestants in England of all degrees and ranks to be void of not only all conscience and honor but of humanity itself." [6]—We may conclude however from other authorities, that in fact only a small minority of these Kirk Ministers took part with the opposition.

In the Highlands the common people at this period busied themselves little with State affairs. In the Low-

[6] Letter dated Edinburgh, Nov. 9, 1706, and printed in the Marchmont Papers, vol. III. p. 303.

lands so far as can be traced they had at the outset no ill feeling to an Union. But every passion was now appealed to, and every prejudice inflamed by a host of pamphlets which the Jacobites put forth. To the Jacobites indeed it seemed a question of life and death. The settlement by law of the Succession in the Hanover line would preclude all uncertainty at the demise of the Crown, and leave no scope for the heir whom they designed.

Directed from a central Junta there now came up Addresses from divers counties and towns praying the Parliament not to pass the Union. These Addresses, though they make a good show in their enumeration, appear to have lacked weight in their signatures. Certain it is that the dominant party paid them no regard. "They will serve to make kites," so speaking in Parliament said the Duke of Argyle.

Edinburgh however was of course the place where the opponents of the measure could make the largest play. There the Union would no doubt entail upon the shop-keepers some loss of custom; upon the burgesses some loss of dignity. There it was natural that some ferment should arise. A crowd had been wont to gather in the High Street in the afternoons, since the meeting of the Parliament, to do honor to the Duke of Hamilton as chief of the Anti-Unionist Peers. It was their habit to escort the sedan-chair of His Grace back to his apartments in Holyrood. On the 23rd of October, as it chanced, there was a larger crowd than usual though consisting chiefly of apprentices and boys. It chanced also that they were disappointed of their Duke who had gone to visit another Peer. Upon this, as the next best pastime in their power, they went to assail the house of a former Lord Provost, a man of the opposite side. The tumult was of the slightest kind and quelled with the utmost ease by a party of soldiers from the Castle, but it was magnified into some importance by the exaggerations of party writers.

By that time the Parliament had already sat three weeks. It had been employed in some preliminary skirmishes on the Minutes of the late Commission—the object being for each party to try its strength and determine its future course. But now the promoters of the measure deemed it right to bring its general principle to a decisive issue. Shall there be an Union on any possible terms?—such was the question raised by a vote to be taken on the 4th of November upon the first Article, with the understanding (in their own words), "that if the other articles of the Union be not adjusted by the Parliament, then the agreeing to and approving of the first shall be of no effect." There ensued a great debate well worthy the solemn occasion. Seton of Pitmedden, one of the Commission, spoke a well-reasoned essay in support of the measure. Against it the Duke of Hamilton delivered a spirited harangue. We may conclude that Argyle and Mar and many others would not be wanting. But beyond all doubt the palm of oratory was borne off by Lord Belhaven. That nobleman then fifty years of age[7] was of Revolution principles, and had commanded a troop of horse for King William at the battle of Killiecrankie. Bluff and burly of aspect—looking like a butcher as his adversaries said—and with little or no experience of

---

[7] Mr. Burton (Hist. of Scotland, vol. 1. p. 450) describes him at the time of his speech as "the young Lord Belhaven." But Douglas's very accurate Peerage of Scotland gives the exact date of his birth as July 8, 1656.

public speaking—he rose undauntedly to the height of this great argument. He was sustained by an inward and impelling sense of right, by the consciousness that he was pursuing no selfish object nor underhand intrigue, by the conviction however unfounded that his country was now on the brink of dishonor and of ruin. His speech against the whole scheme of Union, carefully elaborated, was among the most striking and successful that the record of Parliament displays.

It is worthy of note that this speech while intended to produce, and in fact producing, a strong popular effect, abounds with refined and classical allusions which do not seem well adapted to the lower classes. Its gloomy prophecies however are within the reach of all. With these the orator sets out. He has thirteen paragraphs, each worked out with artistic skill, to show how the divers ranks and classes in Scotland would suffer from an Union if it passed; and each commencing "I think I see." Of these paragraphs here follow (with one exception) the four last.

"I think I see the honest industrious tradesman loaded with new taxes and impositions, disappointed of the equivalents, drinking water in the place of ale, eating his saltless pottage, petitioning for encouragement to his manufactories and answered by counter-petitions.—I think I see the laborious ploughman with his corn spoiling upon his hands for want of sale, cursing the day of his birth, dreading the expense of his burial, and uncertain whether to marry or do worse. —I think I see the incurable difficulties of the landed men, fettered under the golden chain of equivalents, their pretty daughters petitioning for want of husbands,

CHAP. VIII.
1706.

and their sons for want of employments.—But above all, my Lord, I think I see our ancient mother Caledonia like Cæsar sitting in the midst of our Senate, ruefully looking round about her, covering herself with her Royal garment, attending the fatal blow and breathing out her last with a ET TU QUOQUE MI FILI!"

In another part of his speech Lord Belhaven exclaims: "We may bruise this Hydra of division, and crush this cockatrice's egg. Our neighbours in England are not yet fitted for any such thing. They are not under the afflicting hand of Providence as we are. Their circumstances are great and glorious; their Treaties are prudently managed both abroad and at home; their Generals brave and valorous, their armies successful and victorious, their trophies and laurels memorable and surprising . . . . and above all, these vast riches, the sinews of war, and without which all the glorious success had proved abortive. . . . It is quite otherwise with us, my Lord. We are an obscure poor people though formerly of better account; removed to a remote corner of the world, without name and without alliances, our posts mean and precarious. . . . What hinders us then, my Lord, to lay aside our divisions, to unite cordially and heartily together in our present circumstances, when our all is at stake? Hannibal, my Lord, is at our gates; Hannibal is come within our gates; Hannibal is come the length of this Table; he is at the foot of this Throne; he will demolish this Throne if we take no notice; he will seize upon these Regalia; he will take them as our SPOLIA OPIMA; and whip us out of this House never to return again. For the love of God then, my Lord; for the safety and welfare of our ancient kingdom, whose sad circumstances I hope we shall convert into prosperity and happiness!"

To this noble piece of declamation there was no counter-argument at the time attempted. Only after a pause the veteran Marchmont rose up and said amidst laughter and cheering: "My Lord, I have heard a long speech and a very terrible one, but I think a short answer will suffice and it may be given in these words: 'Behold he dreamed; but lo! when he awoke, he found it was a dream.'"

The division that ensued, like most other divisions in our Parliamentary annals, seemed to be scarcely at all affected by the preceding eloquence. There were 116 votes in favor of the Article and 83 against it. Hence we see that the Flying Squadron, of which the force is given by one of its chiefs as 24,[a] held at the outset the fate of the measure in its hands.

But although the speech of Lord Belhaven might not convince nor even charm his audience it was far otherwise with his readers. The speech was immediately printed and reprinted in thousands of copies. It flew from mouth to mouth and from hand to hand. Scarce any broad-sheet that did not reproduce some passages. Chiming in as it did with many noble sentiments and also with some narrow prejudices, it made a lasting impression upon the Scottish people; and is to be ranked as one main cause of the unpopularity into which shortly afterwards the Act of Union fell.

Up to this time the opponents of the Union had prevailed upon one point only which the Ministerial party did not care to risk the displeasure of the Kirk

---

[a] Earl of Marchmont to Lord Somers, Nov. 9, 1706.

by gainsaying. This was the appointment of a solemn fast in expiation of the sins of the land. The day of fasting and humiliation was held accordingly on Thursday the 7th of November; and among the sermons then delivered were some which upbraided the chosen people for lukewarmness. This was especially the case at Glasgow the stronghold of the Cameronians. One zealous preacher closed his discourse with the words. "Wherefore up and be valiant for the city of our God." The drum was beat in the back-streets that very afternoon. Next day it grew to a riot, when the mob assailed and broke open the Provost's house, while the Provost himself, as we are told, with infinite prudence "retired for a while out of town, not knowing what the issue of these things might be."[9] The rioters were however satisfied with compelling signatures to an Address against the Union. On the morrow they quietly dispersed and the Provost who had fled to Edinburgh came home again.

Timidity in high places produced the usual fruits. Within a few days there was a renewal of the riot, this time fiercer than the last. The Provost on this occasion hid himself in a bed, which seems to have been by far the fittest place for him; and then he fled to Edinburgh for the second time. For some time the rabble were masters of the streets. They challenged every man they met with the question: "Are you for the Union?" and no man durst avow it but at

---

[9] De Foe's History of the Union, part III. p. 61. The author goes on to praise this Provost, Mr. Aird, most highly as "an honest, sober, discreet gentleman, who was exceedingly beloved." He might have completed the character by a line from Dryden:

"And ever, save in time of need, at hand."

great peril. Nevertheless the outrages committed were extremely few, and not a drop of blood was shed.

In a few other places also there were some attempts at disturbance, but far slighter than at Glasgow and by no means such as to imply as yet any general aversion to the pending measure. Even in the accounts of Glasgow there is reason to suspect some exaggeration. Both parties had a motive for it: the Tories to enhance the popularity of their opposition; the Whigs to excuse the pusillanimity of their magistrates.

In the meantime the Commission of the General Assembly of the Church which was sitting at Edinburgh sent in petitions to the Parliament, praying that there should be some further safeguards for "the true Protestant Religion as by law established," and also representing "the increase of Popery, profanity and other irregularities." It was thereupon resolved that instead of leaving the Presbyterian Church wholly untouched by the Act of Union, and of course secured by the preceding Acts of Parliament, there should be new legislation of the most stringent kind to declare its permanency. There was introduced and carried through what was termed the Act of Security, with a stipulation that it should be repeated as part of any Act adopting the treaty of Union both in Scotland and in England. It provided that the Presbyterian Church government as then by law established should be for ever unalterable, and be the only government of the Church within the kingdom of Scotland. Still further to secure this object an oath in accordance with it was required from the Sovereign, not as in England at the Coronation but at his or her accession to the Throne;

and there was also a test of conformity imposed on the Professors of the Scottish Universities and the teachers at the Scottish schools.

It was rather to the surprise of the zealous Presbyterians when they found this Act of Security even in its most stringent clauses readily supported by the Jacobites. The motives of the last named party are not hard to fathom. They foresaw that to establish for evermore the Presbyterian form in Scotland, and to declare it at the same time "the true Protestant Religion," would give great offence to all English High-Churchmen, and might incline them to resist the measure as a whole.

Besides the Act of Security, the Scottish Parliament was at this time busy with the Articles of Union discussed one by one. Considering the principle of the measure as affirmed by the great division taken on the first, the leading politicians next applied themselves to matters of detail. During the whole remainder of this year, they were keenly debating small points of excise and finance. They succeeded in gaining several advantages for Scotland beyond those of the Government scheme. Thus for instance they carried an addition to the sixth article with the view of extending the bounties on divers kinds of grain to the case also of oats which had been passed by as of small account in England. We must remember that the common Scottish use of this their national food had in past times drawn upon them many an ungenerous and unseemly taunt from their richer neighbours. So late as 1755 even so great a mind as Dr. Johnson's could stoop to this silly prejudice. It is well known that in the first edition of his Dictionary there was a description as follows appended to the article OATS: "A grain which in England is generally given to horses, but in Scotland supports the people."

It might be said however that at this juncture the English statesmen were less intent on Legislative than on Ministerial changes. The great question of Lord Sunderland's appointment was now brought to a decisive issue. Godolphin had for a long time pressed it, and subsequently Marlborough also. They were moved by the increased necessity of securing Whig support. But Anne had been resolute against it. Besides some unfavourable rumours that had reached her as to the young Earl's impetuosity of temper, she remembered with no unnatural bitterness the treachery of his father to hers. The Duchess of Marlborough had sought during many months to overcome these scruples. There is still extant the ample and curious correspondence on this subject between her and the Queen.

It would seem from this correspondence and from the accounts of her conduct and demeanour about this time, as if elated by the long possession of favor, she had gradually lost the arts by which that favor was acquired. She forgot the respect that was due to her Royal mistress. She gave the rein more and more to her imperious temper and her railing tongue. No wonder then if Anne, though tenacious of ancient friendships, felt her affection for the Duchess cool. No wonder if in this sharp controversy the foundation was laid for that entire estrangement which shortly afterwards ensued.

On this occasion however the return from the Continent of Marlborough who added his personal en-

CHAP. VIII.
1706.

treaties, and a renewed threat of resignation from Godolphin, wrought the desired effect. The Queen though with the utmost reluctance consented to the appointment of Sunderland in the place of Hedges. The new Secretary of State was announced on the 3rd of December; the very day that Parliament met. This Session so long deferred was opened by the Queen herself. Then on the surface at least there appeared great unanimity. The expressions in the Royal Speech on the projected Union were warmly re-echoed. The supplies required for the public service were rapidly passed. There was a general assent to Votes of Thanks to the Duke of Marlborough for his splendid victory at Ramillies; and to a Bill by which, on the failure of a son, his Dukedom and domain were settled on his daughters in succession and their issue male. There were also on account of these successes two triumphal processions before the close of the year; the one when the standards and colours taken in the battle were set up as trophies in Guildhall; the other when on the day appointed for a General Thanksgiving the Queen attended by the great officers of State and by both Houses of Parliament went in person to St. Paul's.

In the course of this December there were also divers promotions and creations in the peerage—all or nearly all in favor of the Whigs. Three Earls—Kent, Lindsey, and Kingston—were raised to Marquesses. The Lord Treasurer was made an Earl, as were also Lord Wharton, Lord Poulett, and Lord Cholmondeley. A peerage with the rank of a Baron was granted to the Lord Keeper and to Sir Thomas Pelham.

The plain tendency of all these favors was, as may be supposed, far from pleasing to the Tories. They were further chafed at the tidings which came to them from Edinburgh, that the Government had yielded the clauses providing for the perpetuity of the Presbyterian Church. No sooner then did Parliament meet after the Christmas holidays than their ire broke forth. On the 14th of January after solemn notice the Earl of Nottingham brought forward this last subject in the House of Lords. "Since," he said, "the Parliament of Scotland has thought fit to secure the Presbyterian Church Government in that kingdom, it becomes the wisdom of the Parliament of England to provide betimes against the dangers with which our Church by law established is threatened in case the Union be accomplished. And therefore I move that the proceedings in Scotland shall be laid before us."

In the debate which followed Nottingham was supported by the other Opposition chiefs—Rochester and Buckingham—while Godolphin argued that the matter was not yet ripe for them to discuss. The leaders of the Whigs—Somers, Halifax, and Wharton—spoke in the same sense; and the independent Peers showed so little favor to the motion that Nottingham was induced to withdraw it.

In the Commons the High Tory resentment found another issue. St. John as Secretary at War produced an Account of some Extraordinary Charges, not provided for in last year's estimates. There were subsidies to the Kings of Portugal and Denmark and to the Duke of Savoy, as also to several of the smaller German Princes; there were services not foreseen arising from the Spanish campaign; and the whole sum fell little short of one million sterling. It was moved that these sums had been advanced "against the common enemy and for the safety and honor of the nation;" but the Tories interposed with the previous question and divided the House, when the Government prevailed by 254 votes against 105.¹

On one point only there was still entire unanimity. All parties joined in the readiness to grant on behalf of the nation some further recompense to the hero of Ramillies. An Act of Parliament was passed on the recommendation of the Queen to settle a pension of 5,000*l.* a year out of the revenue of the Post Office, upon the Dukes of Marlborough in due descent for ever. But on other matters, so sharp had been the altercation between the High Tories and the Ministers, that it seemed to render the breach between them irreparable. The Queen was prevailed on by the last to visit the former with a signal mark of her displeasure. Accordingly the names of Buckingham, Nottingham, and Rochester, with some others, were struck off from the list of the Privy Council.

At Edinburgh meanwhile, the Scottish Parliament going through the Articles of Union had nearly approached the termination of its labours. There was rising by degrees much popular discontent against the measure, which the leaders of the Jacobites observed with joy and reported with exaggeration. They urged in secret letters and messages to Versailles and St. Germain's that no moment could be so opportune for the invasion of the kingdom by a well-appointed French force. To await the result of these representations their great object in the Legislature was delay,

¹ Commons Journals, January 27, 1707. These numbers are wrongly given in the Parliamentary History, vol. vi. p. 551.

but that object being seen through by the other parties was but seldom permitted to prevail.

The crisis at Edinburgh was now at hand. A few days more and the Act of Union would have passed. The Jacobites saw that they must relinquish their hopes of foreign invasion. But there still remained to them the chance of civil war. To clear the way to this there was prepared on the part of the Jacobites and at the Duke of Hamilton's house, it is not certain by whose hand, an able state-paper which is still preserved. It bears the form of a Protest, and sets forth that the members of a legislature are mere temporary administrators of their trust, and not the owners or masters of a people. They are not entitled to bargain away the nation they represent, or make it cease to exist. Therefore they of the minority, entertaining these sentiments, would now secede from the others protesting against what it was designed to do, and in their secession, would consider themselves the centre of a new Scottish Parliament.

The time selected for this manifestation was the debate on the twenty-second Article, which fixed and limited the Scottish share in the Imperial legislature. As such it was most fiercely fought, renewing in divers forms the animosities which had recently raged. It bore within it moreover the germ of religious as well as of political contests, since, in the declaration which it required from the Peers and Commoners to be hereafter chosen, it rigidly adhered to the terms of the English Act of Charles the Second, "by disabling Papists from sitting in either House of Parliament." No more favourable time could be found for the minority to break away.

It was further intended, though perhaps not expressly stipulated, it being assumed as almost a matter of course that the Duke of Hamilton the Premier Peer should be the person to present, or as termed in Scotland "table" the Protest. The leader after performing this office was then to walk out of the House followed by the Opposition in a body. Towards that body the popular risings might henceforth be directed; around it might gather men of the most opposite opinions on all other subjects —Republicans and Royalists, Roman Catholics and Cameronians. Beyond doubt it was a well concerted scheme. Some rumours of it had been allowed to go abroad; and thus on the appointed day the avenues of the Parliament House were thronged with eager crowds, while the members of the Opposition sat ranged on their benches and ready for the move. But at the last moment their chief His Grace of Hamilton failed them. Some among them have imputed his failure to his tortuous machinations; far more probably it was owing only to his timid character. First he sent word that he had a toothache and could not come. Next when he did appear he asked some of his confederates with an innocent air whom they had appointed to table the Protest —since he certainly could not, though ready when tabled to give it his adherence. The other members, confounded by this check and suspecting some treachery behind it, lost all heart and spirit and gave up all thoughts of their scheme.

Of these Articles of Union, twenty-five in all, the twenty-second was the last that presented any difficulties or provoked any trial of numbers. But on several points in this, the contention was long and keen. On the first day six separate Protests were presented by dissentient members; on the next a Protestation against the Protests from the Earl of Marchmont; then again a counter-Protestation against Marchmont's from Lord Balmerino. Among the Amendments moved to this Article, there was one that the Parliament of Great Britain should hold its Session once every third year in Scotland. A very judicious writer of our own day, Mr. Burton, has pointed out that this motion was not prompted by any popular feeling, it being scarcely even mentioned in the histories or pamphlets of the time. It was, he thinks, made only as a matter of form and not at all pressed.[a]

The passing of this twenty-second Article was marked by a tragical incident.—John Dalrymple, Master of Stair, only too well known by that time in the dark deed of 1692, had succeeded his father the first Viscount in 1695 and been created Earl of Stair, greatly to the discredit of the Government, in 1703. As one of the Scottish Commissioners for the Treaty of Union, and afterwards as a Peer in the Scottish Parliament, he had zealously applied himself to forward and promote that measure. Thus on the sitting of the 7th of January in this year, amidst the fierce storm of anger with which the twenty-second Article was assailed, he had spoken in its support with his usual force and fluency, and with far more earnestness than might have been expected from a man of his lax principles and unscrupulous character. But his nerves appear to have been over-wrought by his anxiety and his exertions, and they failed him just as his object was attained. He returned home suffering from illness when the second

---

[a] History of Scotland, vol. 1. p. 482.

paragraph of the Article had been successfully carried, and in the course of the next day he expired. Thus he had the honor which a better man might envy, to die in the service of his country—striving to the last by voice and vote to carry through a measure essential at that period as he knew to its peace and welfare. It requires some such thought to reconcile us, however slightly, to a memory on which such a load of infamy rests—a memory stained so deeply, with the blood of the Macdonalds of Glencoe.[3]

The Articles having passed one by one, there was next introduced the measure which should give validity to all; the Act of Ratification as it was usually called. Upon this Act and on the 16th of January was taken the final division against the Treaty of Union—110 votes to 69. Then the Lord High Commissioner having touched the Act with the Royal Sceptre, it became the law.

But although the Scottish Estates had thus passed the Treaty of Union they continued to sit as a Sovereign Legislature pending the acceptance of that Treaty on the part of England. And they had still some weighty duties to perform. It was by this time understood as the desire of the Government, that the existing Parliament of England should remain as the English portion of the united legislature, and the Scottish Estates now resolved that, should the Queen so determine, then the Representative Peers as well as the Commoners for Scotland should be chosen from their existing Parlia-

---

[3] The character of Lord Stair is traced in full detail though with most favourable colours, in the Complete History of Europe for 1707, p. 519. Lockhart of Carnwath says of him that he had "a peculiar talent of dissimulation, so that he was seldom or never to be taken unawares."

ment. Other questions came up for decision. Should all the Scottish Peers go up to Parliament in their turn by a system of rotation, or should representatives be elected for each Parliament? The latter plan was carried. Then again should the election of these Peers be by ballot or by open voting? After some discussion open voting was preferred, and proxies of the absent were allowed.

In distributing the forty-five Seats reserved for the Scottish Commons, the Estates resolved to give thirty to the counties and fifteen to the towns. Edinburgh as the capital was to enjoy the privilege of electing its representative singly; but the other boroughs, sixty-six in all, were joined together in groups, to the number of fourteen. Each borough was to elect a Commissioner; and the Commissioners of each group were to meet as a Committee and elect the member of Parliament. Papists were expressly shut out both from the representation and the franchise.

There was also great jealousy of the Scottish Peers. It was proposed to enact that they should not be capable of being elected to the House of Commons, for any shire or borough in Scotland; and so far the exclusion seems only natural and reasonable; but it was also desired, in accordance with what was then the law of Scotland, to apply the same exclusion to their eldest sons. To limit in this manner the absolute choice of the electors, where no privilege of actual peerage intervenes, seems not easily defensible; nevertheless, at the time, the principle was not nearly so much debated as the form. When the exclusion was moved in plain terms, and in so many words, it was keenly resisted and could not be carried, but a large majority affirmed it in an indirect shape, agreeing to limit the representative right to "such as are now capable by the laws of this kingdom to elect or be elected." It is worthy of note that this legal incapacity of Peers' eldest sons to sit for any Scottish shire or borough continued down to the Reform Act of 1832.

It was also the business of the Estates before they separated to apportion the Equivalent which was left at their disposal. More than half of the whole, namely the sum of 232,000*l.*, went to the stockholders of the Darien Company for capital and interest. Another portion was employed in paying off certain outstanding claims; another, to the just dissatisfaction of the public, in remunerating the Commissioners—not only those who had concluded the late Treaty, but those who had attempted it in vain four years ago. Finally the Estates passed an Act for the encouragement of the growth of wool—an Act which, considering the total revolution in the ideas of trade, may seem to us at present not only inexpedient but grotesque. It provided that woollen shrouds should be always used, and none of any other fabric be allowed in burials.

In London, the Queen went to the House of Lords on the 28th of January; and in a Royal Speech announced the passing of the Treaty of Union by the Parliament of Scotland. She expressed her hope that the House of Commons would be willing to provide for the Equivalent which had been stipulated, and to the Legislature at large she commended the opportunity "of putting the last hand to a happy Union of the two kingdoms." The formal documents were on the same day presented to both Houses.

Politicians—or at least the most far-sighted among

them—observed with some anxiety that as yet the measure was by no means clear of the rocks and shoals. The amendments in the Articles carried by the Scottish Parliament had been neither few nor inconsiderable. But were the English Parliament now to follow its example—were controversies in consequence to arise between the Legislatures of both kingdoms—the national prejudices would ere long grow embittered and irreconcileable, and the enemies of the Union would infallibly prevail. Godolphin and his colleagues clearly saw the danger and wisely determined to save the principle by sacrificing some of the details. As Secretary Johnstone could report to his friends in Scotland, "the Whigs are resolved to pass the Union here without making any alteration at all, to shun the necessity of a new Session of yours." Members of the House of Commons might indeed complain. "Why," said some of them to Johnstone, "why are we not to make alterations as well as you?" [4]

There was however one addition which the more zealous Churchmen were resolved to make. As the Scots had embodied with the measure an Act for the security of their Presbyterian settlement, so should the English for the security of their Episcopal Church. A Bill for this object, framed on the model of the precedent at Edinburgh, and seeking in like manner to provide for the perpetuity of the Establishment, was brought in by the Archbishop of Canterbury; and the Queen and Prince were present at the discussion upon the Second Reading. Then the High Church party, even yet not fully satisfied, endeavoured to render the Bill more stringent by inserting in it an Act of Charles

[4] Letter dated January 4, 1707, and published in the Jerviswood Correspondence.

the Second against Popish Recusants; but the proposal was rejected by a large majority; and the Bill passed in its original form.

On the Union itself, the debates in both the Houses might have seemed to us of considerable interest had they been preserved. But in the scanty records of that period, scarce more than two or three sentences are commonly assigned to any speech that is mentioned, and in general, even the names of the speakers are left out. The reports seem to be given at length only in the few cases when the orator himself sent his oratory to the press; and this was not the practice of the best. Thus the vain and pushing Lord Haversham, held as of little account by his contemporaries, took care to publish his speech against the Union, while we find no trace of the weightier remarks that may have fallen from Somers or Cowper in the one House, from St. John or Harley in the other.

In the Commons there was great dispatch in passing the Articles of Union. The discussion upon them in Committee was commenced upon the 4th of February, and all amendments being strongly discountenanced by the Government, the Report in their favor was presented to the House upon the 8th. Members of the Opposition complained of what they called the posthaste speed with which a measure of so much importance was being hurried through, but they were overruled. Still some of them continued to cry out "post-haste! post-haste!"—"Not so," said Sir Thomas Lyttleton; "we do not ride post-haste but a good easy trot, and for my part so long as the weather is fair, the roads good, and the horses in heart, I am of opinion that we ought to jog on, and not take up till it is night."

Of the opponents to this measure in the Commons, Sir John Packington was perhaps the most bitter. He did not indeed bring forward any arguments, for of these he had seldom much store; but he dealt largely, as was his wont, in random accusations. The Union, he said, had been carried through the Scottish Parliament by the bribery and corruption of its members, and he left it to the House to consider, whether men guilty of such conduct were fit to sit amongst them. These expressions, as might be expected, provoked great resentment and some sharp replies. It is strange, I may observe in passing, that Sir John Packington should ever have been supposed by later writers the original of Sir Roger de Coverley. Both were staunch High Tories and both lived in Worcestershire, but there the resemblance ends. Sir John was throughout his life a most rancorous partisan, delighting in coarse invectives and spiteful attacks, and bearing no trace of the gentle and kind-hearted Knight whom Addison has so well portrayed.

When in due course the Articles came before the Lords, it was moved and carried that Bishop Burnet should take the Chair in the Committee—a well-merited compliment to an early and earnest promoter of the Union. There was another Prelate who seems to have done it good service during the debate, as we may judge from an able speech made public by himself. This was Doctor William Talbot then Bishop of Oxford, subsequently by translation of Salisbury; and at last of Durham. He was father of Lord Chancellor Talbot, and ancestor of the Earl Talbot who in our own times, on the failure of his elder line, inherited the honors of Shrewsbury.

CHAP.
VIII.
1707.

The Bishop in his speech especially applied himself to allay the unfavourable impression produced by the Act of the Scottish Parliament which declared—and asked our assent in declaring—the Presbyterian form to be the true Protestant religion. "I would suppose" he said "that we were treating with the French King; those that should act for him would be sure to give him the stile of the Most Christian King; but would it follow that if we ratified the treaty agreed on, in some part whereof he was to be so stiled, that we assented to this proposition that Louis the Fourteenth is Most Christian?" Perhaps the Bishop might have found a like illustration even nearer home. How long did the Sovereigns of England continue to bear in their Acts and Treaties the title of King of France after they had lost every shred and particle of its dominion, and Foreign Powers had ceased to attach the least importance to that empty name.

In the debates which now ensued the lead against the Union was taken by the usual High Tory chiefs, Nottingham, Rochester, and Buckingham. There were other speakers besides. Thus Lord North and Grey took great exception to the inadequate amount of Land Tax which the Scots were to pay, considering the number of representatives which was assigned them. He was answered by Lord Halifax, whose speech seems worthy of note, when we recollect that it needed a century and a quarter before the idea of Parliamentary Reform which it implied could ripen into legislation. "In fixing taxation" said Halifax "the number of representatives is no rule to go by. Why, even now in England, there is the county of Cornwall that pays not near so much towards the Land Tax as the county of Gloucester, and yet sends up to Parliament almost five times as many members."

The arguments urged against the measure had at least in some cases the merit of novelty. Thus Nottingham objected to the name of Great Britain, which he said was such an innovation in the monarchy as must totally subvert all the laws of England; and he moved that the opinion of the Judges should be taken on this point. Strange to say other Peers also whose names are not recorded expressed their concurrence in this view. They prevailed so far that it was agreed to consult the Judges. Being asked their opinion one by one, the Judges unanimously declared that the Act of Union would not in any respect alter or impair the Constitution of the realm, nor put an end to any laws except such as it expressly repealed.

The Articles having passed, there now remained only as in Scotland the Act of Ratification. It was expected by the Opposition that they should be able to renew the contest Article by Article; and the Ministers foresaw with dismay not only the chance of interminable delays, but the risk that the Houses might be tempted on second thoughts to disallow on some points the alterations made in Scotland, and to bring back the Treaty nearer its original form. An expedient to secure both despatch and uniformity was devised by the ready wit of Sir Simon Harcourt, one of the moderate Tories who with Harley and St. John still adhered to the Ministry, and who in the gradations of office had recently become from Solicitor, Attorney General. By his advice, there was placed in the preamble a recital of the Articles as they were passed in Scotland, together with the Acts made in both Parliaments for the security of their several Churches; and in conclusion there came one enacting clause ratifying all. "This" adds Bishop Burnet "put into great difficulties those who had resolved to object the several Articles; for they could not object to the recital, it being merely matter of fact; and they had not strength enough to oppose the general enacting Clause." In this form, the Bill passed rapidly through its stages in the Commons, before its opponents had well recovered their surprise. They reserved themselves for a final effort on the Third Reading in the House of Lords, when Lord North and Grey moved as a Rider: "Provided always that nothing in this ratification contained shall be construed to extend to an approbation or acknowledgment of the truth of the Presbyterian way of worship, or allowing the religion of the Church of Scotland to be what it is stiled the true Protestant religion." But this Rider was rejected by 55 Peers against 19; and thus had the great measure passed the Parliament of both the kingdoms, and needed only the Queen's assent to make it law.

The Queen determined—or rather the Queen's advisers determined for her—to give that Assent with all the solemnity becoming the occasion. On the 6th of March Her Majesty, seated on her throne in the House of Peers, and having in due form summoned the Commons to the Bar, addressed her Parliament in some well-weighed and high-spirited words: "My Lords and Gentlemen," she said, "I consider this Union as a matter of the greatest importance to the wealth, strength, and safety of the whole island; and at the same time a work of so much difficulty and nicety in its own nature that till now all attempts which have been made towards it, in the course of above a hundred years, have proved ineffectual; and therefore, I make no doubt but it will be remembered and spoke of hereafter, to the honor of those who have been instrumental in bringing it to such a happy conclusion.—I desire and expect from all my subjects of both nations, that from henceforth they act with all possible respect and kindness to one another, that so it may appear to all the world, they have hearts disposed to become one people. This will be a great pleasure to me."

In this manner, and over a thousand obstacles was this great and healing measure carried through. Looking back to it at this distance of time, and as part of that posterity to which Queen Anne appealed, we should not find perhaps a single man in either country to deny the blessings it has brought on both. It has given to the Scottish people that equal share so long desired, in our colonies and trade. It has opened to them new avenues of wealth, and by that wider scope, has quickened and stirred their industry. It has raised a petty huckster town upon the Clyde into a mart of manufacture, numbering its inhabitants no more by hundreds but by hundreds of thousands, sending forth its cargoes into the furthest regions, and inferior at this time in importance to no other mart in the world. Along the Firth of Forth, it has changed the crops of oats with which the Scots were formerly taunted into a wheat-culture so perfect in its farming skill as greatly to surpass the harvest, of some more genial climes. In the Highlands, it has driven sterility and famine and their fit companion ignorance, step by step before it. It has clothed with growing forests the slopes of the

CHAP. VIII.
1707.

bare hills; it has reclaimed to luxuriant pasture the bleak moor-lands. Nor has this mighty progress been attended with any decline of that national spirit for which Scotland is renowned. There are still and in the same numbers, Scotsmen who, like their own Sir Walter, guard every ruin, cherish every memory, hold sacred every record, of their by-gone ages; Scotsmen with as much pride in their country as their fathers, and with still more reason to be proud.

The benefits of the Union to England though perhaps less apparent were not less real. It freed us from a rival Legislature always in jealousy of ours; and far less eager to promote the common good than to prove its independence. It enabled Chatham, when he desired to recruit our armies in his gigantic struggles against France, when he sought as he said for valour, to find it in the mountains of the north, and to call to our service the descendants of the Celtic race. It has brought us to regard the Highlanders not as aliens as King William's Government thought them, or as one at least among their tribes is described, in that letter which King William signed, "a sect of thieves to extirpate," but, on the contrary, as most gallant fellow countrymen, whose loyalty to the Reigning Family is no longer doubtful but devoted, and to whose hardihood and daring through many a toilsome campaign, through many a hardfought battle, we have been and we are much beholden. Thus also in the arts of peace, there is no department in which the sagacity and enterprise of Scotsmen have not most signally availed us. In the council chamber or the counting house, in the discoveries of science, or in the master-pieces of imagination, the Scots have most ably aided in our common

QUEEN ANNE.   319

objects and enhanced our joint renown. All honor
then to the statesmen by whom this great work was
planned and accomplished. All honor to that good
Queen who had not indeed the genius to take part in
any schemes of statesmanship, but who honestly loved
her people, and who gave to this Act her cordial good
wishes, and her constant favor.

CHAP. VIII.
1707.

There remains on the other hand to be noticed, the painful accusation that the Union was carried through by bribery—direct payments in money for their votes to divers members, Peers and Commoners, of the Scottish Parliament. This charge does not rest merely on vague words of vituperation like Sir John Packington's, uttered in the heat of debate. Lockhart of Carnwath in his Memoirs made public a list of thirty-two names with a certain sum of money assigned to each, the entire sum amounting to upwards of 20,000*l.* This actual sum was advanced in an irregular manner and without the customary forms, from the Treasury of England, as was proved before the Commission of Public Accounts in 1712, of which Commission Lockhart was himself a member, and he infers that the money was designed and applied for the purchase of votes. On his authority, the accusation passed current in that age with the Jacobite writers, and in later years with those who felt more or less sympathy with them. But admitting his list to be entirely authentic, the inference which he drew from it is shown by subsequent research to be entirely erroneous.[s]

In the first place then, it appears that of the entire sum more than one moiety, namely 12,325*l.*, was ad-

[s] See especially the full details and the able arguments of Mr. Burton in his History of Scotland, vol. I. p. 484-494.

vanced to the Lord High Commissioner "for equipage and daily allowance;" and there was evidence before the Commission of 1712 that, after the Union, this money was repaid, although the point is not perfectly clear. We have therefore to account only for the remaining balance of 7,675*l.*—certainly no vast treasure with which to bribe an entire Parliament! It is admitted by Lockhart that the entire sum was asked for and conceded as a loan to pay arrears of salary. Have we then any grounds for doubting that such was the real fact? Arrears of salary in those days were constantly recurring and not obtained without much solicitation, as is shown especially by the diplomatic correspondence in this and the preceding reign. It was natural also that at the Union, upon the winding up of the separate accounts for Scotland, it should be thought proper to adjust all such outstanding claims.

This general view appears to be fully confirmed by an examination of particular instances, so far as that examination after a lapse of time is practicable. Next to the Lord Commissioner's, the highest payment in the list is of 1,104*l.* to the Earl of Marchmont. Now it so happens that there is extant a private letter of that time from Marchmont to Argyle, bitterly complaining that the arrears of his salary when Chancellor of Scotland remain unpaid. The editor of his papers has supplied some further calculations, and made clear that the payment to him which Lockhart cites was no gratuity, but simply the discharge of a legal obligation.[6]

---

[6] Compare in the Marchmont Papers the letter at vol. III. p. 294, with the "Defence" by Sir George Rose, at vol. I. p. CXI. See also a note in Somerville's Queen Anne, p. 232.

In like manner there appears among the last "Acts of the Scots Parliament" a petition from Major Cunninghame of Ecket, praying that he may be repaid the sum of 275 *l.* expended out of his own means, in the subsistence of officers under his command. Cunninghame is on the list of Lockhart as having received 100 *l.*—clearly either a final composition of his claim or a first payment on account of it.

As against the charge of bribery, however, there still remains to be stated the strongest argument of all. Some of those who figure upon Lockhart's list as in receipt of public money did not vote for the Union but on the contrary against it. Such was the case with Major Cunninghame of Ecket whom I have just named, and also with the Duke of Athol to whom was paid 1,000 *l.*

It is true however that of the remaining items there are some of small amount that do not seem to be connected with arrears. These however were in no sense presents for votes; they were only in the modern phrase payments for the conveyance of voters. Thus we find Mr. William Hunter, the Minister of Banff, write as follows to Carstairs: "My Lord Banff upon declaring himself Protestant has a mind to go south and take his place in Parliament; and withal because his circumstances require it his Lordship requires your kind influence for his encouragement that he may undertake his journey. My Lord's circumstances are but low."[7] When therefore in the subsequent list we find Lord Banff's name credited for 11 *l.* 2 *s.* we may safely conclude that this was the sum allowed his Lordship for his travelling expenses.

[7] Carstairs Papers, p. 736.

We are therefore, I conceive, entitled to cast aside as an utter calumny the allegation of bribery against the members of the Scottish Parliament. Exactly the same allegation, and on just as flimsy grounds, was, on occasion of the Irish Union a century afterwards, brought against the members of the Irish Parliament.

There is yet another charge. It is said that even admitting the members of the Scottish Parliament to have acted from pure and honourable motives they acted against the wishes and the feelings of the Scottish people. But of this there is no proof at all. There is no reason to doubt that in this as in most other cases it was the majority of the people that prevailed over the minority. So far only may be granted, that in Scotland the minority against the Union was warm and eager, while the majority accepted it with some degree of hesitation, and on a balance of advantages, as a sacrifice of certain objects for the attainment of other and greater.

It seems also to be true that the aversion to the Treaty of Union, which was not at the outset considerable, much increased while the measure was passing, and increased further still after it had passed. By degrees and only by degrees that aversion again receded. Many years elapsed ere it was finally consigned to the book-shelves of the antiquaries, and ceased to have the least effect in common life. It was supported so long, not by any experience of the predicted evils, but mainly perhaps, from an overweening confidence of national superiority. This point in the character of Scotsmen during the last century has been touched with great humour by one of themselves—Dr. Moore, the able and accomplished author of Zeluco.

That work, first published in 1789, brings before us the conversation of two servingmen in Italy, both of Scottish birth; but the former long absent as a follower of the Stuarts; and the latter just arrived. The one long absent will by no means allow that any good has been gained by the Union. "On the contrary" he says "the Union has done a great deal of harm to the Lowlands of Scotland."—"How so?"—"By spreading luxury and effeminacy of manners. Why I was assured by Serjeant Lewis Mac Neil, a Highland gentleman in the Prussian service, that the Lowlanders in some parts of Scotland are now very little better than so many English!"—"Oh fie!" cries the other Scotsman in alarm, "things are not come to that pass as yet; your friend the Serjeant assuredly exaggerates."[8]

The 1st of May had been fixed as the date on which the Act of Union should commence, and a Proclamation from the Queen had directed that day to be observed as one of Public Thanksgiving for the happy conclusion of the Treaty. During the interval the two kingdoms were still distinct; and both the Legislatures might continue to sit if required by the public service. Meanwhile Addresses of Congratulation to the Queen came in from various parts of England. But it was noticed that the University of Oxford, taking great offence at the formal recognition of the Presbyterian Church, remained resolutely silent. Nor yet was there any Address from any place in the northern kingdom.

[8] *Zeluco*, vol. II. p. 156. Some readers may recollect the observation of Æneas Sylvius, when visiting Scotland three centuries and a half before: "nihil Scotos audire libentius quam vituperationes Anglorum." See the *Concilia Scotiæ* as edited with admirable skill by the late Mr. Joseph Robertson (Preface, vol. I p. xcii.).

The Scottish Estates had by this time brought their labours to a close. On the 25th of March they were addressed by the High Commissioner in a short concluding speech, and they were then adjourned never to meet again. His Grace soon afterwards set out for England that he might place their Act in Her Majesty's hands. On his entry into London he was received with great state and magnificence by a solemn procession of the High Officers of the realm in coaches and on horseback; and in this manner he was escorted to St. James's.

But even yet the difficulties of the Union were not entirely surmounted. In the concluding weeks of the English Parliament which was still in Session, there arose, in connection with the pending measure, a serious entanglement between the two Houses. The question came from some frauds apprehended in Scotland where advantage was sought to be taken of the remaining interval before the 1st of May. Then the duties on import would be common to both countries, but meanwhile it would be possible to land prohibited goods in Scotland, ready to be transshipped to England as soon as the Union took effect. A Bill was presented to the House of Commons to prevent the expected abuse; and on the third reading, Harley proposed and carried a Clause rendering the measure more complete by a retroactive effect. When however the Bill with this addition reached the House of Lords, they were apprised that the Scots in general would regard it as an infringement of the Articles of Union, and thus forewarned the Peers were firm against it.

Under these circumstances the Queen by the advice of her Ministers prorogued the Parliament for a week

—from the 8th to the 14th of April—so as to afford to both parties leisure for reconsideration. The Whigs were full of wrath against Harley. Already in the preceding autumn they had striven to obtain his dismissal conjointly with Sunderland's appointment, but they could not prevail with Marlborough and Godolphin who might still be ranked as Tories. Now all their accusations were renewed. "I believe"—so writes Sunderland to Marlborough who had already reached the Hague, "you will be surprised at this short Prorogation. It is entirely occasioned by him who is the author of all the tricks played here."[9]

The Prorogation had not however the healing effect that was designed. The Commons were stirred by an earnest petition from the fair traders praying to be secured from the Scottish contrabands, and thus incited they passed for the second time their Bill, which the Lords as before were unwilling to let through. It only remained therefore for the Queen to end the dispute by closing the Session, as was done with a short speech from Her Majesty on the 24th of the same month.

It was provided in the Act of Union that "there be one Great Seal for the United Kingdom, which shall be different from the Great Seal now used for either kingdom." As the 1st of May drew near a new Great Seal was accordingly prepared, and Lord Cowper to whom it was committed was promoted to the post of Chancellor—the first Lord Chancellor of Great Britain. In like manner Prince George and Lord Godolphin received new patents, and took the oaths respectively,

[9] Coxe's Marlborough, vol. III. p. 122 and 149.

CHAP.
VIII.
1707.
as Lord High Admiral and Lord Treasurer of Great Britain, and no longer of England only.

In the Scottish Peerage both the Marquess of Montrose and the Earl of Roxburgh were raised to the rank of Dukes. Their patents bearing date the 24th and 25th of April were the last effort of an expiring Prerogative, since the right of the Crown to make either creations or promotions of Scots Peers was held to cease on the day of Union. It is strange that this cessation was not stated by any express clause to that effect, and was only taken as implied by the words of the twenty-second article, that "of the Peers of Scotland at the time of the Union sixteen shall be the number to sit and vote in the House of Lords."

END OF VOL. I.

PRINTING OFFICE OF THE PUBLISHER.

CONTENTS.

PART I. — *Ancient and modern ITALY compared.*

The following Poem is thrown into the form of a Poetical Vision. Its scene, the ruins of ancient Rome. The Goddess of Liberty, who is supposed to speak through the whole, appears, characterized as British Liberty. Gives a view of ancient Italy, and particularly of Republican Rome, in all her magnificence and glory. This contrasted by modern Italy; its valleys, mountains, culture, cities, people: the difference appearing strongest in the capital city Rome. The ruins of the great works of Liberty more magnificent than the borrowed pomp of Oppression; and from them revived Sculpture, Painting, and Architecture. The old Romans apostrophized, with regard to the several melancholy changes in Italy: Horace, Tully, and Virgil, with regard to their Tibur, Tusculum, and Naples. That once finest and most ornamented part of Italy, all along the coast of Baiæ, how changed. This desolation of Italy applied to Britain. Address to the Goddess of Liberty, that she would deduce from the first ages, her chief establishments, the description of which constitute the subject of the following parts of this Poem. She assents, and commands what she says to be sung in Britain: whose happiness, arising from freedom, and a limited monarchy, she marks. An immediate Vision attends, and paints her words. Invocation.

PART II. — *GREECE.*

Liberty traced from the pastoral ages, and the first uniting of neighbouring families into civil government. The several establishments of Liberty, in Egypt, Persia, Phœnicia, Palestine, slightly touched upon, down to her great establishment in Greece. Geographical description of Greece. Sparta and Athens, the two principal states of Greece, described. Influence of Liberty over all the Grecian states; with regard to their Government, their Politeness, their Virtues, their Arts, and Sciences. The vast superiority it gave them, in point of force and bravery, over the Persians, exemplified by the action of Thermopylæ, the battle of Marathon, and the retreat of the Ten Thousand. Its full exertion, and most beautiful effects in Athens. Liberty the source of free Philosophy. The various schools which took their rise from Socrates. Enumeration of Fine Arts: Eloquence, Poetry, Music, Sculpture, Painting, and Architecture; the effects of Liberty in Greece, and brought to their utmost perfection there. Transition to the modern state of Greece. Why Liberty declined, and was at last entirely lost among the Greeks. Concluding Reflection.

PART III. — *ROME.*

As this part contains a description of the establishment of Liberty in Rome, it begins with a view of the Grecian Colonies settled in the southern parts of Italy, which with Sicily constituted the Great Greece of the Ancients. With these colonies, the Spirit of Liberty, and of Republics, spreads over Italy. Transition to Pythagoras and his philosophy, which he taught through those free states and cities. Amidst the many small Republics in Italy, Rome the destined seat of Liberty. Her establishment there dated from the expulsion of the Tarquins. How differing from that in Greece. Reference to a view of the Roman Republic given in the First Part of this Poem; to mark its Rise and Fall the peculiar purport of this. During its first ages, the greatest force of Liberty and Virtue exerted. The source whence derived. The Heroic Virtues of the Romans. Enumeration of these Virtues. Thence their security at home; their glory, success, and empire abroad. Bounds of the Roman empire geographically described. The states of Greece restored to Liberty, by Titus Quintus Flaminius, the highest instance of public generosity and beneficence. The loss of Liberty in Rome. Its causes, progress, and completion in the death of Brutus. Rome under the emperors. From Rome the Goddess of Liberty goes among the Northern Nations; where, by infusing into them her Spirit and general principles, she lays the groundwork of her future establishments; sends them in vengeance on the Roman Empire, now totally enslaved; and then, with Arts and Sciences in her train, quits earth during the dark ages. The celestial regions, to which Liberty retired, not proper to be opened to the view of mortals.

PART IV. — *BRITAIN.*

DIFFERENCE betwixt the Ancients and Moderns slightly touched upon. Description of the dark ages. The Goddess of Liberty, who during these is supposed to have left earth, returns, attended with Arts and Science. She first descends on Italy. Sculpture, Painting, and Architecture fix at Rome, to revive their several arts by the great models of antiquity there, which many barbarous invasions had not been able to destroy. The revival of these arts marked out. That sometimes arts may flourish for a while under despotic governments, though never the natural and genuine production of them. Learning begins to dawn. The Muse and Science attend Liberty, who in her progress towards Great Britain raises several free states and cities. These enumerated. Author's exclamation of joy, upon seeing the British seas and coasts rise in the vision, which painted whatever the Goddess of Liberty said. She resumes her narration. The Genius of the Deep appears, and addressing Liberty, associates Great Britain into his dominion. Liberty received and congratulated by Britannia, and the Native Genii or Virtues of the Island. These described. Animated by the presence of Liberty, they begin their operations. Their beneficent influence contrasted with the works and delusions of opposing Demons. Concludes with an abstract of the English history, marking the several Advances of Liberty, down to her complete establishment at the Revolution.

PART V. — *The PROSPECT.*

THE author addresses the Goddess of Liberty, marking the happiness and grandeur of Great Britain, as arising from her influence. She resumes her discourse, and points out the chief Virtues which are necessary to maintain her establishment there. Recommends, as its last ornament and finishing, Sciences, Fine Arts, and Public works. The encouragement of these urged from the example of France, though under a despotic government. The whole concludes with a prospect of future times, given by the Goddess of Liberty; this described by the author, as it passes in vision before him.

LIBERTY.

PART I.

ANCIENT AND MODERN ITALY COMPARED.

O my lamented Talbot! while with thee
The Muse gay roved the glad Hesperian round,
And drew the inspiring breath of ancient arts;
Ah! little thought she her returning verse
Should sing our darling subject to thy Shade.
And does the mystic veil, from mortal beam,
Involve those eyes where every virtue smiled,
And all thy Father's candid spirit shone?
The light of reason, pure, without a cloud;
Full of the generous heart, the mild regard;
Honour disdaining blemish, cordial faith,
And limpid truth, that looks the very soul.
But to the death of mighty nations turn
My strain; be there absorpt the private tear

   Musing, I lay; warm from the sacred walks,
Where at each step imagination burns:
While scatter'd wide around, awful, and hoar,
Lies, a vast monument, once glorious Rome,
The tomb of empire! Ruins! that efface
Whate'er, of finish'd, modern pomp can boast.

   Snatch'd by these wonders to that world where thought
Unfetter'd ranges, Fancy's magic hand
Led me anew o'er all the solemn scene,
Still in the mind's pure eye more solemn dress'd:
When straight, methought, the fair majestic Power
Of Liberty appear'd. Not, as of old,

Extended in her hand the cap, and rod,
Whose slave-enlarging touch gave double life:
But her bright temples bound with British oak,
And naval honours nodded on her brow.
Sublime of port: loose o'er her shoulder flow'd
Her sea-green robe, with constellations gay.
An island-goddess now; and her high care
The Queen of Isles, the mistress of the main.
My heart beat filial transport at the sight;
And, as she moved to speak, the awaken'd Muse
Listen'd intense. Awhile she look'd around,
With mournful eye the well known ruins mark'd,
And then, her sighs repressing, thus began:
  'Mine are these wonders, all thou seest is mine;
But ah, how changed! the falling poor remains
Of what exalted once the Ausonian shore.
Look back through time: and, rising from the gloom,
Mark the dread scene, that paints whate'er I say.
  'The great Republic see! that glow'd, sublime,
With the mix'd freedom of a thousand states;
Raised on the thrones of kings her curule chair,
And by her fasces awed the subject world.
See busy millions quickening all the land,
With cities throng'd, and teeming culture high:
For Nature then smiled on her free-born sons,
And pour'd the plenty that belongs to men.
Behold, the country cheering, villas rise,
In lively prospect; by the secret lapse
Of brooks now lost, and streams renown'd in song;
In Umbria's closing vales, or on the brow
Of her brown hills that breathe the scented gale:
On Baiæ's viny coast; where peaceful seas,
Fann'd by kind zephyrs, ever kiss the shore;
And suns unclouded shine, through purest air:
Or in the spacious neighbourhood of Rome;
Far shining upward to the Sabine hills,
To Anio's roar, and Tibur's olive shade;

To where Preneste lifts her airy brow;
Or downward spreading to the sunny shore,
Where Alba breathes the freshness of the main.

'See distant mountains leave their valleys dry,
And o'er the proud Arcade their tribute pour,
To lave imperial Rome. For ages laid,
Deep, massy, firm, diverging every way,
With tombs of heroes sacred, see her roads;
By various nations trod, and suppliant kings;
With legions flaming, or with triumph gay.

'Full in the centre of these wondrous works,
The pride of earth! Rome in her glory see!
Behold her demigods, in senate met;
All head to counsel, and all heart to act:
The commonweal inspiring every tongue
With fervent eloquence, unbribed, and bold;
Ere tame Corruption taught the servile herd
To rank obedient to a master's voice.

'Her Forum see, warm, popular, and loud,
In trembling wonder hush'd, when the two Sires,
As they the private father greatly quell'd,
Stood up the public fathers of the state.
See Justice judging there, in human shape.
Hark! how with freedom's voice it thunders high,
Or in soft murmurs sinks to Tully's tongue.

'Her tribes, her census, see; her generous troops,
Whose pay was glory, and their best reward
Free for their country and for me to die;
Ere mercenary murder grew a trade.

'Mark, as the purple triumph waves along,
The highest pomp and lowest fall of life.

'Her festive games, the school of heroes, see;
Her Circus, ardent with contending youth:
Her streets, her temples, palaces, and baths,
Full of fair forms, of Beauty's eldest born,
And of a people cast in virtue's mould:
While sculpture lives around, and Asian hills

Lend their best stores to heave the pillar'd dome:
All that to Roman strength the softer touch
Of Grecian art can join. But language fails
To paint this sun, this centre of mankind;
Where every virtue, glory, treasure, art,
Attracted strong, in heighten'd lustre met.
    'Need I the contrast mark? unjoyous view!
A land in all, in government and arts,
In virtue, genius, earth, and heaven, reversed,
Who but these far famed ruins to behold,
Proofs of a people, whose heroic aims
Soar'd far above the little selfish sphere
Of doubting modern life; who but inflamed
With classic zeal, these consecrated scenes
Of men and deeds to trace; unhappy land,
Would trust thy wilds, and cities loose of sway?
    'Are these the vales, that once, exulting states
In their warm bosom fed? The mountains these,
On whose high-blooming sides my sons, of old,
I bred to glory? These dejected towns,
Where, mean and sordid, life can scarce subsist,
The scenes of ancient opulence and pomp?
    'Come! by whatever sacred name disguised,
Oppression, come! and in thy works rejoice!
See nature's richest plains to putrid fens
Turn'd by thy fury. From their cheerful bounds,
See razed the enlivening village, farm, and seat.
First, rural toil, by thy rapacious hand
Robb'd of his poor reward, resign'd the plough;
And now he dares not turn the noxious glebe.
'T is thine entire. The lonely swain himself,
Who loves at large along the grassy downs
His flocks to pasture, thy drear champaign flies.
Far as the sickening eye can sweep around,
'T is all one desert, desolate, and grey,
Grazed by the sullen buffalo alone;
And where the rank uncultivated growth

Of rotting ages taints the passing gale.
Beneath the baleful blast the city pines,
Or sinks enfeebled, or infected burns.
Beneath it mourns the solitary road,
Roll'd in rude mazes o'er the abandon'd waste;
While ancient ways, ingulf'd, are seen no more.
　'Such thy dire plains, thou self-destroyer! foe
To humankind! thy mountains too, profuse,
Where savage nature blooms, seem their sad plaint
To raise against thy desolating rod.
There on the breezy brow, where thriving states
And famous cities, once, to the pleased sun,
Far other scenes of rising culture spread,
Pale shine thy ragged towns. Neglected round,
Each harvest pines; the livid, lean produce
Of heartless labour: while thy hated joys,
Not proper pleasure, lift the lazy hand.
Better to sink in sloth the woes of life,
Than wake their rage with unavailing toil.
Hence, drooping art almost to nature leaves
The rude unguided year. Thin wave the gifts
Of yellow Ceres, thin the radiant blush
Of orchard reddens in the warmest ray.
To weedy wildness run, no rural wealth
(Such as dictators fed) the garden pours.
Crude the wild olive flows, and foul the vine;
Nor juice Cæcubian, nor Falernian, more,
Streams life and joy, save in the Muse's bowl.
Unseconded by art, the spinning race
Draw the bright thread in vain, and idly toil.
In vain, forlorn in wilds, the citron blows;
And flowering plants perfume the desert gale.
Through the vile thorn the tender myrtle twines:
Inglorious droops the laurel, dead to song,
And long a stranger to the hero's brow.
　'Nor half thy triumph this: cast, from brute fields,
Into the haunts of men thy ruthless eye.

There buxom Plenty never turns her horn;
The grace and virtue of exterior life,
No clean convenience reigns; e'en sleep itself,
Least delicate of powers, reluctant, there,
Lays on the bed impure his heavy head.
Thy horrid walk! dead, empty, unadorn'd,
See streets whose echoes never know the voice
Of cheerful hurry, commerce many-tongued,
And art mechanic at his various task,
Fervent, employ'd. Mark the desponding race,
Of occupation void, as void of hope;
Hope, the glad ray, glanced from Eternal Good,
That life enlivens, and exalts its powers,
With views of fortune — madness all to them!
By thee relentless seized their better joys,
To the soft aid of cordial airs they fly,
Breathing a kind oblivion o'er their woes.
And love and music melt their souls away.
From feeble Justice, see how rash Revenge,
Trembling, the balance snatches; and the sword,
Fearful himself, to venal ruffians gives.
See where God's altar, nursing murder, stands,
With the red touch of dark assassins stain'd.
    'But chief let Rome, the mighty city! speak
The full-exerted genius of thy reign.
Behold her rise amid the lifeless waste,
Expiring nature all corrupted round;
While the lone Tiber, through the desert plain,
Winds his waste stores, and sullen sweeps along.
Patch'd from my fragments, in unsolid pomp,
Mark how the temple glares; and artful dress'd,
Amusive, draws the superstitious train.
Mark how the palace lifts a lying front,
Concealing often, in magnific jail,
Proud want; a deep unanimated gloom!
And oft adjoining to the drear abode
Of misery, whose melancholy walls

Seem its voracious grandeur to reproach.
Within the city bounds the desert see.
See the rank vine o'er subterranean roofs,
Indecent, spread; beneath whose fretted gold
It once, exulting, flow'd. The people mark,
Matchless, while fired by me; to public good
Inexorably firm, just, generous, brave,
Afraid of nothing but unworthy life,
Elate with glory, an heroic soul
Known to the vulgar breast: behold them now
A thin despairing number, all-subdued,
The slaves of slaves, by superstition fool'd,
By vice unmann'd and a licentious rule;
In guile ingenious, and in murder brave.
Such in one land, beneath the same fair clime,
Thy sons, Oppression, are; and such were mine.
  'E'en with thy labour'd Pomp, for whose vain show
Deluded thousands starve; all age-begrimed,
Torn, robb'd, and scatter'd in unnumber'd sacks,
And by the tempest of two thousand years
Continual shaken, let my ruins vie.
These roads that yet the Roman hand assert,
Beyond the weak repair of modern toil;
These fractured arches, that the chiding stream
No more delighted hear; these rich remains
Of marbles now unknown, where shines imbibed
Each parent ray; these massy columns, hew'd
From Afric's farthest shore; one granite all;
These obelisks high-towering to the sky,
Mysterious mark'd with dark Egyptian lore;
These endless wonders that this sacred way
Illumine still, and consecrate to fame;
These fountains, vases, urns, and statues, charged
With the fine stores of art-completing Greece.
Mine is, besides, thy every later boast:
Thy Buonarotis, thy Palladios mine;

And mine the fair designs, which Raphael's soul
O'er the live canvass, emanating, breathed.
  'What would you say, ye conquerors of earth!
Ye Romans! could you raise the laurel'd head;
Could you the country see, by seas of blood,
And the dread toil of ages, won so dear;
Your pride, your triumph, your supreme delight!
For whose defence oft, in the doubtful hour,
You rush'd with rapture down the gulf of fate,
Of death ambitious! till by awful deeds,
Virtues, and courage, that amaze mankind,
The queen of nations rose; possess'd of all
Which nature, art, and glory could bestow:
What would you say, deep in the last abyss
Of slavery, vice, and unambitious want,
Thus to behold her sunk? your crowded plains,
Void of their cities; unadorn'd your hills;
Ungraced your lakes; your ports to ships unknown;
Your lawless floods, and your abandon'd streams;
These could you know; these could you love again
Thy Tiber, Horace, could it now inspire,
Content, poetic ease, and rural joy,
Soon bursting into song: while through the groves
Of headlong Anio, dashing to the vale,
In many a tortured stream, you mused along?
Yon wild retreat, where superstition dreams,
Could, Tully, you your Tusculum believe?
And could you deem yon naked hills, that form,
Famed in old song, the ship-forsaken bay,
Your Formian shore? Once the delight of earth,
Where art and nature, ever smiling, join'd
On the gay land to lavish all their stores.
How changed, how vacant, Virgil, wide around,
Would now your Naples seem? disaster'd less
By Black Vesuvius thundering o'er the coast
His midnight earthquakes, and his mining fires,

Than by despotic rage: that inward gnaws
A native foe; a foreign, tears without.
First from your flatter'd Cæsars this began:
Till, doom'd to tyrants an eternal prey,
Thin peopled spreads, at last, the syren plain,
That the dire soul of Hannibal disarm'd;
And wrapt in weeds the shore of Venus lies.
There Baiæ sees no more the joyous throng;
Her bank all beaming with the pride of Rome:
No generous vines now bask along the hills,
Where sport the breezes of the Tyrrhene main:
With baths and temples mix'd, no villas rise;
Nor, art-sustain'd amid reluctant waves,
Draw the cool murmurs of the breathing deep:
No spreading ports their sacred arms extend:
No mighty moles the big intrusive storm,
From the calm station, roll resounding back.
An almost total desolation sits,
A dreary stillness, saddening o'er the coast;
Where, when soft suns and tepid winters rose,
Rejoicing crowds inhaled the balm of peace;
Where citied hill to hill reflected blaze;
And, where, with Ceres Bacchus wont to hold
A genial strife. Her youthful form, robust,
E'en Nature yields; by fire, and earthquake rent:
Whole stately cities in the dark abrupt
Swallow'd at once, or vile in rubbish laid,
A nest for serpents; from the red abyss
New hills, explosive, thrown; the Lucrine lake
A reedy pool: and all to Cuma's point,
The sea recovering his usurp'd domain,
And pour'd triumphant o'er the buried dome.
  'Hence, Britain, learn; my best establish'd, last,
And more than Greece, or Rome, my steady reign;
The land where, King and People equal bound
By guardian laws, my fullest blessings flow;
And where my jealous unsubmitting soul,

The dread of tyrants! burns in every breast:
Learn hence, if such the miserable fate
Of an heroic race, the masters once
Of humankind; what, when deprived of ME,
How grievous must be thine? in spite of climes,
Whose sun-enliven'd ether wakes the soul
To higher powers; in spite of happy soils,
That, but by labour's slightest aid impell'd,
With treasures teem to thy cold clime unknown;
If there desponding fail the common arts,
And sustenance of life: could life itself,
Far less a thoughtless tyrant's hollow pomp,
Subsist with thee? against depressing skies,
Join'd to full spread oppression's cloudy brow,
How could thy spirits hold? where vigour find,
Forced fruits to tear from their unnative soil?
Or, storing every harvest in thy ports,
To plough the dreadful all producing wave?'
   Here paused the Goddess. By the cause assured,
In trembling accents thus I moved my prayer:
'Oh first, and most benevolent of powers!
Come from eternal splendours, here on earth,
Against despotic pride, and rage, and lust,
To shield mankind; to raise them to assert
The native rights and honour of their race:
Teach me, thy lowest subject, but in zeal
Yielding to none, the progress of thy reign,
And with a strain from THEE enrich the Muse.
As thee alone she serves, her patron, THOU,
And great inspirer be! then will she joy,
Though narrow life her lot, and private shade:
And when her venal voice she barters vile,
Or to thy open or thy secret foes;
May ne'er those sacred raptures touch her more,
By slavish hearts unfelt! and may her song
Sink in oblivion with the nameless crew!

Vermin of state! to thy o'erflowing light
That owe their being, yet betray thy cause.'
  Then, condescending kind, the heavenly Power
Return'd: — 'What here, suggested by the scene,
I slight unfold, record and sing at home,
In that bless'd isle, where (so we spirits move)
With one quick effort of my will I am.
There Truth, unlicensed, walks; and dares accost
E'en kings themselves, the monarchs of the free!
Fix'd on my rock, there, an indulgent race
O'er Britons wield the sceptre of their choice:
And there, to finish what his sires began,
A Prince behold! for me who burns sincere,
E'en with a subject's zeal. He my great work
Will parent-like sustain; and added give
The touch the Graces and the Muses owe.
For Britain's glory swells his panting breast;
And ancient arts he emulous revolves:
His pride to let the smiling heart abroad,
Through clouds of pomp, that but conceal the man;
To please his pleasure; bounty his delight;
And all the soul of Titus dwells in him.'
  Hail, glorious theme! but how, alas! shall verse,
From the crude stores of mortal language drawn,
How faint and tedious, sing, what, piercing deep,
The Goddess flash'd at once upon my soul.
For, clear precision all, the tongue of gods
Is harmony itself; to every ear
Familiar known, like light to every eye.
Meantime disclosing ages, as she spoke,
In long succession pour'd their empires forth;
Scene after scene, the human drama spread;
And still the embodied picture rose to sight.
  Oh thou! to whom the Muses owe their flame;
Who bidd'st, beneath the pole, Parnassus rise,
And Hippocrene flow; with thy bold ease,
The striking force, the lightning of thy thought,
And thy strong phrase, that rolls profound and clear;
Oh, gracious Goddess! reinspire my song;
While I, to nobler than poetic fame
Aspiring, thy commands to Britons bear.

LIBERTY.

PART II. — GREECE.

Thus spoke the Goddess of the fearless eye;
And at her voice, renew'd, the Vision rose:
'First, in the dawn of time, with eastern swains,
In woods, and tents, and cottages, I lived;
While on from plain to plain they led their flocks,
In search of clearer spring, and fresher field.
These, as increasing families disclosed
The tender state, I taught an equal sway.
Few were offences, properties, and laws.
Beneath the rural portal, palm-o'erspread,
The father senate met. There Justice dealt
With reason then and equity the same,
Free as the common air, her prompt decree;
Nor yet had stain'd her sword with subjects' blood.
The simpler arts were all their simple wants
Had urged to light. But instant, these supplied,
Another set of fonder wants arose,
And other arts with them of finer aim;
Till, from refining want to want impell'd,
The mind by thinking push'd her latent powers,
And life began to glow, and arts to shine.
'At first, on brutes alone the rustic war
Launch'd the rude spear; swift, as he glared along,
On the grim lion, or the robber wolf.
For then young sportive life was void of toil,
Demanding little, and with little pleased:
But when to manhood grown, and endless joys,
Led on by equal toils, the bosom fired;
Lewd lazy rapine broke primeval peace,

And, hid in caves and idle forests drear,
From the lone pilgrim, and the wandering swain,
Seized what he durst not earn. Then brother's blood
First, horrid, smoked on the polluted skies.
Awful in justice, then the burning youth,
Led by their temper'd sires, on lawless men,
The last worst monsters of the shaggy wood,
Turn'd the keen arrow, and the sharpen'd spear.
Then war grew glorious. Heroes then arose;
Who, scorning coward self, for others lived,
Toil'd for their ease and for their safety bled.
West, with the living day, to Greece I came:
Earth smiled beneath my beam: the Muse before
Sonorous flew, that low till then in woods
Had tuned the reed, and sigh'd the shepherd's pain;
But now, to sing heroic deeds, she swell'd
A nobler note, and bade the banquet burn.
 'For Greece my sons of Egypt I forsook;
A boastful race, that in the vain abyss
Of fabling ages loved to lose their source,
And with their river traced it from the skies.
While there my laws alone despotic reign'd,
And king, as well as people, proud obey'd;
I taught them science, virtue, wisdom, arts;
By poets, sages, legislators sought;
The school of polish'd life, and human kind.
But when mysterious Superstition came,
And, with her Civil Sister leagued, involved
In studied darkness the desponding mind;
Then Tyrant Power the righteous scourge unloosed:
For yielded reason speaks the soul a slave.
Instead of useful works, like nature's, great,
Enormous, cruel wonders crush'd the land;
And round a tyrant's tomb, who none deserved,
For one vile carcase perish'd countless lives.
Then the great Dragon couch'd amid his floods,
Swell'd his fierce heart; and cried, "This flood is mine,

'T is I that bid it flow." But, undeceived,
His frenzy soon the proud blasphemer felt;
Felt that, without my fertilizing power,
Suns lost their force, and Niles o'erflow'd in vain.
Nought could retard me: nor the frugal state
Of rising Persia, sober in extreme,
Beyond the pitch of man, and thence reversed
Into luxurious waste: nor yet the ports
Of old Phœnicia; first for letters famed,
That paint the voice, and silent speak to sight;
Of arts prime source, and guardian! by fair stars,
First tempted out into the lonely deep;
To whom I first disclosed mechanic arts,
The winds to conquer, to subdue the waves,
With all the peaceful power of ruling trade;
Earnest of Britain. Nor by these retain'd;
Nor by the neighbouring land, whose palmy shore
The silver Jordan laves. Before me lay
The promised Land of Arts, and urged my flight.
   'Hail, Nature's utmost boast! unrival'd Greece!
My fairest reign! where every power benign
Conspired to blow the flower of human kind,
And lavish'd all that genius can inspire.
Clear sunny climates, by the breezy main,
Iönian or Ægean, temper'd kind:
Light, airy soils: a country rich, and gay;
Broke into hills with balmy odours crown'd,
And, bright with purple harvest, joyous vales;
Mountains, and streams, where verse spontaneous flow'd;
Whence deem'd by wondering men the seat of gods,
And still the mountains and the streams of song.
All that boon Nature could luxuriant pour
Of high materials, and my restless Arts
Frame into finish'd life. How many states,
And clustering towns, and monuments of fame,
And scenes of glorious deeds, in little bounds?
From the rough tract of bending mountains, beat

By Adria's here, there by Ægean waves;
To where the deep adorning Cyclade Isles
In shining prospect rise, and on the shore
Of farthest Crete resounds the Libyan main.
  'O'er all two rival cities rear'd the brow,
And balanced all. Spread on Eurotas' bank,
Amid a circle of soft rising hills,
The patient Sparta one: the sober, hard,
And man-subduing city; which no shape
Of pain could conquer, nor of pleasure charm.
Lycurgus there built, on the solid base
Of equal life, so well a temper'd state;
Where mix'd each government, in such just poise;
Each power so checking, and supporting each;
That firm for ages, and unmoved, it stood,
The fort of Greece! without one giddy hour,
One shock of faction, or of party rage.
For, drain'd the springs of wealth, Corruption there
Lay wither'd at the root. Thrice happy land!
Had not neglected art, with weedy vice
Confounded, sunk. But if Athenian arts
Loved not the soil; yet there the calm abode
Of wisdom, virtue, philosophic ease,
Of manly sense and wit, in frugal phrase
Confined, and press'd into Laconic force.
There too, by rooting thence still treacherous self,
The Public and the Private grew the same.
The children of the nursing Public all,
And at its table fed; for that they toil'd,
For that they lived entire, and even for that
The tender mother urged her son to die.
  'Of softer genius, but not less intent
To seize the palm of empire, Athens rose.
Where, with bright marbles big and future pomp,
Hymettus spread, amid the scented sky,
Ilis thymy treasures to the labouring bee,
And to botanic hand the stores of health;

Thomson.

Wrapt in a soul-attenuating clime,
Between Ilissus and Cephissus glow'd
This hive of science, shedding sweets divine,
Of active arts, and animated arms.
There, passionate for me, an easy moved,
A quick, refined, a delicate, humane,
Enlighten'd people reign'd. Oft on the brink
Of ruin, hurried by the charm of speech,
Inforcing hasty counsel immature,
Totter'd the rash Democracy; unpoised,
And by the rage devour'd, that ever tears
A populace unequal; part too rich,
And part or fierce with want or abject grown.
Solon at last, their mild restorer, rose:
Allay'd the tempest; to the calm of laws
Reduced the settling whole; and, with the weight
Which the two senates to the public lent,
As with an anchor fix'd the driving state.

'Nor was my forming care to these confined.
For emulation through the whole I pour'd,
Noble contention! who should most excel
In government well poised, adjusted best
To public weal: in countries cultured high:
In ornamented towns, where order reigns,
Free social life, and polish'd manners fair:
In exercise, and arms; arms only drawn
For common Greece, to quell the Persian pride:
In moral science, and in graceful arts.
Hence, as for glory peacefully they strove,
The prize grew greater, and the prize of all.
By contest brighten'd, hence the radiant youth,
Pour'd every beam; by generous pride inflamed,
Felt every ardour burn: their great reward
The verdant wreath, which sounding Pisa gave.

'Hence flourish'd Greece; and hence a race of men,
As gods by conscious future times adored:
In whom each virtue wore a smiling air,

Each science shed o'er life a friendly light,
Each art was nature. Spartan valour hence,
At the famed pass, firm as an isthmus stood;
And the whole eastern ocean, waving far
As eye could dart its vision, nobly check'd.
While in extended battle, at the field
Of Marathon, my keen Athenians drove
Before their ardent band a host of slaves.

'Hence thro' the continent ten thousand Greeks
Urged a retreat, whose glory not the prime
Of victories can reach. Deserts, in vain,
Opposed their course; and hostile lands, unknown;
And deep rapacious floods, dire bank'd with death;
And mountains, in whose jaws destruction grinn'd;
Hunger, and toil; Armenian snows, and storms;
And circling myriads still of barbarous foes.
Greece in their view, and glory yet untouch'd,
Their steady column pierced the scattering herds,
Which a whole empire pour'd; and held its way
Triumphant, by the sage-exalted Chief
Fired and sustain'd. Oh light and force of mind,
Almost almighty in severe extremes!
The sea at last from Colchian mountains seen,
Kind-hearted transport round their captains threw
The soldiers' fond embrace; o'erflow'd their eyes
With tender floods, and loosed the general voice
To cries resounding loud — "The sea! The sea!"

'In Attic bounds hence heroes, sages, wits,
Shone thick as stars, the milky way of Greece!
And though gay wit, and pleasing grace was theirs,
All the soft modes of elegance, and ease;
Yet was not courage less, the patient touch
Of toiling art, and disquisition deep.

'My spirit pours a vigour through the soul,
The unfetter'd thought with energy inspires,
Invincible in arts, in the bright field
Of nobler Science, as in that of Arms.

Athenians thus not less intrepid burst
The bonds of tyrant darkness, than they spurn'd
The Persian chains: while through the city full
Of mirthful quarrel and of witty war,
Incessant struggled taste refining taste,
And friendly free discussion, calling forth
From the fair jewel Truth its latent ray.
O'er all shone out the great Athenian Sage,
And Father of Philosophy: the sun,
From whose white blaze emerged, each various sect
Took various tints, but with diminish'd beam.
Tutor of Athens! he, in every street,
Dealt priceless treasure: goodness his delight,
Wisdom his wealth, and glory his reward.
Deep through the human heart, with playful art,
His simple question stole; as into truth,
And serious deeds, he smiled the laughing race;
Taught moral happy life, whate'er can bless,
Or grace mankind; and what he taught he was.
Compounded high, though plain, his doctrine broke
In different Schools: the bold poetic phrase
Of figured Plato; Xenophon's pure strain,
Like the clear brook that steals along the vale;
Dissecting truth, the Stagyrite's keen eye;
The exalted Stoic pride; the Cynic sneer;
The slow-consenting Academic doubt;
And, joining bliss to virtue, the glad ease
Of Epicurus, seldom understood.
They, ever candid, reason still opposed
To reason; and, since virtue was their aim,
Each by sure practice tried to prove his way
The best. Then stood untouch'd the solid base
Of Liberty, the liberty of mind:
For systems yet, and soul-enslaving creeds,
Slept with the monsters of succeeding times.
From priestly darkness sprung the enlightening arts
Of fire, and sword, and rage, and horrid names.

'O Greece! thou sapient nurse of finer arts!
Which to bright science blooming fancy bore;
Be this thy praise, that thou, and thou alone,
In these hast led the way, in these excell'd,
Crown'd with the laurel of assenting Time.
  'In thy full language, speaking mighty things;
Like a clear torrent close, or else diffused
A broad majestic stream, and rolling on
Through all the winding harmony of sound
In it the power of Eloquence, at large,
Breathed the persuasive or pathetic soul;
Still'd by degrees the democratic storm,
Or bade it threatening rise, and tyrants shook,
Flush'd at the head of their victorious troops.
In it the Muse, her fury never quench'd,
By mean unyielding phrase, or jarring sound,
Her unconfined divinity display'd;
And, still harmonious, form'd it to her will:
Or soft depress'd it to the shepherd's moan,
Or raised it swelling to the tongue of gods.
  'Heroic song was thine; the Fountain Bard,
Whence each poetic stream derives its course.
Thine the dread moral scene, thy chief delight!
Where idle Fancy durst not mix her voice,
When Reason spoke august; the fervent heart
Or plain'd, or storm'd; and in the impassioned man,
Concealing art with art, the poet sunk.
This potent school of manners, but when left
To loose neglect, a land-corrupting plague,
Was not unworthy deem'd of public care,
And boundless cost, by thee; whose every son,
E'en last mechanic, the true taste possess'd
Of what had flavour to the nourish'd soul.
  'The sweet enforcer of the poet's strain,
Thine was the meaning music of the heart.
Not the vain trill, that, void of passion, runs
In giddy mazes, tickling idle ears;

But that deep-searching voice, and artful hand,
To which respondent shakes the varied soul.
 'Thy fair ideas, thy delightful forms,
By Love imagined, by the Graces touch'd,
The boast of well pleased Nature! Sculpture seized,
And bade them ever smile in Parian stone.
Selecting Beauty's choice, and that again
Exalting, blending in a perfect whole,
Thy workmen left e'en Nature's self behind.
From those far different, whose prolific hand
Peoples a nation; they for years on years,
By the cool touches of judicious toil,
Their rapid genius curbing, pour'd it all
Through the live features of one breathing stone.
There, beaming full, it shone; expressing gods:
Jove's awful brow, Apollo's air divine,
The fierce atrocious frown of sinewed Mars,
Or the sly graces of the Cyprian Queen.
Minutely perfect all! Each dimple sunk,
And every muscle swell'd, as nature taught.
In tresses, braided gay, the marble waved;
Flow'd in loose robes, or thin transparent veils;
Sprung into motion; softened into flesh;
Was fired to passion, or refined to soul.
 'Nor less thy pencil, with creative touch,
Shed mimic life, when all thy brightest dames,
Assembled, Zeuxis in his Helen mix'd.
And when Apelles, who peculiar knew
To give a grace that more than mortal smiled,
The soul of beauty! call'd the Queen of Love,
Fresh from the billows, blushing orient charms.
E'en such enchantment then thy pencil pour'd,
That cruel-thoughted War the impatient torch
Dash'd to the ground; and, rather than destroy
The patriot picture, let the city scape.
 'First, elder Sculpture taught her sister art
Correct design; where great ideas shone,

And in the secret trace expression spoke:
Taught her the graceful attitude; the turn,
And beauteous airs of head; the native act,
Or bold, or easy; and, cast free behind,
The swelling mantle's well adjusted flow.
Then the bright Muse, their eldest sister, came;
And bade her follow where she led the way:
Bade earth, and sea, and air, in colours rise;
And copious action on the canvass glow:
Gave her gay Fable; spread Invention's store;
Enlarged her View; taught Composition high,
And just Arrangement, circling round one point,
That starts to sight, binds and commands the whole.
Caught from the heavenly Muse a nobler aim,
And scorning the soft trade of mere delight,
O'er all thy temples, porticos, and schools,
Heroic deeds she traced, and warm display'd
Each moral beauty to the ravish'd eye.
There, as the imagined presence of the god
Aroused the mind, or vacant hours induced
Calm contemplation, or assembled youth
Burn'd in ambitious circle round the sage,
The living lesson stole into the heart,
With more prevailing force than dwells in words.
These rouse to glory; while, to rural life,
The softer canvass oft reposed the soul.
There gaily broke the sun-illumined cloud;
The lessening prospect, and the mountain blue,
Vanish'd in air; the precipice frown'd, dire;
White, down the rock, the rushing torrent dash'd;
The sun shone, trembling, o'er the distant main;
The tempest foam'd, immense; the driving storm
Sadden'd the skies, and, from the doubling gloom,
On the scath'd oak the ragged lightning fell;
In closing shades, and where the current strays,
With Peace, and Love, and innocence around,
Piped the lone shepherd to his feeding flock:

Round happy parents smiled their younger selves;
And friends conversed, by death divided long.
  'To public virtue thus the smiling arts,
Unblemish'd handmaids, served; the Graces they
To dress this fairest Venus. Thus revered,
And placed beyond the reach of sordid care,
The high awarders of immortal fame,
Alone for glory thy great masters strove;
Courted by kings, and by contending states
Assumed the boasted honour of their birth.
  'In Architecture too thy rank supreme!
That art where most magnificent appears
The little builder man; by thee refined,
And, smiling high, to full perfection brought.
Such thy sure rules, that Goths of every age,
Who scorn'd their aid, have only loaded earth
With labour'd heavy monuments of shame.
Not those gay domes that o'er thy splendid shore
Shot, all proportion, up. First unadorn'd,
And nobly plain, the manly Doric rose;
The Ionic then, with decent matron grace,
Her airy pillar heaved; luxuriant last,
The rich Corinthian spread her wanton wreath.
The whole so measured true, so lessen'd off
By fine proportion, that the marble pile,
Form'd to repel the still or stormy waste
Of rolling ages, light as fabrics look'd
That from the magic wand aërial rise.
  'These were the wonders that illumined Greece,
From end to end' — Here interrupting warm,
'Where are they now? (I cried) say, goddess, where?
And what the land, thy darling thus of old?'
'Sunk! (she resumed) deep in the kindred gloom
Of Superstition, and of Slavery, sunk!
No glory now can touch their hearts, benumb'd
By loose dejected sloth and servile fear:
No science pierce the darkness of their minds;

No nobler art the quick ambitious soul
Of imitation in their breast awake.
E'en to supply the needful arts of life,
Mechanic toil denies the hopeless hand.
Scarce any trace remaining, vestige gray,
Or nodding column on the desert shore,
To point where Corinth, or where Athens stood.
A faithless land of violence, and death!
Where commerce parleys, dubious, on the shore;
And his wild impulse curious search restrains,
Afraid to trust the inhospitable clime.
Neglected nature fails; in sordid want
Sunk, and debased, their beauty beams no more.
The sun himself seems, angry, to regard,
Of light unworthy, the degenerate race;
And fires them oft with pestilential rays:
While earth, blue poison steaming on the skies,
Indignant, shakes them from her troubled sides.
But as from man to man, Fate's first decree,
Impartial Death the tide of riches rolls,
So states must die and Liberty go round.
  'Fierce was the stand, ere Virtue, Valour, Arts,
And the soul fired by me (that often, stung
With thoughts of better times and old renown,
From hydra-tyrants tried to clear the land)
Lay quite extinct in Greece, their works effaced
And gross o'er all unfeeling bondage spread.
Sooner I moved my much reluctant flight,
Poised on the doubtful wing: when Greece with Greece
Embroil'd in foul contention fought no more
For common glory, and for common weal:
But false to Freedom, sought to quell the free;
Broke the firm band of Peace, and sacred Love,
That lent the whole irrefragable force;
And, as around the partial trophy blush'd,
Prepared the way for total overthrow.
Then to the Persian power, whose pride they scorn'd,

When Xerxes pour'd his millions o'er the land,
Sparta, by turns, and Athens, vilely sued;
Sued to be venal parricides, to spill
Their country's bravest blood, and on themselves
To turn their matchless mercenary arms.
Peaceful in Susa, then, sat the Great King;
And by the trick of treaties, the still waste
Of sly corruption, and barbaric gold,
Effected what his steel could ne'er perform.
Profuse he gave them the luxurious draught,
Inflaming all the land: unbalanced wide
Their tottering states; their wild assemblies ruled,
As the winds turn at every blast the seas:
And by their listed orators, whose breath
Still with a factious storm infested Greece,
Roused them to civil war, or dash'd them down
To sordid peace — Peace! that, when Sparta shook
Astonish'd Artaxerxes on his throne,
Gave up, fair-spread o'er Asia's sunny shore,
Their kindred cities to perpetual chains.
What could so base, so infamous a thought
In Spartan hearts inspire? Jealous, they saw
Respiring Athens rear again her walls:
And the pale fury fired them, once again
To crush this rival city to the dust.
For now no more the noble social soul
Of Liberty my families combined;
But by short views, and selfish passions, broke,
Dire as when friends are rankled into foes,
They mix'd severe, and waged eternal war:
Nor felt they, furious, their exhausted force;
Nor, with false glory, discord, madness blind,
Saw how the blackening storm from Thracia came.
Long years roll'd on, by many a battle stain'd,
The blush and boast of Fame! where courage, art,
And military glory shone supreme:
But let detesting ages, from the scene

Of Greece self-mangled, turn the sickening eye.
At last, when bleeding from a thousand wounds,
She felt her spirits fail; and in the dust
Her latest heroes, Nicias, Conon, lay,
Agesilaus, and the Theban friends:
The Macedonian vulture mark'd his time,
By the dire scent of Cheronæa lured,
And, fierce descending, seized his hapless prey.

'Thus tame submitted to the victor's yoke
Greece, once the gay, the turbulent, the bold;
For every grace, and muse, and science born;
With arts of War, of Government elate;
To tyrants dreadful, dreadful to the best;
Whom I myself could scarcely rule: and thus
The Persian fetters, that inthrall'd the mind,
Were turn'd to formal and apparent chains.

'Unless Corruption first deject the pride,
And guardian vigour of the free-born soul,
All crude attempts of Violence are vain;
For firm within, and while at heart untouch'd,
Ne'er yet by force was freedom overcome.
But soon as Independence stoops the head,
To Vice enslaved, and vice-created Wants;
Then to some foul corrupting hand, whose waste
These heighten'd wants with fatal bounty feeds:
From man to man the slackening ruin runs,
'Till the whole state unnerved in Slavery sinks.'

LIBERTY.

PART III. — ROME.

Here melting mixed with air the ideal forms
That painted still whate'er the goddess sung.
Then I, impatient. — 'From extinguish'd Greece,
To what new region stream'd the Human Day?'
She softly sighing, as when Zephyr leaves,
Resign'd to Boreas, the declining year,
Resumed. — 'Indignant, those last scenes I fled;
And long ere then, Leucadia's cloudy cliff,
And the Ceraunian hills behind me thrown,
All Latium stood aroused. Ages before,
Great mother of republics! Greece had pour'd,
Swarm after swarm, her ardent youth around.
On Asia, Afric, Sicily, they stoop'd,
But chief on fair Hesperia's winding shore;
Where, from Lacinium to Etrurian vales,
They roll'd increasing colonies along,
And lent materials for my Roman reign.
With them my spirit spread; and numerous states,
And cities rose, on Grecian models formed;
As its parental policy and arts
Each had imbibed. Besides, to each assign'd
A guardian Genius, o'er the public weal,
Kept an unclosing eye; tried to sustain,
Or more sublime, the soul infused by me:
And strong the battle rose, with various wave,
Against the tyrant demons of the land.
Thus they their little wars and triumphs knew;
Their flows of fortune, and receding times,
But almost all below the proud regard

Of story vow'd to Rome, on deeds intent
That Truth beyond the flight of Fable bore.
 'Not so the Samian sage; to him belongs
The brightest witness of recording Fame.
For these free states his native isle forsook,
And a vain tyrant's transitory smile,
He sought Crotona's pure salubrious air;
And thro' Great Greece his gentle wisdom taught;
Wisdom that calm'd for listening years the mind,
Nor ever heard amid the storm of zeal.
His mental eye first launch'd into the deeps
Of boundless ether; where unnumber'd orbs,
Myriads on myriads, through the pathless sky
Unerring roll, and wind their steady way.
There he the full consenting choir beheld;
There first discern'd the secret band of love,
The kind attraction, that to central suns
Binds circling earths, and world with world unites.
Instructed thence, he great ideas form'd
Of the whole-moving, all-informing God,
The Sun of beings! beaming unconfined
Light, life, and love, and ever active power:
Whom nought can image, and who best approves
The silent worship of the moral heart,
That joys in bounteous Heaven, and spreads the joy.
Nor scorn'd the soaring sage to stoop to life,
And bound his reason to the sphere of man.
He gave the four yet reigning virtues name;
Inspired the study of the finer arts,
That civilize mankind, and laws devised
Where with enlighten'd justice mercy mix'd.
He e'en, into his tender system, took
Whatever shares the brotherhood of life:
He taught that life's indissoluble flame,
From brute to man, and man to brute again,
For ever shifting, runs the eternal round;
Thence tried against the blood-polluted meal,

And limbs yet quivering with some kindred soul,
To turn the human heart. Delightful truth!
Had he beheld the living chain ascend,
And not a circling form but rising whole.
　'Amid those small republics one arose
On yellow Tiber's bank, almighty Rome,
Fated for me. A nobler spirit warm'd
Her sons; and, roused by tyrants, nobler still
It burn'd in Brutus; the proud Tarquins chased,
With all their crimes; bade radiant eras rise,
And the long honours of the Consul-line.
　'Here from the fairer, not the greater, plan
Of Greece I varied; whose unmixing states,
By the keen soul of emulation pierced,
Long waged alone the bloodless war of arts,
And their best empire gain'd. But to diffuse
O'er men an empire was my purpose now:
To let my martial majesty abroad;
Into the vortex of one state to draw
The whole mix'd force, and liberty, on earth;
To conquer tyrants, and set nations free.
　'Already have I given, with flying touch,
A broken view of this my amplest reign.
Now, while its first, last, periods you survey,
Mark how it labouring rose, and rapid fell.
　'When Rome in noon-tide empire grasp'd the world,
And, soon as her resistless legions shone,
The nations stoop'd around; though then appear'd
Her grandeur most; yet in her dawn of power,
By many a jealous equal people press'd,
Then was the toil, the mighty struggle then;
Then for each Roman I a hero told;
And every passing sun, and Latian scene,
Saw patriot virtues then, and awful deeds,
That or surpass the faith of modern times,
Or, if believed, with sacred horror strike.
　'For then, to prove my most exalted power,

l to the point of full perfection push'd,
To fondness and enthusiastic zeal,
The great, the reigning passion of the free.
That godlike passion! which, the bounds of self
Divinely bursting, the whole public takes
Into the heart, enlarged, and burning high
With the mix'd ardour of unnumber'd selves;
Of all who safe beneath the voted laws
Of the same parent state, fraternal, live.
From this kind sun of moral nature flow'd
Virtues, that shine the light of humankind,
And, ray'd through story, warm remotest time.
These virtues too, reflected to their source,
Increased its flame. The social charm went round,
The fair idea, more attractive still,
As more by virtue mark'd; till Romans, all
One band of friends, unconquerable grew.

'Hence, when their country raised her plaintive voice,
The voice of pleading Nature was not heard;
And in their hearts the fathers throbb'd no more;
Stern to themselves, but gentle to the whole.
Hence sweeten'd Pain, the luxury of toil;
Patience, that baffled fortune's utmost rage;
High-minded Hope, which at the lowest ebb,
When Brennus conquer'd, and when Cannæ bled,
The bravest impulse felt, and scorn'd despair.
Hence Moderation a new conquest gain'd:
As on the vanquish'd, like descending heaven,
Their dewy mercy dropp'd, the bounty beam'd,
And by the labouring hand were crowns bestow'd.
Fruitful of men, hence hard laborious life,
Which no fatigue can quell, no season pierce.
Hence, Independence, with his little pleased
Serene, and self-sufficient, like a god;
In whom Corruption could not lodge one charm,
While he his honest roots to gold preferr'd;
While truly rich, and by his Sabine field,

The man maintain'd, the Roman's splendour all
Was in the public wealth and glory placed:
Or ready, a rough swain, to guide the plough;
Or else, the purple o'er his shoulder thrown,
In long majestic flow, to rule the state,
With Wisdom's purest eye; or, clad in steel,
To drive the steady battle on the foe.
Hence every passion, e'en the proudest, stoop'd
To common good: Camillus, thy revenge;
Thy glory, Fabius. All submissive hence,
Consuls, Dictators, still resign'd their rule,
The very moment that the laws ordain'd.
Though Conquest o'er them clapp'd her eagle-wings,
Her laurels wreath'd, and yoked her snowy steeds
To the triumphal car; soon as expired
The latest hour of sway, taught to submit,
(A harder lesson that than to command)
Into the private Roman sunk the chief.
If Rome was served, and glorious, careless they
By whom. Their country's fame they deem'd their own;
And above envy, in a rival's train,
Sung the loud Iös by themselves deserved.
Hence matchless courage. On Cremera's bank,
Hence fell the Fabii; hence the Decii died:
And Curtius plunged into the flaming gulf.
Hence Regulus the wavering fathers firm'd,
By dreadful counsel never given before;
For Roman honour sued, and his own doom.
Hence he sustain'd to dare a death prepared
By Punic rage. On earth his manly look
Relentless fix'd, he from a last embrace,
By chains polluted, put his wife aside,
His little children climbing for a kiss;
Then dumb through rows of weeping, wondering friends,
A new illustrious exile! press'd along.
Nor less impatient did he pierce the crowds
Opposing his return, than if, escaped

From long litigious suits, he glad forsook
The noisy town a while and city cloud,
To breathe Venafrian, or Tarentine air.
Need I these high particulars recount?
The meanest bosom felt a thirst for fame;
Flight their worst death, and shame their only fear.
Life had no charms, nor any terrors fate,
When Rome and glory call'd. But, in one view,
Mark the rare boast of these unequal'd times.
Ages revolved unsullied by a crime:
Astrea reign'd, and scarcely needed laws
To bind a race elated with the pride
Of virtue, and disdaining to descend
To meanness, mutual violence, and wrongs.
While war around them raged, in happy Rome
All peaceful smiled, all save the passing clouds
That often hang on Freedom's jealous brow;
And fair unblemish'd centuries elapsed,
When not a Roman bled but in the field.
Their virtue such, that an unbalanced state,
Still between Noble and Plebeian tost,
As flow'd the wave of fluctuating power,
Was then kept firm, and with triumphant prow
Rode out the storms. Oft though the native feuds,
That from the first their constitution shook,
(A latent ruin, growing as it grew,)
Stood on the threatening point of civil war
Ready to rush: yet could the lenient voice
Of wisdom, soothing the tumultuous soul,
Those sons of virtue calm. Their generous hearts
Unpetrified by self, so naked lay
And sensible to Truth, that o'er the rage
Of giddy faction, by oppression swell'd,
Prevail'd a simple fable, and at once
To peace recover'd the divided state.
But if their often cheated hopes refused
The soothing touch; still, in the love of Rome,

The dread Dictator found a sure resource.
Was she assaulted? was her glory stain'd?
One common quarrel wide inflamed the whole.
Foes in the forum in the field were friends,
By social danger bound; each fond for each,
And for their dearest country all, to die.
  'Thus up the hill of empire slow they toil'd:
Till, the bold summit gain'd, the thousand states
Of proud Italia blended into one;
Then o'er the nations they resistless rush'd,
And touch'd the limits of the failing world.
  'Let Fancy's eye the distant lines unite.
See that which borders wild the western main,
Where storms at large resound, and tides immense;
From Caledonia's dim cerulean coast,
And moist Hibernia, to where Atlas, lodged
Amid the restless clouds and leaning heaven,
Hangs o'er the deep that borrows thence its name.
Mark that opposed, where first the springing morn
Her roses sheds, and shakes around her dews:
From the dire deserts by the Caspian laved,
To where the Tigris and Euphrates, join'd,
Impetuous tear the Babylonian plain;
And bless'd Arabia aromatic breathes.
See that dividing far the watery north,
Parent of floods! from the majestic Rhine,
Drunk by Batavian meads, to where, seven-mouth'd,
In Euxine waves the flashing Danube roars;
To where the frozen Tanais scarcely stirs
The dead Meotic pool, or the long Rha,
In the black Scythian sea, his torrent throws.
Last, that beneath the burning zone behold:
See where it runs, from the deep-loaded plains
Of Mauritania to the Libyan sands,
Where Ammon lifts amid the torrid waste
A verdant isle, with shade and fountain fresh;
And farther to the full Egyptian shore,

To where the Nile from Ethiopian clouds,
His never drain'd ethereal urn, descends.
In this vast space what various tongues, and states!
What bounding rocks, and mountains, floods, and seas!
What purple tyrants quell'd, and nations freed!
  'O'er Greece, descended chief, with stealth divine,
The Roman bounty in a flood of day:
As at her Isthmian games, a fading pomp!
Her full-assembled youth innumerous swarm'd.
On a tribunal raised, Flaminius sat:
A victor he, from the deep phalanx pierced
Of iron-coated Macedon, and back
The Grecian tyrant to his bounds repell'd.
In the high thoughtless gaiety of game,
While sport alone their unambitious hearts
Possess'd; the sudden trumpet, sounding hoarse
Bade silence o'er the bright assembly reign.
Then thus a herald: — "To the states of Greece
The Roman people, unconfined, restore
Their countries, cities, liberties, and laws:
Taxes remit, and garrisons withdraw."
The crowd astonish'd half, and half inform'd,
Stared dubious round; some question'd, some exclaim'd.
(Like one who dreaming, between hope and fear,
Is lost in anxious joy,) 'Be that again,
Be that again proclaim'd, distinct, and loud.'
Loud, and distinct, it was again proclaim'd;
And still as midnight in the rural shade,
When the gale slumbers, they the words devour'd.
A while severe amazement held them mute,
Then bursting broad, the boundless shout to Heaven
From many a thousand hearts ecstatic sprung.
On every hand rebellow'd to their joy
The swelling sea, the rocks, and vocal hills:
Through all her turrets stately Corinth shook;
And, from the void above of shatter'd air,
The flitting bird fell breathless to the ground.

What piercing bliss, how keen a sense of fame,
Did then, Flaminius, reach thy inmost soul!
And with what deep-felt glory didst thou thou
Escape the fondness of transported Greece?
Mix'd in a tempest of superior joy,
They left the sports; like Bacchanals they flew,
Each other straining in a strict embrace,
Nor strain'd a slave; and loud acclaims till night
Round the Proconsul's tent repeated rung.
Then, crown'd with garlands, came the festive hours;
And music, sparkling wine, and converse warm,
Their raptures waked anew. "Ye gods! (they cried)
Ye guardian gods of Greece! and are we free?
Was it not madness deem'd the very thought?
And is it true? How did we purchase chains?
At what a dire expense of kindred blood?
And are they now dissolved? And scarce one drop
For the fair first of blessings have we paid?
Courage, and conduct, in the doubtful field,
When rages wide the storm of mingling war,
Are rare indeed; but how to generous ends
To turn success, and conquest, rarer still:
That the great gods and Romans only know.
Lives there on earth, almost to Greece unknown,
A people so magnanimous, to quit
Their native soil, traverse the stormy deep,
And by their blood and treasure, spent for us,
Redeem our states, our liberties, and laws!
There does! there does! Oh saviour, Titus! Rome!"
Thus thro' the happy night they pour'd their souls,
And in my last reflected beams rejoiced.
As when the shepherd, on the mountain-brow,
Sits piping to his flocks and gamesome kids;
Meantime the sun, beneath the green earth sunk,
Slants upward o'er the scene a parting gleam:
Short is the glory that the mountain gilds,
Plays on the glittering flocks, and glads the swain;

To western worlds irrevocable roll'd,
Rapid, the source of light recalls his ray.'
   Here interposing I — 'Oh, Queen of men!
Beneath whose sceptre in essential rights
Equal they live; though placed for common good,
Various, or in subjection or command;
And that by common choice: alas! the scene,
With virtue, freedom, and with glory bright,
Streams into blood, and darkens into woe.'
Thus she pursued: — 'Near this great era, Rome
Began to feel the swift approach of fate,
That now her vitals gain'd: still more and more
Her deep divisions kindling into rage,
And war with chains and desolation charged.
From an unequal balance of her sons
These fierce contentions sprung: and, as increased
This hated inequality, more fierce
They flamed to tumult. Independence fail'd;
Here by luxurious wants, by real there;
And with this virtue every virtue sunk,
As, with the sliding rock, the pile sustain'd.
A last attempt, too late, the Gracchi made,
To fix the flying scale, and poise the state.
On one side swell'd aristocratic Pride;
With Usury, the villain! whose fell gripe
Bends by degrees to baseness the free soul;
And Luxury rapacious, cruel, mean,
Mother of vice! While on the other crept
A populace in want, with pleasure fired;
Fit for proscriptions, for the darkest deeds,
As the proud feeder bade; inconstant, blind,
Deserting friends at need, and duped by foes;
Loud and seditious, when a chief inspired
Their headlong fury, but of him deprived,
Already slaves that lick'd the scourging hand.
   "This firm republic, that against the blast
Of opposition rose; that (like an oak,

Nursed on feracious Algidum, whose boughs
Still stronger shoot beneath the rigid axe,)
By loss, by slaughter, from the steel itself,
E'en force and spirit drew; smit with the calm,
The dead serene of prosperous fortune, pined.
Nought now her weighty legions could oppose;
Her terror once, on Afric's tawny shore,
Now smoked in dust, a stabling now for wolves;
And every dreaded power received the yoke.
Besides, destructive, from the conquer'd East,
In the soft plunder came that worst of plagues,
That pestilence of mind, a fever'd thirst
For the false joys which Luxury prepares.
Unworthy joys! that wasteful leave behind
No mark of honour, in reflecting hour,
No secret ray to glad the conscious soul;
At once involving in one ruin wealth,
And wealth-acquiring powers: while stupid self,
Of narrow gust, and hebetating sense,
Devour the nobler faculties of bliss.
Hence Roman virtue slacken'd into sloth;
Security relax'd the softening state;
And the broad eye of government lay closed.
No more the laws inviolable reign'd,
And public weal no more: but party raged;
And partial power, and license unrestrain'd,
Let Discord through the deathful city loose.
First, mild Tiberius, on thy sacred head
The fury's vengeance fell; the first, whose blood
Had since the consuls stain'd contending Rome.
Of precedent pernicious! with thee bled
Three hundred Romans; with thy brother, next,
Three thousand more: till, into battles turn'd
Debates of peace, and forced the trembling laws,
The Forum and Comitia horrid grew,
A scene of barter'd power, or reeking gore.
When, half-ashamed, Corruption's thievish arts,

And ruffian force begin to sap the mounds
And majesty of laws; if not in time
Repress'd severe, for human aid too strong
The torrent turns, and overbears the whole.
　'Thus Luxury, Dissension, a mix'd rage
Of boundless pleasure and of boundless wealth,
Want-wishing change, and waste-repairing war,
Rapine for ever lost to peaceful toil,
Guilt unatoned, profuse of blood Revenge,
Corruption all avow'd, and lawless Force,
Each heightening each, alternate shook the state.
Meantime Ambition, at the dazzling head
Of hardy legions, with the laurels heap'd
And spoil of nations, in one circling blast
Combined in various storm, and from its base
The broad republic tore. By Virtue built
It touch'd the skies, and spread o'er shelter'd earth
An ample roof: by Virtue too sustain'd,
And balanced steady, every tempest sung
Innoxious by, or bade it firmer stand.
But when, with sudden and enormous change,
The first of mankind sunk into the last,
As once in Virtue, so in Vice extreme,
This universal fabric yielded loose,
Before Ambition still; and thundering down,
At last, beneath its ruins crush'd a world.
A conquering people, to themselves a prey,
Must ever fall; when their victorious troops,
In blood and rapine savage grown, can find
No land to sack and pillage but their own.
　'By brutal Marius, and keen Sylla, first
Effused the deluge dire of civil blood,
Unceasing woes began, and this, or that,
Deep-drenching their revenge, nor virtue spared,
Nor sex, nor age, nor quality, nor name;
Till Rome, into a human shambles turn'd,
Made deserts lovely. — Oh, to well earn'd chains,

Devoted race! — If no true Roman then,
No Scævola there was, to raise for me
A vengeful hand: was there no father, robb'd
Of blooming youth to prop his wither'd age?
No son, a witness to his hoary sire
In dust and gore defiled? no friend, forlorn?
No wretch that doubtful trembled for himself?
None brave, or wild, to pierce a monster's heart,
Who, heaping horror round, no more deserved
The sacred shelter of the laws he spurn'd?
No: — Sad o'er all profound dejection sat;
And nerveless fear. The slave's asylum theirs:
Or flight, ill-judging, that the timid back
Turns weak to slaughter; or partaken guilt.
In vain from Sylla's vanity I drew
An unexampled deed. The power resign'd,
And all unhoped the commonwealth restored,
Amazed the public, and effaced his crimes.
Through streets yet streaming from his murderous hand
Unarm'd he stray'd, unguarded, unassail'd,
And on the bed of peace his ashes laid;
A grace, which I to his demission gave.
But with him died not the despotic soul.
Ambition saw that stooping Rome could bear
A master, nor had virtue to be free.
Hence, for succeeding years, my troubled reign
No certain peace, no spreading prospect knew.
Destruction gather'd round. Still the black soul,
Or of a Catiline, or Rullus, swell'd
With fell designs; and all the watchful art
Of Cicero demanded, all the force,
All the state-wielding magic of his tongue;
And all the thunder of my Cato's zeal.
With these I linger'd; till the flame anew
Burst out, in blaze immense, and wrapt the world.
The shameful contest sprung; to whom mankind
Should yield the neck: to Pompey, who conceal'd

A rage impatient of an equal name;
Or to the nobler Cæsar, on whose brow
O'er daring vice deluding virtue smiled,
And who no less a vain superior scorn'd.
Both bled, but bled in vain. New traitors rose.
The venal will be bought, the base have lords.
To these vile wars I left ambitious slaves;
And from Philippi's field, from where in dust
The last of Romans, matchless Brutus! lay,
Spread to the north untamed a rapid wing.
 'What tho' the first smooth Cæsars arts caress'd,
Merit, and virtue, simulating me?
Severely tender! cruelly humane!
The chain to clinch, and make it softer sit
On the new-broken still ferocious state.
From the dark Third, succeeding, I beheld
The imperial monsters all. — A race on earth
Vindictive, sent the scourge of humankind!
Whose blind profusion drain'd a bankrupt world;
Whose lust to forming nature seems disgrace;
And whose infernal rage bade every drop
Of ancient blood, that yet retain'd my flame,
To that of Pætus, in the peaceful bath,
Or Rome's affrighted streets, inglorious flow.
But almost just the meanly patient death,
That waits a tyrant's unprevented stroke.
Titus indeed gave one short evening gleam;
More cordial felt, as in the midst it spread
Of storm, and horror. The delight of men!
He who the day, when his o'erflowing hand
Had made no happy heart, concluded lost;
Trajan and he, with the mild sire and son,
His son of virtue! eased awhile mankind;
And arts revived beneath their gentle beam.
Then was their last effort: what sculpture raised
To Trajan's glory, following triumphs stole;

And mix'd with Gothic forms, (the chisel's shame)
On that triumphal arch, the forms of Greece.
  'Meantime o'er rocky Thrace, and the deep vales
Of gelid Hæmus, I pursued my flight;
And, piercing farthest Scythia, westward swept.
Sarmatia, traversed by a thousand streams,
A sullen land of lakes, and fens immense,
Of rocks, resounding torrents, gloomy heaths,
And cruel deserts black with sounding pine;
Where nature frowns: tho' sometimes into smiles
She softens; and immediate, at the touch
Of southern gales, throws from the sudden glebe
Luxuriant pasture, and a waste of flowers.
But, cold-compress'd, when the whole loaded heaven
Descends in snow, lost in one white abrupt,
Lies undistinguish'd earth; and, seized by frost,
Lakes, headlong streams, and floods, and oceans sleep.
Yet there life glows; the furry millions there
Deep dig their dens beneath the sheltering snows:
And there a race of men prolific swarms,
To various pain, to little pleasure used;
On whom, keen-parching, beat Riphæan winds;
Hard like their soil, and like their climate fierce,
The nursery of nations! — These I roused,
Drove land on land, on people people pour'd;
Till from almost perpetual night they broke,
As if in search of day; and o'er the banks
Of yielding empire, only slave-sustain'd,
Resistless raged; in vengeance urged by me.
  'Long in the barbarous heart the buried seeds
Of Freedom lay, for many a wintry age;
And though my spirit work'd, by slow degrees,
Nought but its pride and fierceness yet appear'd.
Then was the night of time, that parted worlds.
I quitted earth the while. As when the tribes
Aërial, warn'd of rising winter, ride

Autumnal winds, to warmer climates borne;
So, arts and each good genius in my train,
I cut the closing gloom, and soar'd to Heaven.
  'In the bright regions there of purest day,
Far other scenes, and palaces, arise,
Adorn'd profuse with other arts divine.
All beauty here below, to them compared,
Would, like a rose before the midday sun,
Shrink up its blossom; like a bubble break
The passing poor magnificence of kings.
For there the King of Nature, in full blaze,
Calls every splendour forth; and there his court,
Amid ethereal powers, and virtues, holds:
Angel, archangel, tutelary gods,
Of cities, nations, empires, and of worlds.
But sacred be the veil, that kindly clouds
A light too keen for mortals; wraps a view
Too softening fair, for those that here in dust
Must cheerful toil out their appointed years.
A sense of higher life would only damp
The schoolboy's task, and spoil his playful hours.
Nor could the child of Reason, feeble man,
With vigour through this infant-being drudge;
Did brighter worlds, their unimagined bliss
Disclosing, dazzle and dissolve his mind.'

LIBERTY.

PART IV. — BRITAIN.

Struck with the rising scene, thus I amazed:
'Ah, Goddess, what a change! is earth the same?
Of the same kind the ruthless race she feeds?
And does the same fair sun and ether spread
Round this vile spot their all-enlivening soul?
Lo! beauty fails; lost in unlovely forms
Of little pomp, magnificence no more
Exalts the mind, and bids the public smile:
While to rapacious interest Glory leaves
Mankind, and every grace of life is gone.'
  To this the Power, whose vital radiance calls
From the brute mass of man an order'd world:
  'Wait till the morning shines, and from the depth
Of Gothic darkness springs another day.
True, Genius droops; the tender ancient taste
Of Beauty, then fresh blooming in her prime,
But faintly trembles through the callous soul;
And Grandeur, or of morals, or of life,
Sinks into safe pursuits, and creeping cares.
E'en cautious Virtue seems to stoop her flight,
And aged life to deem the generous deeds
Of youth romantic. Yet in cooler thought
Well reason'd, in researches piercing deep
Through nature's works, in profitable arts,
And all that calm Experience can disclose,
(Slow guide, but sure), behold the world anew
Exalted rise; with other honours crown'd;
And, where my Spirit wakes the finer powers,
Athenian laurels still afresh shall bloom.
  'Oblivious ages pass'd; while earth, forsook

By her best Genii, lay to Demons foul,
And unchain'd Furies, an abandon'd prey.
Contention led the van; first small of size,
But soon dilating to the skies she towers:
Then, wide as air, the livid Fury spread,
And high her head above the stormy clouds,
She blazed in omens, swell'd the groaning winds
With wild surmises, battlings, sounds of war:
From land to land the maddening trumpet blew,
And pour'd her venom through the heart of man.
Shook to the pole, the North obey'd her call.
Forth rush'd the bloody power of Gothic war,
War against human kind: Rapine, that led
Millions of raging robbers in his train:
Unlistening, barbarous Force, to whom the sword
Is reason, honour, law: the foe of arts
By monsters follow'd, hideous to behold,
That claim'd their place.   Outrages mix'd with these
Another species of tyrannic rule;
Unknown before, whose cankerous shackles seized
The envenom'd soul; a wilder Fury, she
Even o'er her Elder Sister tyrannized;
Or, if perchance agreed, inflamed her rage.
Dire was her train, and loud: the sable band,
Thundering;—"Submit, ye Laity! ye profane!
Earth is the Lord's, and therefore ours; let kings
Allow the common claim, and half be theirs;
If not, behold! the sacred lightning flies!"
Scholastic Discord, with a hundred tongues,
For science uttering jangling words obscure,
Where frighted reason never yet could dwell:
Of peremptory feature, cleric Pride,
Whose reddening cheek no contradiction bears;
And holy Slander, his associate firm,
On whom the lying Spirit still descends:
Mother of tortures! persecuting Zeal,
High flashing in her hand the ready torch,

Or poniard bathed in unbelieving blood;
Hell's fiercest fiend! of saintly brow demure,
Assuming a celestial seraph's name,
While she beneath the blasphemous pretence
Of pleasing Parent Heaven, the Source of Love!
Has wrought more horrors, more detested deeds,
Than all the rest combined. Led on by her,
And wild of head to work her fell designs,
Came idiot superstition; round with ears
Innumerous strow'd, ten thousand monkish forms
With legends ply'd them, and with tenets, meant
To charm or scare the simple into slaves,
And poison reason; gross, she swallows all,
The most absurd believing ever most.
Broad o'er the whole her universal night,
The gloom still doubling, Ignorance diffused.
  'Nought to be seen, but visionary monks
To councils strolling, and embroiling creeds;
Banditti Saints, disturbing distant lands;
And unknown nations, wandering for a home.
All lay reversed: the sacred arts of rule
Turn'd to flagitious leagues against mankind.
And arts of plunder more and more avow'd;
Pure plain Devotion to a solemn farce;
To holy dotage Virtue, even to guile,
To murder, and a mockery of oaths;
Brave ancient Freedom to the rage of slaves,
Proud of their state, and fighting for their chains;
Dishonour'd Courage to the bravo's trade,
To civil broil; and Glory to romance.
Thus human life, unhinged, to ruin reel'd,
And giddy Reason totter'd on her throne.
  'At last Heaven's best inexplicable scheme,
Disclosing, bade new brightening eras smile.
The high command gone forth, Arts in my train,
And azure-mantled Science, swift we spread
A sounding pinion. Eager pity, mix'd

With indignation, urged her downward flight.
On Latium first we stoop'd, for doubtful life
That panted, sunk beneath unnumber'd woes.
Ah, poor Italia! what a bitter cup
Of vengeance hast thou drain'd? Goth, Vandals, Huns,
Lombards, barbarians broke from every land,
How many a ruffian form hast thou beheld?
What horrid jargons heard, where rage alone
Was all thy frighted ear could comprehend?
How frequent by the red inhuman hand,
Yet warm with brother's, husband's, father's blood,
Hast thou thy matrons and thy virgins seen
To violation dragg'd, and mingled death?
What conflagrations, earthquakes, ravage, floods,
Have turn'd thy cities into stony wilds;
And succourless, and bare, the poor remains
Of wretches forth to Nature's common cast?
Added to these the still continued waste
Of inbred foes that on thy vitals prey,
And, double tyrants, seize the very soul.
Where hadst thou treasures for this rapine all?
These hungry myriads, that thy bowels tore,
Heap'd sack on sack, and buried in their rage
Wonders of art; whence this grey scene, a mine
Of more than gold becomes and orient gems,
Where Egypt, Greece, and Rome united glow.

'Here Sculpture, Painting, Architecture, bent
From ancient models to restore their arts,
Remain'd. A little trace we how they rose.

'Amid the hoary ruins, Sculpture first,
Deep digging, from the cavern dark and damp,
Their grave for ages, bid her marble race
Spring to new light. Joy sparkled in her eyes,
And old remembrance thrill'd in every thought,
As she the pleasing resurrection saw.
In leaning site, respiring from his toils,
The well known Hero, who deliver'd Greece,

His ample chest, all tempested with force,
Unconquerable rear'd. She saw the head,
Breathing the hero, small, of Grecian size,
Scarce more extensive than the sinewy neck:
The spreading shoulders, muscular, and broad;
The whole a mass of swelling sinews, touch'd
Into harmonious shape; she saw, and joy'd.
The yellow hunter, Meleager, raised
His beauteous front, and through the finish'd whole
Shows what ideas smiled of old in Greece.
Of raging aspect, rush'd impetuous forth
The Gladiator: pitiless his look,
And each keen sinew braced, the storm of war,
Ruffling, o'er all his nervous body frowns.
The dying other from the gloom she drew:
Supported on his shorten'd arm he leans,
Prone, agonizing; with incumbent fate,
Heavy declines his head; yet dark beneath
The suffering feature sullen vengeance lours,
Shame, indignation, unaccomplish'd rage,
And still the cheated eye expects his fall.
All conquest-flush'd, from prostrate Python, came
The quiver'd God. In graceful act he stands,
His arm extended with the slacken'd bow:
Light flows his easy robe, and fair displays
A manly soften'd form. The bloom of gods
Seems youthful o'er the beardless cheek to wave:
His features yet heroic ardour warms;
And sweet subsiding to a native smile,
Mix'd with the joy elating conquest gives,
A scatter'd frown exalts his matchless air.
On Flora moved; her full proportion'd limbs
Rise through the mantle fluttering in the breeze.
The Queen of Love arose, as from the deep
She sprung in all the melting pomp of charms.
Bashful she bend, her well taught look aside
Turns in enchanting guise, where dubious mix

Vain conscious beauty, a dissembled sense
Of modest shame, and slippery looks of love.
The gazer grows enamour'd, and the stone,
As if exulting in its conquest, smiles.
So turn'd each limb, so swell'd with softening art,
That the deluded eye the marble doubts.
At last her utmost masterpiece she found,
That Maro fired; the miserable sire,
Wrapt with his sons in fate's severest grasp:
The serpents, twisting round, their stringent folds
Inextricable tie. Such passion here,
Such agonies, such bitterness of pain,
Seem so to tremble through the tortured stone,
That the touch'd heart engrosses all the view.
Almost unmark'd the best proportions pass,
That ever Greece beheld; and, seen alone,
On the rapt eye the imperious passions seize:
The father's double pangs, both for himself
And sons convulsed; to Heaven his rueful look,
Imploring aid, and half accusing, cast;
His fell despair with indignation mix'd,
As the strong curling monsters from his side
His full extended fury cannot tear.
More tender touch'd, with varied art, his sons
All the soft rage of younger passions show.
In a boy's helpless fate one sinks oppress'd;
While, yet unpierced, the frighted other tries
His foot to steal out of the horrid twine.
'She bore no more, but straight from Gothic rust
Her chisel clear'd, and dust and fragments drove
Impetuous round. Successive as it went
From son to son, with more enlivening touch,
From the brute rock it call'd the breathing form;
Till, in a legislator's awful grace
Dress'd, Buonaroti bid a Moses rise,
And, looking love immense, a Saviour God.

Thomson.

'Of these observant, Painting felt the fire
Burn inward. Then ecstatic she diffused
The canvass, seized the pallet, with quick hand
The colours brew'd; and on the void expanse
Her gay creation pour'd, her mimic world.
Poor was the manner of her eldest race,
Barren, and dry; just struggling from the taste,
That had for ages scared in cloisters dim
The superstitious herd: yet glorious then
Were deem'd their works; where undeveloped lay
The future wonders that enrich'd mankind,
And a new light and grace o'er Europe cast.
Arts gradual gather streams. Enlarging This,
To each his portion of her various gifts
The Goddess dealt, to none indulging all;
No, not to Raphael. At kind distance still
Perfection stands, like Happiness, to tempt
The eternal chase. In elegant design,
Improving nature: in ideas fair,
Or great, extracted from the fine antique;
In attitude, expression, airs divine;
Her sons of Rome and Florence bore the prize.
To those of Venice she the magic art
Of colours melting into colours gave.
Theirs too it was by one embracing mass
Of light and shade, that settles round the whole,
Or varies tremulous from part to part,
O'er all a binding harmony to throw,
To raise the picture, and repose the sight.
The Lombard school, succeeding, mingled both.
    'Meantime dread fanes, and palaces, around,
Rear'd the magnific front. Music again
Her universal language of the heart
Renew'd; and, rising from the plaintive vale,
To the full concert spread, and solemn quire.
    'E'en bigots smiled; to their protection took
Arts not their own, and from them borrow'd pomp:

For in a tyrant's garden these awhile
May bloom, though Freedom be their parent soil.
  'And now confess'd, with gently growing gleam
The morning shone, and westward stream'd its light.
The Muse awoke. Not sooner on the wing
Is the gay bird of dawn. Artless her voice,
Untaught and wild, yet warbling through the woods
Romantic lays. But as her northern course
She, with her tutor Science, in my train,
Ardent pursued, her strains more noble grew:
While Reason drew the plan, the Heart inform'd
The moral page, and Fancy lent it grace.
  'Rome and her circling deserts cast behind,
I pass'd not idle to my great sojourn.
  'On Arno's fertile plain, where the rich vine
Luxuriant o'er Etrurian mountains roves,
Safe in the lap reposed of private bliss,
I small republics raised. Thrice happy they!
Had social Freedom bound their peace, and arts,
Instead of ruling Power, ne'er meant for them,
Employ'd their little cares, and saved their fate.
  'Beyond the rugged Apennines, that roll
Far through Italian bounds their wavy tops,
My path, too, I with public blessings strow'd:
Free states and cities, where the Lombard plain,
In spite of culture negligent and gross,
From her deep bosom pours unbidden joys,
And green o'er all the land a garden spreads.
  'The barren rocks themselves beneath my foot,
Relenting bloom'd on the Ligurian shore.
Thick swarming people there, like emmets, seized
Amid surrounding cliffs, the scatter'd spots,
Which Nature left in her destroying rage.
Made their own fields, nor sigh'd for other lands.
There, in white prospect from the rocky hill
Gradual descending to the shelter'd shore,
By me proud Genoa's marble turrets rose.

And while my genuine spirit warm'd her sons,
Beneath her Dorias, not unworthy, she
Vied for the trident of the narrow seas,
Ere Britain yet had open'd all the main.
  'Nor be the then triumphant state forgot;
Where, push'd from plunder'd earth, a remnant still
Inspired by me, through the dark ages kept
Of my old Roman flame some sparks alive:
The seeming god-built city! which my hand
Deep in the bosom fix'd of wondering seas.
Astonish'd mortals sail'd, with pleasing awe,
Around the sea-girt walls, by Neptune fenced,
And down the briny street; where on each hand,
Amazing seen amid unstable waves,
The splendid palace shines; and rising tides,
The green steps marking, murmur at the door.
To this fair Queen of Adria's stormy gulf,
The mart of nations! long, obedient seas
Roll'd all the treasure of the radiant East.
But now no more. Than one great tyrant worse
(Whose shared oppression lightens, as diffused,)
Each subject tearing, many tyrants rose.
The least the proudest. Join'd in dark cabal,
They jealous, watchful, silent, and severe,
Cast o'er the whole indissoluble chains:
The softer shackles of luxurious ease
They likewise added, to secure their sway.
Thus Venice fainter shines; and Commerce thus,
Of toil impatient, flags the drooping sail.
Bursting, besides, his ancient bounds, he took
A larger circle: found another seat,
Opening a thousand ports, and, charm'd with toil,
Whom nothing can dismay, far other sons.
  'The mountains then, clad with eternal snow,
Confess'd my power. Deep as the rampant rocks,
By Nature thrown insuperable round,
I planted there a league of friendly states,

And bade plain Freedom there ambition be.
There in the vale, where rural plenty fills,
From lakes, and meads, and furrow'd fields, her born,
Chief, where the Leman pure emits the Rhone,
Rare to be seen! unguilty cities rise,
Cities of brothers form'd: while equal life,
Accorded gracious with revolving power,
Maintains them free; and, in their happy streets,
Nor cruel deed, nor misery, is known.
For valour, faith, and innocence of life,
Renown'd, a rough laborious people, there,
Not only give the dreadful Alps to smile,
And press their culture on retiring snows;
But, to firm order train'd and patient war,
They likewise know, beyond the nerve remiss
Of mercenary force, how to defend
The tasteful little their hard toil has earn'd,
And the proud arm of Bourbon to defy.
  'E'en, cheer'd by me, their shaggy mountains charm,
More than or Gallic or Italian plains;
And sickening Fancy oft, when absent long,
Pines to behold their Alpine views again:
The hollow-winding stream: the vale, fair spread
Amid an amphitheatre of hills;
Whence, vapour-wing'd, the sudden tempest springs:
From steep to steep ascending, the gay train
Of fogs, thick-roll'd into romantic shapes:
The flitting cloud, against the summit dash'd;
And, by the sun illumined, pouring bright
A gemmy shower; hung o'er amazing rocks,
The mountain ash, and solemn sounding pine:
The snow-fed torrent, in white mazes tost,
Down to the clear ethereal lake below:
And, high o'ertopping all the broken scene,
The mountain fading into sky; where shines
On winter, winter shivering, and whose top
Licks from their cloudy magazine the snows.

'From these descending, as I waved my course
O'er vast Germania, the ferocious nurse
Of hardy men, and hearts affronting death,
I gave some favour'd cities there to lift
A nobler brow, and through their swarming streets,
More busy, wealthy, cheerful, and alive,
In each contented face to look my soul.
　'Thence the loud Baltic passing, black with storm,
To wintry Scandinavia's utmost bound;
There, I the manly race, the parent hive
Of the mix'd kingdoms, form'd into a state
More regularly free. By keener air
Their genius purged, and temper'd hard by frost,
Tempest and toil their nerves, the sons of those
Whose only terror was a bloodless death,
They, wise and dauntless, still sustain my cause.
Yet there I fix'd not. Turning to the south,
The whispering zephyrs sigh'd at my delay.'
　Here, with the shifted vision, burst my joy:—
'O the dear prospect! O majestic view!
See Britain's empire! lo! the watery vast
Wide waves, diffusing the cerulean plain.
And now, methinks, like clouds at distance seen,
Emerging white from deeps of ether, dawn
My kindred cliffs; whence, wafted in the gale,
Ineffable, a secret sweetness breathes.
Goddess, forgive!—My heart, surprised, o'erflows
With filial fondness for the land you bless.'
As parents to a child complacent deign
Approvance, the celestial brightness smiled;
Then thus—'As o'er the wave resounding deep,
To my near reign, the happy isle, I steer'd
With easy wing; behold! from surge to surge,
Stalk'd the tremendous Genius of the Deep.
Around him clouds, in mingled tempest, hung;
Thick flashing meteors crown'd his starry head;
And ready thunder reddened in his hand,

Or from it stream'd compress'd the gloomy cloud.
Where'er he look'd, the trembling waves recoil'd.
He needs but strike the conscious flood, and shook
From shore to shore, in agitation dire,
It works his dreadful will. To me his voice
(Like that hoarse blast that round the cavern howls,
Mix'd with the murmurs of the falling main,)
Address'd, began — "By Fate commission'd, go,
My Sister-Goddess now, to yon bless'd isle,
Henceforth the partner of my rough domain.
All my dread walks to Britons open lie.
Those that refulgent, or with rosy morn,
Or yellow evening, flame; those that, profuse,
Drunk by equator suns, severely shine;
Or those that, to the poles approaching, rise
In billows rolling into Alps of ice.
E'en, yet untouch'd by daring keel, be theirs
The vast Pacific; that on other worlds,
Their future conquest, rolls resounding tides.
Long I maintain'd inviolate my reign;
Nor Alexanders me, nor Cæsars braved.
Still, in the crook of shore, the coward sail
Till now low crept; and peddling commerce ply'd
Between near joining lands. For Britons, chief,
It was reserved, with star-directed prow,
To dare the middle deep, and drive assured
To distant nations through the pathless main.
Chief, for their fearless hearts the glory waits,
Long months from land, while the black stormy night
Around them rages, on the groaning mast
With unshook knee to know their giddy way;
To sing, unquell'd, amid the lashing wave;
To laugh at danger. Theirs the triumph be,
By deep Invention's keen pervading eye,
The heart of Courage, and the hand of Toil,
Each conquer'd ocean staining with their blood,
Instead of treasure robb'd by ruffian war,

Round social earth to circle fair exchange,
And bind the nations in a golden chain.
To these I honour'd stoop. Rushing to light
A race of men behold! whose daring deeds
Will in renown exalt my nameless plains
O'er those of fabling earth, as hers to mine
In terror yield. Nay, could my savage heart
Such glories check, their unsubmitting soul
Would all my fury brave, my tempest climb,
And might in spite of me my kingdom force."
Here, waiting no reply, the shadowy power
Eased the dark sky, and to the deeps return'd:
While the loud thunder rattling from his hand,
Auspicious, shook opponent Gallia's shore.
  'Of this encounter glad, my way to land
I quick pursued, that from the smiling sea
Received me joyous. Loud acclaims were heard;
And music, more than mortal, warbling, fill'd
With pleased astonishment the labouring hind,
Who for a while the unfinish'd furrow left,
And let the listening steer forget his toil.
Unseen by grosser eye, Britannia breathed,
And her aërial train, these sounds of joy.
For of old time, since first the rushing flood,
Urged by almighty power, this favour'd isle
Turn'd flashing from the continent aside,
Indented shore to shore responsive still,
Its guardian she — the Goddess, whose staid eye
Beams the dark azure of the doubtful dawn.
Her tresses, like a flood of soften'd light
Through clouds imbrown'd, in waving circles play.
Warm on her cheek sits Beauty's brightest rose,
Of high demeanour, stately, shedding grace
With every motion. Full her rising chest;
And new ideas, from her finish'd shape,
Charm'd Sculpture taking might improve her art.
Such the fair Guardian of an isle that boasts,

Profuse as vernal blooms, the fairest dames.
High shining on the promontory's brow,
Awaiting me, she stood; with hope inflamed,
By my mixed spirit burning in her sons,
To firm, to polish, and exalt the state.
  'The native Genii, round her, radiant smiled.
Courage, of soft deportment, aspect calm,
Unboastful, suffering long, and, till provoked,
As mild and harmless as the sporting child;
But, on just reason, once his fury roused,
No lion springs more eager to his prey:
Blood is a pastime; and his heart, elate,
Knows no depressing fear. That Virtue known
By the relenting look, whose equal heart
For others feels, as for another self:
Of various name, as various objects wake,
Warm into action, the kind sense within:
Whether the blameless poor, the nobly maim'd,
The lost to reason, the declined in life,
The helpless young that kiss no mother's hand,
And the grey second infancy of age,
She gives in public families to live,
A sight to gladden Heaven! whether she stands
Fair beckoning at the hospitable gate,
And bids the stranger take repose and joy:
Whether, to solace honest labour, she
Rejoices those that make the land rejoice:
Or whether to Philosophy, and Arts,
(At once the basis and the finish'd pride
Of government and life) she spreads her hand;
Nor knows her gift profuse, nor seems to know,
Doubling her bounty, that she gives at all.
Justice to these her awful presence join'd,
The mother of the state! no low revenge,
No turbid passions in her breast ferment:
Tender, serene, compassionate of vice,
As the last woe that can afflict mankind,

She punishment awards; yet of the good
More piteous still, and of the suffering whole,
Awards it firm. So fair her just decree,
That, in his judging peers, each on himself
Pronounces his own doom. O happy land!
Where reigns alone this justice of the free!
Mid the bright group Sincerity his front,
Diffusive, rear'd; his pure untroubled eye
The fount of truth. The thoughtful Power, apart,
Now, pensive, cast on earth his fix'd regard,
Now, touch'd celestial, launch'd it on the sky.
The Genius he whence Britain shines supreme,
The land of light, and rectitude of mind.
He, too, the fire of fancy feeds intense,
With all the train of passions thence derived:
Not kindling quick, a noisy transient blaze,
But gradual, silent, lasting, and profound.
Near him Retirement, pointing to the shade,
And Independence stood: the generous pair,
That simple life, the quiet-whispering grove,
And the still raptures of the free-born soul,
To cates prefer by Virtue bought, not earn'd,
Proudly prefer them to the servile pomp,
And to the heart-embitter'd joys of slaves.
Or should the latter, to the public scene
Demanded, quit his silvan friend awhile;
Nought can his firmness shake, nothing seduce
His zeal, still active for the commonweal;
Nor stormy tyrants, nor corruption's tools,
Foul ministers, dark-working by the force
Of secret-sapping gold. All their vile arts,
Their shameful honours, their perfidious gifts,
He greatly scorns; and, if he must betray
His plunder'd country, or his power resign,
A moment's parley were eternal shame:
Illustrious into private life again,
From dirty levees he unstain'd ascends,

And firm in senates stands the patriot's ground,
Or draws new vigour in the peaceful shade.
Aloof the bashful virtue hover'd coy,
Proving by sweet distrust distrusted worth.
Rough Labour closed the train: and in his hand
Rude, callous, sinew-swell'd, and black with toil,
Came manly Indignation. Sour he seems,
And more than seems, by lawless pride assail'd;
Yet kind at heart, and just, and generous, there
No vengeance lurks, no pale insidious gall:
Even in the very luxury of rage,
He softening can forgive a gallant foe;
The nerve, support, and glory of the land!
Nor be Religion, rational and free,
Here pass'd in silence; whose enraptured eye
Sees Heaven with earth connected, human things
Link'd to divine: who not from servile fear,
By rights for some weak tyrant incense fit,
The God of Love adores, but from a heart
Effusing gladness, into pleasing awe
That now astonish'd swells, now in a calm
Of fearless confidence that smiles serene;
That lives devotion, one continual hymn,
And then most grateful, when Heaven's bounty most
Is right enjoy'd. This ever cheerful Power
O'er the raised circle ray'd superior day.

'I joy'd to join the Virtues, whence my reign
O'er Albion was to rise. Each cheering each,
And, like the circling planets from the sun,
All borrowing beams from me, a heighten'd zeal
Impatient fired us to commence our toils,
Or pleasures rather. Long the pungent time
Pass'd not in mutual hails; but, through the land
Darting our light, we shone the fogs away.

'The Virtues conquer with a single look.
Such grace, such beauty, such victorious light,
Live in their presence, stream in every glance,

That the soul won, enamour'd, and refined,
Grows their own image, pure ethereal flame.
Hence the foul Demons, that oppose our reign,
Would still from us deluded mortals wrap;
Or in gross shades they drown the visual ray,
Or by the fogs of prejudice, where mix
Falsehood and truth confounded, foil the sense
With vain refracted images of bliss.
But chief around the court of flatter'd kings
They roll the dusky rampart, wall o'er wall
Of darkest pile, and with their thickest shade
Secure the throne. No savage Alp, the den
Of wolves, and boars, and monstrous things obscene,
That vex the swain and waste the country round,
Protected lies beneath a deeper cloud.
Yet there we sometimes send a searching ray,
As, at the sacred opening of the morn,
The prowling race retire; so, pierced severe,
Before our potent blaze these Demons fly,
And all their works dissolve — the whisper'd tale,
That, like the fabling Nile, no fountain knows.
Fair-faced Deceit, whose wily conscious eye
Ne'er looks direct. The tongue that licks the dust,
But, when it safely dares, as prompt to sting:
Smooth crocodile Destruction, whose fell tears
Ensnare. The Janus-face of courtly Pride;
One to superiors heaves submissive eyes,
On hapless worth the other scowls disdain:
Cheeks that for some weak tenderness, alone,
Some virtuous slip, can wear a blush. The laugh
Profane, when midnight bowls disclose the heart,
At starving Virtue, and at Virtue's fools.
Determined to be broke, the plighted faith;
Nay more, the godless oath, that knows no ties.
Soft-buzzing Slander; silky moths, that eat
An honest name. The harpy hand, and maw,
Of avaricious Luxury; who makes

The throne his shelter, venal laws his fort,
And, his service, who betrays his king.
 ' Now turn your view, and mark from Celtic night
To present grandeur how my Britain rose.
 ' Bold were those Britons, who, the careless sons
Of Nature, roam'd the forest-bounds, at once
Their verdant city, high-embowering fane,
And the gay circle of their woodland wars:
For by the Druid taught, that death but shifts
The vital scene, they that prime fear despised;
And, prone to rush on steel, disdain'd to spare
An ill saved life that must again return.
Erect from Nature's hand, by tyrant force,
And still more tyrant custom, unsubdued,
Man knows no master save creating Heaven,
Or such as choice and common good ordain.
This general sense, with which the nations I
Promiscuous fire, in Britons burn'd intense,
Of future times prophetic. Witness, Rome,
Who saw'st thy Cæsar, from the naked land,
Whose only fort was British hearts, repell'd,
To seek Pharsalian wreaths. Witness, the toil,
The blood of ages, bootless to secure,
Beneath an empire's yoke, a stubborn isle,
Disputed hard, and never quite subdued.
The North remain'd untouch'd, where those who scorn'd
To stoop retired; and, to their keen effort
Yielding at last, recoil'd the Roman power.
In vain, unable to sustain the shock,
From sea to sea desponding legions raised
The wall immense, and yet, on summer's eve,
While sport his lambkins round, the shepherd's gaze.
Continual o'er it burst the northern storm,
As often, check'd, receded; threatening hoarse
A swift return. But the devouring flood
No more endured control, when, to support
The last remains of empire, was recall'd

The weary Roman, and the Briton lay
Unnerved, exhausted, spiritless, and sunk.
Great proof! how men enfeeble into slaves.
The sword behind him flash'd; before him roar'd,
Deaf to his woes, the deep. Forlorn, around
He roll'd his eye, not sparkling ardent flame,
As when Caractacus to battle led
Silurian swains, and Boadicea taught
Her raging troops the miseries of slaves.
  'Then (sad relief!) from the bleak coast, that hears
The German ocean roar, deep-blooming, strong,
And yellow-hair'd, the blue-eyed Saxon came.
He came implored, but came with other aim
Than to protect: for conquest and defence
Suffices the same arm. With the fierce race
Pour'd in a fresh invigorating stream,
Blood, where unquell'd a mighty spirit glow'd.
Rash war, and perilous battle, their delight;
And immature, and red with glorious wounds,
Unpeaceful death their choice: deriving thence
A right to feast, and drain immortal bowls,
In Odin's hall; whose blazing roof resounds
The genial uproar of those shades, who fall
In desperate fight, or by some brave attempt;
And though more polish'd times the martial creed
Disown, yet still the fearless habit lives.
Nor were the surly gifts of war their all.
Wisdom was likewise theirs, indulgent laws,
The calm gradations of art-nursing peace,
And matchless orders, the deep basis still
On which ascends my British reign. Untamed
To the refining subtleties of slaves,
They brought a happy government along;
Form'd by that freedom, which, with secret voice,
Impartial Nature teaches all her sons,
And which of old through the whole Scythian mass
I strong inspired. Monarchical their state,

But prudently confined, and mingled wise
Of each harmonious power: only, too much,
Imperious war into their rule infused,
Prevail'd their General-King, and Chieftain-Thanes.
   'In many a field, by civil fury stain'd,
Bled the discordant Heptarchy; and long
(Educing good from ill) the battle groan'd;
Ere, blood-cemented, Anglo-Saxon saw
Egbert and peace on one united throne.
   'No sooner dawn'd the fair disclosing calm
Of brighter days, when lo! the North anew,
With stormy nations black, on England pour'd
Woes the severest e'er a people felt.
The Danish Raven, lured by annual prey,
Hung o'er the land incessant. Fleet on fleet
Of barbarous pirates unremitting tore
The miserable coast. Before them stalk'd,
Far seen, the Demon of devouring Flame;
Rapine, and Murder, all with blood besmear'd,
Without or ear, or eye, or feeling heart;
While close behind them march'd the sallow Power
Of desolating famine, who delights
In grass-grown cities, and in desert fields;
And purple-spotted Pestilence, by whom
E'en Friendship scared, in sickening horror sinks
Each social sense and tenderness of life.
Fixing at last, the sanguinary race
Spread, from the Humber's loud resounding shore
To where the Thames devolves his gentle maze,
And with superior arm the Saxon awed.
But Superstition first, and monkish dreams,
And monk-directed cloister-seeking kings,
Had eat away his vigour, eat away
His edge of Courage, and depress'd the soul
Of conquering Freedom, which he once respired.
Thus cruel ages pass'd; and rare appear'd
White-mantled Peace, exulting o'er the vale,

As when, with Alfred, from the wilds she came
To policed cities and protected plains.
Thus by degrees the Saxon empire sunk,
Then set entire in Hastings' bloody field.
  'Compendious war! (on Britain's glory bent,
So fate ordain'd) in that decisive day,
The haughty Norman seized at once an isle,
For which, through many a century, in vain,
The Roman, Saxon, Dane, had toil'd and bled.
Of Gothic nations this the final burst;
And, mix'd the genius of these people all,
Their virtues mix'd in one exalted stream,
Here the rich tide of English blood grew full.
  'Awhile my Spirit slept; the land awhile,
Affrighted, droop'd beneath despotic rage.
Instead of Edward's equal gentle laws,
The furious victor's partial will prevail'd.
All prostrate lay; and, in the secret shade,
Deep stung but fearful Indignation gnash'd
His teeth. Of freedom, property, despoil'd,
And of their bulwark, arms; with castles crush'd,
With ruffians quarter'd o'er the bridled land;
The shivering wretches, at the curfew sound,
Dejected shrunk into their sordid beds,
And, through the mournful gloom of ancient times
Mused sad, or dreamt of better. E'en to feed
A tyrant's idle sport the peasant starved:
To the wild herd, the pasture of the tame,
The cheerful hamlet, spiry town, was given,
And the brown forest roughen'd wide around.
  'But this so dead, so vile submission, long
Endured not. Gathering force, my gradual flame
Shook off the mountain of tyrannic sway.
Unused to bend, impatient of control,
Tyrants themselves the common tyrant check'd.
The Church, by kings intractable and fierce,
Denied her portion of the plunder'd state,

Or tempted, by the timorous and weak,
To gain new ground, first taught their rapine law.
The Barons next a nobler league began,
Both those of English and of Norman race,
In one fraternal nation blended now,
The nation of the Free! press'd by a band
Of Patriots, ardent as the summer's noon
That looks delighted on, the tyrant see!
Mark! how with feign'd alacrity he bears
His strong reluctance down, his dark revenge,
And gives the Charter, by which life indeed
Becomes of price, a glory to be man.

'Thro' this, and thro' succeeding reigns affirm'd
These long-contested rights, the wholesome winds
Of Opposition hence began to blow,
And often since have lent the country life.
Before their breath Corruption's insect-blights.
The darkening clouds of evil counsel fly;
Or should they sounding swell, a putrid court,
A pestilential ministry, they purge,
And ventilated states renew their bloom.

'Though with the temper'd Monarchy here mix'd
Aristocratic sway, the People still,
Flatter'd by this or that, as interest lean'd,
No full protection knew. For me reserved,
And for my Commons, was that glorious turn.
They crown'd my first attempt, in senates rose
The fort of Freedom! Slow till then, alone,
Had work'd that general liberty, that soul
Which generous nature breathes, and which, when left
By me to bondage, was corrupted Rome,
I through the northern nations wide diffused.
Hence many a people, fierce with freedom, rush'd
From the rude iron regions of the North,
To Libyan deserts swarm protruding swarm,
And pour'd new spirit through a slavish world.
Yet, o'er these Gothic states, the King and Chiefs

Retain'd the high prerogative of war,
And with enormous property engross'd
The mingled power. But on Britannia's shore
Now present, I to raise my reign began
By raising the Democracy, the third
And broadest bulwark of the guarded state.
Then was the full the perfect plan disclosed
Of Britain's matchless constitution, mix'd
Of mutual checking and supporting powers,
King, Lords, and Commons; nor the name of free
Deserving, while the vassal-many droop'd:
For since the moment of the whole they form,
So, as depress'd or raised, the balance they
Of public welfare and of glory cast.
Mark from this period the continual proof.
  'When Kings of narrow genius, minion-rid,
Neglecting faithful worth for fawning slaves;
Proudly regardless of their people's plaints,
And poorly passive of insulting foes;
Double, not prudent, obstinate, not firm,
Their mercy fear, necessity their faith;
Instead of generous fire, presumptuous, hot,
Rash to resolve, and slothful to perform;
Tyrants at once and slaves, imperious, mean,
To want rapacious joining shameful waste;
By counsels weak and wicked, easy roused
To paltry schemes of absolute command,
To seek their splendour in their sure disgrace,
And in a broken ruin'd people wealth:
When such o'ercast the state, no bond of love,
No heart, no soul, no unity, no nerve,
Combined the loose disjointed public, lost
To fame abroad, to happiness at home.
  'But when an Edward, and a Henry breathed
Through the charm'd whole one all-exerting soul:
Drawn sympathetic from his dark retreat,
When wide-attracted merit round them glow'd:

Then counsels just, extensive, generous, firm,
Amid the maze of state, determined kept
Some ruling point in view: when, on the stock
Of public good and glory grafted, spread
Their palms, their laurels; or, if thence they stray'd,
Swift to return, and patient of restraint:
When regal state, pre-eminence of place,
They scorn'd to deem pre-eminence of ease,
To be luxurious drones, that only rob
The busy hive: as in distinction, power,
Indulgence, honour, and advantage, first;
When they too claim'd in virtue, danger, toil,
Superior rank; with equal hand, prepared
To guard the subject, and to quell the foe:
When such with me their vital influence shed,
No mutter'd grievance, hopeless sigh, was heard;
No foul distrust through wary senates ran,
Confined their bounty, and their ardour quench'd:
On aid, unquestion'd liberal aid was given:
Safe in their conduct, by their valour fired,
Fond where they led victorious armies rush'd;
And Cressy, Poitiers, Agincourt proclaim
What Kings supported by almighty Love,
And People fired with Liberty, can do.

'Be veil'd the savage reigns, when kindred rage
The numerous once Plantagenets devour'd,
A race to vengeance vow'd! and, when oppress'd
By private feuds, almost extinguish'd lay
My quivering flame. But, in the next, behold!
A cautious tyrant lend it oil anew.

'Proud, dark, suspicious, brooding o'er his gold,
As how to fix his throne he jealous cast
His crafty views around; pierced with a ray,
Which on his timid mind I darted full,
He mark'd the Barons of excessive sway,
At pleasure making and unmaking kings;
And hence, to crush these petty tyrants, plann'd

A law, that let them, by the silent waste
Of luxury, their landed wealth diffuse,
And with that wealth their implicated power.
By soft degrees a mighty change ensued,
E'en working to this day. With streams, deduced
From these diminish'd floods, the country smiled.
As when impetuous from the snow-heap'd Alps,
To vernal suns relenting, pours the Rhine;
While, undivided, oft, with wasteful sweep,
He foams along; but through Batavian meads,
Branch'd into fair canals, indulgent flows;
Waters a thousand fields; and culture, trade,
Towns, meadows, gliding ships, and villas mix'd,
A rich, a wondrous landscape rises round.
His furious son the soul-enslaving chain,
Which many a doting venerable age
Had link by link strong twisted round the land,
Shook off. No longer could be borne a power,
From Heaven pretended, to deceive, to void
Each solemn tie, to plunder without bounds,
To curb the generous soul, to fool mankind;
And, wild at last, to plunge into a sea
Of blood and horror. The returning light,
That first thro' Wickliff streak'd the priestly gloom,
Now burst in open day. Bared to the blaze,
Forth from the haunts of Superstition crawled
Her motley sons, fantastic figures all;
And, wide dispersed, their useless fetid wealth
In graceful labour bloom'd, and fruits of peace.

'Trade, join'd to these, on every sea display'd
A daring canvass, pour'd with every tide
A golden flood. From other worlds were roll'd
The guilty glittering stores, whose fatal charms,
By the plain Indian happily despised,
Yet work'd his woe; and to the blissful groves,
Where Nature lived herself among her sons,
And Innocence and Joy for ever dwelt,

Drew rage unknown to pagan climes before,
The worst the zeal-inflamed barbarian drew.
Be no such horrid commerce, Britain, thine!
But want for want, with mutual aid, supply.
  'The Commons thus enrich'd, and powerful grown,
Against the Barons weigh'd. Eliza then,
Amid these doubtful motions, steady, gave
The beam to fix. She! like the secret Eye,
That never closes on a guarded world,
So sought, so mark'd, so seized the public good,
That self-supported, without one ally,
She awed her inward, quell'd her circling foes.
Inspired by me, beneath her sheltering arm,
In spite of raging universal sway
And raging seas repress'd, the Belgic states,
My bulwark on the continent, arose.
Matchless in all the spirit of her days!
With confidence, unbounded, fearless love
Elate, her fervent people waited gay,
Cheerful demanded the long threaten'd fleet,
And dash'd the pride of Spain around their isle.
Nor ceased the British thunder here to rage:
The deep, reclaim'd, obey'd its awful call;
In fire and smoke Iberian ports involved,
The trembling foe even to the centre shook
Of their new conquer'd world, and, skulking, stole
By veering winds their Indian treasure home.
Meantime, Peace, Plenty, Justice, Science, Arts,
With softer laurels crown'd her happy reign.
As yet uncircumscribed the regal power,
And wild and vague prerogative remain'd;
A wide voracious gulf, where swallow'd oft
The helpless subject lay. This to reduce
To the just limit was my great effort.
  'By means that evil seem to narrow man,
Superior Beings work their mystic will:

From storm and trouble thus a settled calm,
At last, effulgent, o'er Britannia smiled.
  'The gathering tempest, Heaven-commission'd came,
Came in the prince, who, drunk with flattery, dreamt
His vain pacific counsels ruled the world;
Though scorn'd abroad, bewilder'd in a maze
Of fruitless treaties; while at home enslaved,
And by a worthless crew insatiate drain'd,
He lost his people's confidence and love:
Irreparable loss! whence crowns become
An anxious burden. Years inglorious pass'd:
Triumphant Spain the vengeful draught enjoy'd:
Abandon'd Frederick pined, and Raleigh bled.
But nothing that to these internal broils,
That rancour, he began; while lawless sway
He, with his slavish Doctors, tried to rear
On metaphysic, on enchanted ground,
And all the mazy quibbles of the schools:
As if for one, and sometimes for the worst,
Heaven had mankind in vengeance only made.
Vain the pretence! not so the dire effect,
The fierce, the foolish discord thence derived,
That tears the country still, by party rage
And ministerial clamour kept alive.
In action weak, and for the wordy war
Best fitted, faint this prince pursued his claim:
Content to teach the subject herd, how great,
How sacred he! how despicable they!
  'But his unyielding son these doctrines drank,
With all a bigot's rage; (who never damps
By reasoning his fire) and what they taught,
Warm, and tenacious, into practice push'd.
Senates, in vain, their kind restraint applied:
The more they struggled to support the laws,
His justice-dreading ministers the more
Drove him beyond their bounds. Tired with the check

Of faithful Love, and with the flattery pleased
Of false designing Guilt, the fountain he
Of Public Wisdom and of Justice shut.
Wide mourn'd the land. Straight to the voted aid
Free, cordial, large, of never failing source,
The illegal imposition follow'd harsh,
With execration given, or ruthless squeezed
From an insulted people, by a band
Of the worst ruffians, those of tyrant power.
Oppression walk'd at large, and pour'd abroad
Her unrelenting train: informers, spies,
Bloodhounds, that sturdy Freedom to the grove
Pursue; projectors of aggrieving schemes,
Commerce to load for unprotected seas,
To sell the starving many to the few,
And drain a thousand ways the exhausted land,
E'en from that place, whence healing Peace should flow,
And Gospel truth, inhuman bigots shed
Their poison round; and on the venal bench,
Instead of justice, party held the scale,
And violence the sword. Afflicted years,
Too patient, felt at last their vengeance full.
  'Mid the low murmurs of submissive fear
And mingled rage, my Hampden raised his voice,
And to the laws appeal'd; the laws no more
In judgment sat, behoved some other ear.
When instant from the keen resentive North,
By long oppression, by religion roused,
The guardian army came. Beneath its wing
Was call'd, though meant to furnish hostile aid,
The more than Roman senate. There a flame
Broke out, that clear'd, consumed, renew'd the land.
In deep emotion hurl'd, nor Greece, nor Rome,
Indignant bursting from a tyrant's chain,
While, full of me, each agitated soul
Strung every nerve and flamed in every eye,
Had e'er beheld such light and heat combined!

Such heads and hearts! such dreadful zeal, led on
By calm majestic wisdom, taught its course
What nuisance to devour; such wisdom fired
With unabating zeal, and aim'd sincere
To clear the weedy state, restore the laws,
And for the future to secure their sway.
  'This then the purpose of my mildest sons.
But man is blind. A nation once inflamed
(Chief, should the breath of factious fury blow,
With the wild rage of mad enthusiast swell'd)
Not easy cools again. From breast to breast,
From eye to eye, the kindling passions mix
In heighten'd blaze; and, ever wise and just,
High Heaven to gracious ends directs the storm.
Thus in one conflagration Britain, wrapt,
And by Confusion's lawless sons despoil'd,
King, Lords, and Commons, thundering to the ground,
Successive, rush'd — Lo! from their ashes rose,
Gay beaming radiant youth, the Phœnix State.
  'The grievous yoke of vassalage, the yoke
Of private life, lay by those flames dissolved;
And, from the wasteful, the luxurious king,
Was purchased that which taught the young to bend.
Stronger restored, the Commons tax'd the whole,
And built on that eternal rock their power.
The Crown, of its hereditary wealth
Despoil'd, on senates more dependent grew,
And they more frequent, more assured. Yet lived,
And in full vigour spread that bitter root,
The passive doctrines, by their patrons first,
Opposed ferocious, when they touch themselves.
  'This wild delusive cant; the rash cabal
Of hungry courtiers, ravenous for prey;
The bigot, restless in a double chain
To bind anew the land; the constant need
Of finding faithless means, of shifting forms,
And flattering senates, to supply his waste;

These tore some moments from the careless prince,
And in his breast awaked the kindred plan.
By dangerous softness long he mined his way;
By subtle arts, dissimulation deep;
By sharing what corruption shower'd, profuse;
By breathing wide the gay licentious plague,
And pleasing manners, fitted to deceive.
 'At last subsided the delirious joy,
On whose high billow, from the saintly reign,
The nation drove too far. A pension'd king,
Against his country bribed by Gallic gold;
The Port pernicious sold, the Scylla since
And fell Charybdis of the British seas;
Freedom attack'd abroad, with surer blow
To cut it off at home; the saviour league
Of Europe broke; the progress e'en advanced
Of universal sway, which to reduce
Such seas of blood and treasure Britain coust;
The millions, by a generous people given,
Or squander'd vile, or to corrupt, disgrace,
And awe the land with forces not their own.
Employ'd; the darling church herself betray'd;
All these, broad glaring, oped the general eye,
And waked my spirit, the resisting soul.
 'Mild was, at first, and half ashamed, the check
Of senates, shook from the fantastic dream
Of absolute submission, tenets vile!
Which slaves would blush to own, and which reduced
To practice, always honest nature shock.
Not e'en the mask removed, and the fierce front
Of tyranny disclosed; nor trampled laws;
Nor seized each badge of freedom thro' the land;
Nor Sidney bleeding for the unpublish'd page;
Nor on the bench avowed corruption placed,
And murderous rage itself, in Jefferies' form;
Nor endless acts of arbitrary power,
Cruel, and false, could raise the public arm.

Distrustful, scatter'd, of combining chiefs
Devoid, and dreading blind rapacious war,
The patient public turns not, till impell'd
To the near verge of ruin. Hence I roused
The bigot king, and hurried fated on
His measures immature. But chief his zeal,
Out-flaming Rome herself, portentous scared
The troubled nation: Mary's horrid days
To fancy bleeding rose, and the dire glare
Of Smithfield lighten'd in its eyes anew.
Yet silence reign'd. Each on another scowl'd
Rueful amazement, pressing down his rage:
As, mustering vengeance, the deep thunder frowns,
Awfully still, waiting the high command
To spring. Straight from his country Europe saved,
To save Britannia, lo! my darling son,
Than hero more! the patriot of mankind!
Immortal Nassau came. I hush'd the deep
By demons roused, and bade the listed winds,
Still shifting as behoved, with various breath,
Waft the deliverer to the longing shore.
See! wide alive, the foaming channel bright
With swelling sails, and all the pride of war,
Delightful view! when Justice draws the sword:
And mark! diffusing ardent soul around,
And sweet contempt of death, My streaming flag,
E'en adverse navies bless'd the binding gale,
Kept down the glad acclaim, and silent joy'd.
Arrived, the pomp, and not the waste of arms
His progress mark'd. The faint opposing host
For once, in yielding their best victory found,
And by desertion proved exalted faith:
While his the bloodless conquest of the heart,
Shouts without groan, and triumph without war.

'Then dawn'd the period destined to confine
The surge of wild prerogative, to raise
A mound restraining its imperious rage,

And bid the raving deep no farther flow.
Nor where, without that fence, the swallow'd state
Better than Belgian plains without their dykes,
Sustaining weighty seas. This, often saved
By more than human hand, the public saw,
And seized the white-wing'd moment. Pleased to yield
Destructive power, a wise heroic prince
E'en lent his aid — Thrice happy! did they know
Their happiness, Britannia's bounded kings.
What tho' not theirs the boast, in dungeon glooms,
To plunge bold freedom; or, to cheerless wilds,
To drive him from the cordial face of friend;
Or fierce to strike him at the midnight hour,
By mandate blind, not justice, that delights
To dare the keenest eye of open day.
What though no glory to control the laws,
And make injurious will their only rule,
They deem it. What tho', tools of wanton power,
Pestiferous armies swarm not at their call.
What though they give not a relentless crew
Of civil furies, proud oppression's fangs!
To tear at pleasure the dejected land,
With starving labour pampering idle waste.
To clothe the naked, feed the hungry, wipe
The guiltless tear from lone affliction's eye;
To raise hid merit, set the alluring light
Of virtue high to view; to nourish arts,
Direct the thunder of an injured state,
Make a whole glorious people sing for joy,
Bless humankind, and thro' the downward depth
Of future times to spread that better sun
Which lights up British soul: for deeds like these,
The dazzling fair career unbounded lies;
While (still superior bliss!) the dark abrupt
Is kindly barr'd, the precipice of ill.
O luxury divine! O poor to this,
Ye giddy glories of despotic thrones!

By this, by this indeed, is imaged Heaven,
By boundless good without the power of ill.
  'And now behold! exalted as the cope
That swells immense o'er many-peopled earth,
And like it free, my fabric stands complete,
The palace of the laws. To the four heavens
Four gates impartial thrown, unceasing crowds,
With kings themselves the hearty peasant mix'd,
Pour urgent in. And though to different ranks
Responsive place belongs, yet equal spreads
The sheltering roof o'er all; while plenty flows,
And glad contentment echoes round the whole.
Ye floods, descend! Ye winds, confirming, blow!
Nor outward tempest, nor corrosive time,
Nought but the felon undermining hand
Of dark Corruption, can its frame dissolve,
And lay the toil of ages in the dust.'

LIBERTY.

PART V. — THE PROSPECT.

HERE interposing, as the Goddess paused; —
'O bless'd Britannia! in thy presence bless'd,
Thou guardian of mankind! whence spring, alone,
All human grandeur, happiness, and fame;
For toil, by thee protected, feels no pain;
The poor man's lot with milk and honey flows;
And, gilded with thy rays, even death looks gay.
Let other lands the potent blessings boast
Of more exalting suns. Let Asia's woods,
Untended, yield the vegetable fleece:
And let the little insect-artist form,
On higher life intent, its silken tomb.
Let wondering rocks, in radiant birth, disclose
The various tinctured children of the sun.
From the prone beam let more delicious fruits,
A flavour drink, that in one piercing taste
Bids each combine. Let Gallic vineyards burst
With floods of joy; with mild balsamic juice
The Tuscan olive. Let Arabia breathe
Her spicy gales, her vital gums distil.
Turbid with gold, let southern rivers flow;
And orient floods draw soft, o'er pearls, their maze.
Let Afric vaunt her treasures; let Peru
Deep in her bowels her own ruin breed,
The yellow traitor that her bliss betray'd, —
Unequal'd bliss — and to unequal'd rage!
Yet nor the gorgeous East, nor golden South,
Nor, in full prime, that new discover'd world,
Where flames the falling day, in wealth and praise,
Shall with Britannia vie; while, Goddess, she

Derives her praise from thee, her matchless charms.
Her hearty fruits the hand of freedom own;
And warm with culture, her thick clustering fields
Prolific teem. Eternal verdure crowns
Her meads; her gardens smile eternal spring.
She gives the hunter-horse, unquell'd by toil,
Ardent, to rush into the rapid chase:
She, whitening o'er her downs, diffusive, pours
Unnumber'd flocks: she weaves the fleecy robe,
That wraps the nations: she, to lusty droves,
The richest pasture spreads; and, hers, deep-wave
Autumnal seas of pleasing plenty round.
These are delights: and by no baneful herb,
No darting tiger, no grim lion's glare,
No fierce-descending wolf, no serpent roll'd
In spires immense progressive o'er the land,
Disturb'd. Enlivening these, add cities, full
Of wealth, of trade, of cheerful toiling crowds:
Add thriving towns; add villages and farms,
Innumerous sow'd along the lively vale,
Where bold unrival'd peasants happy dwell:
Add ancient seats, with venerable oaks
Embosom'd high, while kindred floods below
Wind through the mead; and those of modern hand,
More pompous, add, that splendid shine afar.
Need I her limpid lakes, her rivers name
Where swarm the finny race? Thee, chief, O Thames!
On whose each tide, glad with returning sails,
Flows in the mingled harvest of mankind?
And thee, thou Severn, whose prodigious swell,
And waves, resounding, imitate the main?
Why need I name her deep capacious ports,
That point around the world? and why her seas?
All ocean is her own, and every land
To whom her ruling thunder ocean bears.
She too the mineral feeds: the obedient lead,
The warlike iron, nor the peaceful less,

Forming of life art-civilized the hond;
And that the Tyrian merchant sought of old,
Not dreaming then of Britain's brighter fame.
She rears to freedom an undaunted race:
Compatriot zealous, hospitable, kind,
Hers the warm Cambrian: here the lofty Scot,
To hardship tamed, active in arts and arms,
Fired with a restless, an impatient flame,
That leads him raptured where ambition calls:
And English merit hers; where meet, combined,
Whate'er high fancy, sound judicious thought,
An ample generous heart, undrooping soul,
And firm tenacious valour can bestow.
Great nurse of fruits, of flocks, of commerce, she!
Great nurse of men! by thee, O Goddess, taught,
Her old renown I trace, disclose her source
Of wealth, of grandeur, and to Britons sing
A strain the Muses never touch'd before.
  'But how shall this thy mighty kingdom stand?
On what unyielding base? how finish'd shine?'
  At this her eye, collecting all its fire,
Beam'd more than human; and her awful voice,
Majestic thus she raised: 'To Britons bear
This closing strain, and with intenser note
Loud let it sound in their awaken'd ear:
  'On virtue can alone my kingdom stand,
On public virtue, every virtue join'd.
For, lost this social cement of mankind,
The greatest empires, by scarce-felt degrees,
Will moulder soft away; till, tottering loose,
They, prone at last, to total ruin rush.
Unbless'd by virtue, government a league
Becomes, a circling junto of the great,
To rob by law; religion mild, a yoke
To tame the stooping soul, a trick of state
To mask their rapine, and to share the prey.
What are, without it, senates; save a face

Of consultation deep and reason free,
While the determined voice and heart are sold?
What boasted freedom, save a sounding name?
And what election, but a market vile
Of slaves self-barter'd? Virtue! without thee,
There is no ruling eye, no nerve, in states;
War has no vigour, and no safety peace:
E'en justice warps to party, laws oppress,
Wide through the land their weak protection fails,
First broke the balance, and then scorn'd the sword.
Thus nations sink, society dissolves;
Rapine and guile and violence break loose,
Everting life, and turning love to gall;
Man hates the face of man, and Indian woods
And Libya's hissing sands to him are tame.
    'By those three virtues be the frame sustain'd
Of British freedom; independent life;
Integrity in office; and, o'er all
Supreme, a passion for the commonweal.
    'Hail! Independence, hail! Heaven's next best gift,
To that of life and an immortal soul!
The life of life! that to the banquet high
And sober meal gives taste; to the bow'd roof
Fair-dream'd repose, and to the cottage charms.
Of public freedom, hail, thou secret source!
Whose streams, from every quarter confluent, form
My better Nile, that nurses human life.
By rills from thee deduced, irriguous, fed,
The private field looks gay, with nature's wealth
Abundant flows, and blooms with each delight
That nature craves. Its happy master there,
The only freeman, walks his pleasing round:
Sweet-featured peace attending; fearless truth;
Firm resolution; goodness, blessing all
That can rejoice; contentment, surest friend;
And, still fresh stores from nature's book derived,
Philosophy, companion ever new.

These cheer his rural, and sustain or fire,
When into action call'd, his busy hours.
Meantime true judging moderate desires,
Economy and taste, combined, direct
His clear affairs, and from debauching fiends
Secure his little kingdom. Nor can those
Whom fortune heaps, without these virtues reach
That truce with pain, that animated ease,
That self-enjoyment springing from within;
That independence, active or retired,
Which make the soundest bliss of man below:
But, lost beneath the rubbish of their means,
And drain'd by wants to nature all unknown,
A wandering, tasteless, gaily wretched train,
Though rich, are beggars, and though noble, slaves.
  'Lo! damn'd to wealth, at what a gross expense
They purchase disappointment, pain, and shame.
Instead of hearty hospitable cheer,
See! how the hall with brutal riot flows;
While in the foaming flood, fermenting, steep'd,
The country maddens into party rage.
Mark! those disgraceful piles of wood and stone;
Those parks and gardens, where, his haunts betrimm'd,
And nature by presumptuous art oppress'd,
The woodland genius mourns. See! the full board
That steams disgust, and bowls that give no joy;
No truth invited there, to feed the mind;
Nor wit, the wine-rejoicing reason quaffs.
Hark! how the dome with insolence resounds,
With those retain'd by vanity to scare
Repose and friends. To tyrant fashion, mark!
The costly worship paid, to the broad gaze
Of fools. From still delusive day to day,
Led an eternal round of lying hope,
See! self-abandon'd, how they roam adrift,
Dash'd o'er the town, a miserable wreck!
Then to adore some warbling eunuch turn'd,

Thomson.

With Midas' ears they crowd; or to the buzz
Of masquerade unblushing: or, to show
Their scorn of nature, at the tragic scene
They mirthful sit, or prove the comic true.
But, chief, behold! around the rattling board,
The civil robbers ranged; and e'en the fair,
The tender fair, each sweetness laid aside,
As fierce for plunder as all-licensed troops
In some sack'd city. Thus dissolved their wealth,
Without one generous luxury dissolved,
Or quarter'd on it many a needless want,
At the throng'd levee bends the venal tribe;
With fair but faithless smiles each varnish'd o'er,
Each smooth as those that mutually deceive,
And for their falsehood each despising each;
Till shook their patron by the wintry winds,
Wide flies the wither'd shower, and leaves him bare.
O far superior Afric's sable sons,
By merchant pilfer'd, to these willing slaves!
And rich, as unsqueezed favourite, to them,
Is he who can his virtue boast alone!

 'Britons! be firm! — nor let corruption sly
Twine round your heart indissoluble chains!
The steel of Brutus burst the grosser bonds
By Cæsar cast o'er Rome; but still remain'd
The soft enchanting fetters of the mind,
And other Cæsars rose. Determined, hold
Your independence; for, that once destroy'd,
Unfounded, Freedom is a morning dream,
That flits aerial from the spreading eye.

 'Forbid it, Heaven! that ever I need urge
Integrity in office on my sons!
Inculcate common honour — not to rob —
And whom? — the gracious, the confiding hand,
That lavishly rewards? the toiling poor,
Whose cup with many a bitter drop is mix'd;
The guardian public; every face they see,

And every friend; nay, in effect themselves.
As in familiar life, the villain's fate
Admits no cure; so, when a desperate age
At this arrives, I the devoted race
Indignant spurn, and hopeless soar away.
 'But, ah too little known to modern times!
Be not the noblest passion past unsung;
That ray peculiar, from unbounded love
Effused, which kindles the heroic soul;
Devotion to the public. Glorious flame!
Celestial ardour! in what unknown worlds,
Profusely scatter'd through the blue immense,
Hast thou been blessing myriads, since in Rome,
Old virtuous Rome, so many deathless names
From thee their lustre drew? since, taught by thee,
Their poverty put splendour to the blush,
Pain grew luxurious, and e'en death delight?
O wilt thou ne'er, in thy long period, look,
With blaze direct, on this my last retreat?
 ''T is not enough, from self right understood
Reflected, that thy rays inflame the heart:
Though virtue not disdains appeals to self,
Dreads not the trial; all her joys are true,
Nor is there any real joy save hers.
Far less the tepid the declaiming race,
Foes to corruption, to its wages friends,
Or those whom private passions, for a while,
Beneath my standard list; can they suffice
To raise and fix the glory of my reign?
 'An active flood of universal love
Must swell the breast. First, in effusion wide,
The restless spirit roves creation round,
And seizes every being: stronger then
It tends to life, whate'er the kindred search
Of bliss allies: then, more collected still,
It urges human kind; a passion grown,
At last, the central parent public calls

Its utmost effort forth, awakes each sense,
The comely, grand, and tender. Without this,
This awful pant, shook from sublimer powers
Than those of self, this Heaven-infused delight,
This moral gravitation, rushing prone
To press the public good, my system soon,
Traverse, to several selfish centres drawn,
Will reel to ruin: while for ever shut
Stand the bright portals of desponding fame.
  'From sordid self shoot up no shining deeds,
None of those ancient lights, that gladden earth,
Give grace to being, and arouse the brave
To just ambition, virtue's quickening fire!
Life tedious grows, an idly bustling round,
Fill'd up with actions animal and mean,
A dull gazette! The impatient reader scorns
The poor historic page; till kindly comes
Oblivion, and redeems a people's shame.
Not so the times when, emulation-stung,
Greece shone in genius, science, and in arts,
And Rome in virtues dreadful to be told!
To live was glory then! and charm'd mankind,
Through the deep periods of devolving time,
Those, raptured, copy; these, astonish'd, read.
  'True, a corrupted state, with every vice
And every meanness foul, this passion damps.
Who can, unshock'd, behold the cruel eye?
The pale inveigling smile? the ruffian front?
The wretch abandon'd to relentless self,
Equally vile if miser or profuse?
Powers not of God, assiduous to corrupt?
The fell deputed tyrant, who devours
The poor and weak, at distance from redress?
Delirious faction bellowing loud my name?
The false fair-seeming patriot's hollow boast?
A race resolved on bondage, fierce for chains,
My sacred rights a merchandize alone

Esteeming, and to work their feeder's will
By deeds, a horror to mankind, prepared,
As were the dregs of Romulus of old?
Who these indeed can undetesting see? —
But who unpitying? to the generous eye
Distress is virtue; and, though self-betray'd,
A people struggling with their fate must rouse
The hero's throb. Nor can a land, at once,
Be lost to virtue quite. How glorious then!
Fit luxury for gods! to save the good,
Protect the feeble, dash bold vice aside,
Depress the wicked, and restore the frail.
Posterity, besides! the young are pure,
And sons may tinge their father's cheek with shame.
  'Should then the times arrive (which Heaven avert!)
That Britons bend unnerved, not by the force
Of arms, more generous and more manly, quell'd,
But by corruption's soul-dejecting arts,
Arts impudent! and gross! by their own gold,
In part bestow'd, to bribe them to give all,
With party raging, or immersed in sloth,
Should they Britannia's well fought laurels yield
To slily conquering Gaul; e'en from her brow
Let her own naval oak be basely torn,
By such as tremble at the stiffening gale,
And nerveless sink while others sing rejoiced,
Or (darker prospect! scarce one gleam behind
Disclosing) should the broad corruptive plague
Breathe from the city to the farthest hut,
That sits serene within the forest shade;
The fever'd people fire, inflame their wants,
And their luxurious thirst, so gathering rage,
That, were a buyer found, they stand prepared
To sell their birthright for a cooling draught.
Should shameless pens for plain corruption plead;
The hired assassins of the commonweal!
Deem'd the declaiming rant of Greece and Rome,

Should public virtue grow the public scoff,
Till private, failing, staggers through the land:
Till round the city loose mechanic want,
Dire prowling nightly, makes the cheerful haunts
Of men more hideous than Numidian wilds,
Nor from its fury sleeps the vale in peace;
And murders, horrors, perjuries abound:
Nay, till to lowest deeds the highest stoop;
The rich, like starving wretches, thirst for gold;
And those, on whom the vernal showers of Heaven
All-bounteous fall, and that prime lot bestow,
A power to live to nature and themselves,
In sick attendance wear their anxious days,
With fortune, joyless, and with honours, mean.
Meantime, perhaps, profusion flows around,
The waste of war, without the works of peace;
No mark of millions in the gulf absorpt
Of uncreating vice, none but the rage
Of roused corruption still demanding more.
That very portion, which (by faithful skill
Employ'd) might make the smiling public rear
Her ornamented head, drill'd through the hands
Of mercenary tools, serves but to nurse
A locust band within, and in the bud
Leaves starved each work of dignity and use.
    'I paint the worst. But should these times arrive,
If any nobler passion yet remain,
Let all my sons all parties fling aside,
Despise their nonsense, and together join;
Let worth and virtue scorning low despair,
Exerted full, from every quarter shine,
Commix'd in heighten'd blaze. Light flash'd to light,
Moral, or intellectual, more intense
By giving glows. As on pure winter's eve,
Gradual, the stars effulge; fainter, at first,
They, straggling, rise; but when the radiant host,
In thick profusion pour'd, shine out immense,

Each casting vivid influence on each,
From pole to pole a glittering deluge plays,
And worlds above rejoice, and men below.
　'But why to Britons this superfluous strain? —
Good nature, honest truth e'en somewhat blunt,
Of crooked baseness an indignant scorn,
A zeal unyielding in their country's cause,
And ready bounty, wont to dwell with them —
Nor only wont — wide o'er the land diffused,
In many a bless'd retirement still they dwell.
　'To softer prospect turn we now the view,
To laurel'd science, arts, and public works,
That lend my finish'd fabric comely pride,
Grandeur and grace. Of sullen genius he!
Cursed by the Muses! by the Graces loathed!
Who deems beneath the public's high regard
These last enlivening touches of my reign.
However puff'd with power, and gorged with wealth,
A nation be; let trade enormous rise,
Let East and South their mingled treasure pour,
Till, swell'd impetuous, the corrupting flood
Burst o'er the city and devour the land:
Yet these neglected, these recording arts,
Wealth rots, a nuisance; and, oblivious sunk,
That nation must another Carthage lie.
If not by them, on monumental brass,
On sculptured marble, on the deathless page,
Impress'd, renown had left no trace behind:
In vain, to future times, the sage had thought,
The legislator plann'd, the hero found
A beauteous death, the patriot toil'd in vain.
The awarders they of Fame's immortal wreath,
They rouse ambition, they the mind exalt,
Give great ideas, lovely forms infuse,
Delight the general eye, and, dress'd by them,
The moral Venus glows with double charms. .
　'Science, my close associate, still attends

Where'er I go. Sometimes, in simple guise,
She walks the furrow with the consul-swain,
Whispering unletter'd wisdom to the heart,
Direct; or, sometimes, in the pompous robe
Of fancy dress'd, she charms Athenian wits,
And a whole sapient city round her burns.
Then o'er her brow Minerva's terrors nod:
With Xenophon, sometimes, in dire extremes,
She breathes deliberate soul, and makes retreat
Unequal'd glory: with the Theban sage,
Epaminondas, first and best of men!
Sometimes she bids the deep-embattled host,
Above the vulgar reach, resistless form'd,
March to sure conquest — never gain'd before!
Nor on the treacherous seas of giddy state
Unskilful she: when the triumphant tide
Of high-swoln empire wears one boundless smile,
And the gale tempts to new pursuits of fame,
Sometimes, with Scipio, she collects her sail,
And seeks the blissful shore of rural ease,
Where, but the Aonian maids, no sirens sing;
Or should the deep-brew'd tempest muttering rise,
While rocks and shoals perfidious lurk around,
With Tully she her wide-reviving light
To senates holds; a Catiline confounds,
And saves awhile from Cæsar sinking Rome.
Such the kind power, whose piercing eye dissolves
Each mental fetter, and sets reason free;
For me inspiring an enlightened zeal,
The more tenacious as the more convinced
How happy freemen, and how wretched slaves.
To Britons not unknown, to Britons full
The Goddess spreads her stores, the secret soul
That quickens trade, the breath unseen that wafts
To them the treasures of a balanced world.
But finer arts (save what the Muse has sung
In daring flight, above all modern wing,)

Neglected droop the head; and public works,
Broke by corruption into private gain,
Not ornament, disgrace; not serve, destroy.
    'Shall Britons, by their own joint wisdom ruled
Beneath one Royal Head, whose vital power
Connects, enlivens, and exerts the whole;
In finer arts, and public works, shall they
To Gallia yield? yield to a land that bends
Depress'd, and broke, beneath the will of one?
Of one who, should the unkingly thirst of gold,
Or tyrant passions, or ambition, prompt,
Calls locust-armies o'er the blasted land:
Drains from its thirsty bounds the springs of wealth,
His own insatiate reservoir to fill:
To the lone desert patriot-merit frowns,
Or into dungeons arts, when they, their chains,
Indignant, bursting; for their nobler works
All other license scorn but truth's and mine.
Oh shame to think! shall Britons, in the field
Unconquer'd still, the better laurel lose?
E'en in that monarch's reign, who vainly dreamt,
By giddy power, betray'd, and flatter'd pride,
To grasp unbounded sway; while, swarming round,
His armies dared all Europe to the field;
To hostile hands while treasure flow'd profuse,
And, that great source of treasure, subjects' blood,
Inhuman squander'd, sicken'd every land;
From Britain, chief, while my superior sons,
In vengeance rushing, dash'd his idle hopes,
And bade his agonizing heart be low:
E'en then, as in the golden calm of peace,
What public works, at home, what arts arose!
What various science shone! what genius glow'd!
    ''T is not for me to paint, diffusive shot
O'er fair extents of land, the shining road;
The flood-compelling arch; the long canal,
Through mountains piercing and uniting seas;

The dome resounding sweet with infant joy,
From famine saved, or cruel-handed shame;
And that where valour counts his noble scars,
The land where social pleasure loves to dwell,
Of the fierce demon, Gothic duel, freed;
The robber from his farthest forest chased;
The turbid city clear'd, and, by degrees,
Into sure peace the best police refined,
Magnificence, and grace, and decent joy.
Let Gallic bards record, how honour'd arts,
And science, by despotic bounty bless'd,
At distance flourish'd from my parent-eye.
Restoring ancient taste, how Boileau rose:
How the big Roman soul shook, in Corneille,
The trembling stage. In elegant Racine;
How the more powerful though more humble voice
Of nature-painting Greece, resistless, breathed
The whole awaken'd heart. How Moliere's scene,
Chastised and regular, with well judged wit,
Not scatter'd wild, and native humour, graced,
Was life itself. To public honours raised,
How learning in warm seminaries spread;
And, more for glory than the small reward,
How emulation strove. How their pure tongue
Almost obtain'd what was denied their arms.
From Rome, awhile, how Painting, courted long,
With Poussin came; ancient design, that lifts
A fairer front, and looks another soul.
How the kind art, that, of unvalued price,
The famed and only picture, easy, gives,
Refined her touch, and, through the shadow'd piece,
All the live spirit of the painter pour'd.
Coyest of arts, how Sculpture northward deign'd
A look, and bade her Girardon arise.
How lavish grandeur blazed; the barren waste,
Astonish'd, saw the sudden palace swell,
And fountains spout amid its arid shades.

For leagues, bright vistas opening to the view,
How forests in majestic gardens smiled.
How menial arts, by their gay sisters taught,
Wove the deep flower, the blooming foliage train'd
In joyous figures o'er the silky lawn,
The palace cheer'd, illumed the storied wall,
And with the pencil vied the glowing loom.
　'These laurels, Lewis, by the droppings raised
Of thy profusion, its dishonour shade,
And, green thro' future times, shall bind thy brow;
While the vain honours of perfidious war
Wither abhorr'd, or in oblivion lost.
With what prevailing vigour had they shot,
And stole a deeper root, by the full tide
Of war-sunk millions fed? Superior still,
How had they branch'd luxuriant to the skies,
In Britain planted, by the potent juice
Of Freedom swell'd? Forced is the bloom of arts,
A false uncertain spring, when Bounty gives,
Weak without me, a transitory gleam.
Fair shine the slippery days, enticing skies
Of favour smile, and courtly breezes blow;
Till arts, betray'd, trust to the flattering air
Their tender blossom: then malignant rise
The blights of Envy, of those insect clouds,
That, blasting merit, often cover courts:
Nay, should, perchance, some kind Mæcenas aid
The doubtful beamings of his prince's soul,
His wavering ardour fix, and unconfined
Diffuse his warm beneficence around;
Yet death, at last, and wintry tyrants come,
Each sprig of genius killing at the root.
But when with me imperial Bounty joins,
Wide o'er the public blows eternal spring;
While mingled autumn every harvest pours
Of every land; whate'er Invention, Art,
Creating Toil, and Nature can produce.'

Here ceased the Goddess; and her ardent wings
Dipt in the colours of the heavenly bow,
Stood waving radiance round, for sudden flight
Prepared, when thus, impatient, burst my prayer:
    'O forming light of life! O better sun!
Sun of mankind! by whom the cloudy north,
Sublimed, not envies Languedocian skies,
That, unstain'd ether all, diffusive smile:
When shall we call these ancient laurels ours?
And when thy work complete?' Straight with her hand,
Celestial red, she touch'd my darken'd eyes.
As at the touch of day the shades dissolve,
So quick, methought, the misty circle clear'd,
That dims the dawn of being here below:
The future shone disclosed, and, in long view,
Bright rising eras instant rush'd to light.
    'They come! great Goddess! I the times behold!
The times our fathers, in the bloody field,
Have earn'd so dear, and, not with less renown,
In the warm struggles of the senate fight.
The times I see! whose glory to supply,
For toiling ages, Commerce round the world
Has wing'd unnumber'd sails, and from each land
Materials heap'd, that, well employ'd, with Rome
Might vie our grandeur, and with Greece our art.
    'Lo! Princes I behold! contriving still,
And still conducting firm some brave design;
Kings! that the narrow joyless circle scorn,
Burst the blockade of false designing men,
Of treacherous smiles, of adulation fell,
And of the blinding clouds around them thrown:
Their court rejoicing millions; Worth, alone,
And Virtue dear to them; their best delight,
In just proportion, to give general joy;
Their jealous care thy kingdom to maintain;
The public glory theirs; unsparing love
Their endless treasure; and their deeds their praise.

With thee they work. Nought can resist your force:
Life feels it quickening in her dark retreats:
Strong spread the blooms of Genius, Science, Art;
His bashful bounds disclosing Merit breaks;
And, big with fruits of glory, Virtue blows
Expansive o'er the land. Another race
Of generous youth, of patriot sires, I see!
Not those vain insects fluttering in the blaze
Of court, and ball, and play; those venal souls,
Corruption's veteran unrelenting bands,
That, to their vices slaves, can ne'er be free.

'I see the fountains purged! whence life derives
A clear or turbid flow; see the young mind
Not fed impure by chance, by flattery fool'd,
Or by scholastic jargon bloated proud,
But fill'd and nourish'd by the light of truth.
Then, beam'd through fancy the refining ray,
And pouring on the heart, the passions feel
At once informing light and moving flame;
Till moral, public, graceful action crowns
The whole. Behold! the fair contention glows,
In all that mind or body can adorn,
And form to life. Instead of barren heads,
Barbarian pedants, wrangling sons of pride,
And truth-perplexing metaphysic wits,
Men, patriots, chiefs, and citizens are form'd.

'Lo! Justice, like the liberal light of Heaven,
Unpurchased shines on all; and from her beam,
Appalling guilt, retire the savage crew,
That prowl amid the darkness they themselves
Have thrown around the laws. Oppression grieves;
See! how her legal furies bite the lip,
While Yorkes and Talbots their deep snares detect,
And seize swift justice thro' the clouds they raise.

'See! social Labour lifts his guarded head,
And men not yield to government in vain.
From the sure land is rooted ruffian force,

And the lewd nurse of villains, idle waste;
Lo! raised their haunts, down dash'd their maddening bowl,
A nation's poison! beauteous order reigns!
Manly submission, unimposing toil,
Trade without guile, civility that marks
From the foul herd of brutal slaves thy sons,
And fearless peace. Or should affronting war
To slow but dreadful vengeance rouse the just,
Unfailing fields of freemen I behold!
'That know, with their own proper arm, to guard
Their own bless'd isle against a leaguing world.
Despairing Gaul her boiling youth restrains,
Dissolved her dream of universal sway:
The winds and seas are Britain's wide domain;
And not a sail, but by permission, spreads.
  'Lo! swarming southward on rejoicing suns,
Gay colonies extend; the calm retreat
Of undeserved distress, the better home
Of those whom bigots chase from foreign lands.
Nor built on rapine, servitude, and woe,
And in their turn some petty tyrant's prey;
But, bound by social Freedom, firm they rise;
Such as, of late, an Oglethorpe has form'd,
And, crowding round, the charm'd Savannah sees.
  'Horrid with want and misery, no more
Our streets the tender passenger afflict.
Nor shivering age, nor sickness without friend,
Or home, or bed to bear his burning load;
Nor agonizing infant, that ne'er earn'd
Its guiltless pangs; I see! the stores, profuse,
Which British bounty has to those assign'd,
No more the sacrilegious riot swell
Of cannibal devourers! right applied,
No starving wretch the land of freedom stains:
If poor, employment finds; if old, demands,
If sick, if maim'd, his miserable due;
And will, if young, repay the fondest care.

Sweet sets the sun of stormy life; and sweet
The morning shines, in Mercy's dews array'd.
Lo! how they rise! these families of Heaven!
That! chief, (but why — ye bigots! — why so late?)
Where blooms and warbles glad a rising age;
What smiles of praise! and, while their song ascends,
The listening seraph lays his lute aside.
  'Hark! the gay muses raise a nobler strain,
With active nature, warm impassion'd truth,
Engaging fable, lucid order, notes
Of various string, and heart-felt image fill'd.
Behold! I see the dread delightful school
Of temper'd passions, and of polish'd life,
Restored: behold! the well dissembled scene
Calls from embellish'd eyes the lovely tear,
Or lights up mirth in modest cheeks again.
Lo! vanish'd monster land. Lo! driven away
Those that Apollo's sacred walks profane:
Their wild creation scatter'd, where a world
Unknown to nature, Chaos more confused,
O'er the brute scene its Ouran-Outangs pours;
Detested forms! that, on the mind impress'd,
Corrupt, confound, and barbarize an age.
  'Behold! all thine again the Sister-Arts,
Thy graces they, knit in harmonious dance.
Nursed by the treasure from a nation drain'd
Their works to purchase, they to nobler rouse
Their untamed genius, their unfetter'd thought;
Of pompous tyrants, and of dreaming monks,
The gaudy tools, and prisoners, no more.
  'Lo! numerous domes a Burlington confess:
For kings and senates fit, the palace see!
The temple breathing a religious awe;
E'en framed with elegance the plain retreat,
The private dwelling. Certain in his aim,
Taste, never idly working, saves expense.

'See! silvan scenes, where Art alone pretends
To dress her mistress, and disclose her charms:
Such as a Pope in miniature has shown;
A Bathurst o'er the widening forest spreads;
And such as form a Richmond, Chiswick, Stowe.
  'August, around, what public works I see!
Lo! stately streets, lo! squares that court the breeze,
In spite of those to whom pertains the care,
Ingulfing more than founded Roman ways,
Lo! ray'd from cities o'er the brighten'd land,
Connecting sea to sea, the solid road.
Lo! the proud arch (no vile exactor's stand)
With easy sweep bestrides the chasing flood.
See! long canals, and deepen'd rivers join
Each part with each, and with the circling main
The whole enliven'd isle. Lo! ports expand,
Free as the winds and waves, their sheltering arms.
Lo! streaming comfort o'er the troubled deep,
On every pointed coast the lighthouse towers;
And, by the broad imperious mole repell'd,
Hark! how the baffled storm indignant roars.'
  As thick to view these varied wonders rose,
Shook all my soul with transport, unassured,
The Vision broke; and, on my waking eye,
Rush'd the still ruins of dejected Rome.

GLOSSARY.

Archimage, the chief, or greatest of magicians and enchanters.
Apaid, paid.
Appal, affright.
Atween, between.
Ay, always.
Bale, sorrow, trouble, misfortune.
Benempt, named.
Blazon, painting, displaying.
Breme, cold, raw.
Carol, to sing songs of joy.
Caurus, the north-east wind.
Certes, certainly.
Dan, a word prefixed to names.
Deftly, skilfully.
Depainted, painted.
Drowsy-head, drowsiness.
Eath, easy.
Eftsoons, immediately, often, afterwards.
Eke, also.
Fays, fairies.
Gear or *Geer*, furniture, equipage, dress.
Glaive, sword. (Fr.)
Glee, joy, pleasure.
Han, have.
Hight, named, called; and sometimes it is used for *is called*. See Stanza vii.
Idless, idleness.
Imp, child or offspring; from the Saxon Impan, to graft or plant.
Kest, for cast.
Lad, for led.
Lea, a piece of land, or meadow.
Libbard, leopard.
Lig, to lie.
Losel, a loose idle fellow.

Louting, bowing, bending.
Lithe, loose, lax.
Mell, mingle.
Moe, more.
Moil, to labour.
Mote, might.
Muchel or *Mochel*, much, great.
Nathless, nevertheless.
Ne, nor.
Needments, necessaries.
Nouriding, a child that is nursed.
Noyance, harm.
Prankt, coloured, adorned, gayly.
Perdie, (Fr. par Dieu), an old oath.
Pricked through the forest, rode through the forest.
Sear, dry, burnt up.
Sheen, bright, shining.
Sicker, surely.
Soot, sweet, or sweetly.
Sooth, true, or truth.
Stound, misfortune, pang.
Sweltry, sultry, consuming with heat.
Swink, to labour.
Smackt, savoured.
Thrall, slave.
Transmew'd, transformed.
Vild, vile.
Unkempt, (Lat. Incomptus) unadorned.
Ween, to think, be of opinion.
Weet, to know, to weet, to wit.
Whilom, ere-while, formerly.
Wight, man.
Wis for *Wist*, to know, think, understand.
Wonne, (a noun) dwelling.
Wroke, wreakt.

Thomson.

26

N. B. The letter Y is frequently placed in the beginning of a word, by Spenser, to lengthen it a syllable, and *en* at the end of a word, for the same reason, as *withouten easten,* &c.

Yborn, born.
Yblent, or *blent*, blended, mingled.
Yclad, clad.
Ycleped, called, named.
Yfere, together.
Ymolten, melted.
Yode, (preter tense of *yede*) went.

THE END.

www.ingramcontent.com/pod-product-compliance
Lightning Source LLC
Chambersburg PA
CBHW051721300426
44115CB00007B/418